Fulfilling the Silent Rules

inside and outside in modern British poetry 1960–1997

Selected previous publications by Andrew Duncan

Poetry

In a German Hotel
Cut Memories and False Commands
Sound Surface
Alien Skies
Switching and Main Exchange *
Pauper Estate *
Anxiety Before Entering a Room. New and selected poems
Surveillance and Compliance
Skeleton Looking at Chinese Pictures
The Imaginary in Geometry
Savage Survivals (amid modern suavity) *
Threads of Iron *
In Five Eyes *
On the Margins of Great Empires. Selected Poems *

Criticism

The Poetry Scene in the Nineties (internet only)
Centre and Periphery in Modern British Poetry **
The Failure of Conservatism in Modern British Poetry **
Origins of the Underground
The Council of Heresy *
The Long 1950s *
A Poetry Boom 1990-2010 *

As editor

Don't Start Me Talking (with Tim Allen)
Joseph Macleod: *Cyclic Serial Zeniths from the Flux*
Joseph Macleod: *A Drinan Trilogy: The Cove / The Men of the Rocks / Script from Norway* (co-edited with James Fountain)

* original Shearsman titles
** revised second editions from Shearsman

Fulfilling the Silent Rules

Inside and outside in modern British Poetry 1960-1997

Andrew Duncan

Shearsman Books

First published in the United Kingdom in 2018 by
Shearsman Books Ltd
50 Westons Hill Drive
Emersons Green
BRISTOL
BS16 7DF

Shearsman Books Ltd Registered Office
30–31 St. James Place, Mangotsfield, Bristol BS16 9JB
(this address not for correspondence)

ISBN 978-1-84861-609-7

Copyright © 2018 by Andrew Duncan.

ACKNOWLEDGEMENTS

The pieces on Kevin Nolan, Grace Lake, Michael Ayres, Nigel Wheale, Adrian Clarke were previously published in *Angel Exhaust* in a different form.
The pieces on Gavin Selerie, Jeff Hilson, Peter Manson and Sean Bonney were published in *Terrible Work* online.
The piece on Helen Macdonald and Paul Holman was published in *Jacket* in a different form.
The piece on Pauline Stainer was previously partially published in *Poetry Review*.

Contents

Introduction   7

The Rules of the Game

Groups and Boundaries: the Poetic Field Around 1995   13
The Lexicon – a common source of unique distinctions   48
Metre   55
The Concatenator   70
Formations of Taste and Attitudinal Learning   81
A Section on Black and South Asian Poetry   108

Points scattered round an invisible field

Noble Relics   124
Christian Poets   136
The Atlantic Periphery   147
Jungian Poets   160
Poetry of the Evanescent Present   165
Occultist, Mantic, and Eccentric   174
Naturalist Poets   190
The Meta-periphery: Arctic Poetry   203
Poets from the *Grosseteste Review*   216
Myth and Deep Narrative   239
The Dominance of the Optical   253
Ludic Poets of the 1980s   261
The Neo-underground   269
Nondiscursive Poetry   277
Expanded Documentary   286
Feminist Poets   289
Conventionally Breaching Conventions   300

Bibliography   309

Index   316

Introduction: Self-bracing Surfaces

This is part of a series of seven volumes on modern British poetry (one on the Internet at www.pinko.org), which are designed not to overlap. The British Council's excellent bibliography of *Poetry in Britain and Ireland since 1970* contains 700 names of British poets (as I laboriously counted, twice). There is a need for a book which explores the *range* of good poetry and gives a glimpse of the *whole cultural field*. The present volume is closest to an overview of the period. To help with shopping, you need to get a grasp of affinities, to tell you which poets are similar to the one you've just enjoyed; and a grasp of blind spots, so that when you reach the end of a vein you grasp where your guide is incomplete, and so where you might search next. The notion of the present volume is to cover the whole range of poetry being written within a short space, making the differences visible and so pointing to possible reasons why a hundred poets differ from each other. We can imagine – without being able to see – the process of differentiation, the stages through which such complex patterns were built up.

The year 1960 was chosen by Eric Mottram as the start of the British Poetry Revival (Wolfgang Görtschacher saw 1959 as a turning-point); the significance of 1997 is that I got a job in that year and had to wind down the research project. Evidently all kinds of poetry has happened since 1997, but I am content with the detachment which the passage of time brings. The purpose of the book is less to calm the present than to calm the past. The evaluation of British poetry of our time has been largely defeated by the material – if not by the external alliances of the critics. The process of winning understanding is essentially collective and it is the work of many minds which makes the poetry in question emerge in its true relations. By my reckoning, some 300 significant books of poetry were published in the period (listed at http://angelexhaust.blogspot.com/2011/07/poetry-shopping-list-2010.html). It is possible to have separate and accurate knowledge of each one. A dim infinity gives way to a place scattered with proper objects. The separation between poets is clear but coherence is less clear. I am wondering whether there is a quality of the age. We can link any given number of dots into a shape, but is it the shape of something?

Can we write prose about poetry? How do we get from the intense but local strips of personal experience to a glimpse of the whole cultural field? The aim of this book is to try and reach that shared picture, through absorbing hundreds of individual books. It is all blocked by my own personality, if that's the right verb. You might well ask why it differs so much from some other views of the period, or ask me to write about the boring central poets to explain why my view of them differs from that of the institutions. I have avoided this, mostly because all the important positions are implicit and not transparent enough for a proper debate to take place. If people don't believe prose about poetry, it is because of the factor of rage and retaliation, corroding shared space. This is a book full of calm objects. This is the part of the trial where evidence is presented. I believe this will move the whole process forward, towards a conclusion which I am unable to foresee.

Any sober account of the events of the period must read like an indictment of a bad subjectivity. With poetry, if you don't get 'with' the text, it doesn't recite itself to you. The reader can expel the poem from the experience by imposing an expectation pattern which the poem simply fails to match. The record of critics doing this to modern poetry is not exactly short. In fact, it seems that there is a lag of about thirty years in the reception of modern styles. I don't want to prejudge the merits of modern poets, but understanding their work is a necessary step *before* making any judgments. Explaining how modern poems work seems to leave little time for explaining why the poets have lax moral standards and have, basically, got their poems wrong.

Consciousness itself is self-referential. It creates the surface it walks on. Making these miraculous paths stable enough to walk upon depends partly on excluding most of the ambiguity from view. Social reinforcement makes this easier. Culture has to do with complicated acts which you carry out without putting a step wrong. It runs over an even more fragile and more perfect surface. This dreamlike confidence has a lot to do with being socially accepted and relaxed. This is easier with small homogeneous groups where everyone knows each other. We should ask whether the extra-verbal knowledge is stored in a two-person boat which holds up the reader and the poet, or alternatively in small-scale social networks. I am not trying to refute other people's artistic experience – and I also don't think they can invalidate mine. The attempts to do so bring us to a central experience in poetry – the area of feeling high, of demolishing someone's high, of grey, dull, and blank states of mind, of rage and negation of other people's words.

To be radically subjective is likely to notch up non-reproducible results, and runs the risk of recording information, indefinitely extensible, of no relevance to the reader. In the past ten years or so I have tried a number of non-qualitative ways of analysing the data. Little trace of these appears in the text, because most of them lead to so little. Without qualitative appreciation, poetry is almost meaningless. To be stubbornly objective runs, again, the risk of recording information, indefinitely extensible, of no relevance. I have tried an analysis which is qualitative and objective at the same time, in the hope of revealing the shape of the cultural field, something vast enough to contain a thousand poets or even more.

The great feature of the period is the large number of excellent poets. This is a permanent threat to the narcissism of the individual poet. I admit that I dislike the damaging of the artistic space in order to assert resentment and claims to attention. This does down the audience, including me, even if it enables the fractions to gouge more resources out of the central institutions. In the end, it's the integrity of that artistic space which allows aesthetic pleasure. Dissent, conflict, interruption, shutting down, prevent the messages from getting through. Of course the disaffected are right to think that the whole process is subjective. This realisation is useless in itself. Could we see the attempt to set up rules of aesthetics (we exclude all poets who *do not write in a realist style*, all poets who *do not innovate*, etc.), as responses by the poets to their feelings of panic? For the reader, the abundance of good poets represents wealth and fulfilment. Why should we identify with this noise of panic and civil litigation? I think the excessive feature of the modern scene is the attempt to draw the poem wholly into the ownership of the poet. The poet is not a child we have to console. We should remember that beauty exists in the world before a poem opens a window on it, and that the capacity to feel beauty, along with a context set aside and protected by custom to enjoy it in, existed before any particular poet seized temporary control of them.

A survey implies that I look at all points in the landscape and then omit most of them in the write-up. Overviewing is pretty close to overlooking. Anybody will tell you that the work a historian has to do is mainly reading the bad books. By doing this, I dug up all kinds of unjustly forgotten literary works. But it wore me down. I can't claim to be familiar with all 7,000 names. This is where the concept of maladministration arrives on the scene. You can't decide which books not to read on an objective basis. I'm not sure what would constitute due process in reading a book. The idea of reading was for me to have a good time, not to allow the poet to exercise quasi-property rights over the experience. A number of significant poets don't feature in this book.

The Rules of the Game

Groups and Boundaries:
The Poetic Field Around 1995

The poet John Hartley Williams asked, in a baffled letter, "Why is there virtually no overlap between three recent anthologies of modern British poetry?" The increased complexity of the scene does seem to have brought about mutual incomprehension, while invalidating the single-point perspective, which – one cannot emphasize this too strongly – gave rise to the puzzling complexity by irritating poets into passionate revolt. Perhaps we can get some glimpse of the overall shape of the cultural field by looking at a number of anthologies; important socialising sites where both poets and readers undergo violent waves of assimilation and dissimilation.

I wondered about the total count of poets active in the period I write about, viz. 1960 to 1997. One way of getting at this is to use sample points which are, or possibly are, counts of the complete numbers of books published in a particular year. Four I found are: 1960: 131; 1976-7: 906; 1994: 1,737; 1997: 2,311. If we make some major assumptions and take the value for each year in between as the average of those data points, we can build a model for the total number of books in the period. This model yields a figure of 40,139 books for the period. A more cautious model would give 28,000 books. If we assume an average of four books per poet (ASSUMPTION), in a 40-year span, this gives us 7,000 poets.

From the imaginary point of a book that covers all the seven thousand, we look down and find every less complete account to be incomplete. If I offer 140 poets, or even a stack of anthologies that give moments of 400 poets, that is amazingly selective. We do well to ask how the set was cut down to allow this reduction. We would find alliances, barriers, gatekeepers, and ideologies, everywhere.

The assumptions in the model above are pretty huge. Anyone is welcome to provide better figures at any time. As you can imagine, collecting and cleaning up the data is pretty tedious. Maybe 'roughly 7,000' means 'more than 4,000 and less than 16,000'. If you swallow the big figure, this also explains why different critics seem to be living in different worlds: we each take a swathe of this huge dark territory and the swathes scarcely overlap. If you see an anthology claiming coverage of the period with 80 poets, it is worth asking if the 80 victors are (a) the best (b) the most conformist (c) the best connected to people the editor wants to be owed favours by (d) the ones who went to the best universities (e) the most marketable (f) a random morass. I have written, here and elsewhere, about poets whose work I like. That is egocentric, I suppose. I heard a radio programme where a musician (the singer with Mercury Rev, in fact) had an hour to play the records which had influenced him most. It was obvious that everything he played sounded just like Mercury Rev. It was as if he had been hearing this music when he was nine years old and it had taken him that long to get the music down on tape. *All* the singers on those records sang just the way he does. This suggested an egocentric regime of art, where everything you like reflects your basic wishes and everything else basically flows past you leaving your head untouched. The ego is to poetry what the fiddle is to bluegrass.

The dataset we are looking at definitely is not the cultural field. Older poets are critically under-represented. I noticed at some point that Christopher Logue was not anywhere in these anthologies, but obviously he was being read by a large number of people. This led to a closer look at ages. The core of this dataset is poets born between 1939 and 1963. I count some 370 of them. The pressure of analogy is overwhelming. The poets of a single generation are present in almost unbearable density. It's just too many. You can be sure that virtually all the poets in the list want to be at centre stage, with their voice coming over loud and clear and distractions, like other poets, kept to the absolute minimum. The analogical field may not be the landscape in which they wish to be filmed.

Method

I looked for names which overlap in 15 anthologies published between 1985 and 1996, including about 450 different poets, by my count. Quite a few significant poets are missed from these anthologies, as well as diverse insignificant ones. A count of the overlaps shows aesthetic distances: out of 156 possible paired links between two anthologies, only 52 actually exist; or, out of about 6,000 possible overlaps of names, about 174 exist. The pattern is sharp and becomes sharper if we go to a second stage and regroup the 15 anthologies into 7 clusters.

This is an attempt to make implicit knowledge visible and shared. It is subject to criticism and modification in order to make it more visible and sharable. Because poets write more than one poem, they may not fit snugly into a point in the space proposed. One may occupy three or four non-adjacent cells in a 3D space. The model proposed here relies on the ability of the editors of anthologies to identify genuine cultural fault lines, or genuine temporary identities if you will. Their errors of judgement would tend to invalidate the relevance of the model to the poetry audience.

The poem is enforced by analogy; isolated by adaptation; structured by choice between averages and extremes; stretching to touch both originality and transparency; interpreted through norms; using shared means to develop something unique.

Groups

A list of anthologies follows. Probably, they show, together, the horizon of 1995, the attitudes which people in 1995 typically held:

1. *the new british poetry*;   2. *Conductors of Chaos*;
3. *The New Poetry*;   4. *Outsiders, Exiles, and Rebels*;
5. *Out of Everywhere*;   6. *60 Women Poets*;   7. *The Stumbling Dance*;
8. *Dream State*;   9. *Contraflow on the Super-Highway*;
10. *Agenda, an Anthology 1959-93*;   11. *Angels of Fire*;
12. *Purple and Green*;   13. *The Urgency of Identity*;
14. *The New Makars*;   15. *A Various Art*.

Boundaries

The groups are as follows. (The parts of *the new british poetry* abbreviated as tnbp 1, tnbp 2, etc.)

(A) feminist / women's / (grading into) young pop-mainstream.
(*Purple, tnbp2, Angels, 60WP, TNP*)

(B) Black and South Asian
tnbp1

(C) intellectual
AVA, tnbp3, tnbp4, CofC, OofE

(D) Scottish
Dream, Contraflow, Makars

(E) young & amateur
The Stumbling Dance

(F) traditional & low
Outsiders, Agenda

(G) Anglo-Welsh

OVERLAPS ANALYSIS	TNBP1	ANGELS	60 WOMEN	PURPLE	TNBP2	TNBP3	TNBP4	CONDUCTORS	A VARIOUS ART
TNBP1	A	5	3	1	0	0	0	0	0
ANGELS OF FIRE		A	4	7	8	3		4	0
60 WOMEN POETS			A		8	0			
PURPLE AND GREEN				5 A					
TNBP2					1 A				
TNBP3					0	0 A		10	6
TNBP4		1	0	0	0	0 A		8	1
CONDUCTORS OF CHAOS				0	1	0		A	5
A VARIOUS ART				0	0	0			A
OUT OF EVERYWHERE				0	1	0			0
DREAM STATE									
CONTRAFLOW			0	0	0	0	0	0	0
NEW MAKARS									
URGENCY OF IDENTITY			2	0	0	0	1	0	0
THE NEW POETRY			13	1	4	1	0		
STUMBLING DANCE			0	0	0		0		0
AGENDA			1	0	0				0
OUTSIDERS, EXILES AND REBELS				1	0				

OVERLAP ANALYSIS	OUT OF EVERYWHERE	DREAM STATE	CONTRAFLOW	NEW MAKARS	URGENCY	NEW POETRY	STUMBLING DANCE	AGENDA	OUTSIDERS
TNBP1	0	1	0	0	0	4	0	1	0
ANGELS OF FIRE	1	1		0	0	8	0	0	2
60 WOMEN POETS		3		0					1
PURPLE AND GREEN		1		0					
TNBP2		2		0					
TNBP3	1	0		0		0	0	0	0
TNBP4	2	0		0				0	0
CONDUCTORS OF CHAOS	5	0	0	0			0	1	0
A VARIOUS ART	0	0		0	0	0	0	0	0
OUT OF EVERYWHERE	A	0		0	0		0	0	0
DREAM STATE		A		0	0		0	0	0
CONTRAFLOW	0	8 A		2			0	0	0
NEW MAKARS		4		A	0				
URGENCY OF IDENTITY	0	0	0	0 A			0		
THE NEW POETRY	0	7	2	1	2 A			0	0
STUMBLING DANCE		0			0	0 A		0	0
AGENDA		0		2	1		A		
OUTSIDERS, EXILES AND REBELS				1	0			9	A

The Urgency of Identity

Poets who "overlap" two clusters are 49/450, or 11%. To put this another way, the poetic groups are 89% sealed tight. This confirms that the boundaries are real. A provisional analysis of another 10 anthologies found that they made the boundaries more robust.

Additions to this array drawn from other sources include (cluster H) the Jungian direction (variously, mythic, Gothic, psychotherapeutic, into primitive religion, based on folklore, etc.) which has produced some very interesting poetry disliked by most editors; on show in magazines like *Temenos, Ore,* and *Memes.* There is no source here for the continuance of the academic mainstream of the 1950s (cluster I), although (10) does include this line. Peter Levi, Geoffrey Hill, and Anthony Thwaite are significant poets in this area. There is no focused collection of Pop poetry, but it is impossible to think about Pop anyway, and its influence is strong in (3). Using this list has the advantage that generalisations can be made on the basis of the named books, not committing anyone to a version of the whole poetry landscape, which is too vast.

**1. *the new british poetry,*
edited Allnutt, D'Aguiar, Mottram, Edwards; 1988, 360pp., 85 poets.**

This will be referred to as the Muckle/Sinclair anthology, since John Muckle conceived it and Iain Sinclair was the overall coordinator after Muckle left. It is divided into four sections, each edited by a different person. The total of 85 poets makes the book tantalising. The alliance of these disparate groups reflects a political association in the wider world, in fact of the New Left with its sporadic fusion of feminists, ethnic minorities, and middle-class Marxists. The harking back to the mid-70s (made explicit by Mottram at p.132) points to a chronological problem with a group that was supposed to be the future: that of having retired exhausted in about 1977, and gone on to be a stable and benign community, avoiding trouble and looking nostalgically back at its heyday. The contrast between oppressed groups practising "identity politics" by asserting themselves, and "arrived" groups regarding cultivated poetry as that which criticises the elementary processes of the self, is striking. It is legitimate to see this arrangement either as the fragmentation of the counter-cultural hopes of 1968 into small and bitterly defended territorial units, or as a magnanimously shared space, open for interactions and contacts across borders. The second stroke whereby the counterculture moved into the centre was by now obviously not going to occur, having been overtaken by the splitting of poetry into a spectrum of independent markets, as throughout mature commodity capitalism. The broad sweep of the anthology disguises the fact that it is distributed along a periphery, the parts separated from each other by the excluded centre, of mainstream poetry, by now a combination of the reformed (and purged?) academic traditionalism of the 1950s with the pop themes of the 1960s.

The different principles of selection of the four sections (splitting neatly into two groups) oppose sociological belonging (being a woman, being in an ethnic minority) to formal skill or risk. These boundaries can be analysed in terms of baffles (blocks which confine energy to a space close to its source) and of fidelity to social geometry. The boundary provides guarantees to the reader that they are not allying themselves with someone who is not on their side. The implication (that some poets expressed their belonging to a group and raised its status, so *raising and belonging*) may have been more of a marketing ploy than a reality. The chiastic implications of the division – that poems which appealed through sociological identity lacked any sense of style, and that women or people from racial minorities who wrote experimentally rather than raisingly were disloyal, that only highly educated white males wrote art poetry, that pleasure depends on a flattering picture of the group to which one belongs – may all be untrue, but they did occupy much of the time spent discussing poetry in this period.

tnbp Section 1. *'Black British Poetry'*, ed. Fred D'Aguiar

"I did try to tell her something of what was oppressing my mind: more than half of all English words directly or indirectly slur blackness – and I was teaching the bloody language and the bloody literature and also actually writing my novels in it." —Dambudzo Marechera, from *The House of Hunger*.

The introduction disclaims completeness in favour of "cross-section and… representation"; says that the poems "tend to argue not just with themselves and with each other, but with society as a whole"; says that although poetry "cuts across race and class" these divisions do not vanish; says that the division between oral and literary poetry is declining. The selections are diverse in style and also mix Urdu with Jamaican poets.

The Black section, carefully partitioned off so that readers don't have to pay any attention to other people's sections, offers the seductive potential of a world periphery, a kind of free trip to a different and exotic topography and sociology. The problem of consuming exoticism is always that, the more exotic the message is, the less comprehensible it is. The more remote Caribbean poetry is from the British cultural context, the more peripheral and ignorable it becomes for a British reader.

The idea of erasing your own code, of pouring yourself out to the periphery, suggests that this experience will be significant: reading Black poetry will not be like reading White poetry, it will take you somewhere and be progressive and unselfish.

Oral poetry (as rapping, toasting, mike chanting, etc.) is popular in the Black community. This has a destructive influence on the printed version, which does not have the added attractions of music, beer, and dance. Contacts with the home islands are very close, and this means a steady flow, not just of reggae records, but also of "dub poetry" and other cultural adaptations from the other side of the ocean.

Caribbean sociolinguistics are peculiarly complex and locally variable. On anglophone Caribbean islands, as I understand it, the upper class speak something very similar to RP English, and the graduations from that to a creolised basilect correspond to social status. Psychological problems follow; this produces an almost ineluctable pressure to stylistic polarization, so that it would become impossible to write about ideas in patois or about intimate feelings in Standard English. On the island, in situ, this elaborate structure supplies rather precise information, useful for characterization, humour, etc.; but transfer the speakers to England, and speech differences no longer supply valid information. The use of patois in poetry in fact aligns with a naïve self-presentation. Patois carries, at least potentially, a nationalist and lower-class charge.

The audience expectation of colonial peoples involves authenticity and untouchedness. Like other myths of the periphery, this involves the concept of depth: in the *depths* of the slums; in the *abyss*; *deep* patois. This expectation of profound homogeneity discourages self-consciousness in the author. We also use the word *deep* of colours.

The funding agencies put indirect pressure on Black artists to be conservative and populist in form, because they want their campaign to promote ethnic arts to be visibly Black and visibly ethnic, and they feel much more secure about this if the art in question involves patois, yams, coloured clothing, and a beat-box. There is a niche for this kind of thing, a circuit. A Black artist who is being conceptual or, heaven preserve us, avant-garde, is likely to vanish from sight.

tnbp Section 2. *"feminist quote unquote poetry"*, ed. Gillian Allnutt

The introduction starts by Allnutt confessing that she no longer knows what "feminist" means and goes on to define "feminist poetry" in terms so vague I can't paraphrase them. "'Objective' and 'representative' are to me man-made words or illusory concepts." She says she has no idea about chronology: the publication of feminist poetry over the past 20 years has been haphazard and piecemeal. She has applied various criteria of choice. The subjects of the poems include "love, death, war, international politics, music, dolphins". There is a "continuity" in the pages selected which is too subtle to be seen clearly.

The poems are diverse but mostly share an aversion to complex syntax, to organised knowledge, and to criticising people: the immediate data of consciousness of a single person are the visible matter of the poem. This is presumably reassuring for people. The external, social, level where different voices are heard, and disagree, or debate, is not taken on. Presumably, in other poems, in other sections of the book, where the immediate data of consciousness are questioned (of which de-natured language is the token), people find this anxiety-making?

The simplicity of the style could be seen as a vast lack of curiosity; but the retort to this is that someone who doesn't want to read about other people's daily life, or is selective about just whose life he wants to consume, is also suffering from lack of curiosity.

tnbp Section 3. *'A Treacherous Assault on British Poetry'*, edited by Eric Mottram

Mottram's introduction identifies his poets with "The British Poetry Revival" (BPR), resisting past metrics and irony; committed to invention or exploration and taking up modern poetics from abroad. He defines a central British poetry from 1956 to 1982, ironical, defensive, and facing away from the world: the Movement and its heirs. He lists some "in" magazines and publishers of the alternative scene. All but two of the poets included were published in *Poetry Review* during his tenure there in 1971-7. As he explains, there was a row at the Poetry Society, which led to the resignation of most of the elected board and to the end of his stint as editor; this was a traumatic event, perhaps the only event one can point to in a landscape where most processes are long-term and statistical in nature. It accelerated the disappearance of Mottram's crew into the underground, and the interruption of the progressive tradition, which exerted remarkably little influence on British poetry in the 1980s. It is the dissatisfaction of very large sections of the reading public with the sanitized alternative which has given rise to the current uncertainty and instability.

The poets in 'A Treacherous Assault' (what Mottram was accused of) represent, therefore, a marginal formation for the retail market; they are not so much as mentioned in books, supposedly about modern British poetry, by Donald Davie, Neil Corcoran, Alan Robinson, or Anthony Thwaite.

The poets included mostly have a strong connection either with Cambridge or with London, or both. The concept of marginality is stylistic; a theory which locates marginality in a geographical area, or in a sociologically defined class, e.g. of non-graduates, is wrong. The public was sold a spatial metaphor in whose terms everybody in London, or in the South, is successful and conventional, and everyone anywhere else is unorthodox and virtuous and neglected. Although these are the great poets who emerged in the Sixties, a glance at almost any survey or anthology from that time will show a completely different picture, a different array of poets; the real picture of that decade only emerged with hindsight.

These poets do not fit well into anthologies; their interest has moved away from fine phrases and instant impact towards deeper aspects of poetic process. In order to make exploration possible, it's necessary to silence the leftovers of the previous aesthetic, to silence the reassuring chatter of the DJ-like figure who fills the space of traditional poems.

> All of your ideas
> begin life again
> when you wake up
> your faithful servants, already at work

> in their accustomed places
> like clothes neatly folded on the chair
> which no one else could wear
> in quite your way, grown fat
> on the success of small ambitions
> which you dream about
> and can't outgrow
> like permanent convalescence
> there's no escaping them.
> The way your friends remember you
> clips over like paper
> cut to fit a larger model
> (...)
> Drop a coin into the slot
> and a kind of truth comes out
> I SPEAK YOUR MIND
> One foot cheating on the ground
> 	(Andrew Crozier, from *High Zero*, a book excerpted in *tnbp*)

To break out of the deadlock of babbling yet cultured inanity, it was necessary to empty the text, shedding surface appeal and recognizability; a new universe of discourse was opened by using rules to generate new procedures. These rules replaced the existing rules of domestic realism; the poet ceases to impersonate himself in the poem, making way for something speculative and new. In excerpt, this poetry is arresting and tantalizing, rather than identifiable or satisfying; it thrives when taken *in extenso*.

tnbp Section 4. *'Some Younger Poets'*, edited by Ken Edwards

This group is, largely, the "alternative" poets born in the 1950s. Almost all the poets included hung out at the same workshop/readings series in North London – which suggests they *weren't* a whole generation. The introduction does little to define them except by pushing them into the story of the older poets who were big in the mythological and defining era of the 1970s. Otherwise, it repeats what Mottram has already said about the BPR and the Poetry Society fracas, gives a negative description of the mainstream poetry of the 1980s, and talks about the means of production. Edwards' definition of their commonality is actually a repeat of what Andrew Crozier said in the Introduction to *A Various Art* (at p.14) about the previous generation. He does say that this generation get their impulse from the previous generation of British writers, and not (as before) by reacting against the established British poets and imitating American models. In this context, it's possible to suspect that this age-group failed to compete with their elders for the scant resources available, weren't aware of each other, didn't get their books out, and weren't very visible even to Ken Edwards at this point in time. Essentially the same group re-appear in *Conductors of Chaos*, eight years later, so we don't have to dwell on them now. He quotes two of the women poets protesting against the restrictive assumptions of some feminists about what liberation or self-assertion mean. He says that poetries now "speak for and to communities" defined by "culture, politics, gender identity and geographical locus(.)" but doesn't define what community section 4 speaks to or how this affects poetic form. He doesn't mention any new innovations since 1976. For a group defined by innovation, this might be a crisis.

2. *Conductors of Chaos*, ed. Iain Sinclair (1996), 484 pp., 35 poets

The introduction says "The work I value most is that which seems the most remote, alienated, fractured" and speaks of "Pulp and poetry, the most extreme cultural responses, trapped in a clandestine marriage." As for selection, it is personal, and he says "The voices here are the ones that have been locked away, those who rather enjoy it."

The poetry included has been described as radical, modernist, experimental, non-realistic, countercultural, dissident, theoretical. The poems are distributed around the edge of something missing: normality. They are exceptionalist poems, protests against restriction, routine, probability, fixed sequences of ideas. We can propose a cluster of features to site this poetry: {contestatory subjective conjectural autonomous individualist ideas-driven constructed montage unrestricted unfamiliar mutated}.

Sinclair offers B. Catling as an exemplar for the collection, and dedicates the whole thing to the late Eric Mottram; the 'names list' suggests that *Conductors* is extremely close to sections 3 and 4 of *tnbp*, but is eight years later and includes a new generation of poets. Within this cluster we can detect two trends, carried out by rival groups known as the Cambridge and London schools. The geographical terms do not describe where the poets live or studied. In the "London" group, we can detect a rejection of convention, replaced by a language-game in which events are monotonous and energetic, as if liberation meant being free from differentiation and qualification. In the "Cambridge" tendency, classically summed up by the collection *A Various Art*, we can point to a reflexive approach, where the poet's self is always present, and the action tends to be the play of nuances within the moral and aesthetic tribunal controlling the self's behaviour towards others. The London school moves towards a state of jumping up and down shouting, whereas the Cambridge school moves towards painting and philosophy. One is a fast and dirty aesthetic, one is a cool aesthetic. In London there is an interest in graphic poetry and sound poetry, the disintegration of words and of phonemes, as if totality were to be reached by breaking down the primary rules of language; seeing Cambridge poetry as not being battered and regressed enough.

The roughness of some of the language leaves it open to being interpreted as careless and badly finished. The superabundance of implicit statements possibly points to a shared identity of the creators and the target audience, as a group which has lived together for twenty years and has unstated common values – which, indeed, would be profoundly bored by the statement of these common values. This can be compared with the greater social and geographical diversity of an anthology like *The New Poetry*, which has minimised the ideas content and simplified the style in order to meet an unprimed audience. Every poet here is extremely stylised; if the start point is improbable, the improbability grows with every successive line, which fits in exactly with the previous ones and does not drift back towards the ordinary. Clearly, the poem is growing out of the idea of itself; it is partly a hypothesis, partly autosuggestion, perhaps an anxiety hallucination; the brain programme which thinks and hypothesises is as much writing the material of the poem as the programme which takes in information, and continually updates it, from the outside world. The observer is the subject as much as the observed. The inside of the poem is as much like a museum or a philosophical argument, as like a length of film of a domestic scene. The principle of association of components in the poem can be either simultaneity in space and time or logical and emotional affinity.

Sinclair reports of his subjects that 'They will recall their contributions to the anthology a dozen times [...] They make impossibly complex demands on the typesetters, are a mass of precise and insane instructions. It matters so much, life and death: the furies have to be appeased/ antagonised on a single page.' The myopia which makes tiny differences of weight visible opens up a new universe, mutated at molecular level. He shows them quarrelling with each other – totally involved with each other's texts and demanding total purity.

The home range of *Conductors* is birth years from 1936 to 1963, but it includes five poets of the Forties – David Jones, J.F. Hendry, W.S. Graham, Nicholas Moore, and David Gascoyne – as ancestors. The absence of any of the poets from *tnbp* 1 and 2 – i.e. the feminists and the racial minorities – can be taken as an indication that Sinclair does not like the work of those poets, or that the target audience does not like it; conversely, the lack of market presence of the poets who do get selected can be interpreted as a mass opting by the left-intellectual audience against left-intellectual poets.

3. *The New Poetry* ed. Michael Hulse, David Kennedy, David Morley (1993); 340 pp., 55 poets

The boundary is poets who have emerged since 1982, the date of an anthology which the editors regard as canonical. The introduction talks of "the hierarchies of values ... disappearing", "flux", "accessibility, democracy and responsiveness", "death of the national consensus", "ironic social naturalism", "the marginal becoming central", "pluralism", "multicultural", "challenge the centre", "a questioning of ideas about poetic authority, sincerity, and authenticity", "above all sceptical", and claims a great diversification of British poetry starting in 1980, ignoring the British Poetry Revival catalogued by Eric Mottram in 1974. Perhaps the most significant point about *The New Poetry* is that it excludes every single poet in *Conductors*; or vice versa; a strip of cognitive dissonance which crackles.

The first two times I wrote about this anthology I stressed the weaker poets. They were distracting, but of course the good ones are what really matters. Examination of the poets closest to the boundary will show that several of the *Conductors* aren't complex or intelligent and that several of the 'light' poets in *The New Poetry* are brilliant and far from simple. Quite obviously there was a breakthrough represented by poets such as John Ash, John Hartley Williams, Robert Crawford, and Jo Shapcott. The timing of this is interesting. The process was defined by Douglas Dunn (*Poetry Review*, April 1978) as "that [...] it is possible to handle traditional expectations and The New in one practice of writing. Indeed, what else has English poetry been working towards during the past decade, if not that? A confrontation of styles is involved, but not a contradiction of styles [.]" This breakthrough could be glimpsed, then, in 1978, and had hit its stride by 1985. This is just the period when the Alternative wing of poetry was in disarray and had lost its ability to reach younger poets. A thesis bound to occur is, how does this new tier relate to the 'persistent underground' poets of *tnbp4*? Did it turn out that the innovative line of English and Scottish poetry was captured in the early 1980s by poets like Hartley Williams and Crawford, and that the new Underground poets were heading down a blind alley? In the media, conventional material is branded as 'experimental' and so the avant-garde has to be suppressed. Most of the innovations of the 1960s and 1970s have been cast aside in a regression to the conversational norm. But was the pursuit of disintegration and arbitrary re-creation of language a line which had run into the sand by 1980? If so, it was not artistically right to load up with all the accumulation of innovations (some of which were negations).

Most of the poets belong to what has been described as the Nincompoop School, because of their expert avoidance of seriousness, stemming from a fear of being authority in an era of popular cynicism; they are products of a Biedermeier era, of flight from an aggressive right-wing ruling group into domestic art and artificially prolonged immaturity. This is a reaction against the moral seriousness promulgated by the new criticism (and which, conventionally, was overrun by Pop hedonism in the 1960s). *TNP* is much tidier and more conventional and helpfully labelled than 'Underground' poetry. It minimises the gap between poetry and stand-up comics or disk jockeys. The connection between {resistance to convention: high educational level: political radicalism: fitness for authority} drawn during the era of 1968 has as fallout that readers find poetry which is more conventional and less morally serious, more relaxing. There is a break point as one rises up the curve of intelligence, at which tidiness ceases to be a mark of intelligence and becomes one of conformism. Of course, this raises questions of prestige (and of the mimicry of prestige behaviour). Poetry which questions everything certainly fulfils one of the imperatives of the education system, certainly minimises repetition of old information, but also faces the breakup of language itself.

4. *Completing the Picture: Exiles, Outsiders, and Independents* (ed. William Oxley); 1995, 185pp, 34 poets

Oxley says in his introduction that the poets have nothing in common except being "a recognizable continuation of the tradition of English poetry" and that they are critically ignored (he does not specify if they are more popular with publishers or readers, or other poets). They don't suffer from "technosis". They are unsuccessful, he says, because the critic cares more about the biography and sociological identity than the poem; because of the 'parlous state' of criticism; because of exile, or internal exile, as a "recluse", which all poets must be, as original people. Such exiled poets tend to 'over-produce'. 'There are no role models here for the poetic lager-lout!'

The anthology exhibits the mediocrity which radical poets daringly and bewilderingly escape from. This proposition of a lumpish and heedless sensibility expands our knowledge even if by dredging scaly monsters from the deep. It is possible that Oxley has chosen their worst poems. Feyyaz Fergar, Anna Adams, or Harry Guest do not show up too badly. Oxley also supplies an introduction to each poet, about another 34 pages.

The rhetoric of the title is curious: the poems in the book are traditional, conventional, and ordinary. The two favoured topics seem to be hedgehogs and King Arthur. An Arthurian poem about hedgehogs would presumably be very popular in this market. The claim to completeness made in the title is not credible.

The poets do not seem confident with their texts, as if getting to the end without disaster were ambitious enough; expressivity would demand more technical command. Positive aesthetic choice is sidelined, to be replaced by a certain loyalty, to the idea of the poem and its familiar tune, and decency. The strain between being unfashionable and being unoriginal dominates the book. Oxley criticises Anna Adams, a gifted contributor, saying "a good poet needs some obsession (…) a sort of message or vision". We need a word for the category which includes {visions, obsessions, fashions, political ideals, and experiments}. The problem with a vision is that it is apodictic, authoritarian, and non-negotiable, and as soon as we make it open for modification and for discussion by more than one person it has become a hypothesis or experiment, the very things Oxley is attacking the modern poetry world for doing. The term *outsiders* suggests two sets of non-mainstream poets; those in contact with other poets, who penetrate the realm of formal experiment; and those who are cut off, and stick to literary devices which are many decades out of date. Someone like cris cheek or Caroline Bergvall, for example, is obviously an insider in the sense that they make a living out of art and are in daily contact with other writers, however small their audience. The decree by which something becomes out of date is arbitrary, emitted by a literary circle, and can be called tyrannical; it is possible to opt out of it at household level, like refusing to pay the Poll Tax. The hypothesis that recluse outsiders write bad poetry because they have no grasp of the reader's sensibility, and so are under-stimulated, and largely uninventive and repetitive, remains a hypothesis. The rejection by the selected poets of literary trends (advances? crazes?) since about 1960 may allow us to identify what these trends have been; permitting a critique of the poetic milieu as being academic, metropolitan, socialistic, anti-romantic, etc. This is one more contest over legitimacy.

5. *Out of Everywhere: linguistically innovative poetry by women in North America and the UK,* ed. Maggie O'Sullivan; 1996; 238 pp.; 30 poets (of whom six are British)

The introduction refers to "challenging, formally significant and progressive work", "formally progressive language practices", "excluded", "cliché-ridden rallying positions of mainstream poetry", "excavating language", "inter- and multi-media work", "intellectually challenging". The Afterword, by the publisher, Wendy Mulford, speaks of "disordering and destructive techniques". The title comes from an exchange where someone in the audience said to one of the participants that she was shut "out of everywhere". Since the credits pages list a torrent of publications, jobs, and awards held by the contributors, this phrase is not literally true; nor should we assume that the magazines and publishing houses listed are regarded by the authors as low-prestige and tainted with failure. Instead, the claim signals upper middle-class status; the exact knowledge of how much institutional success they should have had signals perfect knowledge of how the institutions work and of the career paths of all of the individuals competing with them for the prizes. These are not the managed but the managers. The abilities to attribute a ranking to all forms of achievement, to rank other people's image of you, to control it following rules, and to criticise them for not following the rules, place this group of poets in a specific cell of the class diagram. To identify this cell with the university milieu would be to blur the fact that the people who are very successful at university behave in this way wherever they are, and to skimp the question of where university *mores* came from. The placing of words in such poetry is precise to within much finer tolerances than in non-academic poetry; the reader is going to have much more precise and refined feelings, unless they have some particular block about academic life and the upper middle class. This elite (of relatively low income) deserves to be viewed as a cultural treat on offer, just like the culture of some Melanesian tribe, but unfortunately, some readers bring projective resentment to the party. Bourdieu has described the academic elite as the state nobility. Because its function is to legitimate, many readers respond to it with anxiety and contest the legitimacy of its social power. Only someone who is free from anxiety does not want legitimation; the more anxious someone is, the more desirable legitimation is. Why would someone not want symbolic legitimation?

If you write poetry which your friends think is unsophisticated, you will become anxious; the most sophisticated friends are found in the graduate schools of English Literature faculties, where they are also the most concerned about nuances of language and, in many ways, the most competitive and insecure. The essential terms, naivety and anxiety, are fixed at the points defined by recent academic publications on literature: exposing emotional identification and the claim to use personal experience to authenticate poems and beliefs. Importantly, the more ambitious the work of literary theory is, the more it spurns these literary methods. These books get written by people from the same graduate schools as those who write sophisticated poetry. Reflexivity starts where the spontaneous ends, is policed by anxiety, and allows competition. The more you internalise the rules of the academic system, the more you are afraid of other people finding out that you can't read French (or whatever it is). It produces a kind of convergent divergence: it is formally necessary to be original, but the rules restricting what you can say are very numerous. Most of the poets in *Out of Everywhere* fall inside the solution zone left clear by all these negative rules. It is either freedom or over-fulfilment.

Why is there no overlap with *60 Women Poets* when this poetry is obviously so good? Only three (of the British poets in *OofE*) are outstanding from an artistic point of view, of whom one has now been published by Penguin Books; the others offer great problems to the conservative reader. The gap corresponds to the gap between the Latin and Greek taste of the educated class up till 1930 or so and the taste of people with a simpler, monolingual, culture. The distinction between *OofE* and either *60 Women Poets* or *Purple and Green* has to do with education: symbolic capital, in Bourdieu's terms. Educated and uneducated read English poetry with a different apparatus. The polarity of symbolic capital: economic capital develops a quadrilateral within which one quadrant has neither symbolic nor economic capital. In order to acquire cultural wealth, you have first to realise that it is not to be found in "accessible" poetry, which in fact causes a certain panic among the upwardly mobile. Poetry which jettisons communal roots and the autobiographical freight is making claims to impersonality and universality typical of the upper middle class, which has mastered role-detachment and does not mistake social games for reality. By becoming a detached observer, you acquire the power of valid utterance, and so professional status.

Reflexivity involves managing your social image, practiced by writing essays, talks, and dissertations and by close contact with your classmates who read them and write similar scripts. It is signalled by talking about: time; subjectivity; language as concepts. The more you see life as a series of roles, subject to choice, which can be talked about, managed, and turned to the best account, the more prestigious you are. Language is a means for becoming reflexive and for reflecting. The difference between "progressive language practices" and "self-expression" or "the truth about my life and our shared life" is that between high and low, just as talking about "language" is high compared to talking about "experience" in discussing poetry; the poetry in *OofE* never deals with concrete situations, with the exception of the poems by Denise Riley. Realism is by now a mark of low educational status, and has been since the 1930s. Not to realise this is another sign of being an outsider.

6. *60 Women Poets*, ed. Linda France (1993, 275 pp., 60 poets)

There is an Introduction: "that communicates itself effectively and unequivocally" "a sense of history" "the honesty of a clearly owned I" "a well-lived life" "small acts of kindness", not "unrealistic, high-minded-ascetic" "the sense of place, of community" "our concerns are essentially very similar" "never any sense of the merely ephemeral, of fashion, 'schools'" "being true to their own nature".

Faced with a reliably predictable environment, one seizes on the moments of deviation and transgression from home-made rules. We find indeed at many points attempts to be unpredictable, to be ambiguous, to offer sensations that aren't immediately classifiable, moments of biography that aren't instantly demonstrations of womanly virtues. Typically, this occurs through smells: because they are elusive yet arousing, physically dispersed yet really there. Smells stand in for abstract ideas.

A repeated image is the fantasy about being a cow, a leitmotif which could have made a good cover image. If your secret dream is to be a cow, this book is for you. A certain massive reliability, indifference to distracting stimuli, physically founded self-confidence, contentment with immediate surroundings, speak for themselves.

Food is constantly being described. This is meant to be sensuous and so superior to abstraction; and is status competition. Imagine a geometer who reconfigured Sainsbury's so you could never leave. A poem about food is not like food, it is made entirely of ideas and has to fulfil the laws of the intelligence or leave us hungry.

With a few exceptions, the poets all seem to write in the same style. Maybe this is just my insensitivity to fine differences in patterns I am weakly motivated to notice, so the verbal differences might be like stylistic differences between a dozen dresses which I am happy to classify as "dress". Perhaps they all cluster in the same few square inches because that enhances differentiation.

60 Women Poets can be related to *Purple and Green* as depoliticised; compared to *Out of Everywhere*, as anti-intellectual and low. It relates to amateur poetry, not in these 15 books, as brighter and more efficient.

Food is *energy* but politics is about *power*. It is possible to argue that ideas are the concern of powerful people, food the concern of ordinary people, so that the exclusion of ideas represents a rejection of elitism and a reaching-out to the mass market. This depoliticisation raised two other topics: first, that the goal of politics could well be a kind of suburban affluence, and apolitical poets, by depicting this material plenty, could claim to have "got over politics", and that freedom from ideas is actually freedom from anxiety. Secondly, that contestation of settled authority became a form of status competition, like having experience of drugs and alcohol; there was a kind of rule that "anyone non-contestatory is an idiot" (concomitantly, "all settled authority is an idiot"), which ceased to be fashionable in the 1980s; the redefinition of the poem away from ideas and towards objects, away from the community towards the household, is in line with what the Conservative Party designed, and which accounts for their electoral success.

7. *The Stumbling Dance*, (ed. Rupert Loydell, 1994); 246 pp., 22 poets

The introduction states that the idea of the anthology was new or young poets, but this turned out not to be the case. The editor does not believe in schools or manifestoes.

A look at the contents list indicates that two of the poets' names are misspelt on the cover. It has been included here as a source of poetry of low standards, as a background against which to examine literary poetry. The contributors seem to have low confidence in their own ability and in the powers of language. They don't ask very much of the reader. They don't put the reader into a specialised state, an elaborate game calling for behaviour which departs widely from everyday norms, and which moves inside a complex symbolic array; this may go along with a suspicious attitude towards ideas, a truculent feeling that things are obstinate and that ideas don't change them very much. If these poems did induce one into an error, it would not be of a captious or treacherous kind. It is hard to date the poems by style, since style of any kind is hard to locate; this does not mean that they are coterminous with reality. Looking at them, one hypothesises that the elementary condition of poeticity is a game shared between writer and readers, which resets the terms of reality, and whose depth depends on the enthusiasm of both sides; a virtual space whose dimensions are specified by the sociolinguistic situation. Being unable to take part in games may imply a criticism of commodity capitalism, the media, or the education system, as sites where games take place. The poets represent situations which they seem to have little control over or stake in; no-one could accuse them of rigging experience to bear out ideas, which they don't have. They often use the word *traipse*, to signal a kind of clumsy reluctance with which they go through life. This stolidity is perhaps a denial of the authenticity of sensibility; both an idea and an emotion seem, here, to depend on a basic distortion of probability, a trick of the brain against the universe, preordained to be found out.

Not all the poetry is uninteresting. Paul Holman is one of the hopes of British poetry, Jope is a mythic-Jungian who has written some beautiful poems; in general the anthology serves to illustrate non-literary poetry, the opposite pole from skilled poetry, whether mainstream or artistic.

There is no overlap between (7) and any of the other anthologies.

8. *Dream State*, (edited Daniel O'Rourke, 1994), 229 pp., 25 poets

The offering is restricted to younger Scottish poets. It covers a wider formal span than the other books here listed, from high to low; while diverse, it is of very uneven quality. I counted 29 poems in Scots out of 156. The introduction refers to the enormous influence of Edwin Morgan, and quotes him on "the other dedication – to a society, to a place, to a nation(.)" All Scottish poets were affected by the withholding of autonomy in 1979 and the fanaticism of the Thatcher government which came to power soon afterwards; but "a kind of queasy quietism seems to have prevailed as far as day-to-day dialectics were concerned." The poets were dreaming a new state, enjoying "a vigorous pluralism" "unprecedented cultural confidence". The poets were born between 1955 and 1967, but the introduction does not relate style to age. "(A)ny statement about Scotland is likely to be true"; a dreamlike state, not quite a dream (and not quite a state); the rest of the introduction is about individual poets and not to our purpose; it merely claims pluralism.

The pressure to break up the spectrum which has led to so many separate markets in England is here ignored – but not quite, for there is no tradition in Scotland of anthologies of younger poets, and this one is therefore an innovation. *The New Makars* includes someone born in 1900. The Scots market is less mature than the English one, where this specialisation of commodity also seems to imply a narrowing of scope for the individual poet. There is also less sense of specialisation inside the poets' work. Whether we read this array of rejection and withdrawal as sophistication or as hostility will influence our judgment on the development of the market. A Scottish anthology is of course a specialised commodity, isolated by nature in bookshops which hold masses of American and English poetry. Regional anthologies are also starting to exist, but mostly including prose; *Fower Brigs til a Kinrik*, an excellent volume, collected poems by four poets from Fife. Whereas such a nationally defined anthology is pictorial, accepting, and identifying, asks readers to think of the society which generated it, using the separate poets as characters, like figures in an illustration showing all the different types that make up a society, a technical anthology like *Conductors* asks us to think about the forces which generate a self; it is critical, isolating, and analytical, it relates to sociological theory (for example, phenomenology) but not to descriptive sociology. Because it narrows views down to those of the poets, it is much more homogeneous than *Dream State*; it claims to be universal, but through being non-faithful to, and outside, actual social experience.

Apart from the Informationists, the poetry included is quite uninteresting.

9. *Contraflow on the Super-highway*
(edited by W.N. Herbert and Richard Price, 1994) 63 pp., 6 poets

This book is effectively self-published, and is a specialist anthology of the group called the Informationists, representing formal ideas worked out in the early 1980s, and climaxing with *Sharawaggi* (1990). Some details on the origin of the idea are given in *interference*, issue 1. The name refers to an interest in the world as information, and in the latter as a commodity, developing the resistance and obstinacy of an object; the daily contrast between Scots and English makes the non-transparency of linguistic form especially obvious in Scotland. The cover sums it up as "the aesthetic manipulation of media and academic jargon". The title page says "information is beauty". The introduction by Richard Price says that "the Informationist (demonstrates) the absurdity of (...) political discourse, cinema, scientific, academic and philosophical jargon, history and (...) cultural kitsch and detritus of all sorts(.)" He wants to provide a communal map of the world of data. He believes in the primacy of discourse; has as heritage John Davidson, Hugh MacDiarmid, and Edwin Morgan; deals with science and contemporary metaphysics.

The essay speaks of "ambiguities, paradoxes, and complexities" beside "urban, littoral, and rural variations in vocabulary and syntax" (littoral refers to generalised differences between West and East Coast Scots). He speaks further of "recontextualised" "substitution of fantastic... elements", "interest in social construction", "fascinated by Scottish kitsch", "the argumentative but also the transcendent". The afterword by W.N. Herbert speaks of "an urban poetry, a scientific poetry".

It is not clear how far the group differs from a number of poets in England; if they are really doing something with language that John Goodby and Ian Duhig are not. An oscillation in the use of Scots is apparent; only W.N. Herbert uses it habitually, Robert Crawford uses it only for occasional *tours de force*, David Kinloch uses it for the odd poem; the others don't use it at all.

The overlap with (3) shows that English editors are now admitting the right to exist of Scottish poetry, but also points in the other direction: Herbert is only used because he is published by Bloodaxe. English editors just ignore Scottish and Welsh poets, and as a result there is no word of mouth about them in England, and so no impulse to start reading them, less from racist arrogance than from a geographical divide between cultural circuits.

10. *Agenda: An Anthology – The First Four Decades 1959-93*, (edited William Cookson, 1994) 281 pages of poetry, more of prose, 53 poets

The introduction describes the editor's contacts with Ezra Pound, the inspiration of the magazine, and not artistic policy. There are only a series of circular statements, to the effect that good poetry is good. There is a horizontal split in the magazine's cultural selection: for poets born before 1900, it chooses the most radical and the most ambitious, but for younger poets it chooses obscure and unambitious figures. Speculatively, Cookson (the editor) was smitten, when he was a teenager, by meeting poets fifty years older than he was; this experience could never happen again, and so he was disappointed with, and resentful of, all later poetic developments (later than 1959). Geoffrey Hill gets proper handling, but he was already established in 1959. *Agenda*'s handling of First World War veterans like David Jones and Giuseppe Ungaretti has been absolutely exemplary. The poetry in *Agenda* is conservative rhythmically, syntactically, in the logical sequence of ideas, in the lack of linguistic effects, in the way the image of the poet is presented, in the lack of contention with established authorities and ideas, in the reserved and low-affect tone, in the lack of conjecture, in the preference for old books and buildings, in the sense of stability, and sometimes in the resort to religious values and a disapproving morality. There are exceptions; for example, the metre of David Jones is not conservative. Other examples of this conservative literate poetry can be found in the 1980 anthology *Eleven British Poets* (edited by Michael Schmidt), and in *PN Review*, where ideological backing for it is sometimes printed. It represents a quadrant where the poet commands neatness, and prestige cultural assets, including good impulse control, but also very limited expressivity.

The set of poets in this anthology represents a double selectivity, that of the editors of *Agenda* and of the poets who submitted material to it. The ambience of *Agenda* is unusually specific, and is the sequel of a position of embitterment – anti-democratic, anti-modern, anti-establishment – and as a response an illuminist conspiracy of the secret elite, in 1959. This has developed by violently rejecting anything new happening since 1959, while striking attitudes of martyrdom (at not being a recognised authority) and exilic condemnation (exercising authority to revile and condemn without having any authority), in a vogue of security and solidarity, the fraternal feelings of the conspirators. The specifics of the Poundian position of the editor are not widely shared, but the magazine's support represents a wider faction, that of an educated group with low upward mobility who resent all the challenges to middle-class authority which have occurred over the past 40 years. The educated public is in fact split between those who accepted the proposals of the New Left in the 1960s, and those who did not.

Jean MacVean wrote only Arthurian poems, perhaps following Charles Williams in around 1935 to 1945; she may well have reasoned that appealing to a collective myth combined with being deeply unfashionable amounted to a worthwhile poetic project; successful poets are generally personal and central at the same time. The reasons why she was simply unfashionable and unoriginal belong to sociology. The long poem by Alan Massey is very good.

11. *Angels of Fire: an anthology of radical poetry in the '80s*, edited Paskin, Silver, Ramsay (1985) 154 pp., 53 poets

The kind of poetry represented in this anthology attacks society for causing personal unhappiness, but demonstrates the possibility for social change by showing individual change; it explores an uncontrolled area, insecure yet available, where neither character nor authority are firm, where new behavioural and psychological patterns can be developed. Most of the poems are in a stylistic zone between pop and agitprop, which we can call agitpop. The start is governed by a medical metaphor, of exercises repeated in order to solve the malady of unhappiness, defined as submission or self-dislike; the outcome is governed by a political metaphor, as a new social contract, with, typically, less hierarchical structures and less aggression.

There is a contrast within *Angels of Fire* between the straight-ahead first-person moral uplift stuff and certain poems which are avant-garde. Paskin is attacking these poets included in her own anthology. When she happily talks, on p.xviii, about the poetry which Eric Mottram used to promote as "disappearing into obscurantism", one has to at least suspect that this darkness visible pours out of editors sealing off the new and demanding. The mainstream response to the avant-garde, the formal periphery, involves four strokes: it's bad; it doesn't exist; we are it; and it used to exist but doesn't any more. It is usual to deploy all four at once. Obscurantism is an active word, whereas obscurity is imposed from outside.

Angels of Fire was the name assumed by a troupe of poets who gave readings together from 1982. The events had very mixed bills; there were some core members, but most of the poets in the anthology were only occasional guests. The selection is based on oral performance rather than radicalism.

Sylvia Paskin attempts, in the Introduction, to establish that formal and social radicalism are really the same thing, and to set up a time sequence for the departure from conventional norms which she believes to be the norm for contributors to this volume. The *terminus a quo* cited (page xviii) is the late 1950s, which is when the Poetry and Jazz events, linked by Jeff Nuttall to the Young Communists, were running. If poetry is progressing, it should have shown changes between 1958 and 1985. The implication is that either the radical Left, or radical poetry, did not exist in 1957.

One version of the arrow of time is that it runs away from written poetry and towards the recitation. In this perspective, simplification, reduction, stridency, and schmalz are progressive. The pressure of the live audience flattens aesthetic differences so that people become insensitive to form, inducing a group loyalty and camaraderie which also means intolerance of outsiders.

Angels of Fire was giving performances in London, so all its staple poets were living in or near there. How is it that the new and progressive, as defined by Paskin, Ramsay, Silver, lives in London when the introduction to *The New Poetry* says that London is the centre of tradition? Is somebody telling a lie? Or do we have a clash over the progress franchise here?

12. *Purple and Green: poems by 33 Women Poets* (no editor, Rivelin Grapheme Press, 1985) 191 pp.

The lack of mention of an editor is a deliberately egalitarian gesture; authority is neither claimed nor accepted. There is a certain Northern slant, due presumably to Rivelin Grapheme's base in Sheffield. The title probably refers to the suffragette colours. The declining of a foregrounded manager-spokesman figure is paralleled within the poems by a particular attitude towards the poet's relative importance and the status of their information – or, how the value of their information relates to the status of the person.

The anthology is pervaded by the changes brought about by feminism, and would be unthinkable without it. Someone who demanded why so could only be rebutted by examining an anthology of women's poetry from the 1950s: but of course there is none such. The whole idea of a swarm of women poets writing in a documentary way, writing about feelings disloyal to their husbands, lovers, employers, the government, capitalism, etc., being forthright, sometimes self-seeking, but never religious, glamorous, refined, or self-denying, didn't exist in the 1950s. Modern feminism effectively didn't start until 1970, and when it did start a lot of people derided it and denied its right to existence.

It is because the feminist position is an attack on the whole social order, not simply on local abuses, that the genre of anthology is peculiarly suited to it. The poems here act to confirm each other: we see, not only one household where bad things are happening behind closed doors, but we see inside all the houses in the street. As in a pop record, hearing the same thing confirmed by many voices gives it an objective reality. This factor points oddly away from individual, differentiated experience, although at the same time every poem is original, and most of the poets make personal experience and feelings the centre of truth, because they are alienated from the way society is run. The critique of the truth of personal experience, so popular in contemporary philosophy, would be unwelcome here: this device is fired once and once only, when the poet-protagonist makes the break from the patriarchal ideology and rebuilds her awareness of the world on different presuppositions. This new awareness is not seen as provisional. In fact the device is kept in the cupboard, to be deployed again when it is a question of discrediting the whole consciousness of a man. There is a latent gap in the fabrication here: if there are two people involved in a situation, and one of them is capable of being wrong, surely they are both capable of being wrong; this leaves us looking for a stable, external yardstick capable of establishing the truth, for the satisfaction of us, as the readers. It would be unreasonable to look for this inside the poem, admittedly written by one of the participants. But further, it opens the possibility that a great deal of consciousness, especially in the spheres of the emotions, may not be subject to truth-testing, because it does not correspond to anything outside itself. When two people clash, not about truth, but about what they want to do, it may be strength that determines the outcome. The poem may then become a vent for unsatisfied desires, one-sided language uncontrolled by the moral resistance of another person to contradict or agree. This flaw does not necessarily matter in the reading of particular poems. Or perhaps, on the other hand, we gauge the character of the poet from the whole tone of the poem, and it is this composite judgment which allows us to evaluate the story the poem tells.

Stylistically, several dozen of these 33 poets merge into each other. But poetic richness is not to be found in experimentation alone; the stress here is on the semantic elements, and on the psychology of the situation being presented. Evidently, all the successes come from detailed linguistic effort all the same; from directness, clarity, precision, concentration, brilliance of imagery. Experimentation is not the only way of dealing with experience in an honest and intellectually fascinating way. We should consider the whole process of verbalization, the indefinable region (a grey void? a featureless plenitude?) it starts with, and how many dimensions the process has. It takes understanding of all dimensions of language, to write such poems as Elizabeth Bartlett and Isobel Thrilling publish here; even if they aren't performing a latent criticism of the rules of poetry.

In a project of confession and repentance, experience is here being verbalized and recounted in order to attain a higher level of consciousness, and this therapeutically, in order to alter one's behaviour and train of life. It is not dead, not like property, but has a progress ideology built into it, and competes with the experimentalist version of progress. The progress ideology implies the rejection of existing experience, as part of the before. Poetry might fall apart along this fault line, that is between bad past and glowing, but unrealised, future. It would be an error to reduce the project of confession to its historical roots in religious meetings, largely those of the Dissenters and Methodists: these are not the source of the wish to rethink one's life in public, but only a historical form which this wish took. The importance both of Dissenters and of women in the development of the English novel is well-known.

Fantasy has an important role in creating meaning, which is self-referential at the level of groups even when it avoids being so at the level of individuals. Poetry starting out from the critique of the social order could end up either with a "grey array", with acts of shaping and highlighting deliberately withheld, or with a sealed autonomy, where the self flows like water across a floor because the world it normally interacts with has been set aside. The threat is that by undefining the self-process you undermine the juridical claims under litigation, disfavouring women as the underdogs who most want change and redistribution of power. The more stiff, unchangeable positions a poem has, the less the total information flow of the poem; and so the less intelligence it visibly has. The original feminist critique was that the social order is the product of male subjectivity, inadequately restrained, and not of objective needs; this tenet could not sustain anything but the idea that social meaning, and social structure, are the products of the imagination. The fruits of victory are meant to be a new way of life, not simply the relief of laying down arms; limiting the imagination, even in order to win disputes, limits the shape a new society can take.

There is an overlap of only 1 poet with *tnbp* section 2. I think this is misleading, and that the two anthologies certainly belong together as feminist statements. I would suggest that the lack of overlaps points to a pattern where individuals do not dominate, being related to the lack of an editor for *Purple and Green*. The ethos of this area is anti-exceptionalist;

the experiences recounted are felt to be typical and to relate to the real social system. We can guess, then, that what is on show is uncultivated poetry, and that it tells us something of what is happening outside the specialised world of people totally committed to poetry. We may wonder what the shared assumptions of highly-invested poets are.

13. *The Urgency of Identity. Contemporary English-language Poetry from Wales*, (edited by John T. Lloyd, 1994) 217pp. (including interviews) 19 poets

The introduction speaks of "colonizer's language", "a colonial or post-colonial condition", where use of English "compromises their sense of identity... a kind of treason" (hence the name of the book), "Welshness", "struggle to preserve the Welsh language", "pressure towards Anglicisation", "a minority language under siege", "fundamentally shaped by Welsh culture, landscape, and language", "clear nationalistic bias (...) has not gained recognition, much less acceptance", "lose its distinctive qualities over time", "language/identity issues", "specifically Welsh times and places", "interested in mythology and in history", "grounded in place and time".

Meic Stephens, interviewed, remarks that reviewers and writers in Wales mostly know each other, and he misses argument and theoretical debate in Wales. The limitation to "poets of the 1980s and 1990s" leaves *Urgency* overshadowed by an earlier generation of Anglo-Welsh poets who were much more interested in ideas and much more interesting. The aesthetic guiding the poems here is one of banality. This is flatness under pressure; it would seem that the preceding political conflict was about the eclipse of normal Welsh life from the Anglo-American media, and perhaps also the polemic version of this, as Welsh nationalists claimed that English-speaking Welsh people were without culture or identity. In this context the portrayal of normality without striving to excel it could become a goal of Anglo-Welsh literati. The plainness is cheerful and inclusive. Another political message behind it is that Welsh society is classless, and the buzz of welcoming if unexciting togetherness is an assertion of this. The older generation had an idealistic view of Welsh life which aspired to revolutionary transformation but could be seen as treating everyday Welsh consciousness as a theory to be argued over and modified.

Though flatness comes across as a low quality, poems by Peter Finch and Chris Bendon are excellent. Your address decides whether you get arts-grant money; one of the rules of a game which I cannot expound, because the committees sit behind closed doors.

14. *The New Makars*
(edited Tom Hubbard, 1991) 211 pages; 65 poets

The qualification for this book is to write in Scots. Virtually all the poems in all the other anthologies (except 8 and 9) are in Standard English. The introduction, 'A Future for Poetry in Scots?' speaks of "the political and cultural dominance of London", "the acquiescence of powerful sections of the Scottish intelligentsia and media", "the oral dimension", "several generations", "fragmentation of the language", "accuse Gaelic and Scots poets of paranoia", "monoglot reviewer", "one's inclinations, one's land, and one's language", "spiritual emptiness", "collective unconscious", "driven underground", "All that has dark sounds has *duende*", "the physicality of Scots language", "the passionless, the super-cool, the clever-clever".

The poems are very diverse, although we can observe that (a) everyone is aiming for a Scottish audience (b) the poets are either from the working-class or, if from a higher class, they have powerful political motives for adopting Scots. The emphasizing of the contrast Scots: English deletes other contrasts, such as old: young, high: low, or even good: bad. Although Scots is marked as {non-standard; lower-class; local; low}, it is also difficult to write and to read, and in that sense high. The choice of a difficult but common medium tends to push the individuality of the artist into the background; the community invoked is one hoped-for, in which power has been decentralised back to Edinburgh, and local power brings about the end of alienation. Just as Scots is barely a written language, so the poets are less sustained by print than by writers' groups and live readings, both tied into local arts subsidies; so that the nation Scotland is a theoretical object. The support prose mentions identity, but also internationalism: the introduction quotes the manifesto of a Yiddish poets' group, brilliantly spotted as another low-status Germanic language. The most ambitious poems in the book tend to be translations, indicating a certain nervousness and attraction towards the folk pole of style (which it turns out is also the conservative pole) on the part of the poets.

The publisher is James Thin, the leading bookshop in Edinburgh. Inspection of the poetry section in the shop shows Scottish poetry segregated, and the keyword SCOTTISH prominent in the packaging of most books. So the Scottish reader partly owns this poetry; a poet who dared to offer something distinctive would forfeit this ownership by other people. The bookshop ambience poses the question of when something you consume constitutes dominance. Rival concepts of culture are split over the ideal of it as transformation, or as something that reminds you of you.

15. *A Various Art*
(edited by Andrew Crozier and Tim Longville, 1987) 372pp., 17 poets

The introduction to this by now classic product is distinctly cagey, but the selection of 17 poets represents the best of a "generation", (i.e. born between about 1936 and 1950), who emerged during the 1960s, refers to a *timenow* of about 1975, and continues the artistic policy of the magazine *Grosseteste Review* (1968-84), edited by Longville and John Riley. The introduction does offer a definition of the poetry, written by academics, which emerged in the 1950s, had almost monopoly power during the 1960s, and "foreclosed the possibilities". It is the variety of the following generation to which the title refers. Many of the poets of this contrasting, sixties generation can be summed up as academic Marxists influenced by the New Left, with high expectations of a reformed society, which beauty and goodness in the here and now are advance guards of. *GR* itself grew out of an interest in the Objectivists, a left-wing group of American poets of the 1930s. Attention, throughout, to how awareness is constructed can be compared with the contemporary films of Antonioni, such as *Blow-up*, in which the whole process of perception is cut off from its result and made problematic. Reflecting a return to the oral, the poems narrate things as they happen, avoiding the certainty of past experience and organised knowledge. This direct address goes along with an absence of compulsion. The poetry aims at the beautiful, and finds this in the present, unstill quick learning rather than accumulated passive knowledge. The conduct of the text is smooth and undisturbed, soaked in light to capture its ambiguities. The conjecture is protected from dispersal by stabilising, but is itself an act of instability. Allen Fisher's review of the book used the term *sprezzatura*; the term means contempt, but as used of 15th-century Italian painting it means a studied casualness; the negligent ease of this poetry is reached by the avoidance of the didactic or the effortful. Space is freed for the action of doubt by the exclusion of higher-energy conflict; thought is made possible by freedom from practical tasks, which in some sense form its grounds. The constant invoking of qualities of light is a way of distancing the contemplating mind from experience: biochemically tied to luminosity levels, but simultaneously detached, because the study of painting has revealed the effect of light on staging and mood, and the speaker is aware of the transience of such moments. The specific distance – light being both transient and immersing – allows the success of the poems, operating in the substantive realm between self-projection and passivity. Greater self-awareness, and finer perception of gradations within this realm are the coveted skills. Naval battles are not on show. The logical structure of some of the poems shows a check and update mechanism; the reader may well point out that the check is just as much subject to fixing by the poet as the conjecture; but the zigzag mechanism does have an effect of psychological reassurance. Politics as the area of feasible change is removed from a governmental site, where the poet can only look on from afar, to the everyday, where the result without projection is denuded of meaning, and the interest has shifted to how projections by different people can be integrated. The drama of frustration and exclusion has been lifted out of these poems; as if the action of the intelligence can only take place where the mind is in control of what it acts on. The kind of Marxism in question owes something to Lefebvre's *The Philosophy of Everyday Life* (etc.), where the stress is less on violent struggle and more on the practice of equity, a flavour suited to the 30-year wave of prosperity in Western Europe, which came to an end around 1975. This poetry could be about affluence, and a time when politics is the fine course-steering which produces consensus and excludes other possibilities. It was a time of dandyism. Despite Crozier's reference to "the discovery of form in language itself", it is not about line-breaks but about the pleasures of social life and afternoons in the country.

Analysis

Out of the 450 names, about 50 are either Irish or North American. Exact data about nationality is not available to me in all cases. The audience in this country certainly reads poetry by Canadians, Irish, etc. However, since the non-appearance of these names across the board is because of their nationality, it says nothing about aesthetic preferences and so adds nothing to the model. It is better to remove them from this analysis.

The divisions which really prove Hartley Williams' point are stylistic ones: *Conductors* and *The New Poetry* are dealing with exactly the same age-range and nation, but there is not even one overlap between the 35 in one pick list and the 55 in the other. We can answer his question by proposing that identification leads to partial loss of insight. A poem grips the reader's mind at many levels – and, so occupied, the mind is less able to transform and identify with other kinds of poetry. Anthologists recognise this and produce *convergent* selections of poems. Some of the clusters are separated by 'identification points' – being Scottish, female, young, etc. – which need not imply any formal differences.

We propose that each anthology is organised around an *ideal*. The divisions of the map are not there because there is a wholly empty space separating each group, but because poets strive towards an artistic ideal and so the areas remote from any single ideal are sparsely populated.

I see the clusters named as similar to genres. In 1956, someone who went to a western one Friday could go to a musical the next Friday and a Doris Day flick the week after that. Genre, even at its height, is not co-extensive with an individual's needs; the concept is more one of *temporary* cultural identity, where someone can form different artistic wishes at different times.

The radius which is the stylistic distance between Sean O'Brien and J.H. Prynne (say) is the most striking feature of the scene. Viewing the scene as a virtual space allows us to see this distance as a monumental quality: the object which contains it is like a mountain or a pyramid, a triumph of scale. The mutual rejection of various individuals (secondarily, of various groups) is the feature of the scene which most calls for explanation. I suppose understanding of it follows only from a grasp of hundreds of individual works. We can suggest that it may follow from a simple quality of speech: we wish to be the only person speaking (when we speak). If we extrapolate this to a field of 400 poets (a minimum figure) the wish for other poets to fall silent may also climb to high levels.

I would wish to deliver the experience of knowing O'Brien's apprehension of Prynne and then at once of knowing Prynne's apprehension of O'Brien.

The field around 1995 doesn't have spaces for poets thriving in the '60s. Although they went on publishing, they disappear from the anthologies – which have a bias towards new commodities. This could represent a downward curve of someone's career: at first part of an age cohort with a dozen others, they disappear when the cohort is centrally 'edited' down to 3 or 4. However, absence from the anthologies does not always mean that someone was not popular.

The anthology itself is a powerful generator of analogies, spectrums, power relations, and sustenance or subversion. The format of anthologies incites the reader to compare poets with each other; it differs from reading a volume all by one poet, which generally follows an act of preference and relies on mutual indulgence. Such reading calls for a sociology of solitude and self-consciousness; the reduction of household size over the last few decades is related to the reduction of the number of people in the average poem. We seem to see in poetry the most extremely original and personalised poets, the furthest from the collective norms, voicing the most advanced collectivist beliefs. The modern poem finds it hard to allow a second voice; the purchase of the anthology is the revenge of the reader on the single self-confirming voice. We can think about the single voice of the poem by looking back at the Ealing comedies, or contemporary soap operas, as if at a matrix from which the individual ran away; where the casting of a variety of different characters allows for constant alternation of tone, lets us realise different parts of ourselves in different roles, and encourages peculiarities while also reassuring us about our physical and moral failings, in a spirit of forgiveness. We don't go into art to become somebody else; we go in to become everybody else.

Why do we pursue specialisation? Why do we form quarrelling bands? Why do we regard some other people's experience as alienation, or again as a covetable commodity? This kind of politics is driven by deep imperatives which are more powerful than the poems, and shape them. Groups fight with each other because they both want the same thing.

Through these anthologies we get brief snatches of 450 poets; it may be useful to emphasize the crudeness of the hope that reading these 15 books (only) would give someone an overview of what is happening in British poetry; this overestimates the power of the poem as against context and presentation. The total field of published poets is not 400 but 7,000. Published poets differ quite systematically from amateur poets.

Other anthologies that could be consulted, to improve the mapping of the conceptual space of poetry, would be *Poetry with an Edge, The Mingling of the Streams, A State of Independence, PN Review #100, Ladder to the Next Floor, The Exact Change Yearbook, Floating Capital, Angel Exhaust #9, Angel Exhaust #15, Other.*

The Lexicon
a common source of unique distinctions

A simple building-block of poetry – although not the simplest – is the word. Cataloguing the English lexicon is rather easy – we simply skip it and point to a finished reference resource such as the Oxford English Dictionary. Meanwhile – grasping the shape of the lexicon as a whole is something beyond our intellects.

The poem is made of words which belong to the common language; they can only work by evoking memories of shared experiences which, if shared, belong then to the common stock. It is unusual to have memories of things that didn't happen. The deception by which poets link worn memories into new series is fragile. It would indeed be paradoxical to claim that the poet can be outside society, while language and knowledge (and what knowledge knows) are inside it.

We need the concept of an archive to describe what is not-original: what is a *fait acquis*, discovered to the court, consensual, bagged and tagged, safely stored. This archive, controlled by all speakers (but to a greater extent, of course, by the educated), stocks the definitions of words, but also commonplaces, a shelf full of facts and opinions. It is organised in fields, of tiered oppositions. A rule of speech is that a familiar notion need not be voiced again; the archive is also a (complete) definition of what we do not want to hear or to utter. An extension of this rule tells us that unoriginal poetry is not good to read. We can conceptualise the poem as defining a sensation which is not in the expanded lexicon; whose absence from the store is constitutive of the poemicity of the poem.

It is much easier to spot what poetry must not do than what it must. The poetry that comes into the post-boxes of magazines is full of clichés; clichés are solid and describe a consensual domain. We fail to react. Negative rules, dulled areas of insensibility, are easy to frame. So perhaps the central area of poetry is really where it must not go. Writing a poem is like painting on a surface composed almost entirely of holes. The question is more how poets find the narrow intact paths.

Uncorrelatedness defines what, in a mass of experiences and verbal material, is worthy of becoming a poem. The poem is interstitial to the nuances of the common lexicon. Its internal parts isolate what is new and set it off against what is familiar; they provide a motive for the attention demanded; they swat aside reasons for treating the event as a freak, misrecognition of what is familiar. The poem and the parts of the poem must be:

(+interstitial, -freakish)

and most parts of poetics can be seen as different ways of reaching this point.

There is a Gaelic folktale in which the hero is told to find wood which is neither crooked nor straight. The riddle is solved by a queen who tells him to go to a saw-pit and pick up a bag of sawdust. Neither straight nor crooked describes a space that seems not to exist – but which actually does. This is an example of how an agreed linguistic code can be used to describe unfamiliar things. Verbal art likes to focus on moments which breach the code from which the verbal art is constructed. The paradox is basic to poetry, and the gap between paradox and nonsense is the most important there is. Riddles often carry out this function – and are one of the bases of poetry. (Kennings, for example, are closely related to the riddles of which the Anglo-Saxons were so fond.) The riddle is the folk, or ancient, version of paradox; it may be the predecessor of stylised language, and is related to taboo languages of obligate non-namings and periphrases.

The principle on which cabinets of curiosities were built is that they breached the rules of classification which were in common use. There is a tight match, such that any object which does bear out these rules will be excluded from the cabinet, and would be viewed with contempt if it were there. A fossil is worth more than the carcass of a familiar beetle. This implies an analogy between the cabinet of curiosities and the poem or book of poems. The curiosity resembles the paradox, as the unit structure of the Metaphysical poem. The paradoxes were pushing against the edges of the folk classification system as embedded in the common language, and perhaps provide a glimpse of its artificiality. The awareness of the arbitrariness of social systems remains a social discriminator.

Strangeness takes us back to a primitive level of acquiring objects. In the later stage of their social pre-eminence – say from 1630 to 1900 – the nobility were much given to collecting rare objects. This was the origin of museums and archaeology – which, at its origin, recouped the object-acquisitions of aristocrats from previous millennia, buried with them. These precious objects were paralleled by equally ornate aristocratic praise-poems, which were the basis for European poetry, and which were still being composed in languages such as Gaelic and

Welsh into the 18th century. One way of thinking about the post-Elizabethan book of poems might be as a collection of rare sensations, paralleling a collection of rare objects but constituting virtual as opposed to real wealth. Modern poetry would then be a recapitulation of immense enterprises of seizure and display by the lords at the apex of the social system. Modern shopping would be a fulfilment of a dim memory of the exploits of total shoppers who owned the countryside and could afford to buy anything in the world. Fashion emerged from a combination of the surplus purchasing power of the nobility and their abiding wish to compete with each other; a set of instructions for change which has also involved poetry in overreaching, a fury for excelling its models, a costly quest for the new and unassimilable. Overfulfilment and over-consumption are related to each other.

We can draw on the work of George Lakoff (citing the work of Eleanor Rosch) on salience and focal membership of sets. Nouns describe categories, sets of phenomena which are bounded by the rules defining the category and, in detail, by the boundaries of adjacent nouns. These nouns are, however, grouped by trees: that is, vertical organising functions, where the topmost noun is more salient than nouns lower down, which are contained inside it and describe finer distinctions. Some objects are more central within categories than others, and are called *focal* members; some distinctions are more primary than others. Any qualifying word belongs in a wordfield embodying a set of distinctions. Complex phrase structure allows offsets not given by single lexical items. Reader expectation is that poetry should be "sensitive", and we can, coarsely, equate this with delicacy of semantic offsets (both via exotic lexis and via qualifications). Claims that the genre system has collapsed are gainsaid by this quality which demarcates poetry. The exceptionalist bias of modern poetry makes us expect a preference for non-focal areas of semantic space; while looking for these, we can use the term *subfocal* to say what we are looking for, i.e. what is secondary, offset from the banal, and piquant. (Exceptionalist was defined above in the discussion on *Conductors of Chaos*.)

The high or low quality of a poem has to do with its mixture of focal and interstitial in vocabulary choice. Height correlates with higher education, with cultural sophistication, and with doing office work as opposed to manual work. The tilt towards interstitiality also reduces the poem's ability to draw on primary psychic energies; the social cachet it brings is bought by a perilous transaction; the poet needs restorative plunges into salience and focality. The exceptionalist poets drew on this model of interstitiality for their model of their own experience, the unique quality which they admired in themselves and offered to the reader. The originality which they enjoyed so much competed with the salience of what they had to say.

The vocabulary we have today is much larger than that of Anglo-Saxon, and probably much more excelling the store of any individual, and probably a much better index of social class than its predecessor of 800 AD. The acquisition of French and Latin words over the last thousand years has largely served as the interstitial filling of native lexical structures, to achieve *fins écarts*. French words are common in areas like millinery and confectionery where fine distinctions and innovation are important to the sales potential. We know (from the work of Edwin Ardener) that colour terms tend to be borrowed from foreign languages, filling out a simple spectrum; thus Welsh (and Cornish and Breton) have the Latin word for green (viridis/gwyrdd etc.) to eke out a native word *glas* which meant "green and blue"; *glas* has not had its range of meaning restricted, so *gwyrdd* is still something of a stranger. *Porffor* (purple) was borrowed at much the same time. This enrichment of the lexicon gives rise to a pedagogic moment when the parent teaches the child a new word (or, corrects its naïve use): what colour is this? No, it's mauve.

These distinctions allow a competitive game and over-fulfilment. We can describe much of schooling as the acquisition of new vocabulary and simultaneously of new semantic distinctions. Each school year is an over-fulfilment of the year before, as the child goes further in the mastery of the English language, without losing the previous gains. Engaging in extremely (competitively) fine distinctions is an obvious move for poets to make. It brings an obvious risk. The availability of the interstitial words allows them to be misused by people without true control of the distinctions. The preciosity of the speakers so nimbly mocked by Shakespeare (Osric, a fantastic fop; various characters in *Twelfth Night*) is only comic because it goes beyond an invisible boundary in carrying out procedures which everyone carries out; the language we use is saturated with French and Latin words and so is clearly precious and fantastic. The decree that sites the line is self-referential; we may suspect that the precious speaker is making a bid for influence and advancedness which is unsuccessful, but otherwise like other bids. The line between a Latinate coinage which we imitate and one which we laugh at resembles the line between a good poem and a bad one. I would think that the trajectory of stylistic devices resembles that of single words, and is controlled by gatekeepers.

There is a moment in *Poems from Afghanistan* where Colin Simms uses the word *grain* to evoke the Afghan clans. *Grain* is a Scandinavian word used in the eastern Borders (and only there, I believe) to mean a patrilineal descent group, or clan, there bound together by possessiveness and military energy for self-defence in a lawless region; it is thus ultra-specific as a description of Afghanistan in the throes of civil war. It originally means a branch of a tree (cf. *grow*), but was early adapted to mean the confluence of two streams, and a look at a map of the Borders will show many features so called. It is hard to see the word without vivid recollections of the Border hills and of Northumbrian antiquity.

In an interview, R.F. Langley evokes his enthusiasm for unusual words, and how much time he spends reading dictionaries. *Gleek* and *mournival* are two words he has used at the necessary moment. His poetry generally sets out from paradox. In 'Tom Thumb', a poem in the pamphlet *Jack*, he writes about swallows disappearing at a height in the twilight; then about a swarm of gnats, and how Jack (a cognitive alter ego, a second "agent" occupying the same brain but following different rules) has never seen them doing it before: he imitates prawns and shrimps, equating (is this paradox or metaphor?) his vertebrate arms and legs with their invertebrate limbs. The swallows are as nimble:

> But he was staring higher at
> the final suggestion of the swifts, rapidly
> dashed off, carelessly punctuated with a run
> of dots that flared, then melted immediately
> into thin air. No doubt the lightning sketches of
> the many different shapes of what he called despair.

The evocation of physiological delicacy shares a poetic project of feeling out distinctions too fine for the senses, to be brought within reach by an act of self-steadying and attention. The dusk opens and the poem closes with another evocation of the imperceptible, just across the boundary:

> Gnats twinkle, and Jack glances down another list
> of items due to be removed from the display.
> Swifts vanish in full flight, against the changing of
> the decorations from pale lemon to pearl gray.

> Stop taking stock, and listen. They have briefly left
> their voices, sharpened to incisive single points,
> the screams of fifty little demons on a spree,
> going home excitedly.

By this time the poem seems to be an extended metaphor for the operation of language; the precise pointing to objects which we cannot perceive (but which we know to be there because we have just stopped perceiving them) evokes both the failure and the success of the retrieval process, which brings up fitting utterance but also sheds what it cannot utter, into a non-place. Attention constantly draws a boundary, and this edge in some way defines a human being, as what is within it and goes up to it. The poem is not limited by inherited distinctions because it is all about distinctions that cannot be made.

We have to renounce the possibility of overall maps of how the lexicon works in poems. Whatever we can say is incomplete. The topics discussed just skim the surface. Looking at the lexicon of the English language gives us something central, which all poets use – but which we can neither find a centre of, nor comprehend consciously without severe fragmentation of the object.

The choice of words offers more information than the critic wants to take on: while leaving the poet nowhere to hide, the problems of processing thousands of lexical choices (say 10,000 words in the typical 2,000 line book of poetry) leave the critic floored. It appears that we now have views of the total world-picture of a language, in the splendid and awesome works of George Lakoff and Richard Rorty, building on many decades of lexical work by anthropologists; the time for a semantic analysis of English, as a matrix with 20,000 (or 100,000?) sites, revealing the mysteries of linkages between inner-body sensations, perceptions, conjectures about other people's minds, and self-awareness, and throwing off analyses of the total world-views of individual poets as a by-product, lies in the future.

Another way of locating the structural level might be to follow up an old idea of Dell Hymes' and look at linguistic routines. These are small-scale patterns in language; possibly involving more than one speaker, possibly implicit rather than fixed and explicit. The term refers to repeated patterns, but also to comic routines, preset dialogues involving two speakers and set moments for switching from speaking to listening. For example, Edwin Morgan writes:

>What is a demon? Study my life.
>What is a mountain? Set out now.
>What is fire? It is for ever.
>What is my life? A fall, a call.
>>(from 'A Little Catechism for the Demon')

This is quite a simple split structure (where A entrains B); perhaps we would find many more routines, many more constructions of anticipation and satisfaction, in a poem. The implication is that the learnt part of language is generative and that speaking involves constantly generating new utterances while using structures which repeat, and which allow other people to understand what we say and when to answer; further, that behaviour is generated by combining and stringing-on simple stored programs into longer, more complex, and unique wholes. We could call these multiple parallel threads. We throw away the idea of *complex* preset patterns and find the element of recurrence in small-scale structures. We can't predict the size and shape of the building, but we can recognise the microstructure of the materials used for building it. Because large structures could not fit inside small poems, perhaps small structures are the only ones worth looking for.

Metre

Phonetics offers us a large number of elements which are clearly held in common. Exit from this shared world is only possible by radical modifications of the text, shattering its relationship to the semantic world which is opened up by the conventional magic of coding. The problem is rather that this world of pure sound offers no differentiation – whereas we are definitely interested in the differences between good and bad poets. Bad poetry has the same sounds, in the same frequency ratios, as good poetry. In the foreground of a poem is a kind of machinery of sounds, essential for the meaning to emerge but incapable of expressivity. It is like the working parts of a cine projector – it makes the pictures, but if you open it up, you won't find any pictures. The distinction between good poets and bad does not start until the semantic tier. Poets may well worry about acquiring distinction when they look at the constraints on distinctiveness. We can list the public or shared elements of poetry, something like this:

   phonemes
   lexicon
   rhythmic patterns
   speech prosody
   classification system (underpinning the lexicon)
   expectations of behaviour
   objects (which enter into classification)
   the landscape (man-made or natural)

Against these, we could list combinatory patterns, and violations of norms, as being personal and 'in private ownership'.

English is an intonation language – pitch is not used for lexical distinctions, and this frees it up for signalling grammatical relationships. The intonation pattern of a poem is not indicated in print, but is implicit in grammatical rules which the reader can use to *construct* it. The patterns within the intonation group are intricated with the directing of attention – they indicate relevance and emphasis, at the same time as giving clues to the grammar of the current clause. In reading print, there is a double movement – we deduce the intonation pattern, including stress, from the grammar of the words, but also use the intonation structure to give us pointers to the structure and emphasis of the text.

English speech is organised in intonation groups which are typically between three and fourteen syllables and which are marked at the beginning. These are the basis in natural language for lines of verse. Linguists have identified a peak syllable, called the nucleus, within the intonation group – the most prominent feature in the acoustic landscape. Since it is the absence of sound, the end of a line is not a very prominent event. It would seem that natural language looks towards the dynamic peak, whereas poets look to the end of a line, and the line-break. Or, perhaps the peak syllable is extremely important in verse, and critics have ignored it because their ideas are largely inherited from Latin metrics. The phonological events are related to semantic ones, as the nucleus is generally in an important word and the end of the sound group often corresponds with the completion of a syntactic unit and of a topic. Many intonation groups are ten syllables long, but this does not make the pentameter 'natural', because speech groups are distributed along a curve of lengths, naturally varying, not clustering at ten. The isometric verse line was more monotonous than speech; a form of stylisation which has now fallen out of use. Recognising that free verse opens literature up to speech rhythms would be so wonderful if only we knew what speech rhythms were. Actually, they are even less well understood than free verse. The number of rhythmic and melodic patterns in speech is inordinately rich, and there are no proper names for most of them. Incidentally, all poetry in any century is a stylisation of speech.

Undoubtedly there are norms of free verse. The task of cataloguing them would yield to analysis based on large-scale counting. I have been unable to do this, or to find other people who have had an interest in doing this. My impression is that the natural extent of a verse line includes exactly one nuclear stress, and ends where the intonation group ends, but that many lines deviate from this pattern for an artistic purpose. Further, that these deviations are heard as deviations by the reader, and this breach of convention is necessary to the artistic effect. The breach is a form of emphasis. It is quite easy to spot the nucleus. Here is a sequence of out of copyright verse to practice on. A slanting stroke marks the end of an intonation group, and the nucleus is shown in bold.

Dear and Great **Angel**, / wouldst thou **only** leave
That child/, when thou hast **done** with him, /for **me**!/

Let me **sit** all the day here, /that when **eve**
Shall find per**form**ed thy special ministry
/And time come for de**par**ture, /**thou**,/ sus**pend**ing
Thy flight, /mayst see another child for **tend**ing,/
An**o**ther still,/ to **qui**et and retrieve./

Then I shall feel thee **step** one step, /**no** more,/
From where thou **stand**est now,/ to **where** I gaze,/
And **sudd**enly my head be covered o'er
With those **wings**, /**white** above the child /who **prays**
Now on that tomb/ – and I shall feel thee **guard**ing
Me/, out of **all** the world/; for **me**/, dis**card**ing
Yon heaven thy home/, that **waits** and opes its door! /

I would not look up **thi**ther past thy head
Because the door opes/, **like** that child/, I **know**,/
For I should have thy gracious **face** instead,/
Thou **bird** of God!/ And wilt thou **bend** me low
Like him/, and **lay**/, like **his**/, **my** hands together/,
And **lift** them up to pray/, and gently **te**ther
Me/, as thy **lamb** there/, with thy **gar**ment's spread?/

(from 'The Guardian-Angel: a Picture at Fano', by Robert Browning)

The match of line and intonation group is not especially good here. The argument about the connection between verse line (literary register) and intonation group (natural language) relies on the belief that a pattern which emerges as a majority result over thousands of lines is really a 'norm', and is heard as a norm even in lines which deviate from it. A comma or full stop usually marks the end of an intonation group. One or two of the nuclei are in doubt – there are two candidate syllables within the group. The syntax and sense can be resolved, but I went through a certain period of ambiguity before I resolved them. Browning was called unharmonious by Victorian critics, notably by Tennyson, possibly because his lines did not match intonation groups. The poem completes with an address to a friend in New Zealand that describes the poem as "translating it [the picture] to song" – an early example of a problematic poem wishing to be innocent and simple. I don't think this poem is easily singable. Indeed, the reference to 'smoothing/ Distortion down till every nerve had soothing' evokes what the poem lacks. The power of the norm was already much in doubt in the Victorian era, with poets drifting towards several different ideals of versification. For example –

> The shout was hush'd on lake and fell,
> The monk resumed his mutter'd spell:
> Dismal and low its accents came,
> The while he scathed the Cross with flame

– this (from 'Marmion', by Scott) is so different from the passage of Browning just quoted as to suggest to us that the era permitted poets to vary the norms of metre as a way of expressing personal attitudes and dispositions. The collapse of a centrally regulated, public, metric was bound to follow.

The linguists further analyse syllables into four levels of stress, described by Cruttenden as the Nucleus, and:

> (ii) SECONDARY STRESS/ACCENT involving a subsidiary pitch prominence in an intonation-group, i.e. a non-nuclear pitch-accent
> (iii) TERTIARY STRESS involving a prominence produced principally by length and/or loudness. (...)
> (iv) UNSTRESSED

It is possible to measure their relative height because we have an intonation group, bounded at start and finish, to act as a frame. That is, they have this value inside this intonation group. Stress organises everything in pairs. Contrast itself implies parallelism as well as distinction. These levels do not feature inside the traditional description of the English line of verse, which is admitted to be based on Latin or Greek norms, and to bear little relationship to the English language. Discriminating the inaudible will always be more prestigious than registering the merely audible.

My interpretation – based on a hasty review of samples – is that pre-Elizabethan English poetry stuck quite rigidly to the equivalence of verse line and intonation group; further, that contemporary non-professional English poetry still cleaves to this equivalence, and possibly the violation of this equivalence is one of the signs of sophisticated poetry. The Elizabethan Age was a deviation from time-honoured patterns. These probably included the unity of the line of verse, and my impression is that enjambement has been seen as a mark of sophistication from that day to this. This simple view can be checked by looking at bodies of verse from earlier centuries, where its prediction would be that each line has exactly one intonation group and one nucleus. Actually, a brief scan of Sidgwick and Chambers' *Early English Lyrics*, which stops in roughly 1500, shows quite a few exceptions, with lines that have either two or zero nuclei. If, however, the verse line does correspond to an intonation group, then we can generate well-formed verse lines for as long as we like simply by producing well-formed intonation groups – and the modern irregularity of length is simply the irregularity of speech, and no more baffling than speech.

Speech cannot give us a norm for the length of a verse – a considerable blow to the argument of conservative poets that the pentameter is natural to English. Either the line corresponds to the intonation group – or it is artificial and corresponds to nothing in speech (as at least one linguist, A.C. Gimson, has claimed). It has been suggested that the norm of "unlearned" poetry is the alternation of three-beat and four-beat lines of folk ballads and songs. (Gasparov p.180). Cruttenden says that intonation groups in read material are generally longer than those in speech. I would claim that extra length of intonation groups is a form of over-fulfilment – one of the striking features wherein poemicity resides. I think verse lines are *systematically* longer than speech groups – but are still intonation groups. In speech, intonation groups are generally much shorter than ten syllables. Chaucer popularised the iambic pentameter, rather late in the history of English poetry; this metre was, quite probably, Europhile, learned, and part of the Renaissance. Short lines make generally less impact. Skeltonics might be an example, nimble but forgettable and often grotesque. Wyatt and Surrey lengthened the line of lyric verse, and this is partly why we tag them as the origin of modern poetry. Perhaps this explains also why we find 15th-century poetry, with some exceptions, unreadable.

One of the poems in *Early English Lyrics* includes longer lines, for example:

With favour in her face far passing my resoun

The quality of this line suggests a principle of a good line: that it should be equitable, with the burden of meaning distributed over the line so that it does not sag anywhere, with runs of banal content.

The intonation group offers a recognisable periodicity of structure. All lines are a variation on a norm established by all lines. They represent, quite probably, a norm of length for a frame of attention. The statistical curve leads us to hear in a short line simplicity, lack of interest, low tension; in a long line, complexity, confusion, intellectual activity, self-importance (possibly bullying), opulence.

My impression is that much modern poetry disrupts natural sentence structure and so the intonation rules can't be applied – for 'natural' we can set 'conventional'. The noun string popular with the London school is an example. Whatever disruptions the poet sets up, the text *as perceived* will revert towards the patterns embodied in natural language, in a regression towards the norm. Our print conventions don't mark the nucleus, so the writer can't displace it – in contrast to the line-break, which is subject to arbitrary redirection. We can locate the nucleus, in printed text containing natural English, without fail, by applying rules which we acquired in childhood.

In Skelton, we find a certain number of lines which lack grammatical structure, for example

> Dug, dug, jug, jug
> Good year and good luck!
> With 'Chuck chuck chuck chuck!"

These are mimetic of a sound (birdsong), and also could be treated as melisma if they were sung. A certain proportion of song has been, over many centuries, non-verbal; this is true both of opera and of soul music. We could consider classifying the non-grammatical lines of the London Group, among others, along with these lines of Skelton. *Dandirly, dandirly, dandirly dan.*

I think we have to say that the regulation of verse has broken down. Much of the experience of poetry relies on convention – so if convention breaks down, this is not just the triumph of spontaneity but an impoverishment of literary experience. When experience is based on expectation, convention is vital; for, there is no expectation without a subject who does the expecting. Subjectivity of word setting invites unfair and personal subjectivity of response from the reader. This rather teenage-style response may be the most significant factor in the scene, but is not easy to describe in an essay like this one. However, subjectivity defeats most would-be poets – this is a competition with many losers.

Free-verse lines can't be metrically defective, but they can be bad. When a poet starts with a long extent of continuous verse and rewrites it radically, unconscious rules are being applied which embody vital intuitive knowledge of the patterning of sound and sense. This considerable mass of decisions would be the crucial evidence – the lines which get rejected are the only way of getting at the rules governing modern verse. To be sure, this evidence is missing. The utterances of poets about this process are unfortunately promotional and vainglorious. I have considerable experience of correcting bad lines, and indeed of writing them, but I doubt that the knowledge acquired from this can be elevated to anything typical and indicative. I think we have to admit that the problem of describing modern metrics, and theorising the immense number of operational decisions which poets make – even the incorrect decisions – has not been much addressed by critics. I think we have to go through a long haul of speculation and daring errors before a tenable descriptive account emerges. Let me suggest, now that a line should:

> have roughly 1 nucleus
> be greater than 7 syllables long
> have meaning spread 'equitably' over all its parts
> not repeat itself
> say something the reader doesn't already know
> not disappoint attention, and be admirable if taken in isolation
> not bring the poem to a dead halt

This gives us an explanatory frame for the reader's sensation that some lines are bad, or for the inchoate sensations which guide a poet revising a poem and looking for weak lines. In detail, these sensations can't be seized, and we don't know how many are unexplained.

The evidence suggests that the reader perceives each new line by comparing it with reference norms. The *nature* of a line is like other lines, and the particular qualities of that line are detected by unconsciously measuring deviations. It follows that a reader who imposes inappropriate norms can destroy the qualities of a line. Indeed, we can say that the line on the page is quite a faint stimulus, and most of the information needed to turn it into a complete signal is supplied by the reader. Poetry is not like television, which rolls on regardless; if the reader becomes inattentive, or refuses to cooperate, the poem simply stops and no real experience takes place.

A quality we can call swing is offered by the interplay of rhythmic expectations which do not quite coincide. Swing in music is the tension caused by two, or more, frames of expectation tugging against each other. We have proposed an ideal norm in which the tone group coincided with the verse line. Further framing expectations are that the length of lines will be constant and that the stress will fall constantly in the same part of the metrical foot. A poem may achieve swing by setting up these expectations and then deceiving them. An adequate description of the poem would include the unrealised expectations. A modern poem is like a tree in a wind – the shape of the foliage is visibly changing at every moment.

It is attractive to say that each line sets a new norm of unconscious expectations. Actually, that is too optimistic. The reader can either reconfigure their expectations or – coarsely, perhaps – fail to do so. Expectations depend on the population of past experiences which any reader brings to bear. A poet may be writing a work as the environment of norms in which each new line of the work is read. The setting aside of inherited norms has, of course, great political resonance. It is the project of freedom, echoing other kinds of freedom. A conservative reader will refuse to adjust their internal pattern generator.

I am saying – I admit – that each line is perceived as an offset from an archetypal line, each poem as an offset from an archetypal poem, much as when we hear the word *and* spoken we recognise it by referring it to the word *and* that we heard, uttered, with tiny differences of voice, on previous occasions. As these norms are not included within the books of poetry, it might well seem that a book such as this one should supply them for inspection – if they are to be found nowhere else. I have found considerable difficulty in doing this. Let me say, at least, that these norms are acquired by reading – and that the experience of someone who has read 100 books of modern poetry and then reads the 101st is very different from someone who reads the same book but has never seen any modern poetry before.

If the poet entrusts the reader to set up 10 patterns, the reader may only set up 4. Reading poetry draws on the energy and intelligence of the reader – this would be a good moment to think about why people fail with modern poetry. Authoritarian critics who boasted of their low centre of gravity, low rate of forward movement, and dislike of modern ideas, were perhaps not the most sensitive test equipment. If you define suggestibility as a character weakness – you end up listening to a poet's proposal about what the rhythm of a poem is, and loftily rejecting it, to say that you know the right rhythm of a poem and this poem is simply wrong.

There is a rock story to the effect that, if someone has played xylophone for four bars somewhere on an album, and they are told to listen to a playback of the entire album looking for mistakes, themes blurred by the mix, etc., they will only hear the four bars of xylophone. Selective attention is a wonderful thing, and indeed is what metre, intonation, and stress are all about. If someone is testing a theory about the line break, and they read 3,000 pages of poetry, they really will hear the line breaks as the dominant factor in the whole. If someone spends several days a week editing a magazine dedicated to rhyming and metrically regular verse, they will undoubtedly hear free verse as being like cement mixers chewing on batches of scrap iron. This evidence is perfectly credible. But, it's quite irrelevant to my auditory imagination. In science, we are inclined to define the *circle* of circular thinking as empty. In poetry, this circle is generally full. Whatever is in your head, that's what you will hear.

Looking at a variety of pattern-breaking lines from past eras strongly suggests that the breach makes the poem more interesting. The clash of two patterns – metrical line and grammatical group – is puzzling but also arresting. It is natural to guess that the quite frequent dislocation of parallel groupings in modern poetry is a deliberate attempt to break down predictability, to produce a polyrhythmic pattern like jazz. We would have to choose between this and a more passive theory: Couper reports an analysis of a corpus of spoken English which finds that intonation groups and meaning groups coincide only one-third of the time. That is, an unpremeditated utterance of large extents of English would produce a jazz-like pattern of non-overlapping groupings. If we see this outcome in poetry, it could either be a sign of virtuosity or of a casual approach and not thinking twice.

If we look at the fully regulated verse of the 19th century, and at modern poetry, it appears that a high proportion of the changes can be summed up as reduced predictability. This is true about the length and stress-pattern of lines, but is also applicable to lexicon, grammar, subject matter, and the linking of parts to form the overall design of a poem. Free verse is accompanied by the collapse of genre. The state is not the absence of norms, but ambiguity where two patterns compete for dominant position. Using a metaphor from textiles, we could call this a moiré effect. Where this is the pattern of poetry, we can gratefully abandon our task of looking for common norms: there are none to find.

There is an interesting question about higher-level rhythms. Since the brain does not shut down and go back to zero at the end of a line, we might well expect to find larger patterns. These would depend on the limits of acoustic memory. Couper refers to a higher level unit of prosodic organisation as paratones (on the analogy of paragraphs). She found, in taped material, a distinctive pitch marker which she recognised as identifying the head of a paratone. The example she quotes pairs two blocks of about 40 syllables. To be sure, this was found in a news bulletin, which is quite an unusual and formal situation.

Couper mentions a melodic equivalent for the line-break. Because tone groups generally start high and drift downwards (a process known as declension), the *step pitch pattern* when a syllable is followed by one of much higher pitch signals the end of a tone group. (When a question ends, the step we hear is actually from higher to lower.) That is, we realise the group has ended just after it has ended.

Since I am not a professional phonologist, I need a check to be sure that the linguists already drawn on are not out of step with scientific opinion. If we turn to Heinz Giegerich's book, *English Phonology*, 1992, published by Cambridge University Press, we find some difficulty in relating it to Couper-Kuehlen. He uses different terminology, and gives little attention to the phonology of blocks longer than the word (which, however, we do find at pp.249-58). In fact, it seems that different phonologists are interested by different things. However, on examination his statements agree with Couper-Kuehlen's. He explains the technique of metrical phonology, with its trees of pairs (= 'branches') in which one member is weaker and one stronger, and observes at p.254 that these trees cover entire syntactic units. That is, within such a unit there is a top stress. He adds one essential detail, which is that in a phrase containing several primary stresses the prominence of the top stress is signalled by pitch emphasis, but all the 'strong' syllables of a lower order are not signalled by pitch prominence (p.251). This would imply that

   a)   you cannot read aloud a line of verse until you have located the top stress, and reading verse involves a search for this syllable, all the time;

b) the most prominent feature of the prosodic block in natural English has always been ignored by writers on verse;
c) the design of any line of English verse includes a pitch contour;
d) the line break is notional and open to discussion, and the climax of any line is in its centre – at the most prominent syllable;
e) an extent of words which has two top syllables is two units; one which has three top syllables is three units; and so on.

It follows from (e) that, if you had an extent of English language without any typographical marking, you could still count exactly how many metrical lines it contains, whether 100, 250, 300, and so on. That is, to repeat, the verse line is part of natural English, and only subject to limited manipulation by a poet.

I am aware that some critics of poetry write of sound as if it were the unconscious of poetry, passionate and decisive. I see so many analyses of modern metrics which seize on a single passage and equate its phonetic sequence with an artistic quality in a manner demanding an assent which I am powerless to give. Why is it that none of these pirouettes of close examination supply a statistical analysis of a whole book? Do we read a single passage, or do we read the whole book? Why is it always one passage? And why is it that the sound sequences alleged to contain mighty virtue are just the same ones that we find in bad poets? If no one ever looks at 2,000 syllable sequences, to describe a book of 2,000 lines, it is because there is really no point. The action is elsewhere. You might as well analyse the sound pattern of a book of poems in a language you didn't know; you can run off all the sound patterns, vowel sequences, stress patterns, whatever, but you will not find out whether the poems are good or bad because the sound layer of the text is not an utterance in itself.

The key thing in the sound pattern is stress. English has lexical stress, falling on different syllables in different words. To locate the stresses in a line when you read it, you have first to recognise the words. When you recognise them, you retrieve their meaning. The stress pattern is detected later, if only marginally so. So there is not even a hundredth of a second when you have the sound pattern but not the meaning. This is a time which is not there.

Probably, there are some lines which are clumsy or clever from the phonetic point of view. Some sequences of words are ugly, for example repeating the same syllable too often. I don't have a thorough picture of this, but I think you would be pretty unlucky to get more than a few of these in a set of 2,000 lines. Since the sound level of the poem is colourless, what people say about rhythm refers to a higher level, where the meaning and the sound pattern are both in play. We need to recognise a later tier, which has time values but which includes attention spans based on semantic analysis as well as phonetic analysis. A frame which appears clumsy is slow because it counts too many syllables in ratio to its psychological interest. What we call clumsiness can be analysed in *non-phonetic*, semantic ways as e.g. repetition, deviation, futile detail, taking too long to make a point, lurches of meaning, putting elements in the wrong order, obscurity, unconvincing arguments, poor match of words to meaning, etc. There are so many ways of betraying a flawed intention – hesitation, omission, abandoning statements which are still incomplete, signals betraying the intent to stop, lack of preparedness, drying up. Intent creates the expectations and so bands the time. We carry out a scan which assesses the interest of any frame of words and which is quick enough to do this before a proper reading of the words. The limiting condition of this is where a scan persuades us that the frame is not worth reading – and our attention switches off. Any passage is a fulfilment of expectations and the attention scans available decide if the passage goes over or not. When information arrives at the rate we take it in, the poem is good; so aesthetic quality is defined by the brain's capacity for processing data, a figure which we are hardly likely to find by counting vowels and consonants: it is outside the poem.

There is a domain without a proper name, which manages time and attention. There is an organ which switches, stages, schedules, focuses, and switches off attention. In a poem, attention is seized by a capture spiral, during which different rules apply than inside the text body, because the reader is asking different questions. Data planes are alerted and switched on; they fade and wink out. Every block of attention staged and mounted has to be dismounted; the number of "winkings out" must be exactly the same as the number of "switch-ons"; the fact that these events are inexplicit does not mean they are unimportant. We can never notice the activations being switched off; they escape notice by definition. But good poets have an intuitive map of these events. After a certain point, a theme has "gone" and reference to it will fail, because it is not there in the lit zone of temporary attention. The size of this zone varies significantly between poetry read aloud and poetry on the page. The closing of a frame does not mean the deletion of its syllables from memory, but rather their liberation into a conceptual form, to use as a contrast. Details are thrown away, but in fact a context is being built up.

The existence of a 'frame', with a beginning, an end, and internal relatedness, is accepted by many writers on behaviour. Couper reports with scepticism a theory that the tone group (a line of verse, in our terms) represents a *motor output planning group*, the effective extent of detailed future planning of spoken 'output'. This is very interesting, but it steps outside the scope of linguistics and proof has not been collected. Probably we have a temporary data store of finite size, as pointed to by our performance mistakes. The reader may like to test this by reading some pages of verse aloud, not looking at the page except at the beginning of a line. The shape of this size would certainly affect aesthetic judgments – it could explain why some lines are bad. Naturally we want a semantic group which gives the sensation of fullness, but gives no sensation of difficulty. Clearly the rate at which information arrives is decisive to the comfort and pleasure of reading, and clearly people disagree wildly about the desirable rate.

Line breaks, clause ends, and stanza breaks, may mark the closing of frames. Quite possibly the hierarchical levels of phonetic grouping correspond to various levels of frames, and block-ends represent successive stages of data absorption. At the end of a segment, data leaves short-term memory and is stored, in some way not identical with its original form. The moment when primary phonetic data are available is transient. This is one reason why thinking about metre is hard – and produces so many odd theories. The data available to intellectual reflection is not exactly the data that was momentarily available during reading at normal speed.

The start of a block, at various levels, is signalled by a marker. Often, this also signals the end of a block – and signals to the listener to wrap up and store the block just ending. This is the realisation of transience – the deleting of a momentary universe of sounds. Such markers often come in pairs, and the second occurrence is an alert that the words now about to follow are in contrast to the previous block, and form a pair with it. So, something is deleted – and something remains.

Grammatical contrasts resemble lexical contrasts – such as black/white – but are more explicit. Rhyme and regularity of line length apparently have little role to play in these contrastive and grouping functions.

There is a wealth of information biologically inherent in language which is missing from the printed text. It governs the subjective interpretation of the words, and involves suprasegmental values (speed, pitch, distribution of emphases, voice quality). The missing information includes the qualities of the human voice – something absolutely fundamental to our life in this world. The situation is, largely, made up of the intentional states of the people in it. Phoneme patterns are common – but a voice is perfectly individual and personal. Much modern poetry acquires a distinctive prosodic signature after you have heard the poet read. Consider the total set of factors in Tom Raworth's voice. Is it realistic to think of any subset of factors? The true melody is cross-spectra – we hear it by scanning all channels of information at once. Because the information omitted from print is so crucial, it is reasonable to think that we construct it, by projection, when we read a poem. Because 'voice quality' is used for recognising individuals, and unlocks interpersonal responses – it is reasonable to speculate that we hear a human voice when we read a poem, and that the sound we 'hear' delivering the poem is soaked in our feelings about the person. That is – projective emotional feelings decide whether we like the 'sound' of the poem. I can't analyse this 'sound' for you because we all hear a different one for a given poet – the information just isn't there in the bare print text. Projective identification is an orchestra that conducts itself – it overwhelms the factors which are objective and are visible to close reading. Poets are probably rather better at manipulating complicity than at manipulating sound so that the percentage of L-sounds is 2.91% rather than 2.89%.

Evidently language is a shared, public, system, which works because we follow the rules; and evidently poetry possesses means by which these public materials can be combined to yield something personal and unique. We are looking for the brink line where the world of thermodynamics gives way to that of objects, or where statistically predictable patterns of language acquire individual definition. The signature of a writer is like this: (repeating a length of pattern [which is not repetitive of the common pattern]). Some levels of language are prescribed, but above these is presumably a level where so many combinations are allowed that signature can emerge. When the signature repeats enough times, we recognise it as signature rather than as uncontrolled variation. At this point, it acquires the role of a voice. The propaganda around free verse has spoken of reaching 'the unique voice of the individual' in a way I can't underwrite. Variation is free, essentially unlimited, and available to all. Imposing a property structure on it repeats colonising acts, and could only express a preset and self-replicating character structure if such a thing actually existed.

The productivity of language is based on spontaneous repetition – nonsense series are merely not-yet-differentiated forms of sensible language. Sound governs the tier of fertility – of cascades of blank lines tumbling down and demanding to be filled with words. Autonomous repeating blocks, self-entraining phonological series, offer endless blank frames into which the syllables are fitted to form lines. A poet who simply lacks fertility will produce few poems. Moreover, those poems will be stumbling, because their writer does not have access to dozens of variants for every phrase, so as to pick the best. A good poem may be the result of irrational acoustic productivity during the phase which led up to its being organised and fixed – in a rational form.

The Concatenator

It looks as if we can imagine beside the phonology which generates the sound structure of poems a behaviour generator which creates and connects situations and sequences of behaviour. For what is generated we can always imagine a generator, even if we cannot describe it.

Linguistics is good at explaining the use of an inventory of sounds to form words, and how words are selected to complete a sentence within a given context, but poor at explaining how human subjects open a new context and make it necessary for language to be deployed in the first place. Selecting the next phoneme within a word already planned is very easy, but opening the next frame is less easy. The practice of speech is widespread, but there is no branch of *linguistics* which explains how speech concatenates. Phonemes are picked and realised from a finite set, numbering perhaps 30, but the idea that behaviour in general is the product of simple operations on a similar matrix of combinatory units was a thrilling delusion rather than the next stage of social science. The planning of speech is the most interesting issue, and it looks as if the planning of the next frame is the stage of maximum uncertainty and activity, with a gradual declension, so that selecting a word in a sentence already half planned is less complex and selecting the next phoneme in a word already chosen is easiest of all.

As language permits an infinite set of utterances to be constructed, so perhaps rules of action allow an infinite set of behaviour sequences to be constructed. It is not enough to describe social structure by producing a list of occupations from the census, which would allocate everyone to an economic role. The central problem of sociology is to explain how behaviour is generated, how people turn time into experience, how human agents select and construct the next action and the next and the next. The question about *structure* uses a metaphor which is already misleading: why should human activity be like a building, something static and massive, when at every point we see behaviour flowing across time? Sociology has in general not asked how people generate behaviour, although there are particular exceptions whose relevance to the problems of poetry is obvious if indirect.

The inhabited dream-night:
Tom Lowenstein, *Filibustering in Saṃsāra* (1987, 73 pp., cluster C)

A complex epigraph says, in part, "In this space there is no absolute down, no right or left, no forward or backward". This is a description of music – but since all these directions have absolutely no meaning outside the human body, the statement could describe what the universe is like with no ego in it, or else the 'frame edges' we impose on perception to turn it into an organ. The book contains only six poems: 'Pages from La Tempestà', 'The Dissociation of Narcissus', 'Lines Written in September', 'Cuisse d'un faune ému', 'Labrys' and 'Filibustering in Saṃsāra'. The title is explained in the notes as "(Saṃsāra) Pāli, *lit.* wandering (of births). More loosely, existence in time, as opposed to the emptiness of space and the unconditioned. In the Tempestà sequence and the final two poems, the notion is that of a voice, part unconscious, projecting into silence a makeshift view of the world's changing identity. The final two pieces attempt a description of life-texture ('the continuous membrane') in the context of internal observation and non-personal history." This coincides fortunately with an essay by John Gray in this week's *New Scientist* (*timenow* August 2002), which says that the brain involves 'complex but essentially discontinuous processes, where consciousness figures only intermittently'. It goes on "The idea that our minds are programmed to generate illusions goes against the grain of philosophers…", and, more cautiously, refers to "The idea that the ordinary sense of selfhood is an error we cannot shake off(.)" This gives a picture of essentially accurate cognitive functions telling us what is going on in the physical world, and a restless centre (in the left hemisphere) reforming the data into partly arbitrary narratives – in great excess of what the cognitive data really says. This is the "filibustering" (understood as a speech of quite unlimited length, without pauses or purpose, often associated with Senators from the Old South, aimed to prevent something else from seizing the right to speak). When Lowenstein speaks of the self as a "continuous membrane", his point is that it is continuous (it heals up all the gaps with plausible narratives), and is a surface (on which something, perhaps cognitive data in verbal form) can walk. 'Labrys' opens with the disconcerting statement, 'Time in the north had been/ frozen onto a view of the sun/ masking the earth's movement…", based on the idea that any visual perspective will do, it won't matter as long as it is internally consistent. Anyway, programs in the brain will supply the missing parts, and mask the fact that they are missing; that's how the membrane is spun. When it comes to the narratives, Lowenstein becomes a Jungian: they are the same ones, all around the world. In fact, it's almost as if the narratives were eternal, and the physical world, fitfully reported by the senses, is samsaric and fleeting. Flimsy or not, Lowenstein's powers of association draw such wonderfully diverse and rich cognitive systems together, the metalanguage with which he speaks in both sets of terms at once is so enthralling, that as we are thrown out of the pattern of our own culture we say that, this is the only way to write great poetry in these times. Which is a temporary failure of memory of the kind we apparently perform all the time. The labrys is the double axe of Crete, a word from some pre-Greek Anatolian language associated with *labyrinth*. It involves a "crisis of freedom" and "faking/ an unused assimilation". A time when we were partly together with "this language costume", with an alternate identity in a masked world of upper spirits. Experimental masculinity attacked in a dream. This was a form of alienation for us? So that "The creation went on raving/ sadly into the crepuscular/ without missing us". Eating animals affirmed our separation from other species. Following the herds in Palaeolithic times, we developed myth as a "powerful grammar of assistance". Shamanic flight in the space between the planets was subject to a monopoly. The weather grew "vaguer and more complex". Thousands of facets dance out of my reach as I do this. If narratives are eternal, why have I never seen one like this one before?

The jacket remarks that "later poems further develop themes arising from the writer's ethnographic work in Alaska and Pāli Buddhist studies." The cover illustration shows an Eskimo shaman mask in wood. Since the writer (b.1941) knows not only the Eskimo language of the part of Alaska where he did fieldwork in 1975-6, but also the post-Sanskrit vernacular in which the Buddhist scriptures were written, and has a thorough knowledge of the symbolic constructs living in those languages, there is no question of my writing a commentary on his work. The associational universe these poems draw on is unimaginably rich – I can just crawl along on the outer edge of what I *can* imagine.

Creating a surface by walking along it

We can afford ourselves the luxury of not trying to systematise and record this generator, instead merely pointing to it as a forerunner of what has been generated. The behaviour plans are timebound, context bound, abundant, serial, fluent, covered by verbal justification, analogous to speech, and capable of mis-realisation. Consciousness is, perhaps, an exceptional faculty switched on where rules conflict. If we reflect on what Lowenstein has said, perhaps we can add that behaviour is a constant improvisation and that consciousness is a continual *post hoc* attempt to produce an explanation for processes which are largely unconscious.

Studying the internal structure of a poem is simple compared to asking how poets handle juncture; if a volume contains fifty poems there are forty-nine key moments of juncture where the poet has to restart the engine, a difficult moment which each time may result in a relapse into banality or in a radical opening of possibilities. This point of strain depends also on the poet's social imagination. I would suggest that filibustering does not always work: one agent holds the floor and discourses, but there may come a point when it loses the right to speak, and another agent takes over. We may think of this as taking over the white rod sometimes used to assign the right to speak. At this point the new agent moves from unconsciousness to consciousness and starts to embroider and filibuster its own thread of discourse. This may explain why a book is divided into separate poems and is not one continuous strip.

I find it impossible to paraphrase what Lowenstein is saying because, really, it's a miracle I can read it at all, and while reading it I feel ten times as intelligent as I actually am. The 'path down' from the Christian religiosity which was deserting poetry in the 19th century led slowly but persistently towards a second form of transcendental knowledge, secular this time, which many poets achieved in fragmentary form. With Lowenstein, we finally have someone who can bring anthropological thinking into the main channel of the poem, and write about myth and history without simply reciting myths and histories. It would be ludicrous for me to form a judgement of these poems when they are beyond my own knowledge.

Works which may help us into the world of these poems are Lowenstein's translations of Inuit myths, and his (prose) work about the same myths. The only poet whose work is comparable is another anthropologist, Martin Thom.

The decline of narrative

We have seen Lowenstein explain consciousness as a self-completing membrane, something that flows seamlessly to create intact and shining surfaces in every direction.

This notion has a history outside Buddhism. Historians studying original sources found with great regularity that the narratives adjusted primary events into a pattern which suited their pre-set bias. Such was this regularity that it was set up as a law underlying narrative and, subsequently, proposed not as a function of writing but of consciousness itself.

In the '70s we heard endlessly about ideology and it seemed the accusation was always convincing, that everyone identified was unconsciously constructing a verbal cloud and a state of awareness which embodied their political and economic and even sexual interests. Disproof never arrived. I suggest that this activity is not always successful, that life is full of failed surfaces, collapsed narratives. The spectre has been wandering around since the 19th century of a perforated state where someone has no longer the ability to construct narratives or to spin the thread of consciousness. It is reasonable to think of unsuccessful poetry as embodying this state. There is the spectre also of an integral text being damaged and vacated by an attack. This is somewhere we can go: the abyss of emptied awareness, an endless plain where all plant life has been eaten and destroyed.

Many people believe – it is one of the contemporary myths – that once ideology is destroyed, once the ego is damaged, there is a cold temperature desert of texts where no poem can be uttered and there is only stalking hostility, a kind of psychic bureaucracy repressing narratives.

It may come as a moment of liberation when an engulfing narrative tilts on its side and you see it as one-dimensional, its internal space exposed and leaking away in one huge bubble.

If we look at the period as a unit, one of the features that stands out is that narrative and dramatic poetry are almost taboo. There is a problem of seriation: the poem evaporates after a certain time, whether it has achieved intensity in that brief span or not.

The great feature of the age is therefore the vignette poem, replacing the story. The modern poem has a very short span, which therefore has high coherence and so high predictability. Surrealism and the whole apparatus of montage are therefore a counterbalance, a way of rescuing unpredictability.

In around 1997 the performance poet Khaled Hakim planned a magazine of theory, *narrative not narrative*, which would address this problem of narrative in poetry. It never reached a first issue: beyond a certain point addressing key inhibitions runs into unconscious blocks which prevent people from talking.

The examples of narrative in the modern period are worth looking at even if their atypical status sets them apart from the typical. Examples are George MacBeth's narratives, 'Driving West' and 'A Light in Winter', Logue's Homer translations, Hughes' *Gaudete*, some poems by Francis Berry. Modern poems also accept narratives in the form of anecdotes – like stand-up comics. These very short narratives are dominated by their punch line.

Khaled had a background in the avant-garde film community, which is typically against narrative and dominated by resistance to commercial narrative film. He used to speak of *structural cinema*, a watchword of Peter Gidal, as an object of terror: Khaled was interested in making avant-garde narrative film and questioning the taboo on narrative. This is why he was fascinated by the taboo on narrative in his other field, poetry. His performances were improvised, which foregrounds the problem of concatenation as the central issue for poetry.

We might well say: to understand these poems you must first understand the English social structure. So that a student in the USA or Canada would have to spend the first year of their course studying how English society works, the silent rules, and only then is allowed to see poetic texts. This does not allow for the possibility that human behaviour is fundamentally unpredictable. Nor does it allow for the possibility that the poet takes the behaviour generator and rewires it to produce scenes and action sequences that never happened and could not happen.

The most tragic misunderstanding would be to go to poetry for an account of how life was led in a certain period. Everything seems to show that poetry leaves out everything basic and factual. It would not tell you who won the elections or who was prime minister at any time. Everything is consistent with the idea that poetry has as its primary need to show something unfamiliar and that it starts with the rules of how society runs and how people generally act as givens. This is like saying: there is no description in contemporary poetry which would allow you to recognise an individual, if you met them after reading it.

There is no description of how society works in this poetry either.

Banality in rhythm, choice of vocabulary, sequence of ideas, etc. can be counterbalanced by originality in the design of scenes and in the actions carried out by the protagonists. Suppose that to the line decision rule that *every new line should add information not already there* we add a poem decision rule that *each new poem should create a situation which is unfamiliar*. Then, the rules of the situation would be defined within the poem. This would mean that the poem takes the laws of how to behave as givens and steps outside them, putting new values in the matrix and discovering what new sequences flow from that.

We oppose the *narrative* or *dramatic* poem with succession, large units, multiple voices, to the flight into *very short forms*, with stress on juncture of ideas, repetition, privatisation, a single focal human subject. The simplest explanation for the exit from large forms is egocentricity, the deal with the reader whereby poetry is the carrier for a personality, and every feature of it is an expression of the unique way of looking at the world stored in that personality. This deal acutely limits the burden of external and objective data which poetry can carry. Objective data are then cold, personalisation's warm. Some modern poetry is post-Symboliste in its dedication to subjectivity and in its use of an original and elaborate style in which the angle of vantage dominates over the data. Yet the lure of a personal point of view is something missing from huge swathes of modern poetry, effectively from most of the mainstream and so from most of the field. Yet narrative and drama are not found here either.

Besides the egoistic and Paterian or Symboliste project of displaying one's personality as the goal of the work of art, there is another possibility of taking the behaviour generator as the unknown quantity and using the poem to trap it in the light and to recover its modes of operation. The poem would catch incomplete scenes and ask how a social drama conspires to complete them, allocating individuals to roles and values to actions. A third possibility is to generate artificial rule-sets and artificial worlds as a game, without critical or didactic intent.

Pure intentionality bumps up against autonomous external agents all the time. The outcome may not be a realisation of anyone's plan – is it then licit to trace it back and announce it the realisation of any schema? Where would we find such a schema?

When speaking of the behaviour generator owned and operated by an individual we encounter the possibility that there is both something generated and something which generates which do not belong to an individual, but which are composed of the actions of all individuals within a scene and of the intervention of the physical world.

Through a knowledge of the behaviour generator which is inevitably latent, until we develop a written form of this tacit apparatus, we decide whether a poem is original or unoriginal with respect to its content as a drama or a situation.

It is not enough to look for originality in the rhythmic or logical structure of poems, one also has to look for it in the events being described. A conventional poem can describe unconventional situations and behaviour and achieve originality in that way. There is a vulgate of the modernists which looks for originality *only* at the levels where looking is consecrated, so that not using iambic pentameters, being irregular, avoiding teleology, criticising the self, etc. are the validated forms of originality. Even though originality is the basic question, we should look for this at every level of the artwork. The interest of the concatenator is that it allows us to make judgements on the originality of poems. At a more immediate level, it is the foreknowledge which allows us to guess the development of a situation in a poem, the basic function of locating predictability. Unique human situations are certainly original, and fund original poems. It certainly amounts to an original experience if the poem is set in an exotic setting and shows exotic customs. This is noticeable in the work of David Dabydeen, for example, set in Guyana, or in the poems of George Mackay Brown, set on Orkney (and the adjacent seas), where the elements of the scene are quite unfamiliar to an urban reader in mainland Britain. Even within an urban and British environment, there are scenes and situations available which qualify as original and avoid, for a longer or shorter run, the ineluctable disappointment of encounters with conventional situations and conventional reactions. Exotic locales are an easy win, we can go further and inquire after an originality of social imagination which invents new poems without always referring back to the same debate about the fallibility of everyday consciousness.

Literature does not necessarily have to assert the events it describes but can suspend their effectiveness by the *critical* affect, which questions events and gives a privileged role to replaying and re-imagining them. So feminist poetry could describe banal events and relationships but recover an intellectual quality by the critical attitude it developed towards the scenes and to the psychological or social and legal process which had cemented them in place. It is not mandatory for poetry to reject the social order and to express commitment to alienation, but it is obvious that imagining the world turned upside down offers employment to the intellect in a way which merely remembering conventional and comforting scenes does not. After a certain point on the map, memory and art are incompatible.

In a way often evoked by Louis Gernet, narratives focus often on objects. The object plays a specific role in the organisation of narratives, probably to do with binding the events in time and with particular reactions, attached to the space immediately around the body, which can only be evoked by objects. The reactions have often to do with acquisition, with status, with certainty, with pleasure, with kinship, and with danger. Gernet speaks of the *agalma*, which can be translated as precious object, something which contains large amounts of human work as part of its making. There is also the *tekmerion*, an object of proof which plays a role in legal trials and other acts of proof. There are also the *spoils*, the equipment of a warrior, generally the product of very elaborate technical procedures, stripped from him as the concrete result of a duel. A decline in the efficiency of narrative may have to do with a dislocation of the economy of objects.

We have to raise the possibility that the collective version of norms and repeatable modules etc. is quite different from the ones owned and put into practice by any or all individuals, so that the recovery of collective norms is irrelevant when considering the behaviour of particular individuals. While secession from structures like the currency, phonology, traffic rules, etc. is unlikely, space has to be left unused for the fundamentalist positions which some agents in the landscape have certainly asserted. These are on the lines of 'the bourgeois cannot possibly understand the proletarian' 'a man cannot possibly understand a woman' 'a person of one race cannot possibly understand someone of another race' and similar. Neither the assertion of incomparability and the failure of language nor its opposite was frequently supported by evidence. Evidently the poet is trying to create a verbal device which mediates the differences and makes them attainable from diverse starting-points, rather than making a stony monument to incomprehensibility. If social structure is not in someone's head, the question is then where is it stored. The study of concatenation does not have to wait for a theory of social structure because it belongs to individuals. It is possible that the versions of social structure in the heads of numerous people are not copies of each other but simply separate entities. The question is then whether the goal of sociology is there to be recovered.

Heinz Piontek's anthology *Neue Erzählgedichte* (New Narrative Poems, 1964) stages the argument without guiding it through to a final verdict. Piontek is an interesting poet, capable of writing in different styles but not scaling the heights in any of them. He was one of the most popular poets of his time. The poems he classifies as narrative do not seem like narratives to me, but the notion that any poem which depicts successive scenes is a narrative is of interest. Effectively, the anthology confirms the death of the narrative poem and demonstrates that the issue is a common one over Western Europe, perhaps over eastern Europe as well. The issue was already well developed in 1964, so that Piontek's title was a surprise and a provocation. The causes must be deep and pervasive.

If you study History at any point after about the age of 14 they keep telling you "don't narrate don't narrate don't narrate; analyse". This may suggest to teenagers that writing poetry which analyses causes is superior to describing situations, characters, and events. Narrative is formally inhibited at History A-level but only because the person marking the papers has seen hundreds of essays about the same subject and is depressingly well informed about it. For a story heard for the first time, analysis is useless and narrative is the desirable mode. Until you have committed to memory the key events, situations, and characters, historical reflection is impossible or a fantasy. Most great historians are narrators, narrative is primary but it works for primary information, with sequences which the reader is not already familiar with. Poetry may have migrated into philosophy for lack of primary narrative material, and because the conditions of the writers' lives were excessively familiar to the readers. The problem with narrating in poetry is found in other countries, as described, and so is not mainly a product of preset ways of teaching history in English schools.

There is a problem with a writer's claim to describe the subjective life of anyone except themselves fully and truly. I will argue further on that the way out of the trap of manipulative fantasy was to depict people – other people – at length. People's true nature emerges in long sequences of behaviour and a snapshot is vulnerable to acute problems of selectivity and preconceived emphases and fitting to preset notions. Yet, we have just been saying that modern poetry rejects long sequences and only accepts short vivid ones. Is the conclusion that John Masefield is more authentic than modern poets? The answer is probably yes, and when I read Masefield or Gibson my feeling is precisely that, that they portray people faithfully and especially people from income groups D and E (to use detached terms) in a way which is no longer fashionable.

The archaeologist Lewis Binford evoked a Mesolithic cold-weather hunting economy based on following the prey species over its migration path, with a territory for the human social unit which was vast in direct ratio to the vast territory percoursed by the prey species. Plants would be exploited through the calories which grazing animals recovered from them. A population increase, so far as not reversed by nutrition crises or other setbacks, could cut down territories. For example, if the band split, because two people wanted to be chief, the territory available for each one would be halved, and access to the migratory species would be reduced. The bands might redirect effort towards other species which had less spatial variation (and were also smaller). So far as this modified economy was efficient, and the weather held, the population increase might continue, and the territory available to each social unit would decrease again, and go on decreasing. The key to the future would be to tap smaller and smaller prey species, and ones which had less spatial range, or could be kept from wandering away. The obvious climax to this process would be to rely on plants. The quantity of production would be assured by intense work on the ground, tearing out weeds, channelling water, digging. The people would be as tied to their fields as the plants. At this point you have invented agriculture.

The great development into style over the last century or 150 years may also be an adaptive response to a smaller territory for poetry. The choice and arrangement of words are subject to developmental involution, intense cultivation within a personalised realm demarcated or restricted by a thousand other personalised realms. The question is still why poetry does not go out into the open spaces.

Formations of Taste and Attitudinal Learning

If you write the history of what didn't happen, you have to make up the evidence.

It is quite plausible that editors, who get their jobs by being cultured, prefer poets who agree with them by being cultured and also white, English, a product of Oxford and a good school. Many of the poets went to the most demanding universities, and this often followed going to an elite school. The first step for them was often having an inspiring teacher at school, one who actually understood modern poetry and would teach it to a class. That is, they began with resources which most children don't get. For one line of analysis, they wrote great poetry because they belonged to the dominant social group and their poems are good because they are credible, that is they assert social authority. At this point good poets are Wicked and people who didn't write poetry at all are Virtuous. One of the factions holds it as self-evident that only poets without any culture should be allowed to speak. This is a version of pastoral, as has been pointed out.

Kenneth Allott's *Penguin Book of Contemporary Verse* (two versions, 1950 and 1960) was in print for more than 30 years. 40.6% of his 85 chosen poets were Oxford graduates, 7% were women. He seemed to have erased Scotland and Wales from the map. Everyone could see the force of these figures, some social mobility took place in the Sixties and Seventies, and the leitmotif of the arts world in the Blair era, as our time-span ends, was to do with uptake and social exclusion. It's no longer "from Beowulf to Eliot" but "from counting NEETs to the Social Exclusion Unit". You can legitimate the people inside poetry because they are insiders, in occupation. Or, you can declare their policies null and void, on the grounds that only 0.1% of the population regularly buys works of modern poetry, and the non-participation, especially of women and ethnic minorities, is not a proper outcome. Arts administrators have set up rules whose core intent was to degrade and inhibit the decision powers of someone like Allott, a connoisseur-expert. However, many people would agree, thirdly, that an anthology, or a publisher's roster, should be based on aesthetic choices, not on a set of well-meaning criteria which suppress the question of whether the poems work as art.

Editors (of anthologies, magazines, etc.) would unanimously say that due to Close Reading and so on they transcend mere enforcing of group identity. We have all the same to ask if literary choice creates insiders and outsiders. There are "silent rules" which suggest to some young people that they are not going to succeed as poets, and the literary scene somehow embodies these rules. A large number of people agree, first, that these rules exist, and secondly, that they are not ideal, they should be changed. The "site" of the rules is in the aspiration of young people to please literary selectors, and in the visible wishes of the selectors. We are going to look at these visible wishes in particular cases.

I can't write the history of people who didn't take part in the poetry world, didn't report feelings that show up in the sources I use, didn't take part in the conversation. All I can do is record the social or intellectual process of the people who succeeded in finding modern poetry. The outcome recalls the learning process which led to it.

The Grand Titration

If we look at Barker's *Bibliography of Poetry in Britain and Ireland since 1970* (1995), we find roughly 20% of the poets listed are women. If we then look back at Allott's Penguin anthology, datelined '1918-60', we find 6 out of 85 are women poets. If we look at Lucie-Smith's 1970 Penguin anthology, *British Poetry since 1945*, we again find 6 out of 85 of the poets are women. These points might offer us proxy indicators for the changing balance within the poetry world. The slight change between Allott and Lucie-Smith is surprising but suggests that the '60s were a macho decade, the watchword was liberation but for women things weren't changing all that much. To sum up, these sources, whatever problems they offer, may cover: 1918–1960; 1945–1970; 1970–1995.

You may wish to challenge the idea that 7% was a fair share in 1960. There may be an idea that there were hundreds of utterly brilliant female poets (names unknown) and that they were being excluded from visibility by evil male critics.

I wanted a time curve for the shifting ratio of women to men in the field of poetic activity. Eventually I hit on a proxy indicator, this one. It deals with the balance of reviews of women and male poets in *Poetry Review*. I went through many issues of *Poetry Review* in the university library in Cambridge. This at least covers the whole span of time I am interested in. It covers 2,236 reviews, which may be only about 7% of the books published during the period. It is a sample taken at one point and other indicators might gave different results. I was expecting a jump in the mid-1980s but this is not there in the figures. The figures I came out with (percentages of women poets in reviews of volumes by individuals) were:

        1960-64 15.36
        1965-69 14.16
        1970-79 10.39
        1980-84 31.28
        1985-89 32.21
        1990-94 27.73
        1995-97 35.02

This is a proxy indicator since it doesn't go directly to the share of women in poetic activity, achievement or popularity, but it is the survivor after several other possibilities failed to work out. Even this one falls silent for a significant part of the 1970s. *PR* stopped carrying reviews from 1971 to 1978, so the figures for the 1970s are less indicative (total of 130 books reviewed). This is also when it was going through an 'underground' phase, carrying non-traditional poetry and being badly designed and printed.

Where I think all this fails is in the equivocation of one person with another. Clearly if you count something you are giving the impression that it is a homogeneous quantity. No two poets believe they are interchangeable so a count involving a lump of several hundred of them must be flawed.

Comparing 1997 and 1960 implies that the same person was choosing books in those years – which is obviously untrue. There were a dozen different editors of the flagship *Poetry Review* during that span. Can we say that the job was the same in 1960 and 1997, a set of institutional rules inside which editors worked, a rigid framework which by its conservatism allows us to find a steady yardstick? Obviously not. The scene in 1997 was totally different from the scene in 1960, so the job was also totally different. The women poets competing in 1960 were different from the ones competing in 1997. Actually, my whole project of writing the history of poetry over those four decades is based on the idea that there was lots of change, and was not worth starting if there was, in the final tally, no history.

The scale of the shift (between Allott and Barker) points to a collective quality of the source. If something changes as a whole then it must *be* a whole. Yet any dealing with these entities that are composed of individuals is slippery. Do poets really react as a collective? And is it sensible to treat 'the scene in 2000' as simply 'the scene in 1960' with a few features changed? The assumption seems to be that the poets of 1960 simply evolve into the poets of 2000, rather than being replaced by autonomous individuals who have separate identities. Most poets would react negatively to these assumptions.

The common interpretation of the weak showing of the female gender in English poetry has to do with role models. In the film *Invasion of the Body Snatchers*, characters keep finding pods growing in a barn which acquire the features of people in the town and gradually grow until they are ready to replace them. At this point the human character disappears. The replacement is an alien but looks exactly like the human did. The idea of *role models* is that you are the Pod and that you observe and gradually grow to resemble the living model. If the human model is modified, you modify to grow like it.

The theory then says that girls need female role models. It follows, within the world of this theory, that, in literature, girls have imitated low-grade women poets, or ineffectively imitated male poets. This changes as effective women poets come on the scene. With a generation's delay, other poets are able to follow them. Pressed to say when things did change, the answer for the poetry world seems to be gradually during the '80s. Feminism was in 1970 a vanguard thing, laughed at by confident TV comics. It disseminated to large numbers of people, acquired a ballast of experience over theory, became credible and robust. It was there for someone who was a teenager, acquiring ethical norms, in 1980. By 1985 it was showing up in a wave of new female poets. However, the PR curve does not show an increase during the 1980s, although it has a sharp jump around 1980. Then it shows another jump around 1995.

Learning the rules

Nothing is compulsory in the poetry world and the partakers are not good at following rules – for example, at moving from the bar so that readings can start on time, or at listening during readings rather than wandering off. Readings might draw people together, but some fraction of the audience is always inattentive or else resistant to the feelings they are supposed to be having. In general, they are people who find it hard to conform and who don't admire conformity. We have to ask if there really are rules and how people find out what they are.

People in the scene don't regard the scene as legitimate. The poetry world has not at any moment satisfied the ambitions of the poets. The resentment of the poets is so overwhelming that objective judgment can only be a fleeting thing, washed away quickly by claims of injustice. I find it problematic to say that there is a consensus view or that anyone is respected as an arbiter. My proposal is that by looking at concrete instances of poetic ideologies we can understand something of the scene.

All we have to do is to ask whether other people like a poem to detect that poetry is a domain where the freedom of any agent is constrained by the freedom of all the others. This already suggests that what show up as cultural rules in one description will show up as the practice of freedom in another one.

The fact that poets converge on recognisable stylistic types suggests that there are rules – where there is a repeating pattern, regression will give us the rules that generated it. Again, the fact that poets can predict the effect of their poems on readers suggests that there are shared reactions. This predictive knowledge is won by empathy – even though there is no set of written rules, they are taught by empathy with other people – teachers in the first instance. The wish for approval teaches them the map. That is not quite enough – the fear of disapproval also structures behaviour. To return to the problem area, this could mean that girls in mid-century rationally feared disapproval if they spoke out in poems, and could not imagine successful poems. Also, they were more other-directed and dependent on approval than boys. Also, perhaps, they were less secure about exposing their feelings than boys, more afraid of ridicule. This could explain the lack of good women poets in mid-century. By my analysis, only one significant woman poet was born in the 1930s. Much of this would change with feminism, and that would explain the radically changed proportion of women poets in the anthologies (and elsewhere). At this point, the traditionally greater levels of insight and empathy of women would turn into an advantage.

A poem is made up of a series of lines, and the process which decides what is the right shape for any line uses memory-based projections of the reader's reaction to them. This is what you have to do to write a poem. Images of other people are the landscape – empathy is the camera which perceives and scans it.

It follows that someone with weak empathy cannot find out what the landscape is. Possibly, they can create something not based on contact and produce forced language. This may grate on the ear, or they may go on to develop something new – and create one of the splits we noticed in the field.

How many ways are there in which a line can be bad? Once you accept that a line is good or bad based on its verbal qualities, you accept that there are rules – even if both readers and writers perceive themselves as being unconstrained. The rules are loose in proportion to the quality of language, that it can generate billions of utterances. You could not make them particular without specifying billions of lines. All of this happens without written rules – which is why they are nowhere to be found. Gratification motivates the brain to retain the knowledge, along with anxiety perhaps. The poems do not spell out the rules – they are picked up by empathy. Empathy is the learning path. This rule acquisition is a noisy process, that is one qualified by inefficiency, loss of signal, waste of power, and (partly) perverse results. Empathy can make wrong guesses. The rules are learnt partly through reading poems – but that only teaches you what your own reactions are. Insight into other people's reactions is also vital – and so hanging out with other people who read modern poetry is indispensable to the development process.

To reiterate, we started from the position that Kenneth Allott's choice set was no longer acceptable. We are departing from freedom as an inviolate principle. This choice raises problems, obviously. We could link the problem to the nature of empathy by saying that it works like heat, that radiates from a centre but dissipates with distance. Allott's standard anthology radiates from him, it gets dark on the way to Scotland. But if you construct an anthology in 1997, it does not follow that you can get to a centre from which everything is equidistant.

To tell a story: in 1950 young women were saying "You didn't like the poems which I didn't write because you didn't like them", but in 1980 they were saying "You didn't like the 10 poems I wrote last week but I don't care." In general, writing a poem involves saying "I own the poem but you own the value of the poem". The focus on empathy doesn't untangle the problems of agency, but does explain why they are tangled.

Undoubtedly, poets start at age 15 with no style, and move gradually towards the point they finally reach. They do follow a map of sorts, and as we watch them moving through it we can claim that there is a cultural field and that they know what it is. Their navigation involves a raft of decisions and by using the devices *compare and contrast* we can recover those decisions in part. The grid slides, it is a net which generates fish rather than one which catches fish. Because the poet halts when they have reached a certain cell on the map, we can surmise that they belong there, and so that we can describe them by describing what is the microclimate of that point. The idea of a home range is important here. That is, that a poet settles down where they belong. The different parts of a style which becomes home sustain each other. Numerous traits are highly correlated with each other. As it follows, a home range is exclusive – someone who belongs in such a category does not belong in any other. That is, successful criticism finds home ranges which are there for the poet, and not imposed categories. It is normal to use living adjectives, the names of people, so "Kathleen Raine is like Edwin Muir", but this has many flaws.

I think we can use this low-resolution information as long as we observe protocols relevant to the low-res world. You can't compile low-resolution data to produce a high-resolution map. We see a number of aesthetic positions which clash with each other. The variety is compatible with a weak field. It is only where a person has determination and coherence that the cultural field appears coherent and determinative. This leaves open the possibility that the cultural field is normally fuzzy, weak and low-res. That is – the strong effects are cones around dominant individuals, not products of the field itself.

Empiricism

If you look up the 1957 volume of *Essays in Criticism* that has the celebrated attack by Charles Tomlinson on the much-hated *New Lines*, you will also see an essay in the January number by Robert Conquest on the Anglican-Arthurian poet Charles Williams, entitled 'Art of the Enemy'. If you take a few minutes off from Proper Research to see what Conquest had to say, you find that he has read Williams' interminable poems and identified in them strong elements of traditional discipline: "Pleasure in and justification of corporal punishment are found throughout." He cites

> The implacable hazel
> (a scar on a slave, a verse in Virgil)

> The hazel of the cattle goad, of the measuring rod
> of the slaves' discipline.

What Conquest is getting at is at a much higher level of validity: "The effects of totalitarian thought on art have been examined by various writers[.] The trouble is that it is very difficult to find really illuminating examples, which alone can show us the full pathology of the infection." "The art of the totalitarian countries themselves, since the first establishment of such regimes, has been wholly contemptible[.]" "In Charles Williams", though, we find "a genuine writer who has fully accepted a closed and monopolistic system of ideas and feelings and, what is more, put it forthrightly with its libidinal component scarcely disguised." He is saying that idealistic systems involve punishment at some point because human subjects do not conform to them, and the more unreal the system the more it has to preserve its patterns by repressing deviance. Williams was plunged in fantasy and mystical speculation and the inherent flimsiness of these dreams was buttressed by the dwelling on beating and discipline. The repression of the physical tier was not thorough, and this keeps emerging throughout his Arthurian poems. He has a round bottom as a symbol of balance in the State, because it has two curves; and has hills symbolising that. The hazel wand is at once the rod of correction and the standard of straightness:

> Merlin grew rigid; down the implacable hazel
> (a scar on a slave, a verse in Virgil, the reach
> of an arm to a sickle, love's means to love)

where the disciplining of a slave is again the function of a rod but this rod is also the canon (canon, literally a reed or cane), the model of a correct verse line as in Virgil. The word *hazel* recurs many times in *Taliessin through Logres*. Conquest is saying that a political system which is not an organic development from inside a society will need intense punishment systems to keep itself upright: the Gulag Archipelago, in fact. ('Merlin grew rigid' presumably just means Merlin grew stiff; which may also define what *love's means to love* is, another 'rod'.) Williams was a fantasist but he is akin to mystical idealists in politics. The more perfect the society Lenin imagined, the more people had to die or be put in camps because they did not conform. I think Conquest is perfectly right about this, and one of the signs of an organic political order is that it has a low crime rate, especially for political and ideological activities. This argument is part of the network of ideas behind the favouring of *empiricism*, which is a word with an extremely complex set of notions behind it. Conquest says that "a lack of humility in the presence of the empirical" is a trait of totalitarian art, and had already used the word in a statement of position in the introduction to *New Lines* the previous year, saying "it submits to no great systems of theoretical construction or agglomerations of unconscious commands. It [...] – like modern philosophy – is empirical in its attitude to all that comes."

As a view of the state of European politics in 1957, Conquest's essay has a lot going for it. He was trying to answer the question "why didn't absolute power in the Soviet realm produce the perfect State" which is better than not even asking the question. In 1957, people like E.P. Thompson and John Berger hadn't realised that Sovietland wasn't the perfect State.

I think it came as a surprise to poets linked to the Underground in the '60s, with their perception of humans as a species that plays, and of culture as a form of play, to be told that they were breaching the dams that protected us all against totalitarianism. In my view this was a massive non-sequitur. What it looks like is a by-blow of a guard posting: Cold War intellectuals were so trained to do one thing that, whatever the stimulus, the response would *always* be to denounce the Communist threat. They formed up as a sort of DEW system, an early warning line for incoming missiles or ideas. The defensive perimeter is tensed against pornography, against communism, against Nazism, against drugs, against speculative thought (in concrete terms, against modernism with its reliance on speculation), and against creative fantasy. Like any perimeter, it embraces itself. Its point is to have no breaches. We suppose from the incidental remarks that Conquest is thinking of art theory as well, that he rejects a kind of poetry which jumps off from exalted speculation and writes something which is not experience. It encounters thousands of practical problems (because it is not based on tentative, learning, advances helped by Tradition) and takes authoritarian and damaging steps to fix these problems. In outcome it may fail as poetry but this can be covered up by clique fashions, by imperious Theory. This poetry has an inorganic feel, it has patterning but lacks credibility. To look at speculative thinking through the example of Charles Williams and C.S. Lewis is odd, but the point Conquest is making is that there is a generic resemblance between them and the haughty artistic legislation of, say, a Le Corbusier.

Perhaps we can legitimately identify a specific type of human consciousness which is creative fantasy, a dreamlike waking state in which imaginary events compose and connect themselves in uncontrolled abundance. Wide if unmeasurable extents of the texts we have would, then, be the product of this lushly flowing state rather than of memory or the senses. In fact, a large share of the information stored in culture is the product of creative fantasy.

Conquest's two best poems are about pornography, and this is not completely coincidental. It is obvious that other people appear in the creative fantasies. Any ideal pattern has the problem of what to do when other people don't agree with it and cross its lines. Both totalitarian thought and pornography involve depersonalisation. He is saying that the role of the proletarian in Stalinist myth is just like the role of women in pornography. His best-known poem is about the *Rokeby Venus*, a picture which comes into the story of feminism because it was damaged by an acid attack, by a concerned feminist, in 1915. She was concerned to subtract herself, we suppose, from stories in which a doppelgänger appears who has our face and speaks with our voice but uses words which are not ours. Yet, other people must appear in poems. It is well-known that feminist thought has frequently uncovered male fantasy about the allocation of individuals to roles, as the elementary cells of the social structure. This line of fantasy has then leaked into reality. Male domination appears then as a by-form of totalitarianism and is subject to interruption just as Conquest offers sceptical interruption to fantasy poetry.

The module 'this Marxist story narrates my life but not in a way which I recognise' is adapted into the feminist thesis that 'this film/novel narrates my life in a way which I do not recognise'. The feminist attack on the credibility of (male) writers as cultural authorities recycled the empirical attack on self-idealising writers.

We know that Conquest was spending his working days reading Soviet publications, which were dominated by propaganda. His job was, roughly, to distil truth from inside those texts. This is why he was moving on totalitarian literature, although he chose Charles Williams as his path. I could have addressed narrative distortion by starting with the other side – the whole industry of pleading that representation in the capitalist West is based on alienation, omission of most of the population, the projection of false needs, and so on.

Egoism is no way out. Faced with these criticisms of art, which have been so widely accepted, the conclusion may be to handle other people at length, in terms set by them, with attention to the fine details of behaviour in which the slightest wishes are visible. This drags the poem out of the dominion of projective fantasy. This claim is not in 'Art of the Enemy' but may be found in 'The Rokeby Venus'.

Conquest offers us *two* faculties, of imagining and critically testing. This proposal only works if we can really analyse real texts in terms of these two faculties, which may show up as schematic and abstract when we try to do that.

Conquest's phrase about 'the persistence and variety of the central current of English verse' in the introduction to *New Lines 2* may have given rise to the phrase *mainstream*.

It is hard to give a comprehensive view of empiricism, because it is so pervasive in English intellectual culture. As usual, I have pulled at one thread to see what colour it is. The definition of it by dissident intellectuals who hated it may be crisper than the phenomenon itself.

Historicism

Historicist theory involves a special view of 20th-century art in which evolution progressed rapidly from 1905 to 1930, was then frozen by the era of political polarisation circa 1933-56, migrated to America, migrated back under the aegis of the CIA and the CCF, and re-started in Europe circa 1960. The movement since 1960 is the long-lost son of the movement which stopped around 1930, and everything in between is not allowed in the game.

It may be helpful here to give a few details of this historicism in the form in which it is most current. Three essential components are that everything which is not avant-garde is kitsch, that artistic innovation is 'world-historical' and so more important than anything else, and that there is a timetable of formal innovation which always goes forward (and which disqualifies anything else as *retro*). A fourth tenet is that artists are engaged in a debate about the formal properties of the art object and that somehow the art is *about* its own formal properties. When the debate moves on, all older artistic practices become obsolete. This continual emptying is very exciting for young poets because it continually creates territory which they can stake out and occupy. The 'timetable' of advance allows for a zone of originality which can be demarcated and turned into private property. Thus the advance into undefined stylistic space is like the occupation of the USA by White Americans. If you destroy the sentence or the line of verse you can claim personal territory which if you stick with the sentence and the line of verse as known to the English language you can't claim. Withdrawal from the zones of known art, including the most fertile and effortless ones, is thus mandated by the territorial metaphor, and to stray outside the boundaries of owned (and sensorily derived) estate would invalidate the idea of ownership and so the whole bundle of historicist metaphors. Moving on thus implies wiping out the past and progression towards grey monochrome painting and white cube rooms was a logical extension of impulse. It was a process of becoming conscious in which climactically the objects of consciousness disappeared.

A painting is said to be 'about' flatness and immobility and so a painting which asserts those properties is preferable to one which deploys illusionistic space and places objects in it as if in a real space. Visual art since the Renaissance is said to be in a process of discovery in which each new phase represents more self-awareness and more rejection of illusionism and laying bare of inherent formal properties of the painted thing. The timetable is thus extended back to the 15th century, at least, and all European artists are supposed to know their places on it or are proven to have misunderstood their allotted role in history. This allows for a whole schema of *who's in / who's out* to be built up for the benefit of the loyalists. Changes in painting during the 20th century are thus part of a philosophical debate and each style became obsolete as its contribution to the debate was made and used up. Few people can keep up with this rapid progress and what is up to date at any moment can only be judged by world-historical experts, in fact a few critics in New York, or perhaps just one critic.

It is hard to apply this model to poetry but in a general way the critique of personal consciousness and its objects of knowledge, as discussed below, played the same role. This critique gives us the historicist scale in two senses: writers who want to reproduce experience are 'out of date' technically and people who approve of English society as it was in the 1950s, or at any later moment, are 'out of date' in the light of Marxist politics.

This bundle of theories, or fantasies, was part of the general 'Lend Lease' shipment of American ideas which reached England along with rock and roll and McKinsey-style management consultancy. The British poets who flocked onto the beaches and bought into it were also the ones who bought into American fashions in poetry. The cargo cult in the visual arts has been described by Patrick Heron (who helped it happen in the 1950s) and John A. Walker (*Cultural Offensive*). Its rollout in poetry is described, not as a process but as an Act of Destiny, by Eric Mottram, in essays now in his archive. A brief inventory check of poetry in the USA shows that the import was extremely selective. Olson, Robert Duncan, Zukofsky, O'Hara, Ashbery, Wieners, Jack Spicer were the main stocks. Later poets did not seem to go over. The visual arts market in the USA was rather well centralised and fashion-dominated. Patrons could feel secure about their investments. Painters who did not run with the AbEx stampede had grave career problems, at least according to various reports on the period. No doubt many of them gave up. The US poetry world, though, did not work in this way *at all*.

The belief many poets cling to is that there is a critique of poetic form taking place among concerned intellectuals and that by violating the rules of language they are simultaneously connecting with this debate among the few and making a break with ordinary and 'greyed out' language or knowledge. The breaches inspire thought about how language works (and maybe society and the brain as well). They create a risk which is held to focus the entire powers of the mind on the moment of the breach and the way it is made. The violation of probability in these various forms lets the poem escape from grey predictability. It is fair to say that this radical gesture is not self-explanatory to most of the poetry reading public. Many people respond to phrases like 'cutting edge' 'leading edge', and in this case we can claim that there is an adrenalin reaction even if the phrases have no meaning.

The evidence has been available for a long time now, and it turns out that there is no international elite with legislative powers, that the highly educated in various countries are following completely different agendas, that the line of progress since 1950 is visible so intermittently that it effectively isn't there, that a considerable amount of excellent poetry has been produced which is not 'innovative' in historicist terms, that the idea of a debate about form as the main subject of art is shared by almost no one, that 'world history' has no front line and finally that there is no 'world-historical art' outside the minds of Hegel and a few over-excitable followers of his. These are commonplace opinions, so widely shared that they do not require proof in this place, at this time.

The group relations of innovative poets are of great interest. The originality depends on an expert audience to be appreciated, and this audience needs a shared game in order for the innovation and temporal breach to be effective, legitimated. The game is never completely shared, the players move in patterns which never quite fit into each other. Ideally the poet develops a unique signal which yet permits large-scale production and deep expressivity.

Jewels and Bones in the Catacomb: AGENDA

William Cookson (1939-2003) reviewed Ezra Pound in a school magazine in 1957 and Pound wrote to him, so that in 1958 he stayed with Pound in a castle in Brunnenburg (in the South Tyrol) for a week. It seems that Pound saw Cookson as an acolyte and told him to found a magazine. The early issues of *Agenda*, the result, are not a poetry magazine but an organ of crank monetary theory and Fascist apologia. In 1997, I was asked to review a special issue of *Agenda* on Geoffrey Hill for the *London Review of Books*. I wrote, "When I picked up this copy of *Agenda*, what fell out of it was a letter from two associate editors resigning because of 'the editor's attempt to whitewash and justify the tyranny of Mussolini and the Rome broadcasts of Pound'." What I didn't know then was that an early co-editor had resigned in 1959 for identical reasons. Cookson never experimented, intellectually, after about 1959, when he was only 20. His cult of Pound was hammered into him like a coin struck by a die. Naturally, his admiration for Geoffrey Hill is to be applauded. From 1960, Pound, now aged 75, took less interest in controlling the magazine and so it evolved into a poetry magazine. It lacked an interest in contemporary poetry and a leader.

Cookson says that he was much influenced in founding *Agenda* (in 1959) by *Nine*; "About this time [1957] I had met the English poet and editor, Peter Russell. He had recently published the final issue of his excellent magazine *Nine*, which I regard in many ways as a precursor of what I have attempted in *Agenda*" so we will start with an account of *Nine*. There was a sister magazine called *Catacomb*, even more explicitly neo-fascist, which was funded by the sugar heir Rob Lyle and subject to a scathing and brilliant satirical poem by Christopher Logue, published in *Nimbus*. *Nine* issue 4 contains a review of a book by Bertrand de Jouvenel, a friend of Otto Abetz and a founder in 1947 of the Mont

Pelerin Society along with Milton Friedman. This was a forerunner of the New Right and so *Nine* had links with neo-conservatism already in 1950 – a pretty smart pace. Abetz was Hitler's ambassador to Paris.

European high culture had been integrated with the lifestyle and reputation of the aristocracy. A sector of opinion had responded negatively to the Enlightenment and the rise of middle-class art, with a revanchist theory in which high social status and the thesis of the degradation implied by non-noble art played vital roles. Bourgeois art was seen as essentially a breach of rules of respect and deference, good art was seen as part of the lives of the powerful; unequal status was seen as a simple reflection of the innate superiority of the top three or four per cent of the population. The rise of the bourgeoisie was limited by the unequal advance of the liberal capitalist culture which they drove. In the 1930s, southern Europe was the site of successful aristocratic reactions against the Enlightenment and its sequels, and was also of course the home of European classic art, which was seen as an asset by the variously fascist, clericalist, and monarchist movements of the time. In around 1931, with the collapse of world trade, Modernism was replaced as the dominant interest among the artistically active in Europe by the more pressing concerns of politics and economics. In Italy, Ezra Pound ceased innovating poetically, invested faith in Mussolini, and became prolifically concerned with crank economics. The rise of the tyrant in early modern Italy had been facilitated by the Machiavellian theory of statecraft, and the existing civic culture was undermined to the advantage of individual autocrats; this structure continued in the cult of the 'Strong Man' in 20th-century Mediterranean politics. Pound chose the tyrant Sigismondo Malatesta as a symbol for his own will to power.

The relict culture of classical Europe was the object of educational investment by middle class families and became a symbol of old possessions and of old middle-class blood. It was by 1950 possible for modernism to be aggregated to the same vault of assets, being taken up by the most highly educated and simultaneously accepted by the institutions as the proper subject for academic teaching, acquisition by museums and millionaires, and staging in State theatres. *Nine* was a magazine of right-wing sympathies which also had an active interest in modernism. Its aim was "to re-establish creative contact with the past" and its name referred to the Muses. It was much concerned with translation, and it also peddled the penalised arrogance of those who dislike the modern world and are defeated by it every day.

The key statement by Cookson, in 1962, still an undergraduate, is "in poetry since 1920 ... each successive group since (apart from isolated exceptions) has fallen into the category of dilution and deterioration". This insensibility is for him a line of pride, and led inevitably to the position that nothing is allowed to be Modern after 1959, so that Agenda *did not notice* the whole wave of innovation encompassed in the British Poetry Revival and fell back on meaningless poetry which they didn't even like. The *Agenda* anthology is mainly a collection of conservatism, and the path from modernist principles to this is truly strange. Freezing a situation relates to territoriality and the sense of power and orthodoxy, and may be one of the most significant processes in the landscape. The freezing-up of *Agenda* is important to their position.

Pound's idea of history was based on a cult structure of groupuscules, as outlined by his friend G.R.S. Mead. Language is the product of small groups, rather than individuals, and weird language is the product of deviant small groups. The whole illuminist theory of history which is the content of the *Cantos*, which relies on a great man who sees the hidden patterns of Time and vouchsafes them to a few select and devout disciples, and which throws away any scaffolding of reason, is conducive to modernism because it allows the development of a private language. As the earth vanishes beneath you, you fall or fly and something completely new can be liberated. The insularity of these closed cells, notably attacked by Robert Conquest, is compatible in its arrogance with the self-regard of the aristocracy as a relict group within a democratic culture. Villiers de Lisle-Adam's *Axel* is the great example of this. French monarchists played a role in the development of the Parisian avant-garde after 1850. The monarchists of 1950 or 1959 did not connect with a line of cultural creativity: it is easy to forget how a young right-winger in those years could be immersed in that world-view and see the future of Europe in the roll-back of democracy as well as Bolshevism.

The Right always had problems in connecting with democracy. In order to attack the democrats as much as you want you have to detest their modern world; you have to scorn its beauties and to develop your own unhappiness as the proof of your tenets. The other effect of being such a minority is that you appeal to those who want to be an elite and so from being a catacomb you can requalify as the apex of the system of cultural consumption. The line of legitimism, revanchism, and permanent exile was pioneered, well before the French Revolution, by the Jacobites. The Jacobite style included that dance of horror and indignation and disdain and denial which *Agenda* joined in. The high status narrative in *Agenda* implies, logically, that another group of people has to experience their own low status very vividly. The sense of legitimacy drew on a surge of indignation at anyone *else* having any privileges. Their idea of culture held that the products of liberal education do not understand aristocratic culture (and also that upward mobility must be headed off). The way not to be despised is to acquire a sage, who is not valued for their ability to explain the course of events but as a Master. Objective scholarship is bourgeois. You connect with a vanished nobility (Renaissance buildings, Provençal poetry) but these are representations of lost power. This is different from hanging out with living rich people, the ones who buy Picassos. Hilton Kramer, the most celebrated "neo-con", obviously did hang out with rich people, the ones who decide the prices of modern art and sit on museum boards. *Agenda*'s time-sense was out, and this was a big handicap in dealing with modernist innovation. The art boom of the 1980s connected to the retreat of the State, handing wealth back to the rich – following Milton Friedman's advice.

Agenda's record for poets sufficiently old is very good. Their competence with European poets born after 1900, English poets born after 1920, cannot be called high. Their finest achievement is in cherishing the work of David Jones. The family of Edmund Gray, associated with Cookson at school and well before *Agenda*, were friends of Jones' patron Helen Sutherland. In this way Jones got past the ferocious defences of *Agenda*, and their loyalty to him was marvellous. In the interests of fairness, we have to point to Alan Massey. His poem 'Leechcraft' (1974, part at pp.171-81 of the anthology) is very good and is written around a left-wing critique. We have to discuss how David Jones could be in *Conductors of Chaos* and also in the *Agenda* anthology, with 24 pages of such great poetry.

Modernism came back in Europe after 1960. The crisis of modernism after the collapse of the apolitical position in 1931 was still the dominant fact in its position in the time of *Nine*, 1949-51. The 1950s were a terrible time for English poetry and the modernist line was no exception. The 'modernist heritage' develops with time. The significance of the Objectivists is that they represented the line of conscious technical revolution taken from Pound but used it for left-wing purposes. Eric Mottram takes on American poetry of the 1950s and updates the 'modernist heritage', in fact this new release was the basis for the revival of British poetry in the 1960s and 1970s. The whole cadre of Objectivists, and Olson, were consciously indebted to Pound: the vital twist is the rejection of his fascist cultural politics and a migration to the Left of the spectrum. *Agenda* can be located on the map quite precisely by its refusal of the left-wing adaptation of Pound which had taken place circa 1931, and its omission of the left-modernism of British poetry after 1959 (Roy Fisher's *City*) or so followed from this location. A restoration of right-wing modernism failed to materialise. In fact the *Grosseteste Review* group took English modernism and integrated it with the Objectivist line while moving it very sharply to the Left.

We spoke of historicism above, and particular technical lines are intersected by time, they develop. But there are many of them.

The paranoid-dissociated position

We spoke of doubting the immediate data of consciousness. Doubting everything is a programme which adolescents are anyway inclined to as part of abandoning childhood. It also forms the nucleus of a distinct poetic position. I say paranoid because it sees society as a collusive enterprise which acts to damage the interests of most individuals caught up in it. The idea of a social system is paranoid (as what the primary data offer is not patterned enough to be systematic).

When Anthony Easthope says, in a description of a well-known 1950s poem, "the speaker of the poem is presented as detached, critical, not self-deceived, confident of submitting the world to a controlling gaze; in other words, very much the poised, individualised, empiricist subject whose voice has been represented as speaking in English poetry for over two centuries. At first on the journey objects viewed from the window – knowable, reassuringly familiar – help to generate the mastery of the experiencing 'I'; a river, canals, and then 'the next town'. [...] Everything in the poem – train journey, landscape and townscape, the couples, the concluding vision – is constructed by a script which represents a speaker who experiences all this for us. And the condition for that is an effacement of the materiality of language, to give the effect of someone 'really' speaking." We are to suppose that all this is very very bad. Even if this text dates from 1999, the critique is recognisable as a tune of the avant-garde from much earlier than that. 'Empiricist' is here a code-word for 'not Marxist', and Marxism is assumed to be the theory *par excellence*. The belief that language is material rather than symbolic (if it's made of matter, how much does it weigh?) points to the same investment; Easthope was rather a Stalinist than a Trotskyite, I think. He is setting up other people's awareness as a set of stupid propositions which the true philosopher refutes. Realist poetry then becomes a mishmash of vulgar errors, to be disintegrated and discarded.

Suppose you reject the social order in Britain altogether. A Marxist is forced to do this. It would follow that you rejected all the behaviour you observed and all the behaviour you carried out. You would reject the contents of consciousness, which may be the initial act which permits theorising to occur. Self-display would no longer be the purpose of poetry; you would record behaviour only to negate it, to lure the reader out from their paralysing identification with a niche in the social order, which you are defining as false consciousness. Where many writers tell stories about characters, and ask us to identify with them, and implicitly underwrite the decisions and feelings of the characters, the dissociated artist does none of these things. The impulse is only to interrogate the behaviour: why is the character acting in this way? What do they know about the alternatives to acting in such a way? What is identification? What happens if you don't identify? Whereas an activist might wade into an area of social life and start arguing whether the rules are equally fair to men and women, someone dissociated would ask: why is there an allocation of any individual into a gender category? How is this allocation carried out? What are the motives for identifying with a gender? If there is a pattern of sensibility granted by innate qualities, or innate developmental programs, how do you know what it is?

In a narration, if the camera moves to show us what a character is giving attention to, it amounts to acceptance of part of the character's consciousness, almost to approval. So a camera not moving focus was attractive to this sector, leaving all possibilities equally closed or equally supported. Film from security cameras was attractive because it made no attempt to frame what was significant or make it clearer. (Haroun Farocki, I believe it was, made a film entirely from security camera footage.) The coldness of this footage was exactly what these people wanted. It had no protagonist and so made visible what the subject adds to the experience of sight. The goal of many agents in this zone of sensibility was to reach a narration with *zero affect*. This damage was supposed to break the chain of knowledge and attachment which leads humans to repeat their history rather than to find the exit from it.

As people have a basic need to be validated by other people, to experience art which tries to invalidate everything can be deeply unpleasant and disturbing. Even people who are enthusiastic about it for a finite period get tired of it and find the qualities of anxiety and depression overwhelming them. Attacking someone's emotional attachments is likely either to be unsuccessful or to make them very unhappy. The critical artist would no doubt answer, 'What right do you have to be happy? What makes your miserable bourgeois consciousness able to distinguish happiness and unhappiness anyway? Why should art make you happy?', and so on.

What is the motive for not writing realist poetry? We see the results but not the founding decision. Motives could be:

a) your consciousness is a set of illusions
b) your consciousness represents capitalist ideas about human conduct which I reject in favour of a socialist society which more or less remains to be brought into existence
c) your consciousness is coherent but tedious and literature starts with making an alternative to tedium

How many of the (fundamentally) non-realist writers start with the particular attack on bourgeois consciousness which Easthope presents? a basic question and the answer is undocumented. This position came closest to taking power in the world of conceptual art. However, to see it as predominant in any body of real conceptual artworks that we can gather is a dangerous simplification. Also, a large number of the people who have invested in dissociation have no sense of fellowship with conceptual artists and recognise more of a link to the works of Theodor Adorno, a kind of Marxist without the optimism. Modifying a phrase of his colleague, Herbert Marcuse, about affirmative culture, we can label the dissociation as negative culture.

An older generation of the Left saw proletarians as authentic. However, if you see alienation as the defining condition of working-class life then the actual experience of the working class is invalid in itself, and the revolutionary impetus you recommend depends precisely on this invalidity. The Adorno line was Marxism which rejected the working class. In order to adapt to its new source of material resources and office, the academic world, it also ejected the idea of revolution. It was then a source of fluent speech which had no faith in any part of existing society and no expectation of relief either by political activity or by a future reform of society. From such a position one can depict events without any self-praise and without a sense of possession, simply showing everyone as trapped by the lives they lead and as having structures of behaviour which, in a loop with three or four stages, reproduce the conditions of their captivity.

It is tempting to reject this line and to assert the idea that a *poet* is someone good at forming attachments to ideas, people, landscapes, etc., and that the role of poetry is to illustrate and celebrate this union of exterior and interior. This is not, on examination, what most contemporary poets are doing. In fact, it sounds rather 19th century. As I think about this I have to concede that critical art actually makes you think. Also, that the taste of disillusion is part of modern literature, and not just among the embittered.

A neo-conservative magazine of the Left: a recovery of Carcanet's history

The magazine *Poetry Nation*, which started in 1973, is partly an argument about the position which the Carcanet publishing concern, then new, was adopting. The magazine was edited by Michael Schmidt and Brian Cox, and in 1976 it became *PN Review* and added C.H. Sisson and Donald Davie to its board. According to Schmidt, reminiscing around 2009 about issue 1, "There follows a symposium in which the editor (the same editor who writes this) contends with the *Partisan Review*, with English and American experimental writing, and seems to propose something like a New Formalism as a radical, even a Marxising antidote to the excesses of experiment and the aftermaths of modernism which trouble him. He sees *Poetry Nation* as a journal of the left. His declaration is followed by suggestive demurring comments from Donald Davie; a densely argued clarification by Terry Eagleton (who was the editor's tutor at university), 'Marxism and Form'; an essay on the poetry of the Vietnam conflict by Robert B. Shaw […] and a remarkable interview with that first great English Marxist editor Edgell Rickword, a neglected poet too. […] It was a rich profusion, and confusion of themes, inherences and generations. *The Guardian* called it a thrust from the cultural right, which seemed at the time like a deliberate misreading." (The quote is from the history of *PN Review* currently at http://www.pnreview.co.uk/ip001.shtml .)

The idea of 'poetry nation' was much more 'we belong to the nation of poetry', which is like 'the domain of the human', 'the realm of art', 'the republic of letters', and so on. Or even 'Woodstock nation', a phrase of the time. Schmidt is Mexican, so the idea that he was an English nationalist does not have much credibility. The claim that *Poetry Nation* was a magazine of the Left is the area which attracts extended analysis here. I cannot find this claim within the pages of that first issue. There is an 'editorial note' which certainly makes no such claim. The symposium mentioned is titled 'The Politics of Form' and could, I suggest, be a position statement for the magazine and for Carcanet Press too.

To go back to the beginning, Brian Cox (C.B. Cox) founded *Critical Quarterly* (the other Manchester magazine) in 1958. He also co-wrote a standard textbook teaching Close Reading of poetry. *Critical Quarterly* was aimed at English teachers, and was anti-ideology, but had a programme favouring academics, the academic view of poetry, close reading, empiricism. (This is the academics of 1958, not 1968.) *Carcanet* the magazine started in 1962 (data taken here from an article on Carcanet's website) and its original aim was to link poets from Oxford and Cambridge universities. Thus healing the major split in English poetry, I suppose! Strange what people were worried about in 1962. Schmidt (b. 1947) travelled from Mexico, joined up with the magazine as an undergraduate in 1967, published a few poetry pamphlets, in 1969, and formed (with Gareth Reeves and Peter Jones) Carcanet Press Limited in 1970-1. The 1973 first issue of *Poetry Nation* is all about ideology and may shed a light on what became the framework for Carcanet – except that *Poetry Nation* was co-founded with Brian Cox, and that Schmidt aged 25 or so could be assumed to supply the eagerness while Cox supplied the ideology. There is another story that Schmidt wanted Edgell Rickword (b. 1898) to be the editor and that this only fell through because Rickword was too old and ill. A light deserves to be shone on this: Rickword had edited an important magazine in the 1920s. Schmidt clearly knew his history and was in awe of old people. Rickword was also a Marxist, and edited worthy Party-line reviews, *Our Time* and *Left Review*; so Schmidt was planning a Marxist masthead. A very large volume of *Essays and Opinions 1921-31* by Rickword was one of Carcanet's first books. Ending at 1931 cuts out his 'committed' period. The whole cultural world was getting into politics in 1931, Communist where not Fascist. Part of being a committed intellectual then was writing to reach the masses and not for other intellectuals. Around 1970, Schmidt was trying to become the deputy to someone born in 1898. The problem is obvious, and one can only wonder what would have happened if he'd met a brilliant Marxist thinker born in 1947 (as he was) instead. Carcanet linked to the preoccupations of English literature teachers, not to Thirties-style political commitment.

Some Contemporary Poets [SCP], Carcanet's 1983 programme anthology, mainly ignores the innovations of the 1960s and 1970s but includes strongly Left poems by Jeffrey Wainwright and a poem by Robert Wells about Pasolini. Wells' style is grey and faded, but thematically these poems could not possibly have been taken by a neo-con editor. In 1983 the neo-cons were hypersensitive even to a Marxist twitch of an eyebrow, as anyone who was around at the time will remember. *SCP* genuinely is a neo-conservative anthology; Carcanet serviced a neo-conservative clientele; *PN Review* carried vicious attacks on English modernist poets; but the oddly inarticulate quality of Schmidt's introduction may indicate a lack of commitment on his part to the neo-con project. He was interested in conserving the heritage of European left-wing culture, for example Peter Huchel. Issue one of *Poetry Nation* includes translations of Huchel, a major East German poet who fell out with the regime but retained a loyalty to a deeper idea of the Left, and who was being published further, in more depth, by Carcanet 30 years later.

There was a particular stratum of the Left which was opposed to modernism in the arts. This is not an undiscovered island – the official policy of the Communist Party and the Socialist Workers' Party, as of any other Marxist groups known to me, has been rigidly anti-modernist but in favour of European classicism, the culmination of 'bourgeois art'. The SWP has a clear vision of a future in which the working class will all take piano lessons, take ballet lessons, listen to classical music, read great novels, etc., and where subversion of the classical standards of, say, 1880, will no longer happen (and nobody will wish for it). This vision is clear partly because that was the official policy in the Warsaw Pact countries (notwithstanding serpentine nuances over the decades). What we are looking at here, though, is a fraction of left-wing academics within the Labour Party, rather than the unelectable Marxist bands. At this point the opposition between libertarian and conventional comes to the forefront. The *Black Papers* on Education, co-edited by Brian Cox, roughly from 1968 to 1977, were attacks on the pupil-oriented approach to teaching in schools, as it affected English in particular.

His position was greeted with enthusiasm by the Right but was not incompatible with being on the Left and with wanting State schools to give first-class educations to pupils from income groups D and E and generally to give the working class access to upward mobility. The pupil-oriented approach was associated with lack of discipline for children and with the encouragement of creativity, and so with the excess of creativity which characterised the cultural scene in the 1960s. All arts, also poetry, were being practised by a new style of creative person who was not promoting morality, saw invention and spontaneity as desirable, was less interested in neatness and concentration as parts of the art experience, was detached from 'social poetry' because of its realism and bonds to the material facts of life, and favoured the 'quality of liberated experience' over memorising facts as the goal of learning. It has often been suggested that a permissive attitude to child behaviour produced this whole generation of wildly creative adults, and the new wave were, for whatever reason, extraordinarily distant from the previous generation. This whole line was unacceptable to someone like Brian Cox. The line in the sand being drawn by *Poetry Nation* was to do with culture and, most probably, methods of teaching, in particular of English. The story being told is that 'bright kids will be taught permissively and never learn how to study and will reach 16 and fail their A level courses because they are too busy having acid trips and listening to pop music and not carrying out Acts of Discrimination and will end up with no exam certificates doing dead-end jobs to the great disappointment of their parents'. This is not uttered in *Poetry Nation* but because of the Black Papers it was in the atmosphere and I think it was present when the contributors talk about form, rigour, etc. Conservation (of the self) is being opposed to extravagance (of the self).

As you can see, it's a story that would appeal to a great many people on the Left and to a great many dedicated teachers. There is a paranoid version of it which sees Pop culture as a way of doping the masses and follows that up to regard the penetration of Pop culture, of play, of not doing things you don't want to do, into the classroom as an identical ruling-class trick for producing compliant and apathetic consumers. This paranoid version would see the trick as being pulled only in working-class districts while schools for the elite continue with nineteenth-century standards of rigour, hard work, doing difficult things, etc.

Because women were the primary child carers, the revolution in child-rearing was a revolution initiated by women; feminism addressing affairs outside the household was a *later* chapter of this story. More liberal teaching for young children was also mainly introduced by women, because primary school teachers were mostly female. It was subversive.

The introduction to the symposium on 'The Politics of Form' refers twice to a symposium in *Partisan Review* (1972) on 'the new conservatism' and gives us firmly to understand that Schmidt regards this 'new conservatism' as the right way to write radical poetry and as the path which *Poetry Nation* will follow. The American symposium is about the "political and cultural shift to the right" as a threat, but many of the invited attack the vacuity of "happenings", the art of "immediacy", of letting it all hang out. Schmidt must have agreed with this. *PN 1* regards anti-Vietnam War poetry with utter horror and claims that England needs a whole cultural policy to prevent that kind of thing from happening here. Robert B. Shaw expresses this in an essay and it is picked up in Schmidt's editorial statement. Protest poetry is equated with 'rhetoric' and infantilism. So, *Poetry Nation 1* is a plea for left-wing neo-conservatism. He says exactly that "the so-called cultural conservative ... reveals always new areas of potential, while consistently keeping alive in himself and in his readers an awareness of origins and integrities." This is clarified by "Perspective is only achieved through form, a prime objectifying tool, or through an accurate sense of time and the effect of time upon the immediate experience, the initial response. A writer communicates the truth of an experience only by objectifying the experience [...] to see around and through it. To grant to the experience its integrity he opposes to it an integrity, a form of words which does not invade or break down the image, idea or experience by imitating response directly[.]" This is a fine passage which however excludes from literature any fantasy or improvisation or even wish. Perception always dominates. The idea that conservatism conserves information and so makes possible complex writing, whereas egocentric spontaneity lets information leak away all the time and remains shallow, is compelling. A text conserves information; it draws on what was already conserved by memory. Yet all political radicalism is oriented towards the uncertain future, as the past cannot be influenced. *PN 1* includes a long essay by the art critic Adrian Stokes (1903-72), whose collected works Carcanet later published, to great acclaim. Stokes followed the Kleinian or object relations variant of psychoanalysis and regarded all art as the enactment of infantile fantasies. How is this compatible with the 'integrity' of 'experience' as a framework? Yet it's right there in issue 1. The talk of objective external form has certain echoes of Charles Maurras, chief of Action Française, and favourite writer of C.H. Sisson, who logically enough was a Franco supporter. For Maurras it has to do with burning Mediterranean light, hard edges, and the desired prevalence of Roman virtues.

How could a magazine of the Left include as editors Sisson and Davie? What on earth did those two have to do with the Left? (Stokes is, concretely, present because he was a research associate of Pound around 1930 and Davie, a Pound scholar, had picked up on his writings.)

I don't think it's a secret that the generation of people who were students in the second half of the '60s, especially during 1968, were globally different from people who had been students in the 1950s or the 1940s. The teachers did not reproduce their own views in their pupils, in this case. It is also no secret that 'child-centred learning' was allied with the rise of readerly subjectivity, as a direction in literary theory. Indeed, the whole return to Nietzsche, deposition of the author, revival of subjectivity, insistence on playing games with literal meaning, is connected, on the ground, with the child-centred approach. The resistance to such looseness, and to the formally new poetry which emerged (mostly) after 1968, was predestined by the organised opposition to freestyle learning which Brian Cox was leading. The intervention of academics in the world of poetry has had a different value in each year and asks for considerable unravelling. Schmidt was visibly a student in 1968, his tutor was a Marxist, but he does not seem to have gone through a Marxist/protest phase. Conservative students were numerous at all times; students were the bourgeoisie of the future and could choose whether to feel guilty about this or to feel calm and even proud. Concomitantly, *Critical Quarterly* represented by 1973 an older tier of EngLit academics and by no means the whole campus.

Being 'Left neo-conservative' sounds like a psychotic condition but could simply mean going back to the Left of the 1950s. "The 'new conservatism' ... the reassertion of standards of form, is anything but socially conservative in quality." Schmidt claims his favoured poets as 'the New Formalism'. Formalism was, as described by Eric Homberger in particular, the dominant mode in English and American poetry from 1947 to 1961. Schmidt's 1983 anthology includes a number of poems in rhyme, or assonating. Nothing about them shows anything unlike the *old* formalism. These are poets who are happy to ignore changes of fashion as identified by Homberger or Mottram; Schmidt chose them because of their mournful, withdrawn, anti-metropolitan quality. *SCP* belongs to 'the long 1950s'. Schmidt gives, then, a number of reasons why ignoring innovations of the period 1961-1982 should be seen as an act of authenticity, a sign of depth. As for 'Marxist ... New Formalism', this did not exist in England, or even in Britain. It could be applied to a number of poets in East Germany at that time, (Karl Mickel springs to mind) and probably to 'official' Russian poets too. But in *England*?

* * *

Poets arriving on the scene generally find that they are in the middle of a drama, staged by editors, in which they have an ascribed role and preset lines. What they actually say is not listened to. Only after a struggle does the drama break down enough for them to deliver lines of their own. The summaries are more hard-edged than daily literary practice.

We looked at five factions of opinion, there are obviously a dozen others which I haven't discussed. However, looking at these five surely makes it clear that there is no literary consensus. The likelihood is that novice poets assimilate to the positions in the literary magazines which they see. Classrooms and writing groups would also figure. The novices may see the deep contradictions as an opportunity, an open space. We didn't see any explicit objections to poets being female, Welsh, uneducated, etc, but this was an act without agency, something like the discouragement which meant that very few people became avid poetry consumers after they left school. Saying that all the problems of the poetry world are due to the limitations of empathy is like saying that you could clear up all the problems of poetry by abolishing the poets.

The English condition is that poetic theorising is not quite distinct from poetry marketing. These jingles or attitudes are linked not only to the process of learning how to read poetry but also to the process of marketing it. The pressure of being accountable for sales returns drives impresarios to creative flights, and the noise of the marketplace forces them to cry out simple concepts.

A Section on Black and South Asian Poetry

The cultural formations just discussed are local and so potentially sum up what an immigrant population does not share. This is a way towards understanding English or Scottish culture more adequately than before – opening the sociological view. Misunderstanding has not wholly been absent. We are going to consider further Section 1 of *the new british poetry (1968-88)*, headed *Black British poetry*, and edited by Fred D'Aguiar. Let's recall something of the cultural past, to explain where this poetry starts from. Aldous Huxley wrote about a night-club:

> Bubble-breasted swells the dome
> Of this my spiritual home,
> From whose nave the chandelier,
> Schaffhausen frozen, tumbles sheer.
> (...)
> What negroid holiday makes free
> With such priapic revelry?
> What songs? What gongs? What nameless rites?
> What gods like wooden stalagmites?
> What steam of blood or kidney pie?
> What blasts of Bantu melody?
>   ('Frascati's', from *Leda*, 1920)

(Schaffhausen, a waterfall in Switzerland). This from the first wave of English Modernist poetry. From around the same time, a poem by the working-class realist Wilfrid Gibson:

> A Negro in a dandy livery
> Of blue and silver, dangling from one hand
> A rose-emblazoned bandbox jauntily,
> With conscious smile of gold and ivory
> He ambles down the side-walk...
>   And I see
> Him naked in a steamy forest-land
> Of dense green swamp beneath a dripping tree,
> Crouched for the spring and grinning greedily.
>   ('In Fifth Avenue' from *Travels*, published 1925)

There is a fearful cultural hangover which hampers the appreciation of Black poetry. The existence of a Black community in the United Kingdom arouses imperious historical associations, going back to English slavers plying their trade in West Africa in the mid-sixteenth century, and then through Cromwell's conquest of Jamaica, the fabulously profitable slave-worked sugar-plantations, the hesitant steps away from a planter-slave society. A poet may not be particularly interested in the past; but unconscious fantasy may not have the good taste to stop on reaching the present.

I don't feel able to reconstruct the text-milieu which produced these Black and Asian poets: instead, I'm trying to use the poems as a window, through which to see a social and cultural archipelago which I live not knowing about. The ground-laying anthology of negritude poetry was called *A heart with multiple voice*, actually vaunting the French language; but the phrase seems apposite for the Black diaspora, since the literary background which these poets have chosen is transnational, a canon constructed out of Black writers from the Caribbean, Africa, the USA, Canada, or wherever. The text milieu, merely a preparation for reading these texts critically, would include Léopold Senghor, Aimé Césaire, Marcus Garvey, Frantz Fanon, Malcolm X, Amilcar Cabral, Walter Rodney, Kamau Brathwaite, Derek Walcott; a shopping list you can fill (in London) just by visiting a Black bookshop. I said *archipelago* because the cultural map seems to show a hundred Black islands linked by a single sea. These islands share a common history, in key elements, and the creators of culture are attuned to their fellows in other countries.

The first issue is that of which language to write in. Certain Black writers, from particular regions and particular social classes, are bilingual: able to move along the space between the two extremes of Standard English and deep patois. Psychological problems follow; as is well known, this opposition produces an almost ineluctable pressure to stylistic polarization, so that it becomes incongruous to write about ideas in patois or about intimate feelings in Standard English.

Just as I'm an inauthentic reader, so the defining characteristic of these poems is their inauthenticity: everything is discrepancy and discontinuity. The recent experience of the author and his or her family may include several different countries. There is no *sociology* of a social formation that is so unstable and provisional: instead, there is a lost, rural-colonial past which exists only as information, and there is a future, wholly uncertain, the thing which is fought over in politics. This favours a poetry which is quick-witted, able to render surfaces, able to work with multiple viewpoints, uncommitted enough to deal with change.

John Agard contributes a poem where he denounces an imaginary person for not admiring him enough. The poem is called 'Oxford Don', with populist rhetoric; the argument is at the level of twisting your face up and saying to your opponent, "Look, this is you". The issue is the difference between the way Mr Agard sees himself and the way someone else sees him; it is the difference which is going to stay, and engage our attention, and not Mr Agard's attempts to erase it. The poem shows two people; one, the poet, is aggrandizing himself, the other is a mere puppet, sketched in with derisory crudeness. How can you attack someone else for having a caricature notion of you when you are offering a caricature of him? What could be more hypocritical? The poem conforms to the didactic hopes of bureaucrats; and has no aesthetic content.

Following on from the idea that a book of poems has a structure like a self, and is effective by being unmediated self-expression, is an idea that poetry is a way for teachers and administrators to acquire understanding of the people they administer. This may actually be a way of selling more books, but it is in violent contrast with the artistic intent of poetry. In fact, this sort of teacher-training module vision seems to arise when the artistic function is dead; it is the product of a mortal vacuum.

I thought, some while ago, about the Georgian poets, and their revolutionary transfer of attention to the poor, both rural and urban (income groups D and E, in modern terms). I reported on this in my *Centre and Periphery*. What I realised was that the arrival of state services for the poor meant quite a large expansion of the middle class, but also a new situation where middle-class people were serving income group E, and not income group A any more. There was the possibility of failure in this new function, and therefore a latent preoccupation, among people who bought poetry, with knowledge about the poor. There is a large tier of the middle class, today, which has to deal with ethnic minorities as pupils, clients, and so on, and which is frightened of making mistakes in these dealings. People who dislike poetry exercise, therefore, a dull pressure on poetry to deliver this package of knowledge. In fact, there is a deep conflict between who want poetry to be art, and people who want it to be a sociological package. The latter group don't actually read poetry, but they may be responsible for buying it (for public libraries, school courses, etc.) and for allocating grants to it.

The ethnic minority poet is thus being asked to deliver information to the administrators, as if filling in a form. If a poem is part of the self and is also a commodity, the process of judging it is handling the poet as a commodity. This literal approach to information devalues subjectivity. All the same, if the poetry is printed and on sale, we have to judge it after reading it, and as part of reading it.

Agard's poem does point to the importance of legitimacy contests – a primal function of speech, even if you don't agree that cats, mice, etc. engage in such territorial struggles. With humans, it's no longer literal space where borders are drawn; somehow space has entered language. The fact that someone can get excited about the challenging of a historical event points out the importance of emotional appropriations. There is no text which recounts cultural myths recognized by most British people as valid, and contemporary poetry does not relate such myths: but they do exist, as becomes clear when some radical denies them. It's difficult to see the self as a kind of vessel, with a containing boundary, on the inside of which are narrative objects like "Drake drubs the Dagoes" or "class society starts here and everything Bad begins to happen" or "girls can't fight properly" or even "T.S. Eliot writes fabulous poetry", which can be pulled out, or destroyed, or made larger and more vibrant, but in some sense this picture is true. We do see, daily, how someone's sense of property and identification can stretch a thousand years into the past, or into some abstract area of biology or social history. And it even seems as if effective poetry has to interfere with these impropriated objects, to make them change size, or colour, to shake free of old patterns.

The sociology of language on former plantation islands reflects the old social structure with a planter class and a slave class. As listeners, these people are confused by English voices, which fit into a quite different status hierarchy. The relation of patois to Standard English presents a writer with problems which didn't hinder Ben Okri and the late Dambudzo Marechera, African writers whose first languages are unrelated to English and don't interfere with it. As for other Caribbean people, the problem is worse, because their accent is familiar and alien at the same time, easy to misinterpret. Patois asserts difference from the White community and denies differences within the Black community; but this very potential predisposes the writer to use it in a simplistic, communalist, way.

An urban immigrant community is vulnerable to nostalgic landscape poetry. David Dabydeen offers some splendid recreations of peasant life in Guyana, for example this evocation of the 'Albion Estate':

> Albion village sleeps, hacked
> Out between bush and spiteful lip of river.
> Folk that know bone
> Fatten themselves on dreams
> For the survival of days.
> Mosquitoes sing at a nipple of blood.
> A green-eyed moon watches
> The rheumatic agony of houses crutched up on stilts
> Pecked about by huge beaks of wind,
> That bear the scars of ancient storms.
> Crappeau clear their throats in hideous serenade,
> Candleflies burst into suicidal flame,
> In a green night with promise of rain
> You die.
> (from 'Coolie Odyssey')

Of course he is not naïve about it, he puts the observer into the poem to emphasize that this is an act of memory from a new place. This is not mere auto-exoticism. Dabydeen's ambitious volume-length discussion of the Atlantic slave trade via a painting of a slave-ship is discussed later on. The political requirement to portray history is in total conflict with the casual and simplified gossip style.

The problem of serving the nostalgia of an exiled audience is that the remembered homeland is flattened, no longer a real place; as the reader is served, in effect, with a tourist's eye view of their own unchanging and lost past. This is not quite separable from a way of outflanking the audience: by using a deeper patois, being more intransigent, more anti-White, more audibly like a Caribbean peasant, the poet can make the audience feel guilty and acquire a kind of moral authority. Serious generational conflict is likely within families that have swapped continents in the past generation. For a British resident, or British-born, person to write about the West Indies is to be conservative, and this is hard to combine with political radicalism. We are creeping closer to the situation where a Black artist who is intelligent and formally critical will be written off as a virtual White.

Black artists are inevitably politicised, and this politics will usually take the form of nationalism; bringing a number of internal problems.

The FLN could cheerfully resort to violence in Algeria, because, if there was going to be a race war, it was clearly the Whites who were going to get massacred. But in Britain, the opposite applies; because if there's a race war, it's the Blacks who are going to do all the suffering. All the lessons of the decolonising era – a glorious and revolutionary time fit to excite anybody – have to be reversed or ignored if you live within the metropolis. But no cultural figure is able to stand up and tell a Black constituency to become less Black. There is a non-artistic issue here, namely that, in a multi-cultural society, nationalism is a trait that threatens the well-being of the community. When the motherlands became independent during the Sixties, it seemed to isolate the immigrant communities in Britain, now legally separate from their homelands. The economic problems of the ex-colonies again suggest the weakness or incompleteness of an analysis based on skin colour. The attainment of its goals has made the anti-imperialist cause obsolete. An anti-British attitude is in plain contradiction with British residence.

The sociological project almost demands belief in nationalism: but inspection does not show the portrait of a society, in microscript, hidden inside an artist's work. The sociological project is doomed to frustration. It might be much more accurate to study artists in terms of much smaller audience formations of aesthetic sensibility and ethical beliefs. Maybe nationalism can deliver the goods; and maybe it can't, in which case writers and politicians are marching, banners waving, in the wrong direction. A political artist will be judged on the quality of his or her political analysis.

The labyrinthine twists of local politics have brought it to pass that South Asians have been redefined as Blacks, in order to form a larger bloc of votes: if minorities are competing with each other, they will all lose. Will we see Chinese and Irish defined as honorary Blacks? or Kurds as honorary Celts? This anthology manages two South Asian writers: both born in Lucknow, both normally writing in Urdu, which means they're both Moslems. Legend has it there are other towns in the subcontinent. Anyway, these Urdu-English poems reveal the presence of a poetic tradition of millennial depth and startling refinement; just look at the self-confidence with which Mahmood Jamal rings the changes on his central image of the Star in 'Work-in-progress'. These, along with David Dabydeen's, are the best poems in this section:

> The stars came out
> one night without
> their faces.
> They had no eyes
> nor spoke to us
> through their dark lips.
> A crippled shadow
> wept over the clouds
> where the moon might have been.
> They said in the village
> that a woman lost her child.
> When the sun came out
> we discovered the unity
>
> of faceless dreamers.
>   ('Work-in-progress')

When I was doing an evening class in Farsi, there was someone else there, a native Urdu speaker who was learning Farsi because it represented his cultural roots. Urdu is a language of recent origin, based on an older dialect spoken in Delhi, but in its full fit-out the product of shifting social strata, migrations, and violent political changes. It used Farsi verse forms. Jamal edited the *Penguin Book of Urdu Verse*. He has written poems in English, but the 1984 pamphlet *Silence in the Mouth of a Gun* seemed at first sight a bit thin to write up as a milestone. *Sugar-Coated Pill* was a 2006 Selected Poems which does reveal that 'Work in Progress' was probably 'Stars', which we have poems "from" in the Selected. How does "gun" relate to "sugar"? Both are oral images, and it is probable that these very striking physical images are what survives in translation – he is thinking in an Urdu tradition and the English language cannot echo that. An image-dominated tenor pushes phonological patterning to the back. By *Sugar-Coated* we have about 20 very very strong poems. Urdu was notoriously a mongrel language, emerging out of the cultural confusion as a social system was tossed up in the air. Bosnian Moslems also wrote poems in the Arabic metres, in Serbo-Croat. Perhaps English will be enriched by the historically elaborated forms of a dozen different immigrant cultures.

    I tried to follow up the writers here, but could find very few publications by the ones I liked. I suspect the anthologies I used were not very helpful as introductions to the poetry of ethnic minorities.

The work of James Berry, as displayed in the 1995 volume *Hot Earth Cold Earth*, has a range of virtues quite incompatible with the Pop register of address. Berry (1924–2017) is serious, obstinate, willing to wrestle with deep memories and emotionally ambiguous situations. He writes like a mature man whose memory is not abnormally empty or sugary. Berry reaches the start-line for serious poetry by eliminating every unoriginal line. As we trace his rigorous tangling with the problems of being faithful to memory we become involved in the multiple planes of experience. Apparently critical and doubtful, it is far more involving than smoother poems with ready-made phrasing and sentiments. So much effort could only be expended on personal experience which is both real and precious. Because it makes me think about history and politics, I have to engage with those topics in order to read the poems; and they do not resolve out into a pleasurable substance, in the way which pop songs, lyric poems, and advertisements, may do. He eschews the simplest and most obvious myth fulfilments, but his work is passionate and direct:

> You staring summer days and shut-eye nights
> on beaten place and dried-up tenants
> all people awaiting no-help
>
> eye of burner sun
> watcher of gunshots outflying stones,
> impartial colluder –
> with your silent walk banish pain
>
> You burner sun you wrinkler
> gripping me into a goner
> having me rotting under dazzle
>
> watching me nakedly pocketless
> watching me wretchedly moneyless
> watching non-weapon loser
> with your silent walk banish pain
>   ('Happy Goodbye Sun')

This rips apart facile nationalist legends by showing the Caribbean homeland as a hostile place, 'rotting under dazzle', with problems on every side. The intent of the whole poem is a ritual goodbye to woe and misery: the speaker describes the plantation he is leaving behind. It has an interesting compromise between Standard English and Creole syntax in a phrase like 'on beaten place'. The omission of some pointing words ('a beaten place' or 'the beaten place', is what I would have said) does not reduce the information flow of the poem. Nor does a Latinate phrase like 'impartial colluder' (syntactically parallel to 'you burner sun you wrinkler') muffle the impact of the passage. The sun colludes with the power of the ruling class by making their crops grow and perhaps by making people seek the shade rather than fight for social change. It dazzles your eyes with the same energy that speeds up any process of organic decay or rot. Berry's assumption is that the residue of having lived, as a conscious being, in two different countries, is enough to forge compelling poems by contrasting, recalling, and analysing that double narrative. He's right.

The low oral style was catastrophically handicapped for dealing with the experience of migrants from New World to Old in any credible or striking way. Conversely, that historical experience was so complex that it did form an exceptional material for poetry. If modernity is about estrangement, it is a good start to have a life where everything is strange. If you are going to be alienated, it's an asset to live in a community where everyone is equally displaced and perplexed. Berry has said, in the introduction to *News for Babylon*, his 1984 anthology of 'Westindian-British poetry', that "Essentially, while other potent features are subdued, the poetry exposes a collective psyche laden with anguish and rage."

'Chain of Days', one of the pivotal poems in *Hot Earth*, describes a moment in the poet's childhood when his father was addressed as 'boy', by a White Jamaican child, and James was staggered. As the incident happened in around 1934, his work is stretching to accommodate more decades than I have been alive. Another poem describes his great-grandfather being a slave:

> I remember
> I am third generation since slavery,
> born into people stricken in traps,
> eight generations departed
> with a last sigh, aware they leave
> offsprings all heirs to losses
>   ('In Our Year 1941 My Letter to you Mother Africa').

This moment breaches the picture plane of the poem. Personal knowledge fails, as intellectual drive leads the poem outside its own possibilities: a form of transcendence which is also horror, also humiliation, also autonomy and pride. Much as I might love poetry, this notion of being kidnapped fettered and enslaved makes the landscape of poetry all around it look unbearably shallow. I would propose first that you have to know about this in order to understand the position of the Afro-Caribbean diaspora, the 'heirs' to those 'losses'; secondly, that it is an understanding we look towards but cannot attain. We simply do not have the intellectual and moral scope.

Two arguments in favour of the simplistic style arise here, in connection with the function of advocacy. First, the issue of historic crime and grievance is so simple that it may not need much argument. There is no 'slavery denial' cult to match the sinister Holocaust denial cult of neo-Nazis. Secondly, our legal system forces everyone to be an individual – rights and the whole legal process work for individuals, one at a time. This connects with an egocentric style – if this simplicity allows focus for a court and the legal machinery, then it does similarly for the arguing process within poetry. Hearsay evidence is disallowed, let alone *imaginative reconstruction*. But Berry's Africa poem is set in 1941, composed probably in 1985-94, and looking back to bloody events of the 18th century; its time-line is an elaborate geometrical form.

Berry's volumes of poetry for adults are *Fractured Circles* (1979), *Lucy's Letters and Loving* (1982) and *Chain of Days* (1985). I have not seen these. However, a selection from the 1985 book is included in *Hot Earth Cold Earth* at pages 120 to 159.

The other poet from Lucknow was Iftikhar Arif, author of *The Twelfth Man* (1989, translated from Urdu by Brenda Walker). I couldn't quite work out from the book jacket whether Arif (born 1943) lives in Britain, although it says he works for the BBC and for an Urdu cultural centre in London. The 'twelfth man' is a spare member of a cricket team of eleven; a support who can replace anyone. Arif's poems represent an aesthetic ideal which is quite strange to us. I can't write interestingly about his work.

Because the zone of distinctiveness is seen as individual property, it may get in the way of group identity at a concert event. Rhetorical, idealised poetry is much more suitable for crowd participation – the loss of self. Urdu poetry readings are by all accounts much more rapturous than English ones. The introduction to *Twelfth Man* speaks of a reading in New Delhi attended by 30,000 people. Adapting the zone of ornament to reflect personality may reduce it to the status of documentation and eliminate spontaneity – and with it the key functions of emphasis on the momentary, responsiveness to the passing moment, making decisions in a timescale which the crowd can share.

Arif's poetry is sublime but poor in local detail, the empirical zone. An English audience is more likely to get with the Urdu tradition via the music of Nusrat Fateh Ali Khan. The crux is whether vivid perception has to pick up what is specific, local, unexpected – or whether vividness also produces idealised and perfect perceptions, and such poetic qualities can also be a *symptom* of vivid states of mind. The western myth is of splitting and self-definition: offsets defined as peaks. This belongs with nuclear families – which perhaps suggests that it belongs to the fringes of Europe; northern France, America, England. It seems almost to mean that the deviation of a poem from an ideal is what attracts us to it. With Arif's poems, just the opposite is true. These writers belong to an ethnic minority, in Britain. People who live in large families surrounded by people similar to themselves may have a stronger sense of self and greater serenity than people who live in artificially small families, leave their home town so they move away from their relatives and friends, and leave home to live alone. The extended family offers more continuity than the nuclear one.

The history of individualism in Western art is alluring and uncertain. The arrival of the non-ideal was a kind of revolution – as if somebody had forgotten the rules. Whatever shifts in customs of self-government and reflexivity cut us off from the past of our own society, act now as barriers to our understanding of spiritual poetry from India and Pakistan. Perhaps self-observation has nothing to do with the rise of scientific observation? Who can say? Tower Hamlets Council put out a press release at one point saying that there were speakers of 150 mother tongues in the borough. I know nothing about Urdu poetry in England, and I am left gaping by the possibility of other ethnic traditions – Cypriot, Ukrainian, Yiddish, etc. – which have not penetrated my awareness. England has been the opposite shoreline to every coast in the world.

One version of the minority politics is simply a demand for more space, prizes, praise, attention, wealth, bypassing questions of artistic validity because these are seen as inherently frustrating. The project based on a metaphor of seizing and owning territory involves ignoring the choices of the market and its consumers. You get space in a bookshop because your books sell, not because you own territory. This leads on to a story about the immigrant or minority population. First, there was a question whether they would be interested in the poetry commodity or possibly react like most other people. Secondly, whether the poets from these arriving groups would be lost among 7,000 other poets who weren't very famous. Thirdly, whether in view of the limited local uptake the new groups would accept that the cultural managers of poetry had any legitimacy – and similarly for the artistic, linguistic, political, etc. standards which they upheld. There is a question whether rejecting these pieces of cultural equipment made for being uncompromised, for radical originality, or for poverty of means.

Perhaps a bigger problem is that in the mosaic of micro-communities any art that delves deep and acquires a serious payload of political narrative is likely to appeal to the micro-community only and achieve micro-sales. Or, can you amplify one strand of micro-identity without signalling to every other kind of micro-identity to stay clear. Minority arts needed State support. To some extent, this meant becoming part of the State.

There is a tier of people called cultural managers whose tortured and compromised situation can only be relieved by torturing and compromising other people. The big issue when I was growing up was social class, with a Marxist State just off stage, like Fortinbras' army in *Hamlet*, allegedly about to sweep all bourgeois people and thoughts away and replace them with something starker and stronger. The EngLit industry got caught up in this essentially theatrical illusion and non-event because the majority of its teachers were facing working-class pupils, and their success in exams could plausibly be linked to bringing 'bourgeois culture' to working-class individuals. Poets got wholeheartedly involved in the left-wing scheme for a better future, perhaps too deeply. In the second half of the '70s, the world of culture pulled away from this zone of symbolic conflict; partly because it was too real, thus destroying the indispensable game quality of cultural activity. People divided into ideological silos, where the people taking part in a realm of discourse shared the same values. This minimised political argument, while introducing a nightmare of finding yourself in the wrong room. This was of interest to EngLit teachers and cultural bureaucrats. An ever higher proportion of income groups D and E were ethnically different from the host population, as well as poorer.

The defenders of the system connected with this group in two ways: through exploitation, confinement to low incomes and areas in cities where people didn't really want to live; and through patronage, handing out of resources in mitigation, but with a dependency relationship as part of the package. Politicians with cultural managers wanted to subsidise minority arts as a display of generosity and harmony. The need to show harmony was greatest where affluence and real harmony were least. In fact, although the Arts Council was originally set up to bring high culture to parts of the country outside London, in the 1980s its director of literature (Alistair Niven) claimed he was focussing on ethnic minority arts as his overriding purpose. The idea that a poem has to be a transparent account of daily experience suits the numerical-bureaucratic view, and when applied to thousands of dull poems gives rise (among the well-informed) to the assumption that the critique of personal awareness is indispensable to a good poem – and a poem not doing this is naïve, almost folky.

I spoke just now of a theatrical illusion. At this point, it seems that, rather than seeing bourgeois culture being swept away, what we saw was the middle class expanding inexorably from 20% of the population to 50% (and, according to one recent poll, 60%). Similarly, everyone in the world of arts management tells the same story about what is happening between Ethnic Minorities and Big British Culture, but when we look back in 20 years' time I think this story will turn out to be soap and fag-ash. If we turn our eyes to the altogether more sordid and operational level of daily life, people in the know assume that any ethnic minority poet is dumbed-down and only being published for institutional reasons. Secondly, if I say any ethnic minority poet is good, no one will believe me; they will simply think that I am posing as a good person. Thirdly, if I say anything by a minorities poet is Rubbish (like most of *News for Babylon*, perchance), people will not respond by thinking 'this is good information' but by thinking that I am a bad person. Fourthly, when someone talks about sharing out access to poetry publishing in terms of proportions of the general population, gender race disability educational disadvantage etc., everyone else assumes they are a cipher and talk sociology because they can never retain any other form of knowledge. The relationship between artistic opinion and pious intent has become overloaded.

I am wondering if the strains of contact between the industrialised world and the Third World have really got away from the problems illustrated in the passages I quoted from Huxley and Gibson. There seems to be a mighty force dragging the art towards pastoral – a state of Arcadian innocence where people sit on the beach all day and pluck fruit from the trees for food. A simplified oral style asks us to regress to simpler cognitive processes, along with the exotic fruit. This goes along with stylised representations of the Old Country which are flattened, because remote from real memory, and lose realism just as they claim maximum authenticity. Nationalism seems to come to the fore as an artistic ideology which complements pastoral, without being less false and archaic.

Points Scattered Round an Invisible Field

Admitting weaknesses in one of the anthologies used points up weaknesses in results based on it. At this point I surrender and concede that the rest of this book is not going to follow the schemes worked out by the anthologies (in chapter 1), or from the anthologies. The work is not going to be coherent in that way. It will break up to deal with a scattered subject. I can see that 34 of the 65 poets I have selected for individual treatment do not feature in the anthologies of the mid-90s which I surveyed at the beginning. It is worthwhile saying something about the choice. The set of books described was reached quite simply. First, I had a "shopping list" of about 350 books published in the period. Next, I cut this list down to a number I could deal with. This was 100 at one point. This process was very emotional and difficult and had no rules. The overall goal was to exhibit the variety of excellent British poetry. This tip to tip predilection had a risk of reducing the emphasis on the text as a purely autonomous thing – by exhibiting the field. This is partly a way of forming a critique of the scene, and also of those anthologies. Evidently they exclude older poets, whereas my subject runs from 1960 on.

Anything I write is limited by the initial input pipe – a narrow slit, perhaps. The question of coherence is a basic one, because coherence may simply reflect the rigidity of a given critic as limiting the diversity of what he perceives. The history of poetry criticism shows a regular pattern of self-directed critics acting also as impresarios, taking a narrow view of a cultural strip which they could personalise. There is no way out of this. A number of academics have abandoned the idea of judgement, where critic means "judge", and stopped being critics. Their writings do not evaluate poetry and suffer from alienation, depersonalisation, and artistic vacuity. I do not think this is, actually, a way out. I can't write about artistic experiences I haven't actually had. I see my poetic tastes as being very broad, but this may not be acceptable to the poets whose work I find boring. (I guess egocentric implies ethnocentric, but the artistic forms which turn you on don't coincide with ethnic patterns, they are of a different order of being.)

The key phrase *balkanisation* means partly that the critic doesn't know what's going on outside their personalised strip. I am not trying to impose coherence on the material because I think that would negate and block out the essential quality of diversity. My project has been more to include as wide a range as possible, as this would offer a critique of each of the "narrow strip" experts. Actually, every public utterance on poetry comes from a particular sector of opinion, with implied zones of intense empathetic accuracy and cultural invisibility/ blindness, and can only be an asset for us if we realise what the limiting framework is.

Classification is a *partly* objective process, a move away from pure emotional impulses towards features of verbal behaviour which can yield repeatable results and be shared by more than one person. Poets are hypersensitive about classification, mainly I think because it connects with the consumer's decision not to read something. That is, most poetry readers are going to ignore you. Classification is a piece of equipment which helps them to do this. This might be a reason why I would want to arrange the same raw material into four or five different classification patterns. The value of abandoning a line of data recovery is that by using a different line we can see more of the landscape and, in fact, recover its fragmentation or balkanisation.

The valid groupings are the ones which correspond to formations of taste, associations of people who like the same thing and who have pursued that goal for years. These groups are based on solidarity and familiarity. They are very powerful. But no one has yet looked at the market and the alliance groups and said they are a good thing for the literary art. It always seems that development in poetry means breaking down hardened patterns of response – and of negative response. The reason I did not re-use the clusters was that I wanted to break up tenacious patterns of reaction and loyalty in order to get to an uncoded space.

The obscure markings in the headers refer to the clusters identified above, and to the anthologies. The poets are not drawn from all the clusters, as I did not find every area equally interesting. Everyone knows that Theory is High whereas actually describing texts is low. This book is now going to be mighty low.

Noble Relics

These poets are survivors from eras predating the 1950s – isolated from each other and from recognised groups. They bear witness to an unthinkably vast range of unrealised but possible styles. The pressure of socialising culture left them without peers or successors. Including them naturally makes the selection less consistent. Perhaps it points to a way out of our pervading assumptions. Other poets around in the 1960s, and standing for more complex possibilities, were Berry, Auden, Sacheverell Sitwell, MacDiarmid, Kathleen Raine.

The unique breach in history:
David Jones, *The Tribune's Visitation* (1969; 23 pp. CC, Agenda)

After the artistic decline of Eliot, Jones (1895-1974) was the most significant poetic figure in England, for probably 20 years. The preface tells us that the poem is related to certain other poems (unpublished at that date), also set in Judaea around AD 30, such as 'The Fatigue' 'The Wall' and 'The Tutelar of Place'. All of these were published in *The Sleeping Lord*, in 1974. According to the Jones scholar Thomas Dilworth, the group they belong to was started in the late 1930s. The books published in 1974 and 1981 were probably written before 1960, I guess. In fact, this poem was broadcast in 1958. The ornamental title-page, lettered by the poet, says 1967 (and, also, 784 years *ab urbe condita*, from the founding of Rome, which gives us a double time – as this gives us 31 AD). Jones was a Roman Catholic convert, and everything he wrote is coloured by his belief in the efficacy of ritual. Actions have to be carried out slowly and in the right order, and symbolism has to be properly worked out and to address fundamental emotional needs. Everything in his poems follows the observation of Mircea Eliade on ritual, that it is happening twice: in the present and *in illo tempore*, in sacred time, where the objects are the original objects in the world and the value of the actions is eternal and removed from the touch of human hands. This poem is happening in Palestine of the 1st century AD, but also refers to the British Empire – and to the Catholic Church, as an entity which is geographical and populous, although it is not a state. Jones believes that nothing is happening for the first time; this is a notion most poets reject; Jones' solution is an escape into reflexivity, and a use of montage so radical that it puts us in two minds at once. There is a relationship between anxiety, and liking for repetition, ritual, and continuity. What his circle were discussing, in the 1920s and in the wake of Spengler, was the overthrow of the western social order – a dire complement to the psychological breakdown he experienced and recovered from, around 1932. One of the *loci* for the Ennius line says, in Latin, 'it is to the sound of trumpets that states are usually overthrown'. This overthrow (mentioned in the Notes on the inscription) has two values: as the collapse with which civilisation is threatened, and as the overthrow of the perceptible world and human state-making by the Day of Judgment. Jones sees the social order as being embodied in certain disciplines, certain set sequences of behaviour, which are learnt with some trouble and can then be repeated for centuries.

The lettering on the title-page (repeated on the cover), in a style whose ligatures etc. recall Roman monumental inscriptions, gives us: the name of the book; the author's name; centrally, the words IDEM IN ME; the name Fulcrum, publisher; and, running round the border, the line *At tuba terribili sonitu taratantara dixit*. This is from the epic poet Ennius, and means 'and the trumpet with fearful sound said, taratantara'.

The poem is the spoken account of an inspection (the visitation), by an officer (the tribune), of an Italian legionary unit stationed in Judaea. Before dismissing them, he admonishes them about cleaning their gear – he specifies the back rivets, and 'under those frogs' – and in general about their duties. The poem is documentary, in a sense; it shows military routine. *Idem in me* is the formula of a recruit giving his military oath before joining a legion. Oath is *sacramentum*, and so Jones means by this the sacraments of the Church, binding a believer to the divine dispensation; but also, the social compact by which large bodies of humans live together as a nation. I believe the Judaean poems attach to a visit Jones made to Mandated Palestine, in the 1930s, when the legionaries were British soldiers – as he had been, in those formative years after 1914. This gave him the link to sensuous and verbal details, without which he cannot write his poems. Also – to subject nations and incessant warfare in the world contemporary with the poem (that is, not 1969).

What the Tribune says is an anguished lament for the levelling effect of the Empire, that 'drains to world-sea all the blessed differences: No longer the Veneti, no more Campanian, not the Samnite summer pipes nor the Apulian winter song(.)' The names are those of linguistic minorities in Italy, whose languages are known from scattered inscriptions, but disappeared with the spread of Latin. He speaks with horror of their reduction to a purely military being ('do we but supervise the world-death/ being dead ourselves/ long since?') He wonders what dawn will redeem them – we know the answer is the Crucifixion, an event necessary for Providence to be fulfilled. The tenor unmistakably resembles that of anti-war speakers in around 1938-45 – resisting Hitler, resisting the militarisation of the Empire to face him, resisting (also) the drowning of the Welsh language in a greater community.

Jones went through four years of the First World War as a frontline infantryman and was something of a psychological casualty – yes, still in 1969. There are some experiences which don't stop. This is quite intimately related to the eternal return of the sacramental events which we are watching happen in 'The Tribune's Visitation'. The address to the troops has to do with repetition and cyclicity – but redemption, the unique breach in history, is there as well. For, this is why we are there in AD 31: mankind is about to be redeemed. And the bugle call heard on the title page is – let there be no mistake about this – the last trump, calling us to our eternal reward, purified by that earlier sacrifice of the Son of God. It is possible to read the poem, in the context of circa 1940, as filled with Apocalyptic hope of the trumpet announcing the overthrow of a state – and the coming of a better, more small-scale, society.

I really got involved in poetry through Jones, when I was 16 and 17, and I can't talk about his work because my feelings about it go back to a moment of my life which I just can't dig up now. I could exchange the whole of modern poetry for Jones. My involvement in Celtic languages and literature came from here and I am still pursuing the lines which *The Anathémata* opened up for me. You can't stand outside what's inside you.

The triumph of depth of field:
Kathleen Nott, *Poems from the North* (1956; 54 pages)

Nott (1905-99) published two vital books of poetry: *Landscapes and Departures* (1947), being the other one. The 'north' is Sweden, where she was living at the time (and about which she wrote a travel book).

She is missing from just about all the sites (anthologies and histories) which legitimised poets of that time. Given the quality of the poetry, the gap in public recognition is painful. Look at this:

> There are no tall engines standing in the polar North
> or none that is ready for use. They are all
> sheeted and hooded with the snow: who could discern them
> among faceless pines
> and blinded firs?
>   Yet there are things and forms
> one would hazard only waiting to be stirred
> among this lumber of petrified halls that look
> by the light ruined, as if time out of mind
> ago, they had lost a vaulted and antique branching
> to this faint modern sky: and these not only
> the crashed, spread-eagled and the near-supine
> that lie unvisored from the snow.
>   For though no visible tombs
> lie out among the pall'd rocks and no steelmen ever
> sprang from old granite, though there has never been
> any clangour and the place breeds
> nothing but silence, then snow upon the silence
> and silence upon the snow, and even the birches
> leaped silver from an igneous vein, one can feel how tense
> this soundless and Spring-agony might be
> to heave, to be wholly altered and removed,
> to flutter, though large, and break in through snow
> and at last to be seen of eyes, at last, though monstrous or
>   monolithic,
> and even though inward darkness be perpetual.
>   (from 'Absolute Zero')

The most obvious stylistic point dominates the whole passage, that is the length of the continuous blocks of meaning, what I have called metaphorically depth of field: the style demands not only a perceptible object worthy of such intellectual profundity but also a mind with the intensity and detachment and even longing needed to search the perceptual field at such length before breaking off. Every state of thought has an end; where you reach that end is a key to what operations your mind is undertaking. It is therefore a psychological signal, showing the interior of the mind quite clearly; as we enter into the poem we enter into such an interior state, and there we are either happy – or we dislike the poem. Much depends, then, on this depth of visual field – which I find throughout the book.

It is far unlike the momentary glimpses and violent syncopated transition which we associate with modernism (not all modernism). I quoted Michael Schmidt above as "'Perspective is only achieved through form, a prime objectifying tool, or through an accurate sense of time and the effect of time upon the immediate experience, the initial response", and this says what Nott is about. This was a central attitude, in the 1950s, and she was in the mainstream in that way. Nott's poem is not an allegory and to some extent it is exhausted by the depth of its gaze: what we see does not promise another world but, in recompense, it is actually there.

> When from a noiseless power of flight,
> pinhead, snakeneck, grow single and alight;
> from a watch of cold eyes which was taller
> than the sun's fire-crawl
> upon either port: and on the extinct
> grey chimneys of rock, each distinct
> meteor startles, with a beating
> belly and limp feet, you can hear
> over tufts the wind has usurped all year,
> shrieks as of winches and cordage.

The second half of the book is mainly poems about love and it is not wholly surprising, given the intensity of the gaze shown in the first half, that the object of love turns out to be disappointing, while this searching gaze gives the poems their emotional reward and a retained promise that emotional intensity is the goal to which our faculties are attuned and is still possible. The development of 'Internecine Love' is not completely clear to me, but the northern sea of the quoted stanzas seems to be a kind of exterior equivalent for a love that did not sustain itself under tests:

> Offence of nature and of place
> powered these hulks with love and grace
> and you in lapping peace will read
> what shook these ribs was love indeed [.]

Repeatedly we read of acts of hearing, but none of them seems to be the desired sound; we are left to guess what that is – the music of amorous harmony perhaps. The sea sounds like the North Atlantic, in high latitudes, perhaps between Faeroes and Iceland; but is perhaps not a literal place. It is there as the medium for a journey which is mainly a journey through time. It is there to supply depth of field. 'Pinhead and snakeneck' describes a sea-bird; perhaps it starts as a pinhead, when far away, and increases in apparent size as it descends towards the observer. The chimneys of rock are known in Gaelic as *stacs* and are offshore islands, such as St Kilda, guarded by high cliffs which are perfect nesting-places for sea-birds. The meteors are birds, again.

One poem, 'Manichee's Black Mass', is unlike the others. It is a political satire on social attitudes towards being Black, racially, equated with a Manichaean view of the world which divides it into light and darkness. It is a remarkable poem. The writer is not consistently interested in unintelligent people and illogical views. The book could not be about them. The book as a whole is a celebration of the intelligence and requires large measures of truth as the air which intelligence must breathe.

The poems are like great waves which have a long fetch, starting far out in the ocean and taking their time; this implies the delay of gratification, or rather succeeds by the depth of involvement and the steadiness of focus which we participate in as we follow the wave onto shore. One of the poems quotes Ugo Foscolo and it may be that the method of constructing very long verse paragraphs was influenced by his example in *Le Grazie* and *Dei sepolcri*. This poetry does not strive to create a linguistic world; it is not self-serving and does not obviously reach its self-set goals. It is a search for truth, as much in the desolate landscapes of rural Sweden as in the emotional passage of arms between two people, representing each other as accurately as the ego allows. (Nott's marriage ended around this point.) The depth of focus is the reward, at the same time that it takes on so much truth that it drowns elementary emotional states and hopes.

This book is outside our temporal limits – but we can bend those for a special reason. Nott, also a philosopher, published a book in the early '50s which attacked Eliot for intellectual regression in clinging on to religion. While it is hardly possible to disagree with Nott about Eliot's relapse into monarchism and Anglo-Catholicism, attacking Eliot in the England of the 1950s was a kind of literary suicide, and this on its own possibly explains why her name does not feature in the sites of consecration. The 1950s audience was more likely to identify with religion; they may have respected her but she made them feel uncomfortable. Existentialism plus Formalism – that does sound like the 1950s of the textbooks. *Poems from the North* might call for a recount on that era – it is surely one of the best books of the decade. I think the abiding fact is the English poetry market having a dread of intellectuals.

Between Łodz and Brody:
F.T. Prince, *Dry-points of the Hasidim* (1975; 17pp.)

On the title page we read, "'Why are the people dancing?' ask the deaf ones. 'Why are they running after the musicians?'" A note tells us that dry-point is a way of making prints, by engraving directly onto metal with a chisel point. 'The reader must not think of dry-point as a thin and meagre art. It may be made to look very rich...' The hand has less freedom than in etching. This long poem adapts Martin Buber's collection and translation of wonder and wisdom-tales about the teachers of the Hasidim, an 18th century sect among the Jews of Eastern Europe. Prince (1912-2003) was half-Jewish, although from a cultural group which is rather remote from the Hassids. The sect arose after the mid-17th century Khmelnitsky revolt in the western Ukraine, a period of such intense violence that it threatened the whole civil order. In particular, Jewish community organisation collapsed, education was interrupted, and there came to be a large Jewish population with no rabbis or religious organisation. This was the setting for a radically populist movement, with untrained priests, and a laconic style of utterance – suitable for being memorised, and for oral transmission among the illiterate. Enthusiasm and feeling were the admired qualities in this revival – like German Pietism. Enthusiasm for the Hassids is a concealed enthusiasm for the uneducated of Europe in general – their enthusiasm, their sociability, their desire for goodness above all things. The sayings of these untaught teachers dealt with the whole human subject, were inexplicit and lapidary, and drew on allover intuition that could not account for itself. Unlike most European priests, the Hassids were keen on dancing – and on drinking to make themselves joyful and praise the Lord in a proper way.

The poem is based largely on Buber's *Tales of the Hasidim* and Louis Newman's *Hasidic Anthology*. We hear stories about the sparks (of souls) in exile, and the shells in which they are hidden; about light shining from the faces of the good; about ghosts and magic; about the breakdown of Menahem Mendel of Kotzk, his silence for 20 years after crying out 'There is no judgment and no judge'. Prince's poem is consciously poor in means, sparse in detail, deals with poor people – to leave space where goodness is visible. The parts of the poem do not read as stories and cannot really be read except in the spirit of seriously trying to grasp human life and seriously trying to be a good person. They are both practical, and belong to a time after organised knowledge and institutions had been dissolved.

This is a great poem because it is about a great subject. Prince does not re-create the alien world of Eastern European Jewry but evokes it by spare allusions which never exhaust anything – precise flecks which show a little fleck of a big mystery.

Prince was born in 1912 and published a first volume in 1938 – when it was subject to a review of annihilatory brutality in *New Verse* by Geoffrey Grigson, one of the ethical low points of the entire century. Prince went on writing significant poetry for the next sixty years.

Fine and mighty sins:
George Barker, *The True Confession of George Barker* (1950, complete edition with 2nd part 1964; 110 stanzas of 8 lines)

This text was written in 1947-8, as it says internally; it was turned down by Eliot at Faber, then published by the Communist Party-backed Fore Publications, and again by David Archer. A second part was added in 1965. The inspiration was Villon's confession (as he points out in the poem, he only had a vague idea of it, as he couldn't read French). The addition 'a true confession', though, throws us into the ambience of scaffold confessions by dire criminals, issued as lurid ballads on broadsheets. The metre is octosyllabic rhyming ABCBBDCD (roughly). The 'confession' bit, though, puts us in a Catholic ambience: the first rule is that we are going to be told things which are normally secret, and the hint is that these are going to be terrible and juicy crimes. As he tells us, there is no point confessing unless you have something to confess; his father was a policeman, and so he likes 'uncivil and even sinister violations'. The title also tells us that a single human is going to be at the centre of events: we are going to be shown the precipices and swamps of the human soul, not to wait around while practical matters occupy centre stage. It is this combination of perfect individualism with the intensity and seriousness of Catholic rhetoric, drawing on the Baroque and ancient stocks of Classical oratory and pagan ceremony, which gives Barker's poem its drama.

The poem starts with a declaration against sex (along with an admission that he has spent 'thirty-four/essentially sexual years'), saying that he now has insight into the other sex for the first time. From a picture of the poet starting the poem, aged 34, it goes logically through birth (in low station); first encounter with a girl, aged five; education at an elementary school called The Oratory, and the priest who taught him; the vileness of the sexual act (stanzas 16-17); how he began with poetry aged 9; how the beginning of any poet is in sexual use of the written word, 'heterae noun-anatomised'; how he had no use for reason; self mocking over the missing inner life we are expecting; how at school he learnt above all to lie (which is perhaps the stimulus to confess now?); how he goes through a teenage phase of idealism and phantasy, of moonstruck love 'Abstracted as a mannequin'. Some 18 stanzas describe, with hysterical guilt, crimes attending his first marriage – which are obscure in the text, but which Robert Fraser's biography tells us had to do with the giving away of his first child for adoption, due to poverty: 'through honey of moon to sup of sorrow'. Indeed, poverty is a main theme of the book. In this allegorical landscape, vultures 'Rule empires of white memories' which I think are suppressed memories. Another section talks about marriage and describes his own marriage, up to a journey to Japan (where he had a proper job for the first time) in 1939. The last two sections deal with remorse, and with his seven children, leading into talk about the misery of the human condition (into which he has introduced them), and a climax of violently alternating emotions in which he retrieves his soul from irony and an unnamed 'Apollyonic power' with its 'dark splendour', but ends with a mediaeval picture in which he goes down eternity chained to all the women he has fornicated with (roughly), 'a frenzy of chained doves' – with a shocking final tableau in which he begs angels to 'execute us with mercies', to come down with rags and stifle us in our cradles – so terrible is incarnation. The tableau Barker draws is close to melodrama – this is poetry with frequent climaxes and reversals of fortune; material which holds back the main fever curve of emotion has been eliminated. We hear the boards creak as he stamps into a new tirade. In its preoccupation with guilt, it reminds us of Hitchcock – his contemporary. It has the blood and thunder style – without which we would not have glimpses of perdition and salvation.

I admit this is outside our period, but it is here to point up what was missing from 1950s poetry in general: how it was impossible to write lyric poetry in an asexual way, but even how theology didn't really develop any momentum in poetry without sexuality as its motive force. Barker is much more about theology (in the wake of Francis Thompson) than about lascivious recall: he has this uncrossed split between the sinful urges of the present and the self-condemning tribunal of recollection. Academic poets had crossed this gap – destroying the gap between divine and human and so expelling the transcendental from the poem. If this is the *true* confession, we could weigh up the possibility that the anarchists, the Trotskyites, and the Liberals were hawking *faked* confessions of George Barker through Seven Dials.

Barker is the poet of high affect and violent uncertainty – the ego itself spinning through a world in which everything affects it, everything means fear or delight. While reading something like this we feel that the only part of other – more secure – poets which matters is the part which resembles Barker.

A circular gallery:
Philip Toynbee, *Pantaloon, or, the Valediction* (1961; 342 pp.)

Toynbee (1915-81) wrote a four-volume novel in verse (1961-8), about a public-school intellectual of the 1930s called Dick Abberville; this is volume 1. The framing device is Dick, aged 86 (this is in 1998, or what was still the future, in 1961) recounting his life to a Norwegian-American researcher. The unreliability of his memories is a major topic. The novel is divided into parts called "the second day", and so on, as days in this collecting of memories. I am interested in *Pantaloon* (the name of a *commedia dell'arte* character, a ridiculous old man, the "plague doctor") because it is so isolated in modern poetry: no-one else writes novels in verse. The appeal of the work has partly to do with the mystery and complexity of the literary process. This volume is about 13,000 lines long – though there are a few passages in prose. I do not like it in the way that I like the other books we are discussing. The events of Abberville's life are rather conventional, and the historical processes he sees (e.g. the decline of British power in Egypt) are rather familiar. He is insignificant, conflicted, and displaced, like so many other young men of his generation, in so many novels. The hope, that a tale about immaturity would prove to be symbolic, of the decline of Empire and of the great middle class which benefited from it, was itself muddled and without fruition. It was narcissistic – far too many young men of this class were able to get their repetitive stories into print. The aesthetic focus is not on plot, but on shifts of perception; alluring and deceptive moments, ambiguities, failures of memory. 'Where I'm happiest is in the brief and almost impatient illumination … My memory… lights only on disjointed events.' He says elsewhere he was 'anxious to eliminate all sense of narrative', and the memories follow each other 'neither temporally nor causally', in 'a circular gallery'.

> Enigmas!
> Not one face has opened to my scrutiny; not one.
> Not a voice I hear from the past without an overtone,
> A slur of the tongue or ambiguity of intonation.
> Yes, even she, my rosy and bustling little grandmother,
> Quick redbreast pecking into rooms and out again,
> Whose language was a fluent undulation of gibberish.
> Why so vague? Why? Why?
> Adopting vagueness with what purpose known to you or unknown?
> I mean nothing sinister, but only
> The evaporation of earlier simplicities,
> The refusal of the dead to be changeless.

Toynbee had earlier written prose novels, compared at the time to Virginia Woolf. This kind of novel was the closest to poetry in its goals – and in its detachment from heroes and events. *Pantaloon* is a collector's item – it is so unlike all the poetry around it, so forgotten, and so self-confident. It was more appealing as an idea than as a text to read. As a guideline, a novel without events should have an appealing central character. Toynbee had worked out how to pace long pieces of verse – using a structure which he could repeat, without effort and apparently endlessly. Volume 2 has a stanza structure, as the Introduction describes: it is in 3-line verses of which the first is 25-35 syllables, and

2 and 3 are 10 syllables. The first should be 'purely descriptive and richly adjectival', the second 'clearly devoted to present action', and in the third 'a transposition is made, by means of association, into a wholly different (state)', a dream or memory. If people are going to write in extended forms, they need schemas like this. He had worked out how to write verse without the tonal climaxes which would disturb its flow – the novels have a sense of ease, they don't try to do things which would detract from their main preoccupations with atmosphere and the passage of time. They genuinely flow – towards their discreet coups. The jacket of volume 4 announces a fifth volume, but so far as I can determine this never appeared. The set finished with a holiday just after the narrator leaves Oxford, but has a 'flash forward' which covers 1933-36; it is essentially about an old-fashioned family, and a young man's immaturity. The appeal of the work is the sense of endless time, the lack of pressure, in which a vast archive of details is laid out as if in old photographs.

Christian Poets

The literary history of the Christian congregations is too complex to be written. At best we can point to a few trends. We spoke earlier on of a cluster I of poets animated by the typical virtues of educated poets formed in the 1950s. While it is easy to talk about cluster I – highly socialized, they shared ideals to a great extent – there were plenty of other Christian poets writing quite differently.

Christian poets formed in the 1950s notably include Geoffrey Hill, Peter Levi, and Anthony Thwaite. I am happy to admit that I missed Thwaite and Levi and had to come back and remap the period after reading them. The error started because the 1950s were a period of fearsome conformism. The Conservatives won three general elections. Weak writers who shared in the Christian-moral preconceptions sounded like the strong ones. If we shift on a few years to the new consumerist and hedonist world, the serious Christians opposed it. The spectre of a collapse of Western Christian values stimulated the poets mentioned to great heights. Poets made huge statements of basic cultural values, which were important to readers. The amazing flourishing of British poetry in the 1970s includes the work of people who were profoundly opposed to libertarian and anarchic social values; notably Mackay Brown, Hill, Levi. This is an example of innovation under pressure – and also of the rigid 1950s thought processes breaking down, with liberatory results. This is at least a tentative result.

I have mixed feelings about the bourgeois guardians (to use Roy Fisher's telling phrase) because I was one of the dominated and the managed. They came in for a lot of criticism, partly because they managed the institutions in which poetry flourished over the next three or so decades: the Christian poets were as intimidated as the modernist ones. In poetry, the war was actually one where ignorant armies clash by night – the Christians were anti-capitalist and opposed to the anti-spiritual nature of hedonistic and libertarian society and its crass individualism. The 'underground' were naturally anti-capitalist and in favour of community and of spiritual values. To this extent the war was one long bombardment of empty positions – not a tactic discussed by Clausewitz. It was a war without casualties. We have to conjecture that, once this war sputtered out (the breaking of the New Right wave in roughly the mid-80s), there was no longer much for the poets to say – and the prevalence of the ludic is a two-edged sword.

Planes of autonomous colour:
Euros Bowen, *Cerddi rhydd* (1961, 103 pp.)

Bowen (1904-88), an Anglican priest, did not write any poetry until the winter of 1947. Bowen is somewhere in between Mallarmé and Morgan Llwyd. He explains in the foreword how this volume is not poetic prose or free verse, but really free poetry. 'I called the volume, thus, FREE POEMS, since the poems in it are free from every trace of the traditional form of poetry except rhythm. The basic difference between them and *vers libre* is that they keep rhythm, but dispense with the line.' What he calls rhythm certainly is not a repeating unit of length, and would be hard to put into precise terms, but seems to mean a certain phonological impulse, pushing the poem forward. In fact, the lack of line breaks and other metrical compulsions gives the poems a dreamlike quality, not just slow of pace but dissolved out of time, so that there is endless room for associations to gather and swirl around.

The poems are exercises on set themes from the world of nature and mythology. Titles include "Four creatures of the Apocalypse' 'Signs of the Zodiac' 'The Prodigal Son' (literally, the reformed one) 'Four horsemen of the Apocalypse' 'The cemetery of Pandy' 'Shining' 'The Dead' 'Stars' 'Rain'. The familiarity of the subject matter allows great freedom in the linguistic means of the poem.

Cynghanedd (cf. Latin *concinnitas*, harmony), a phonetic pattern where the consonants are repeated within the line, and within the couplet, is present in primitive form in the oldest Welsh poetry, is still used today, and is dear to readers of Welsh poetry. As Bowen explains, in these free poems there is an occasional use of cynghanedd. Suspending it from the fixed metre was a radical step, which empties the stage of anything but consonantal variation, and, by making it easier, allows it to go much further. Take this passage:

> Diau yr hed i dy yr haul, o gywilydd am gau heulwen gan niwl
> dig ein heolydd oddi wrth elw ar ddiwarth aelwyd.

In terms of classical European poetry, we would call this this wonderfully lush and interlaced total sonic creation Futurist. In terms of contemporary poetry, we would think of Michael Haslam. However, it clearly belongs with cynghanedd. See also:

A llewych y ser ar y dwr segur sy'n lluwchio ei sawr a drysu eigion.

(And a flash of the stars on the slack water which is rolling its flavour along and puzzling the ocean.)
(from 'Sodiac')

And:

daw fel taro ar erwau dyfal Tryweryn

Tryweryn is a river in North Wales of whose valley about one square mile was flooded, in the late 1950s, to make a reservoir. It was, before, partly rough pasture and partly rather richer hay-meadows, lower down. This conversion to use for storing water is not a very big grievance, but even a very small grievance can be comforting.

The prose poem (from which the use of rhythm distinguishes the *Cerddi Rhydd*) was developed by the Symbolistes in mid-19th century France, and Bowen has been deeply drawn into the Symboliste style. The title 'Alchemy of the poem' must be a deliberate echo of 'Alchimie du verbe'. The volume makes considerable use of words like *gweledig, gweledigaeth*, referring to 'vision', and this must represent the Symbolist preoccupation with the poet as voyant, 'seer'. "Where there is the seer, there the invisible is visible" (Lle mae'r gweledig, yno mae'r anweledig yn weladwy.) With Bowen, this is not demarcated from the visions of John of Patmos, and of other Biblical prophets.

The first poem is 'The Three Doves', subtitled 'remembering T Gwynn Jones', and this may suggest a connection with this early 20th C poet, who was perhaps the closest thing to Symbolisme in Wales – he is close to the Pre-Raphaelite poets. Jones wrote narrative poems which were dissolving because of the elaboration and delicacy of his language; with Bowen, the narrative has vanished altogether, myths are reduced to visual form and the refraction and diffusion of language is at centre stage. Here is one of the shorter poems.

The Seven Trumpets

As I was grazing in the land of the newspaper on the blade of a slope in a high place, slowly watching the signs of our times which now may be seen and heard from the countries, a cloud of pain moved and carried crime and its violence angrily across the news, bare words gathering the dead, shouting and crying out, to the valley of the grave.

All at once in terror of the breeze and its shivering, behold the cloud of crime moving away, and behold (hoving) into view a parish giving sustenance to pure beams, the place having been left in guileless colours by the seven coloured tumult of the stiff white-top lighting up the day.

The colour red and its echo sang in the mind of the valley, orange voice crying from the invisible, yellow of the shine above precipice and valleys, and the roads in hearing of the lost green, the eloquent blue of the azure, the resonance of indigo carrying, and beneath it travelled the violet variants of the colour on the skin of the gravel.

The vale is like a pageant of the leisure of some old sabbath day, the place of borders towards the woods in innocence, like the day of resurrection, since now from sea and from bare moors seven trumpets are calling with one mouth their passion to glorify and praise.

So the poet reads a newspaper, which is full of the woes deriving from our fallen state. But the valley prospect in front of him makes him see an ideal parish, as promised by the rainbow, appearing after the great woe of the Deluge as the sign of the Covenant made by God. It is combined with a Symboliste, synaesthetic, version of the colour spectrum. We find the seven trumpets in Revelations, and also a rainbow (standing on an angel's head). Although the degree of stylisation is extreme, the poem may actually be about the woes of international politics in the 1950s. Bowen was a committed Christian as well as a nationalist. The preoccupation with reading signs, as the language in which the will of God is made detectable to human senses, leads to an interest in number, as one element of structure that may lead us to analogies.

Alan Llwyd wrote a book called *The Poetry of Euros Bowen* which analyses all the poems in his first book, *Cerddi*, of 1957. Bowen riposted with *Trin cerddi*, a book which points out mistakes in Llwyd's analyses – without offering any overall explanations. *Trin* in this case does not mean arranging, but causing a fuss or scolding – and the title could mean something like "Chiding my book of poems". With all these explanations available, maybe I chose the wrong book. Llwyd said that Bowen was influenced by Dylan Thomas – I think this is a vital truth even if it alienated Bowen. Also, I think there is a post-Thomas phase, after about 1970, when his poetry was quite different. The errors fail to worry me – the sonic mix is too overwhelming, the reader is unable to fix every detail and the point is to be swept away. This is the aesthetic focal point. The organisation of sentences shows a reliance on equation or analogy as opposed to classification or interest in causal or production processes. This prevents differentiation, lingering in the zone of miracles rather than meteorology. The undifferentiated is also the sublime and also where all things are interchangeable. The primal multi-sensory flow is like a magma preceding a landscape. In the foreword to *Trin cerddi*, Bowen says "The legend of obscurity, so far as I know, in connection with my poems, has had its investiture as a story by now. At least that's what is said to me by friends who know what's what in Welsh poetry today." In that foreword, he points us towards the *Bible Dictionary* and to *Myth and Ritual* (edited Samuel Hooke, 1933) for his sources. *Myth and Ritual* is the book version of a series of lectures which Bowen attended as an undergraduate at Oxford in 1932. It is looking for the explanations of myth in rituals, formalised archaic actions taking place in public and often connected to points on the calendar. This could appeal to an Anglican priest, bound to connect liturgical actions to a body of myth and to a calendar, and, of course, Bowen is writing Christian myth. He has a liking for set scenes fixed by a calendrical rhythm – the Zodiac poem, for example, and the 'times' of Christian myth which appear in other poems. He seems to be taking Christian myth and adapting it to a Symboliste view of the poem, with the pictorial and fantastic elements of the Bible being assimilated to myths like those of the signs of the Zodiac. There is no material about the poet's everyday experience – the foreground is left empty so that the remote, fantastic, and wonderful can come close to us.

The ritual is a public act which seizes a unique moment to make eternal relationships visible. This corresponds to the liturgy, and to rhythm, as a series of unique and dynamic moments within a poem, and may also argue for writing Christian poetry in a style suited to the sound of the 1940s (rather than writing in hymn form – and in 3rd century Greek). Bowen translated a book by Athanasius on the incarnation into Welsh – also a moment where the eternal enters the world of the transient and sensory, and significant to anyone wishing to combine personal experiences with theology. One of the lecturers in *Myth and Ritual* is E.O. James, a clergyman and anthropologist, who continued to work along the lines of relating anthropology to Christian myth.

Bowen is determined to separate himself both from Catholicism and from the pagan kind of Symbolism. Tillich wrote "Religious thought and action visibly represent what is hidden in profane thought and action. (…) Without such an expression profanity becomes empty and the sacrifice to demonic self-destruction. (…)" Also, "Cult should give the everyday its ultimate sense. Not the creation of new liturgies is important, but penetrating into the deeps of what happens every day(.)" Rejecting Catholic sacramentalism allows the Protestant to find the sacred hidden in all the materials of the exanimate world – the profane is nowhere cut off from the transcendent, and the Christian poet can find valid symbols everywhere.

Bowen perhaps belongs to a moment of Christian confidence after the War had discredited the process of modernity and brought people closer to first and last things. In the 1950s, people thought that Christianity was making a come-back, and Auden and Eliot were the dominant voices in poetry. There is also a possible hangover from the Apocalyptics, trying to make myth the natural idiom of the poem.

With the blind helmsman:
George Mackay Brown, *Fishermen with Ploughs* (1971; 100 pp.; cluster D)

The book tells the story of Rackwick, a valley on an island in the Orkneys, from the time of its settling in the 9th century, by a fisher people from Norway, to the future. They are fleeing 'starvation, pestilence, turbulent neighbours (what the poet calls, in the shorthand of myth, the Dragon)'. They are guided by a blind helmsman. In the hold is a jar of seed corn – they are going to take up agriculture for the first time. The prose summary says we see 'how the climate of their existence changed with such things as the Reformation, annexation to Scotland, foreign wars, compulsory education' – but we don't. Most of the poems show "'the wheel of bread', that is at once brutal and holy" – he likes calendrical cycles, whether weeks or months. In the 20th century, the valley loses its population: 'Perhaps… the quality of life grows poorer as Progress multiplies its gifts on a simple community' – but we do not see this either. In the late 20th century, a nuclear war ('Black Pentecost') means that people return, fleeing by boat. They have seed corn, but it rots on the ear – they must become fishermen. This reverses the innovation at the beginning of the book (and explains the title). They are in the power of the Dragon. The book ends with an evocation of a post-nuclear society which is gripping and quite terrifying. One man dominates everyone else, and it is a tyranny. This plot is reminiscent of Edwin Muir's poem 'The Horses'. (Muir, also from Orkney, was Brown's teacher.)

Titles include 'Then Four Great Angels, Air, Water, Fire, Earth, being summoned, fell from their eternal circuits unto poverty at his single station, to be his servitors', 'Ikey crosses the Ward Hill to the Spanish Wreck', 'Sea Runes' 'The Scarecrow in the Schoolmaster's Oats'. The poems are like illustrations in a mediaeval manuscript: highly stylised, simple, arresting, naive, binding. Each deals with a decisive moment in a seasonal cycle or a human life. They are consciously modelled on the New Testament and the less heroic parts of the sagas (set in a society close to that of Orkney). Numbers are important; Thorkeld leads them westwards but has suffered twelve wounds in fighting off the onslaught from the next district – just twelve. 'Steel came unclouded from stiffening mouth' means that Thorkeld has died (they looked if his breath clouded the most polished steel they had, but there was no breath). This style expresses a notion of a fate transcending human volition (which we also find in the sagas); Brown, also, dislikes talking about any inner life, preferring physical signs as an indirect language. Here, it is fate which is unpredictable – not human thoughts and reactions. (This is also why you would choose a blind, but lucky, helmsman.) The first section is modelled on Norse scaldic poetry, an elaborate riddling style – Thorkeld says 'Into his fires, long sharp fish', talking to his sword. With its ornaments and taboos, this may be a relic of an old ritual language. The other sections just aren't as ornate. Two weaknesses of the book are that most of the poems do not contribute to the main theme, since they are just sketches of customs, so that we can't really differentiate between the 9th century and the 19th; and that the poems don't support the claims made about social change in the prose summary. This opens up the suspicion that the poems are honest, and what the prose says is a prejudice without life – for example, when in section V he conflates economic progress with the arrival of the atomic bomb. His poetry is strong because it covers the whole of society, and because he can make everything visible, in a state where economic activities are physical (fishing, housework, etc.); but not only is it non-analytical, but it does not accommodate thought. Somehow the texture of the poetry does not fit into the schematic design of the book, and Brown's thinking about the course of Orkney history (which we can guess to be based on Muir's sense of a lost mediaeval unity) has not found its way into words. The 'decline theory' has an evidence base in the decline of folk creation, above all the loss of the ability to create new ballads. After the black Pentecost, the teacher says that he will not teach the children to count beyond 100 – 'beyond that, the black circle of Mephistopheles'. Brown's diction also has its taboos. The Orkneys once spoke a West Norse language, and he is genuinely close to Scandinavian writers, in fact those who are drawn to folklore and religion, rejecting European culture. (Muir also provided ideas and a style for Kathleen Raine, q.v.)

The appeal of Brown's poetry is its sense of beauty and the reduction of all events shown to a pattern. He starts with something already heavily aestheticised and stylizes it even more. One needs to relax into Brown's setting in which roles are far more rigid than in real life, so that characters are complete externalisations of their roles, like painted figures whose faces are complete showings of their inner nature. *Fishermen* is more like a set of ceramic figurines than a realist novel. This rigidity becomes comforting. This is the translation of human beings into a pattern. I can't see any results of Catholicism in this. It is the product of intense contemplation on Muir's *Variations on a Time Theme*. When Brown says 'the same people appear and reappear through many generations', following Muir, is this true, or is it just that the bound forms of old-fashioned writing cannot register complexity, and use stylisation instead? I don't know.

We could situate Brown in the religious crisis of the 1950s, when people could either choose to go with sociology (which destroyed the inherited literary forms) or to abide with (say) rigorously 15th century forms (and reject anything modern). Brown's obituary revealed that he had only once been to England.

We have to consider the comments of Christopher Whyte where he singles out the aestheticisation of violence as basic to Brown's art. Whyte objects to this, but we also have to ask what is the source of this compulsive patterning. There is a death every three or four pages. In terms of body count, Brown is closer to Hughes than anyone else.

Trail-marks cut in salt:
Geoffrey Hill, *Speech! Speech!*
(2000; 60 pp., 120 x 12 lines Agenda; cluster I)

The 120 poems in the book stand for the 120 days of Sodom – more probably as a symbol of the corrupt society he lives in than an indulgent reference to the Marquis de Sade's novel of that name. The book's name is just a pun – the speech is literally the content of the book. However, the cover shows a Daumier lithograph of an enthusiastic Parisian audience, applauding and quite conceivably shouting 'speech! speech!'. The book is ruled by immediacy – whatever crosses Hill's mind, he writes about, like a jazz musician who has to fill a concert of two hours without too many constraints on musical form except what turns him on at that moment. The book is dedicated to the memory of David Wright, a deaf poet; this may be a gesture to the New Romantic poetry of the 1940s, which Wright was part of as a very young man and whose later stages he anthologised in a key 1960 selection. They wanted to make individual life into a myth. The book is dedicated to the great German novelist Günter Grass, with the epigraph 'curtain, before you understand the applause', which obviously is connected with the cover picture. The first epigraph is the quote from Ennius (about the trumpet speaking with frightful sound) which we have already seen in David Jones' poem. That is – we enter the book at the end of some performance to enjoy the aftermath; while also we hear the trumpet which surely summons us to drastic action. Steeped in the context of Jones' inscription, perhaps it is the signal of impending death – or of the day of redemption. If a city is being overthrown – perhaps it is Sodom, brought to its term by a rain of fire. Already we find the pointers pointing inward – the text is about itself, it shows the poet in the act of reflecting on what he is saying, and on his own consciousness. It may be the end of consciousness is what the Daumier audience is so freely applauding – the end of the performance. Consciousness is like a billion billiard balls ricocheting off each other – not only is it self-starting, but also when the balls come to a final stop the whole performance vanishes. The speed at which Hill dissolves and cuts is unnerving, but it is also the source of excitement – and of conviction; the speed is like someone photographing a storm, dementedly transient effects of light. What we are looking at is a self-shaped object – a storm full of shapes which resemble our own selves. It is both abrupt and direct.

In poem one, we have an evocation of the composition starting: 'Erudition. Pain. Light.' He imagines the PEOPLE rejecting it (as heroic verse is a 'non-starter', a horse that fails to reach the start line). In confusing and repetitive contexts, he says, choose 'self-emulation': that is, simplify and repeat your effects so that they become a theme tune, with a high recognition factor. He lists some of the kinds of theme music our society likes; one is for two fingers, which could either mean a pianist of paltry skills, or else a typically English rude gesture, made with two fingers raised. Two others are cremation and taxiing to take-off – which are rapidly picked up, as in l.12 he imagines a final auto-da-fé – this ('act of faith') is what the Inquisition called the burning of Jews; he is saying that such a heroic project may go through take-off to crash, incineration, and martyrdom to a (misplaced?) faith. In 9-10 he says that 'archaic' (as a judgment on poetry of the kind he is writing) means that files will be destroyed within a generation – the entire cultural knowledge of a society reclassified and laid waste in a kind of Mongol Invasion from within. The use of themed music (*ritournelles*, as Guattari calls them) to signal the identity of a situation is, however, related to the way this poem is composed – with leitmotifs linking all its parts with very rapid signalling which is a pleasure – if we catch it as it fleets by.

Poem 2 starts with interposing a fire-curtain to stop the applause getting through. Presumably, this is again the poet talking about the poem he hasn't written yet – if he listens to his fans, he will never bring it to completion. He wonders if Grass would accept the dedication; and if Grass sits late beside the Aga (kitchen range giving 24-hour warmth) picking up clues from Marconi (i.e. the radio), from Imre Nagy (leader of the 1956 Hungarian Uprising, executed by more pro-Moscow Communists), from Scott (incompetent explorer who died young and was made a hero for English schoolboys). The last eleven words seem to have Heinrich Böll (other Nobel Prize-winning German novelist) ask why he is dead – and not Günter. Mortality again the theme. When Hill says (poem 108) 'Cite your own stiff going-price', the going-price is not only the current price (of the poet's work) but also its price at the moment when he goes; stiff because it is high – but also because it is the price of his going, the cost of mortality (becoming a *stiff*). The 'stiff' ties back to a confusion of *script* and *prescription* in the previous line – a stiff prescription is like a stiff drink, a very strong one, but also like a stiff penalty. I suppose the pun was always a way of drawing on the flow of speech itself, a self-referentiality taken from the metaphysicals and raised here to a principle of construction. But the self-referentiality is also one of generous self-will: cite (name) your own price, create what you want; you can only lose (the price of going) what you have won. The poem is all about choice.

Poem three tackles directly the problem of emotional instability, with a reference to the lithium with which doctors stabilise Hill's depression. He says farewell to his *daimon* or familiar spirit – they are parting because of death.

What this poem possesses is *flow* – complete malleability to the stirrings of the poet's consciousness, and complete access to verbal expression for wherever he jumps to next. It conjures up great figures for the poet to speak to – like Grass – and conjures up the poet in our living-room. A barrage of verbal means – puns, shifts of context, the constant conscious definition of what the context actually is – throws us into the poet's arms, in these rapids of language; compressed, mercurial, incalculable, lashing to and fro, humorous, unconfined. As with Donne, the paradoxes of incarnation and imminent disincarnation are turned into something intelligent, poignant, and funny at the same time. Hill is a poet of the same magnitude as Donne.

The Atlantic Periphery

These poets from Wales and Scotland are separated so as to draw attention to the different social, linguistic, and geographical background to their work. Incidentally, large parts of their audience are also found outside England. Although the devolution of power to national assemblies in Cardiff and Edinburgh happened right at the end of our period, an upsurge of nationalist opinion in the 1960s had made devolution and regional autonomy vital political issues for the cultural creators in those countries. Most people here go around with a "dual optic" whereby they are indulgent to work from their own loyalty group, and feel vaguely threatened and uninvolved by art from other groups. My own loyalty group is Scotland, although my loyalty is not unconditional – which makes me a traitor in some people's eyes. Noisy protest has publicly exposed the private fact that many people regard cultural glamour as confined to a few streets, really, in a few great cities, and simply don't want to know about experience which happens in unfashionable places. Research has revealed that being inside a cultural elite makes you deeply conformist; that the periphery of the world is also the depth of the world; and that you can reach freedom by living away from the control centres. However, cultural pleasure does mean going where you want and indulging your own loyalties.

Harry Guest, *Lost and Found. Poems 1975-82.* (1983; 126 pp.) (Completing; cluster G)

The integrity of the schema requires that I include one poet from *Completing the Picture*. However much I disliked that anthology, Guest (b. 1931) is a major talent and we have to investigate how his stylistic decisions relate to the excellence of his poems. Section titles are 'History/Prehistory', 'English Poems' and 'Elegies', a sequence roughly 430 lines long and the weightiest part of this volume. The title refers to a reminiscence of time past; each poem mentions a ghost somewhere. The theme is recurrence and the poetry suspends the elements of the lived world in a sight outside time:

> The cuckoo flew hooting above the rowan-tree
> where the stone avenue points downhill to the spring
> that trickles from the grass. You have seen this

and gone over marsh ground in winter to find
the last brooklime unshrivelled and the crow's
shadow on a litter of bones. The danger
lies not in loneliness but in absorption
leading to self-absorption.
    ('The Sixth Elegy')

This loving evocation of the world we live in also defines what is lost: *Open the fingers/ and spill forever on the ground/ what seemed to be*. The title *Lost and Found* refers to 'Elegies' and its theme of past experience, past tranquillity. However, 'Grave-Goods' is about archaeology – whose subject matter is by definition what was lost, as rubbish or other deposition, by its owners, and which was found in modern times by digging, erosion, etc.

It was time for the offerings.
One box made of oak
held bronze axes. Another,
flint arrowheads. Another, made of elmwood,
was crammed with daggers.
All were unused.
A ritual wound nicked each blade.
They too had died.
    ('Brittany, c. 2300 BC')

  I don't think Guest can be securely categorized in a group. He is Welsh but any list of the inevitable features of Anglo-Welsh poetry would fail to describe him. If you check the original definition of the "British Poetry Revival" by Eric Mottram, the poets he lists include Harry Guest. Does this locate him? No, because he is too close to the border with the mainstream. He is not dealing with abstractions, but writing pictorial poetry, full of objects. The deliberate damage to the Bronze Age blades is soaked in symbolism but visible and physical at the same time. Across a taxonomic border, he would have to show us abstractions, shapes distorted and enhanced by montage. But Eric (following John Matthias' game-changing anthology) could see that Guest was important, and acknowledged this. A schema is an abstraction. No, you can't abolish the visual in favour of ideas. No, you can't fit numerous poets into a schema without falsifying. Guest is uninterested in montage and shock juxtapositions, not much concerned with emphasis, but good at transitions and at continuity of impulse. There is a whole line of poetry which deals with dramatic reversals, as a political leader is found unfit for office or an idea founding institutions is subverted. This makes for drama, and after all intellectual exchange is animated by these exciting moments of loss. But there is another line of poetry which has stability as its central idea, where the attentiveness which gives the experience its artistic identity is nourished by the refusal to damage the objects of attention, and the depth of time is revealed by the stability of the objects themselves. This is a form of social imagination which expresses a view of politics, one that starts from humans and respect for the human subject. It is presenting an ethos that is applicable to schools and housing, for example, and is indirectly a protest against agglomerations of power that make most individuals into losers. The priority is artistic values, but the poems themselves record a view of human affairs. There may be an affinity with Kathleen Nott and Mimi Khalvati – the line of constancy and softness which leaves intact experiences and human subjects.

'Memories of the Sinagua' describes a tribe in 11th century Arizona who suffer from a volcanic eruption but then find that the ash has made their land supremely fertile:

> Seasons passed with rainfall and snow on the mountain
>   the land stayed dark and silent beneath the wind
> and our fathers saw green shoots on the blackness
>   wondering they saw flowers
> speckling the soft blackness like blue stars

Although the book includes many short poems, a trait that stands out is the interweaving of themes and the emergence of more complex wholes out of numerous images. The presence of multiple themes creates an atmosphere of expectation which is more important than the exact burden of the argument. The ambiguity and density of information are autonomous features and effort to get through them and freeze them is misplaced. His clarity of focus, a typical feature of '50s poets, is highly effective in allowing this suggestibility.

One poem is titled 'Enchanted Acres' and this would no doubt arouse the contempt of the rough modernist lads in the back row. There is a line which says that poetry must be unpleasant in order to incite a contest which will overthrow authority, responsible for things being bad, and then lead to a better society. I am still wondering, how unpleasant does poetry have to be. The poem is about Eden and says that there was no time in Eden, no remorse and no anxiety.

The heron of oblivion:
Alexander Hutchison, *Deep Tap Tree;*
(1978, 61 pp.; Scots, Makars; cluster D)

Hutchison (1943–2015) was born in north-east Scotland, which means his dialect is quite difficult for most Scots; there is only one dialect poem in this collection (which was published in Massachusetts). An epigraph runs 'he is called the heron of oblivion'. The title refers to old living things able to survive long periods of drought by drinking (via 'taproot') into deep buried water; I associate this with the north-eastern dialect, but this may be wrong. The cover design shows a snake-shaped band, taken from a Norse rune stone and carved with runes. Norse is also germane to the north-east, and to the Moray Firth (credited on the jacket as his birthplace), where a local Norse dialect was spoken until quite recent times. I really have to guess about the epigraph – but, since I have to take a fling, my guess is that a poet seizes bright things (from the waters of oblivion) as a heron seizes fish and frogs from the waters of a stream. Titles include 'Mr Scales walks his dog' 'In Brass and Brimstone I Burn like a Bell' 'Construct by Simple Succession' and 'The Dead-*carn* Shifting Slowly in the Drift'.

I think what I like about Hutchison is the combination of scorchingly arresting phrasing and an open approach to the semantic frame of the poem, so that you never feel it has settled down to a set of limits, it is always drawing on further and further resources. He doesn't seem concerned to build a personality on the page – obviously, this would give us a sense of limits. Although there are, in the end, a lot of words in the volume, he always seems about to stop – there is an extreme separation of the poem from the poet, and a withdrawal from the plane of ordinary discourse. Technically, this allows for a great sense of dynamics – we don't feel that decasyllabic lines and even quatrains are going to trundle on and on. Stylistically, it is the sound of someone's voice – people from the north-east are not known for superfluous talk. The book opens with 'Impresa' –

Iron on iron; and so we sharpen
each other's countenance;

Skin to skin; so we kindle
each day's heart.

The first couplet is based on a Biblical phrase about iron sharpening iron (i.e. only a hard substance can whet a hard substance). In the context of intimacy between two people, it seems to point to conflict. They are both hard; perhaps they make each other's faces sharper (i.e. with a keen expression, alert). This is laconic and disturbing. The second couplet is more conventionally about sexuality. So, after 19 words altogether, the poem falls silent. The first couplet mirrors the second; in each couplet a physical contact mirrors a psychological one; the two people mirror each other. This arrangement is ornate – but also close to oral poetry, with its typical symmetries (phonetic where not structural). An 'impresa' is a device, an Italian word for an emblematic picture, resembling a riddle and often punning, best known from Alciati's 16th-century book of them; they were the basis for very many Mannerist and Baroque poems. The condensed and riddling tone gives the impression of pride. The fitting of sense onto an image is like the device which gives us 'iron sharpeneth iron', and like the fitting of the runic inscription onto the twining band of the serpent, in the cover picture.

The 'crowd pleaser' in the volume is 'Mr Scales walks his dog', a very funny poem about the burlesque decrepitude of the dog – built on a simple incremental and parallel structure. The comic exaggeration of 'tall tales' is another feature of oral culture – it isn't surprising this poem is well known. 'Scales dog was buried with the Pharaohs, with the Aztecs; draws social security from fourteen countries; travels with his blanket; throws up on the rug; has a galaxy named after him(.)' The binding principle is quite simple, but it binds the audience as well as the poem. No doubt if you recited this in a pub the company would listen and laugh. 'Construct by Simple Succession' has a similar principle – the storeys of an imaginary building are described one by one, going up to twenty, with surprising and incongruous and disconcerting things at every stage. Explaining the longer poems here would just take too long; we can say that one poem is about the Moghul emperor Akbar, and several draw on old Norse forms. A major theme is north-east Scotland. It may be that the hyperbole, delirious imagination, grotesque erudition, and eerie humour are related to Thomas Urquhart, perhaps the major writer of the north-east – a 17th-century 'avant gardist' who is unaccountable in terms of the time, but who may have been drawing on the ornate eccentricity of Gaelic shannachies.

Paradox and depth perception:
Roland Mathias, *Snipe's Castle* (1979; 77 pp., cluster G)

Mathias (1915-2007) debuted in the 1940s, with a brilliant first volume – at a high point for Anglo-Welsh poetry. He had some legal problems as a conscientious objector. His profession was a history teacher. The title refers to a poem about a ridge in Pembrokeshire – with, I think, a 'secret acre', hidden from the authorities and so untaxed. It is a symbol of the hidden and marginal. We read:

> Every tack,
> Island to island, thundersmack,
> Boiling sand, leviathan
>
> In mid-marvel, nudges profanely
> Homeward.
>   ('The Anchorite').

The poem describes the voyage of Maelduin through a North Atlantic full of religious allegories – the original psychogeography, and why the voyage homeward is 'profane'. The words are spoken by the anchorite, so half-riddle – and half-prophecy. Which brings us back to the Apocalyptic style of the 1940s – riddling and prophetic; its impossible yokings of words have here changed to subtle clashes. A 'tack' is a change of course; 'thundersmack' is simply thunderclap; Dylan Thomas once spoke of sand 'boiling' with cockles; leviathan is the whale. The stanza form involves three rhyming lines and three assonating ones – a reference to the forms of Gaelic or Welsh poetry. The setting of words is cunning, plaited, minimalist. Almost all the poems in *Snipe's* are set in Welsh history. Some titles are 'La Tène' 'Guénolé' 'The Arming of Aberdaugleddau' 'Pwll Llong, Pwll Whiting'. A poem in Mathias' first volume, *Break In Harvest* (1946) starts:

> Comfort in centuries with broken feet
> Limps off this hill of recapture, where meet
> Interminable bournes of fight
> Mapping the brain. The rules of blood that maze
> And wall the sight
> Meet here. I gaze and the spread blood goes back –
> From the wall, runs hard into the hand
> And the brain stops. Only the boundaries stand.
> (from 'Lowbury Hill')

Terminus means boundary stone, as does *bourne*, and so *interminable bourne* is a paradox. The word *exterminatos,* meaning driven beyond the boundaries, was used about the British being cleansed by the Saxons. The boundaries must be the frontier between the Saxons and the British, in fact the definition of what was to become Wales. Wall, the Romans defined the Empire by walls even if that did not apply to England where the invaders arrived by boat. The blood must have to do with ethnic identity, also perhaps with warfare. The recapture must be a rally by the British. Lowbury is in Oxfordshire and may be on an old ethnic border between Saxon and Cymro. In Mathias we find a mixture of style-levels: first, the paradox/frame shift, borrowed from Dylan Thomas (from Donne). Stripping away layers of projective legend to reveal a dissonant reality. And locating a singular reality where everything is intriguing because that mirrors the needs of the brain and is its nutrient medium. The fourth element is intense historical projection – the deletion of the ego. Mathias is besotted with the past and always with themes connected to Wales. His style is comparable to Lynette Roberts, Glyn Jones, Christopher Fry, as well as Thomas.

'Tide-reach' is a sequence talking about characters from Pembroke. The nationalist storybook sees Henry VII (the poem is 'His Nurse to Young Harri Tudur') as a hero, who beat the English, and as a traitor, because he did not 'liberate' Wales. But do the causes in litigation touch at any point the conscious activity of the characters? Was Henry Tudor even aware of a cause which did not exist as an interest and which was constituted centuries later, in retrospect? Or was he a 15th-century magnate, preoccupied with kinship relations, with his enemies, and with a Britain-wide perspective on territory and alliance? The answers involve a knowledge of a myriad details of the human world – the names, kinships, dispositions of parties, conflicts over land or ideas, means of struggle, inside which humans do their thinking and planning. Accuracy shows the Welsh past as less than perfectly harmonious. The deviations from idyll are of course the psychological content of the poems. Mathias is saturated in the documents of the past, landscapes, writing, and implements. This information, we could almost say, would not matter if you did not start with generalising theses about north-west European history, uninsured against structural damage as the facts flow in. The 1960s saw, we could say, the death of myth, for the Irish Sea Province.

One poem is about Mathias' grandfather, the son of a water-bailey, moving into Wales and bidding at an auction for tools and stock, to work his leased farm with, as his neighbours collaborate to bid against him and force him to ruin himself. Each shot seems to expose the faded and stained hues, the unidentifiable and irregular textures, of unstaged reality. This is a world where each cell is different. Who would invent a poem where someone is the son of a water-bailey? (Someone who controls the size of mesh in fishing-nets, breaks down illegal fish-weirs, and enforces the upkeep of bridges and flood defences). In this space littered with obstacles and the motions of irrelevant things, trajectories are critical and dynamic. Avoiding the static portrait-shots of the traditional Anglo-Welsh poem – isolated, benign, and essentialised– Mathias shows characters in action – in the world of uncertainty, of unrevealed complexity, of conscious planning, and of success. Where Bobi Jones' historical world is flimsy, hygienic, and moulded to an ideology, Mathias' is tangled and substantial.

La Tène in Switzerland is the type-site of the second major phase of what archaeologists of an older generation used to call Celtic culture (most of the objects were found underwater, in fact) – and a poem where continuity between La Tène and even early mediaeval Wales is left an open question. All the same, he went to the rural museum there – and his knowledge of the forms and series is minutely accurate. Critical accounts of Mathias' work are missing partly because Tony Conran rejected his work as not being properly nationalist. Late Conran, however, gets increasingly like Mathias' poetry.

In Wales, attitudes towards the past are levelling – they involve very heavy recognition and occupation of chosen heroic figures, adopted into a sense of the present which feels itself as eternal, and so does not recognise changes. I realise most people prefer the stock footage – the images on the biscuit tins. I admire people who think about history. We ask 'who's winning' because we are not following the game. If history consists of big, bold, simple stories – the details can be dispensed with. The point of Mathias' poems is initially of denial – of childish nationalist myths. By this means he breaks open a simple narrative to allow something far more complex and autonomous to emerge – the past itself, human behaviour in its mixture of conscious and unconscious. This is a poetry of ideas which appeals to me. Perhaps nationalism was invented to fill the gaps in a picture made thin by incuriosity, to fill a deficit of interest in the mountains of evidence dug up by Victorian zeal.

The thousand eyes of Dr Marcuse:
Walter Perrie, *By Moon and Sun* (1980; 83 pp.; cluster D)

The book is one continuous poem – characterised by montage of diverse streams of data, from diverse viewpoints. This technique has analogies in England (among an elite group), but is almost unknown in Scotland.

By moon and sun sounds like a periphrasis for 'all the time, without pause'. However, there is an epigraph from the orthodox Christian patristic philosopher, Origen, which runs 'understand then that you are a second world in miniature, and that the sun and moon are within you, as are the stars.' So we could translate the title: by his own lights. The theme might be one of exploring the whole human subject – as something split by analytical, partial, Enlightenment ways of describing human behaviour. The alchemical illustrations suggest that the topic is also of completing the human personality – sending it through transformations to reach its highest possible state. A note on p.90 tells us that 'the fantasy products' recorded in the 16th-century woodcuts used 'chart a process of unselfconscious integration of conflicting psychic contents'. Typical imagery is hunting, alchemy, the streets of Edinburgh, Biblical imagery to do with brides and bridegrooms, highlights from Gaelic poetry, oppression, making love. It deals with panic, vulnerability, and the obstacles to love.

The first section is called 'Passionnelle to Jonathan', and a note glosses the first word as 'a litany of the sufferings of the saints'. When I first read this, it seemed homoerotic to me – but I couldn't believe this was the intention. Since then, a gay friend has pointed that Perrie 'came out' as being gay in the mid-1970s, and that this split the Edinburgh literary scene in two. So in fact *Moon and Sun* is a paean to gay self-realisation. No wonder Perrie does not appear in any of the representative Scottish anthologies, or the surveys of the period. The second section is called 'Creation'. When we look at the woodcut which completes the book, on page 84, we see an androgynous person – the figure of integration of male and female sides of the personality, the soul integrated and complete in itself. We should indeed see this as an icon of the homosexual being – in whom are 'both moon and sun'. David and Jonathan were the closest of friends, and a traditional byword for the closeness of male friendship. The second part is called 'Creation'. The woodcuts show the soul leaving the body, the purification of the latter by a sexual act of conjunction, and the return of the soul to the body now without blemish – and androgynous. There is a great deal about the oppression of the Palestinians, and we are to suppose that David and Jonathan symbolise the Jews and the Palestinians, who ought to be united. At one level, the whole book is about an evening which two lovers spend together before making love.

The layout of the text is a variant on the 'three-stepped verse', with the line breaks marking the end of feet rather than of complete rhythmic units. This gives a great deal of poise and separation. The parts even of a line are floating – incomplete, charged to attract association and refractions. For example:

>   Always obstructions
>   bramble thickets
>   tangles
>   snags among the undergrowth
>   and higher up
>   the rockfalls
>   body-breaking crags
>   and cold
>   for all that I wrap well
>   in malice and anger
>   drawing my self-coloured coat
>   close about me

The style is closer to Lawrence – with a version of Biblical narration in which the personal spiritual tale of the poet has replaced the hero of patriarchal times – than to Pound. A preface quotes (Herbert) Marcuse twice, and offers a radical critique of the split subject. It says 'The language of dream, with its unlimited lexicon of image, situation, gesture, and utterance, is capable of a discourse continually multivalent, fluid and ambiguous.' Perrie's theoretical definition of the value of ambiguity is the clearest I know.

A section of the poem deals with an ascent of the mountain called Schiehallion. This means 'hill of the Caledonians', and acts as a symbol of Scotland; while the ascent is an act of physical endurance which arouses ardour and leads to a sense of triumph. The mountainside is a place to look down from, and this becomes a kind of nationalist hymn, where he calls Scotland 'Protean harlot', invokes the two greatest modern Scottish poets (MacLean and MacDiarmid), and lyrically apostrophises the whole country, and hours where he has 'seen you sifting/dreams of wind and wave/ against the long sea-wall.'

The back jacket of his 1982 book of essays says, 'he is now working on a major sequence of poems on the theme of Orpheus' – which has yet to appear. The front cover shows a four-lobed device in which the rounds are labelled 'MacDiarmid', 'Poetry', 'Homosexuality' and 'Politics'.

There are problems with Perrie's work, with its combination of intense emotions and a manner – rhythmic and constructional – which leads in the opposite direction, towards detachment. My urge to write about Perrie is partly due to the anomaly of someone in Scotland daring to reject the pseudo-folk manner and write modern poetry, partly due to the collusive removal of his work from the public record over the last 30 years.

The concept of the style which combines the lack of finished meaning of individual parts with radical montage of data from differing areas of experience is that its impact is undefined, unbounded, but disturbing. We are put in a challenged state. At the same time, the poem keeps coming at us – unlike a conventional magazine poem, it does not peter out quickly. This kind of poem does not give a packed, fixed, dead list of meanings, but instead opens an area, emotionally and semantically charged, inside which we move around and devise our own reactions. This poem moves around topics of great importance to me – and where verifiable knowledge fails, to be honest. Questions like, could John MacLean have changed Scotland by leading it with a radical Socialist plus Gaelic nationalist policy, what would the Highlands be like if their affairs had been given political priority rather than being reduced to odd minutes of left-over parliamentary time, do not have literal answers. You may not wish to think about them – but I definitely do. The forces Perrie conjures up are difficult to control – at best, they open up a radical subjectivity mighty enough to change legal institutions.

In Trance as Mission: Robert Crawford, *Spirit Machines* (1999; 65 pp. TNP, Contraflow, Dream State; cluster D)

The book is divided into five sections: 'Pollen', 'A Life-exam', 'Highland poems', 'Impossibility', 'Spirit Machines'. Typical imagery is stars, place-names, recording media, seabed creatures, the ocean, pollen, cultural transmission, eccentric knowledge, the history of technology, virtualisation, banks. Crawford's typical quality is smoothness, and this disguises from conservative critics how bizarre and original his procedures are. Even the weird procedures have acquired, locally, a sheen of respectability from association with Edwin Morgan, a 'deep' avant-gardist who happens to be the best Scottish poet of the last half-century or so, and consequently lent (at least after his 60th birthday) tones of loyalty and patriotism to techniques which, in certain countries, were getting people arrested. Take 'Life-Exam'. A list of 71 questions in an exam in life skills, it is something like a description of the whole social order in terms of cognitive and behavioural abilities. It is extremely funny, invites our collusion, seduces us, reminds us of halcyon and formative Morgan-reading experiences. Yet there is no description of the subject in the poem – no direct statement. It is a work of conceptual art – of the kind which had whiskered literary conservatives shedding stage tears over the nihilistic drug-soaked degradation of contemporary existentialist bohemians not so very long ago and in buildings like these. No. 71 simply asks us 'From here on you may add optional questions', which is what we would, scarcely daring to breathe, term an *open procedure*. What can you say about the meaning of a poem which is simply a set of instructions which each reader carries out in a different way? Is it too much to compare this open set to a 16th-century poem by a Gaelic poet named Duncan which is a series of farcical records of objects which a deceased parasite (sorner) begged from other people, and to which everyone is enjoined to add a line? (Which implies that Duncan is not the real author). The swirl of Scottish place-names, throughout the book, harks back to a poem in *The Second Life* composed entirely of place-names (schiehallion! schiehallion! schiehallion!) – a habit of Crawford's which he plays a virtuosic variation on, in the final poems, by using it to evoke the branch banks of central Scotland which are simultaneously where his father spent his life, and the sites of the automatic teller machines, which were closing the rural branches. However, the words also compose a sound poem, as practised by

Concretists like Haroldo de Campos or Ernst Jandl – or indeed Raoul Hausmann. Crawford was one of the founders of the Informationists (whose type-anthology we have already described) – who could equally well have been named 'morganists'.

The invocation of Scottish geography relates to a notion (neatly set out in the book *Mental Maps*, which recorded the subjective geography which people really carried in their heads) that English people had endless power over the fate of Scotland and were governed by fictitious ideas. The virtual history and landscapes which Informationists specialise in are ironic parodies of this master virtual landscape. One of the comic recitatives in 'Highland Poems' is about Wendy Wood, a famous extreme nationalist who is offered, in the poem, as an *agent provocateur*. Thus, certain key events and court cases are shown as virtual events – scripted by MI6. 'Impossibility', a long poem departing from the life of the 19th century novelist Margaret Oliphant, and set largely on the bed of the ocean (she translated works on marine zoology), plays through a bewildering set of variations on its themes of ambition, the souls of lost children, and invertebrate anatomy, almost infinite in its richness and arbitrariness, almost a schematic of Impossibility itself.

So far as I can make out, the title refers to automatic teller machines: the section after which the book is named tells us that 'Money burns the body of everything, so it can become spirit.' The ATMs were thus spirit machines – and by virtualising the act of doling out cash to bank clients made all of his father's friends unemployed. The whole section is dedicated to the memory of his father, who worked in a bank. 'Deincarnation' has the glens being downloaded, 'the tangible spirited away' – an ambiguous poem. However, it is not totally unrelated, at the end of our book, to 'Pollen', at the beginning, where the difficult poem 'Columban' connects radio to Saint Columba – and so transmission to mission. Columba came over the sea from Ireland to convert the Scots to Christianity (a voyage to which oblique reference is made in the image of a seabird with a wireless transmitter on its leg). The arrival of this culture, and of the Gaelic language from Ireland, made Scotland the place it was to be. The image of pollen (genetic material redefined as information) and of the Incarnate Word seems to offer an answer to what comes at the end of the book, in 'Disincarnation': information is not the dissolution of society, but what sustains it.

Jungian Poets

I pointed out, earlier on, that the category of poets influenced by Jungian conceptions of archetypes, personal myths, individuation, etc., did not feature in the map of anthologies but had to be added – as it obviously existed – as a Cluster H. I presume the reader is familiar with the outlines of his theory. I have not been able to find a historical account of the penetration of Jungian ideas into British culture, but three obvious milestones are the publication of Maud Bodkin's book *Archetypal Patterns in Poetry* (1934), Christopher Caudwell's *Illusion and Reality* (1936; which, despite its Marxist exterior, is really an exploration of Jung), and *The Lady of the Hare* (John Layard, 1944). Two high-points for the belief in myth, ritual as abreaction, deep personal symbolism, etc., were in the 1940s and in the later 1960s – the New Age movement.

Actually, it is possible to argue that myth is no more prominent in late-20th-century poetry than it was in 19th-century poetry. And many poets who use myth are not influenced by Jung, but got it straight from Symbolisme, for example. However, the migration away from Christian myth left an empty space which has not been filled by collective myths – this gave a head start to any theory which announced that individualised myths were valid, as jungianism does. In two and a half thousand years of literary adaptation of myth, the themes chosen were collective, traditional, and inherited from a Bronze Age stratum of oral culture whose creativity leaves us gasping. A major exception to this repetition was the East Mediterranean littoral during the late Roman Empire, an era of sectarian creativity which was neither Christian nor simply a retelling of ancient themes. The variety of this religious culture defies description, but even in this difficulty and confusion we can, or think we can, detect similarities to our own time – a saying of G.R.S. Mead which was copied by Jung. Kathleen Raine spent the 1950s researching in the field of neo-Platonism, theurgy, the Corpus Hermeticum, etc., and her poetry based on this research is a milestone on the way to the era of individually owned myth in which we now find ourselves.

Centuries of fertility:
Peter Redgrove, *The Apple-Broadcast* (1981; 133 pp., cluster H)

The title comes from a poem (subtitled 'a meditation experience') describing the spread of apples from a tree as being like a broadcast (which itself is a word for sowing seed transferred to radio waves). As a keynote, it points to an optimistic view of natural processes of fertility, and of human acts related to fertility, drawing on a level of being where apple-trees show analogies to mammals; and to a psychedelic use of language, or at least one which constantly brings different perceptual frames into contact, and which ignores the restrictions of traditional verse. It is hard to resist this work because of its insistent lyricism, the flood of images with which it draws us into the experiences described, the affirmative mood of all the poems, the lack of conflicts or restraints, the amazing self-confidence and flawlessness of the language. His music is dithyrambic and pours like tea. This title poem describes a valley full of apples, its stream like straw on fire because of the reflected apples, it is blushing (red), the hill roads are 'cobbled' with lumpy fallen fruit. A bird calls, hoarse as a fly walking in the foliage of the tree it is under, the fly's swishing skeleton, its footsteps that crackle over the leaves which are 'tusked' (jagged, oak-leaves), it is as hoarse as 'broken bone'. We might pause here (because the poem goes on for 120 lines like this) to take stock: it's not really happening (because it's a meditation vision), there is a plethora of imagery, it's all primary visual or audial, there are no complex classifiers, it's brilliantly organised and set in rhythmic groups, it doesn't change mood. These qualities continue throughout the book. The poem goes on to say that strings of water draw the air taut as it is ridden by blimps of thunder; the insects shake in the lightning, and their shutters shine. The bird calls again from the oak full of green caverns, where the 'dew' forms eyes, opening because the water is 'waking up'. With a reversal of figure and ground, we see the falling rain as a 'water-being' whose outline is drawn by the fretted outline of the trees. The speaker lies 'intensified' on the grass, he is a (detecting) instrument like the birds and insects; like the spider whose cobweb is an 'aerial' catching the transmissions of the insects, coughing dryly (the sound of their wings?), their dry eyes are full of moisture (the rain) which the spider 'blots up' with its 'tusks'. A bird makes a sound like 'crackling porcelain', or the crunching of its own shell. Lightning flashes again. The speaker lies in the sharp grass near the spider in her 'glass ladder' of web. A lorry from the quarry hits a bump so that its load gives off sparks and makes a noise. So far we've only got to the end of the first section, out of four. In section three the light of the moon is a broadcast, it shines on the skin of all the apples, it is a voice beating in echoes whose curves are like cobwebs. In section 4, the speaker compares the conception of a baby, in the house with him, to the interception of a broadcast; and many moths arrive, of whom the spiders eat some.

Other titles include 'The Eye of Dr Horus', 'The Occultist', 'Grimmanderson on Tresco', 'Renfield before his master', 'Pheromones', 'The White, Night-Flying Moths Called "Souls"', 'Short serpentine at the Lizard', 'Mad Speech concerning dress'. Favourite imagery includes fertility, radio waves, unconscious responses to natural stimuli, the occult, dreams, thunderstorms, insects.

One of his book-jackets claims over 900 published poems, and after all basic melodic lines do recur. His work is an exploration of fantasy or personal mood, and does not touch on human relationships and interactions, which give depth to a poem. Still, if someone is so up the whole time that does count as a social grace. He would argue that the exploration of fantasy uncovers the real self, and so also releases the other person's real self. All the same, the predominance of self-absorbed fantasy does mean a missing bandwidth in the area of dialogue and dialectic.

His work partly resembles that of D.H. Lawrence and John Cowper Powys.

Fleming in psychedelic flight:
Jane Draycott and Lesley Saunders,
Christina the Astonishing (1998; 86 pp., cluster A)

The *Calendar of Saints* (quoted) tells the story: 'she suddenly rose from her open coffin and sped up into the rafters of the church. ... She dressed in rags bound together with saplings. She liked being swung round and round mill wheels and never seemed to get hurt doing so.' Further on, 'her body was so subtle and light that she would walk on any dizzy height or precipice, and hang suspended like a sparrow from the topmost twigs of the loftiest trees.' A postface tells us that 'This book came into being over a period of some years as the two of us ... delved deeper and deeper into contemporary and modern meanings of Christina's life.' There are two epigraphs, of which one is from Alban

Butler's *Lives of the Saints* and reads 'there is little in the life of Christina of Brusthem to make us think she was other than a pathological case.' Christina lived (in Flanders) between 1150 and 1224, and the authors know about her life from a Latin vita of 1232. The book of poetry is therefore in dialogue with a text almost 8 centuries older, where every passage dug out releases its literary devices and the structures of its world-view, while trying to hold the events captive. The encounter is a kind of duel. Some 15 of 51 pieces are translations or quotations – giving us high-points from a wide range of mediaeval spiritual texts. Some are quoted as an act of exposure, because they show clerics being anti-feminist or sceptical of Christina.

What is irresistible is the primal impact of the plain violation of the physical conditions governing a human body, its musculature, its weight and lifting capacity. Perhaps this violation is essential to poetry – the fuel which drives its delicate and elaborate transformations.

The way the material is captured means the two poets do not intrude as devisers of the material. Their role is to translate and organise. The avoidance of a critical attitude is most important. As a remake of traditional religious material into modern poetic terms, it can be compared to *Dry-points of the Hasidim*. The versification is often awkward, bedraggled by the traces of the Latin prose. The structure is not completely satisfactory, as it has no logical development or climax; Christina's legend was not structured as a story. It also lacks an account of how her special experience started – something unusual in a vita. The authors use their heroine's aversion to eating and 'lightness' to discuss anorexia – the ambiguous demands to be delicate and spiritual – and draw analogies with the wish for virginity. It was drawn to my attention by someone (Harry Gilonis) who had reviewed a translation of the Irish text *Buile Suibhne Geilt* for us, and was bemused to discover a contemporary poem which had the same theme of flying and living in the tops of trees. Perhaps this is a basic category of the folk-tale, an image existing in collective memory which Christina came along and inhabited. The comparison to the unusual experiences expected of a lyric poet is also interesting. We also have to consider psychedelic flight, how saints' lives can be re-read in the light of experiences in trips or trance states in the now-time. Because there is an opposition in natural semantics between birds and people, who are also similar in some ways (as warm-blooded bipeds who forage for food, care for their young, sing, are in some ways conscious, etc.), we find it equally natural that, in the world of dream or fantasy, the opposition is crossed to eject a being who is in both categories. What is at stake is creation as a projection of 'personality' versus creation as the lawful result of a fertile combinatory logic which anyone can continue – and which our unconscious selves practice as soon as we fall asleep. In 'And will our daughters fly?', Christina is merged with female aviators such as Amy Johnson; and this image of flight is combined with folk sayings about fledglings, soaring, high-flyers and flying the nest (focussing on nurture and autonomy) to be a wonderfully optimistic prayer about 'our daughters' and their flights being as free and splendid as possible. The imagery also uses the swan transformation of the Irish legend of the Children of Lir.

We might set up an opposition between variance of physical law and variance of the linguistic code (which prohibits the former?), as rival bases for poetry. We learn, in 'Tongues', that Christina could speak beautiful Latin without ever having been taught it – a miracle which reminds us of twentieth-century people who could recount myriad details of their past lives, or talk in 1st century Aramaic. These people are also called hysterics – and, hysteria and unusual artistic talent may have something in common. When we consider that modern poets regard exceptional language as proof of the legitimacy of what someone is saying, we recall that Christina's fans also saw her verbal gifts as a form of legitimation. This poetry does not quite reach a style, but is in touch with fundamental bodily experiences of the impossible – the stuff of dream.

Both Draycott and Saunders have had separate careers as poets.

Poetry of the Evanescent Present

**Rapture of the desert:
Rosemary Tonks, *Iliad of Broken Sentences*; (1967; 24 pp.)**

Titles include 'The Sofas, Fogs, and Cinemas', 'Epoch of the Hotel Corridor', 'Orpheus in Soho' 'The Ice-cream Boom Towns', 'Black Kief and the intellectual', 'The Desert Wind Elite'.

The jacket text (quite possibly written by her, since she was best qualified to do it) says 'Her poetry has a dramatic but spontaneous texture, enabling it to carry vast and timeless themes lightly within it (…) the deserts of the Middle-East are again equated with city life; and this is a handbook to its sofas, hotel corridors, cinemas, underworlds, cardboard suitcases, self-willed buses, banknotes, soapy bathrooms, pork-filled newspapers – and to its anguish, its enraged excitement, its great lonely joys.' I can't improve on that. The poetry has perhaps a narrow range, and is brittle – in exchange for its complete immersion in the present moment, the complete identity of intents and effects. I'm not sure if I can quote her poetry. There were only two books before she got religion and quit the scene. I am not sure about the 'vast' themes – they seem rather intimate to me.

I think the 'Middle Eastern' bit is related to a phase described in her novel *Emir*, where the heroine hangs out in a Greek restaurant (East Mediterranean food, then) and with a man who is referred to as 'like an Emir with a beloved prisoner'. It's a kind of Camden Town 1963 style Middle East. In 'Badly-Chosen Lover', she speaks of a piece of her life wasted, time 'In the clear muscles of my brain/ I have the lens and jug of it!' She is explaining this softly, so with reservations we imagine. 'Half Europe, spent like a coarse banknote,/ You took it(.)'

Her dislike of the work ethic puts me off a technical analysis. Maybe instead we could speak of the '60s and presence. This wonderful quality is based on very firm grasp of a frame – either the long view, or the torrent of data concerning everybody else in the room, are excluded. Imagine a microphone that is equally close to 30 people in a room talking. Listening is unbearable. Now imagine a mike that only picks up two people, very close to you – it's intimate, but of course it's selective. The yearning for sociology let all the information back in. Of course, you can't be political unless you're listening to all 30 people. It's true most of her poems can be read as complaints about the male object of interest – but the effect is so different from generalised complaints, expressing a critical attitude and grievance theory. Perhaps the poems survive because they're describing face to face conflict? And because they are implicit dialogues – the male object isn't simply being beaten up and thrust into a cupboard. Trying to speak for and about a whole community is perhaps a terminal experience for poetry – so that lyric is defined by moments of untouched self-awareness in life, unsplit by the demands of other people, by jobs and knowledge structures. Maybe the three-minute single was actually better than the ambitious album. Tonks (1928–2014) is a charming writer – maybe injecting bulk information, or striking the pose of an advocate in litigation, instantly makes the charm vanish. If you're going to be narcissistic – you need a light touch.

I walk the line: John James, *Berlin Return*; (1983; 74 pp., 3; AVA, tnbp 3, CC; cluster C)

The title describes a trip to Berlin. Titles include 'Shakin all over', 'Sister Midnight', 'Craven Images', 'Cambridge', 'Chute de Pierres'. 'One for Rolf' is for Rolf-Dieter Brinkmann, a German Beat poet who died in 1975. One poem runs:

four excessive moves I made today

1. Ate too much lunch

2. Ate too little dinner

3. Talked too much

4. Retired sober

– which sums up the problems of doing a detailed analysis without overloading. Key adjectives would include romantic, charming, volatile, insouciant, hedonistic, energetic, and international. The scenery includes bars, trains, cafés, bedrooms, Berlin, Cambridge, Cardiff, London. I have a copy of *Resuscitator*, number two: from 1965, with a poem by James which represents for me the moment of British poetry becoming fun, after the drab and dismal days of the

1950s. The date is problematic – because we have already seen a volume by Rosemary Tonks, who published *Notes on Cafés and Bedrooms* in 1963, which is quite closely related to James and has most of the same virtues. The poem I am thinking of is set in a café in Clifton, which is where James had gone, from Cardiff, to study – and from where he edited *Resuscitator*. He moved from there to Cambridge, the centre of English poetry at that time. The mobility and enthusiasm seem to sum up the spirit of the time – a kind of security which is not tied to geographical roots. If we look at a child's painting, there is a possibility that the simplicity of features actually corresponds to how we perceive the world from moment to moment – we just don't bother with the immense stores of information in the visual field, and in the archives of memory; which we can draw on if we need them. The minimum needed to produce a satisfactory picture, or poem, is really very little. In a state of flow, where there is no split between the conscious mind and the actions of the body, where the body is like the piece being moved in the game which the symbolic part of the mind is processing at natural speed, the frames of perception may also be very simple – although they have deep complexity around them, and apparently available at any moment. A train ride might be an example, with a landscape opening out at every moment without actually being touched. Fielding shiploads of explicit information might actually damage the poem by closing down the sense of flow. James' poems possess flow – a quicksilver run of images; action in the present; constant physical movement. Whereas a static observer gathers static knowledge, scarce, suitable to be turned into property, a moving observer sees perpetually shifting information, constantly being destroyed and opening up in unseizable complexity on every side. As I have set out elsewhere with regard to *The Welsh Poems*, I think he has also drawn in detail on the boastful and ornamental qualities of mediaeval Welsh poetry, with its largely self-contained lines and constant physical details:

> the linen spattered with honey & lager
> the dawn spouting with little birds & pressing
> a shoulder-blade to the mattress

Something else in the Zeitgeist is rock music – where also great simplicity of form is combined with spontaneous bursts of ornament, and display is the key factor. Naming poems after rock songs (by Iggy Pop and

Johnny Kidd and the Pirates) is a fairly strong clue – but then, a line like 'dusty smell of old red velvet cinema seats' sounds like pure Tonks, and it's impossible to imagine Tonks listening to a rock and roll song. The common point with Tonks is presumably Apollinaire (and Breton? and Prévert?) – where he got those great soaring lines from. The trip to Berlin re-enacts Apollinaire's trip to Prague. A few more references. 'I'm puzzling over the influence of the Stickies' refers to the Official IRA, the ones the Provisionals broke away from because they had given up violence in favour of class analysis and revolution. The Richard Long who appears in a credit ('after Richard Long and Johnny Cash') was a sculptor who manipulated infinite space: by walking through a field of flowers, he created a pattern (caught on a photograph) which was a permanent record of his body in movement across time, and in which almost all the material thus 'signed' was untouched by his body – and unaffected. Invisibly, square miles of countryside formed themselves into sculptures at his gesture of command. This should remind us of the full empty gestures of rock and roll. James may not use as many words as some poets, but his command of the warm and mimetic channel of suggestibility (the missing energy which balances the universe?) is greater than anyone else's.

Dead cormorants held rigid by her rosy breast:
Brian Marley: *Springtime in the Rockies* (1978; 59 pp.; cluster C)

The cover says "Marley is a young Newcastle poet who has been writing subversive poems since adolescence – subversive in the area of language and syntactical coherence". The word subversion is seriously intended. It was demolishing an academic poetry, rooted in the 1950s but still hegemonic in 1978, which, discreetly or less so, offered organised knowledge, confident in its price and in the price of the old universities which had conferred their seal on the verse practitioner. The jacket blurb describes the activities of Marley (b.1953) as a publisher, of Asa Benveniste and Tony Jackson among others. Benveniste was the publisher of Trigram (and printed most of their books, although not this one); he put out a book called *Dense Lens* (1975) of which half was written by Marley and half by him, and it may be that these three knew each other; from the stylistic point of view, I am not sure I could tell their work apart. The key element in this style is rapid shifts of perspective, and, as I have argued elsewhere, these discontinuities derive from the Theatre of the Absurd, very prominent in the 1950s, which itself was a variant on Surrealism. The sudden replacements wipe out the past from the area of discourse, an implicit attack on organised knowledge which also covertly characterises the poet, not wiped out, as someone quick-witted and light-hearted. Because Marley's style mocks accumulated knowledge, and because it is sociable, living in a continuous present, it can be assimilated to a general revolt towards immediacy in the poetry of the sixties. Marley was a latecomer to this style, but had an incomparable skill in using it. It succumbed to the deep politicisation of the 1970s and the gloom caused by the right-wing backlash of 1979, so *Springtime in the Rockies* is a late example, before that package of volatile impulses changed its shape radically. Marley has published little since. He says in the blurb "Smaller editions of his poetry are too numerous to list. This selection of poems can be viewed as the start of a spectacular but admirable decline." This is not a very accessible book, so I will quote a whole poem, 'Three' of the 'Bargain Basement Sonnets'.

> Receptive to bludgeoning generated by white-
> hot voltage (love, wired on a dual circuit) but
> dead cormorants held rigid by her rosy breast
> the motions of small craft during persistent
> storm, piloted on the dread continuum – he was
> conceived during such a gross slash across the
> daylight hours and hung by the legs – leaning
> over the insufferable slops, flung leeward
> lonely as a mute in the wailing psychic down-
> pour: O merry month of May, the hamstrung morn
> the merry harvesters scuttle dutifully towards
> riches in the next life (for now it is permissible
> to nail planks over the dying eyes' milky whites) –
> holding was enough; to grasp frozen amphibians
> chipped from ice and hold them in the mouth (was
> it her hand chewing the skirt folded most beautifully?)

Let me say that I find this poetry more enjoyable than almost anything else in the whole field of culture. It has the virtues of good conversation. In fact, if it represents anything, it is probably the rapid shifts of attention and ease of mutual understanding which indicate hilarity and close friendship. It is like shopping, because we have the sense of an abundance of choice and of perfect liberty in choosing; we explore the slight details of the lines, because we are granted such freedom and leisure. Indeed, ugly and stupid poetry is the antithesis of sociability, whatever its political side-arms.

Much as I enjoy this poetry – much as almost everyone who reads it enjoys it – the style has sometimes been imitated to bad effect. An adequate appreciation would therefore recognise that each line is unique, just as Marley has realised this. We could also characterise it by negatives. It is the negation of work; it is not trying to teach us facts we don't know about the nature of objects, like a grocer instructing a dull apprentice. It does not focus on things; it floats in calm if curious detachment from them, taking it that this *dégagé* quality is requisite for gaiety. It does not argue. It does not describe the author's life.

> *The Luminous Band of Stars*
>
> Recant or distil in double vision
> the amorphic odes thoroughly cauterised as
> a wound not quite held from scar – the
> women aroused with stitches
> a feather boa being removed precipitating
> the wearer (assuasive towards the good things
> in life) to scientific terminology, spirals
> located in the back-brain shooting arrows
> over parkland where Marcel Wave (the protagonist)
> test drives a virginal Chevrolet –
> wringing their hands over and over I
> notion his scent is masked in blood

Springtime is the sort of literary classic which disappeared from the scene almost as soon as it was published, and which justifies reading long tedious books by literary historians. I have just been reading Jeremy Over's first book (of 2001), which strikes me as rather similar to Marley.

Brass-o-rama:
Karlien van den Beukel, *Pitch Lake* (1996, 21 pp.)

The author is Dutch, but spent her childhood in Trinidad – hence the memories of the Pitch Lake, of La Brea, in Trinidad. The title page has a citation from Walter Raleigh about the qualities of the 'stone pitch' to be won from La Brea. The poems seem then to be a flash-back to childhood – as is conventional for authors from tropical countries writing in England. This is why a perambulator appears twice. I counted three Dutch words in the text (*treurspel, weer,* and *opstand.*) Titles include 'Prelude' 'Colibri Play' 'Hush of Mas' 'Hot Inroads' 'Fancy Suit'.

The author is a dance historian by profession, and the key to the style seems to be movement – the verse steps are a virtual body image of the poet, and the verse line is light and constantly moving forward. The dance manner seems to offer a social force – music – made visible; display and flight; poise pushed out to risk; visual rules and non-functionality; quickness of divisions; applause and pressure; levity and fondness for clothes. Short lines and constant shifts of emphasis put the brightest possible light on each phrase – slight enough to give way rapidly, clever enough to sustain the high lights. Indenting of the lines into the page slows the eye down while also emphasizing the movement of the point of focus across a symbolic area – a virtual stage. The semantic context never comes down to earth by being explicit – instead we move rapidly on. The dance metaphor was one frequently used during the early days of *vers libre* in England, around the time of the First World War, and the style seems to owe something to Ezra Pound or Mina Loy. The intensity of registration of such poets – the close focus on a sensibility on a scale small enough to register its movements as alterations to the whole frame of reference of the poem – encouraged childhood as a subject, and was related to the long accounts of childhood in psychological novels of the period, having absorbed Symbolisme into a realist framework. A repeating motif is the colibri or humming-bird, evoking a tropical garden with luxuriant flowers, but also great dexterity and manoeuvrability. The impetus which keeps the balance of the poems at risk is sustained by not pausing to register a large stable reference frame laden with data and relationships. Instead, we get a single, silver thread, in incessant motion. It isn't too surprising if a young girl is preoccupied with dancing – and so several of the poems deal with the Carnival, one of the great events of the year in Trinidad, a Catholic festival into which African cultural energies have been abundantly poured. 'The Spectacle is a Map of This New World', for example, is about the Carnival, referred to in the first line as 'J'ouvert' (short for *jour ouvert*, or Mardi Gras).

> And tarmac lurexed.
> Bring your own body
> to the brass-o-rama
> abandon its orbit
> on slaking pitch.
>
> Bring your love
> o, to the fooling:
> mirth as music
> of division lets
> the rest be his.
>
> To the savannah
> pasquinaded hot-
>
> pants shot through
> nebular hypotheses,

The poem is set in the middle of carnival, with people dressed up as mythical archetypes, in elaborate costumes chosen for maximum visual impact, demigods, acting out primal impulses with fantastic displays of energy. Both *tarmaced* and *pitch* are teasing references to the tutelar Lake of Pitch. The abandoning of orbit relates to the nebular hypothesis – which holds that planets were formed by concretion of dust from a nebula (or, dust-cloud). The rotation is about the dancers going round and round – and the idea of heavenly bodies is the glitter and bright lights. 'Brass' is the horns of the band; if 'panorama' is a tracking shot, then 'brass-o-rama' might be 'a brass band marching in a procession'. Savannah takes us back to Africa, and the roots of the ceremony. 'Fooling' is the imperative of the street party. The rest is 'his' (your love's), because when you're dancing it's with someone else. A pasquinade is a kind of political libel in verse, attached traditionally to a certain statue in Rome – this implies that satire plays a role in the

Carnival, a loosed time where social respect is forgotten. Later, we have another quote from Raleigh, describing the gold idol of Eldorado – who may be in the carnival, as a gilt and not quite divine image; and the phrase 'ship-hopped' echoes 'trip-hop', a dance genre of the '90s (Portishead, Sneaker Pimps, etc.). Although the phrasing is difficult to tease out, and 1920s modernism is an obvious model, the fondness for dance also brings the poems close to popular music. We can wonder whether the interest in exotic clothing attaches to scholarly pursuit of the Ballets Russes, of costumes by Bakst as inspirations for dance movements – or to disco culture.

The book is from rem.press and has an exceptionally beautiful design.

O ice of under-earthly redness:
Occultist, Mantic, and Eccentric

The idea of art as an autonomous world was stimulated by the collapse of shared cosmological frameworks in the 1950s, but had been around since the later 19th century – as brilliantly described by James Webb in *The Occult Revival*. There are a thousand ways you could get at this (excessively?) rich stream of ideas, but the most prominent local representative was W.B. Yeats and the grand rediscovery was William Blake. Of all the people who admired these two, a few accepted that they wanted to write in a similar way. One key issue was rejecting documentary observation and scepticism in favour of suggestibility and the imagination. After 1968, this stream emerged from the shadow of heresy, from reason, delusion, etc. into a new mainstream of psychedelia and New Age.

Spiral influences from the stars:
The Hollow Hill, by Kathleen Raine
(1965; 70 pages; Agenda; cluster H)

Poem titles include 'Two reflections on the *Magia*' 'Beinn Naomh' 'A Certain Moist Nature' 'The Hollow Hill' – a phrase from Scottish folklore, where the hill has Fenian champions inside it, who may return from magical sleep to carry out useful feats. There is a mixture of personal experience, descriptions of landscape, and neo-Platonic theology. Typical imagery is waves, stars, labyrinths, Scottish hills, boundless spaces, endless Time, megalithic tombs, rays. The title page adds the detail "poems 1960-64", and the jacket describes this as her first new book for 13 years – we can interpret this as a problem with the 1950s. Hostility produces silence – which can then be hostilely glossed as self-doubt. There are five large groups of poems. 'Eilean Chanaidh' is a poem in five parts. The title means the island of Canna, in the Hebrides, to the west of Scotland. The sequence is dedicated to Margaret and John Lorne Campbell, the latter of whom lived on Canna collecting Gaelic folklore. The rocky landscape of the Atlantic seaboard is very different from the soft alluvial terrain of south-eastern England. Poem 1 evokes the speech of the isles and evokes work patterns which she says were embodied in the Gaelic speech. 2 is about a graveyard, communal continuity, the tenuity of personal identity. 3 is about a carved Celtic stone cross. 4 is about islets even smaller than Canna, nameless, which are homes to souls. Poem 6 says that she falls as 'a shadow' on the landscape because she is not a Gael, and has a powerful sense of loss. Her style is based on Edwin Muir, who was already Platonic, vague, and serene. Poem 5, 'Stone on High crag' includes a run of 12 adjectives, each occupying a line, describing a carved rock: "wing-spanned... Lichen-roughened/ Granite-grained/ Rock-red/ Rain pocketed" (etc.) – this is a homage to Gaelic poetry. The run is based on the strings of compound adjectives which are common in a type of Gaelic bardic ballad, composed certainly in the 15th and 16th centuries (perhaps earlier and later), and collected (mainly from oral recitation) on a grand scale in J.F. Campbell's *Lebor na Feinne*. Raine made much more extensive use of another genre of Gaelic poetry, the "charms" or prayers collected in Carmichael's *Carmina Gadelica*. This calls to mind the current of folk influence on poetry, which reached quite a peak in around 1951, when Raine's *The Year One* is saturated in it. This preceded the Folk Revival in music, held to have started around 1958. 1951 saw also an interest in folk art as one strand in the national celebration in the Festival of Britain. The exhibition *Black Eyes and Lemonade: British Popular Art* was curated by Barbara Jones for the festival, and Enid Marx and Margaret Lambert published *English Popular Art*, again in 1951. This atmosphere seems to have given George Mackay Brown his point of stylistic departure. There is a relationship between the simple forms of folksong and the more elaborate forms of mythology: English folk culture was as if a scaled-down version. Poets recovering folksong in 1951 anticipated poets capturing full-scale mythology in the 1970s. There is a separate realm of visual naïve art; if poetry does not face a recapture of naive virtues, it is because the reintegration of the naïve had happened in the 1950s and been pursued.

Raine's life as a researcher was significantly parallel to Frances A. Yates, following similar trajectories into a lost wealth of occult texts and doctrines. During the 1950s Raine made a move to a cluster of magical thinkers of the late Roman Empire, known as neo-Platonists, and including those collected in the *Corpus Hermeticum*. That is, by the standards of the Anglican Church she is a heretic – the doctrinal crisis is being solved by a step which also makes that crisis permanent. Authors she refers to include Plato, Plotinus, Blake, the Vedas, and the mediaeval mystic Julian of Norwich; the *Magia* is certainly a reference to a book on 'natural magic' by Giordano Bruno, a believer in magic. The doctrine she has to impart to us is of static eternal configurations, governing the universe and our minds. The eternal truths are rigid when it comes to individual sensations and individual moments – they offer serenity, but verge on the authoritarian, and discourage liveliness of rhythm. How can there be movement from one line to another when they are describing truths which have held immovable for thousands of years? Raine's poems were frequently compared to crystals, according to *Poetry London*'s 1948 review. In fact, this time she seems to have extended the crystal into the whole universe, where astral rays are its vast axes. This 'frozen world of rigid form' is alien to uncertainty and knows movement only in cycles.

Another way of looking at Raine sees melodrama. The Near Eastern material is radically converted into a set of metaphors for states of mind – entirely passionate and even amorous ones. The poems include coded references to love affairs with all narrative account gracefully removed, as that would have given too much away, in a small poetry world. They are quite close to melodramas like 'A Love Story' or 'They Were Sisters', features of which were that they raised the performers in them to Stars, taking their feelings so seriously as to monumentalise them – within the limits of popular cinema. It may help to imagine the poems being read aloud by Phyllis Calvert or Margaret Lockwood.

Something underfoot is not quite steady here – because the "neo-Platonics" had beliefs which are simply bad physics, such as the belief that influences flow spirally down from the stars (making a noise, called *rhoizos*) to control human events, we are forced to select which beliefs we are going to believe. Raine wants her poems to possess authority and orthodoxy but cannot make the transition from heresy and individualism. Sometimes these poems seem to be hidden behind indefinite and vast shapes in the foreground, as opposed to sharp foreground objects receding to the indefinite behind it. The poems take place against these two subjective infinities: the wilderness of the Hebrides, with the Atlantic behind it, and the astral-astrological world of Hermes Trismegistus. These supply a space of vague, indefinite, and sublime shapes within the poems.

Folk gave us the singer-songwriter, and the book marks an early stage of what would, later, be called New Age beliefs. The style is hymn-like – although in long irregular lines, it does float in a world of eternal concepts and interstellar spaces and does expound a doctrine. She uses the second reality of dreams to express disbelief in the body and the evidence of the senses – transient distractions of the eternal soul. If we say that the folk line evolved into rock and roll, and the supernatural line developed into Hammer horror films, it seems that Raine was on the brink of an explosion.

With age, Raine (1908–2003) became increasingly dogmatic and less able to write poetry. However, *The Hollow Hill* was a creative peak and draws you into a world where the whole cosmos is visible, vast events of dazzling beauty and strangeness as if in a photograph from a space ship. It reminds me of the hymns of Proclus – admittedly some of the most beautiful poetry ever written. The Neoplatonist cosmos is so obviously beautiful that a simple, pious evocation of it from any point within it will suffice to make beautiful poetry audible. The Neoplatonist world-view is even more amazing and more beautiful than the Christian one. In times when we associate being lost in music and starstruck with taking drugs, we actually underrate the most important experiences.

The Intermittence of the Stars: 'Astronomy Domine'
(written by Syd Barrett; performed by Pink Floyd)

In her classic interpretation of psychedelic music, *The Space Between the Notes*, Sheila Whiteley points out that Pink Floyd were younger than the pioneers of psychedelic music, and therefore able to form their style in an atmosphere already saturated with the new sounds, and so with the influence of blues, with its folk/Christian framework, minimised. They were consequently able to pursue the new style for longer than the others. Whiteley says of 'Astronomy Domine', the first track on their first album, *Piper at the Gates of Dawn*, in 1967: 'the dip shapes in the guitar solo create a strong feeling of floating around the beat and this is reinforced by the lazy meandering around the notes(.) [...] The chord sequence moves against any formal organisation and (...) there is no real resolution. Instead, there is a movement towards a disorientation of the norm...' The lyrics run in part:

> Lime and limpid green, a second scene
> A fight between the blue you once knew
> Floating down

The sound resounds around the icy waters underground
(…)
Neptune, Titan, stars can frighten

The repetition of the syllable 'ound' echoes the musical sensation of time failing to run forward, and the third verse mutates one of the lines to 'surround the icy waters underground', a near-echo but with the syllable break shifted and the voiced -s- unvoiced – a 'tripping' effect of cognitive dissonance and the semantic tier being eroded. The sequence 'Miranda and Titania' sounds when sung like "Mi ran da ran dTitania', breaking up into nonsense – a later line runs 'Blinding signs flap flicker flicker blam', and this could be a description of these irresoluble, shifting phonetic patterns. The *second scene* is attracted by the *tighten* and *frighten* sounds below it to second sight – the psychedelic insight into a hidden and private world of symbolism, enabling you to see fairies like Oberon and Titania. It also contains the acoustic shape of (for a) *second seen* – which relates to the *flickering* a few lines later. The vision is blinding but intermittent – as shaky as the ghost words of which these lyrics are so full. The equation between the skies above and the icy waters beneath suggests a dissolution of the observer's point of view, the loss of the human scale of a body, on a horizontal surface, as the stable ground for a mind; the hyper-vivid description of the infinite expanses through their colours (blue for the sky, green for the waters, we suppose) does nothing to restore scale. Whiteley quotes a medical source about LSD's effect of dissolving the bounds between the self and the outside world or other people; the notion of 'cosmic rock' arose from the photographs taken in outer space (universal in the media at that time), partly from the 'weightless' music dreamed up for the soundtracks of science fiction films in the 1950s, largely from the projection of this depersonalisation into a place without persons or objects: a feeling of the dissolution of boundaries was sited, mythographically, in a place that had no boundaries and was mere extension. Oberon and Titania are not stars – they mislead, they have the power of flight, and they command potions which delude reason – significant images for psychoactive drugs. Their servant, Puck, is also a will of the wisp – a light that misleads travellers (hence *blinding* signs). Miranda also awoke into a new world: O brave new world, that hath such people in it! – an obvious drug reference. Saturn and Titan are not names of stars, but are perhaps not randomly chosen. Both are names of mythical figures who were thrown down from heaven – the sensation of falling is a terror involved in psychedelic 'flight'. Titan is a moon of the 'leaden planet' Saturn – a frozen body which may contain the 'icy waters'. Its shining rings are a sly reference to light-shows. (Miranda, Titania, and Oberon are moons of Uranus.) The word 'Titan' sounds, ambiguously, like 'tighten' – a reference to tension which anticipates the word *frighten*, in the next half-line. Saturn and Titan were both rockets, both deployed as carriers for nuclear warheads – deterrents which "frighten". These lines are closely packed – a product of hyperassociation, which is the main event in the psychedelic experience. Their refusal of a character to identify with, a feeling to isolate, leads to a loss of orientation. The beloved pop song vanished, replaced by a trick surface, with a slight malice or slyness. We advance onto shifting grounds and don't know if we're falling or 'tripping'.

Early Floyd 'experimented with improvising around one chord used in a drone-like way, seeing how they could extend it. On March 27 [1966], Floyd played a number lasting half an hour.' This static immersion was aided by 'using electronic feedback in continuous controlled waves which added up to complex repeating patterns' (Whiteley). The effect was, obviously, timelessness – a loss of boundaries and orientation to complement the loss of spatial reference points. The Floyd spent the next thirty years exploring these ideas of timelessness and immensity, through varying drones, heartbeat-like bass riffs, repetition, and barely punctuated, engulfing, emptiness. Essentially in parallel to this, poetry moved into the long poem, in which the exploration of inner space, the capture of emptiness, reflexivity (=feedback), and the approach towards timelessness, were all vital.

Poetry sited boundlessness in the free reaches of Inner Asian space (or, the North Atlantic, or, the prairies of the north-western USA) rather than in space beyond the earth's atmosphere or under the ground. Yet the dry air and flat horizons make the stars perilously close: *A true /night of pale registrations / spread out coldly above /the nomadic line* (Martin Thom). The 'icy waters underground' (so close to *blue with the reflected coldness of strangeness* in Thom's poem) bear a puzzling resemblance to the imagery of Northern icy waters in *Malcolm Mooney's Land* and Hendry's *Marimarusa*. The ocean was evidently chosen as the expression of 'lifting' of the body image into the boundless and weightless – which resembles the radical use of the body as the source of all imagery, in 1940s poetry. We are bound to compare this interstellar space with the spiral influences of the stars as they flow, serenely, in Kathleen Raine's poetry.

The proof sheets of Paul Celan's first book include a poem 'Schwarze Flocken', with the part-line 'O Eis von unterirdischer Röte' – O ice of under-earthly redness. This would be a clear anticipation of 'icy waters underground'. However, the reproduction (in *Gesammelte Werke*, volume 3) of the sheets shows that it was the printer's mistake, and the line really reads 'O ice of unearthly redness'.

Eucalyptus skies: Peter Redgrove and Penelope Shuttle, *The Hermaphrodite Album*; (1973; 105 pp. 60WP, TNP; cluster H)

Theologically, this poetry is close to the pagan cults which Christianity got rid of – which laid stress on first-person experience, and on saving transformation through ritual. The book was published by Fuller D'Arch Smith, the imprint of two occultist booksellers, owners of the shop Atlantis Books. The money to pay for it may well have come from Jimmy Page's composing royalties, exchanged for occult books of the Golden Dawn era. The title derives from the dual authorship – the volume is composed of uncredited poems by both poets. It also refers to a transformation in esoteric alchemy, the *conjunctio* – which we have also seen described in Walter Perrie's poem. It is an 'album' like a photograph album into which snapshots are pasted. The hermaphrodite signifies completeness via the reconciliation of opposites. The use of alchemy – a set of knowledge thoroughly discredited by modern science – points quite strongly to Carl Gustav Jung, who wrote a lot about alchemy and its symbols. As a source framework, it declares the dominance of subjectivity within the book. Perhaps we should interpret it as an acceptance of objectivity in the realm of technology, but with the suggestion of energetic subjectivity in the private realm, the realm of leisure which successful technology has opened up for us. We have something else to do other than work the whole time.

The promise is of psychological photographs which are much more sharp and revealing than ones filtered through objectivity – ones which capture the whole furniture of inner worlds rather than just conventional segments. These photographs are of momentary worlds – ones which are only there for a flash. The issue is about credibility and honesty – do we want someone who is rigorous and rigid about self-reporting, or someone who is enthusiastic and trusting and free about it. Surely there is a division of domestic labour whereby we want work thinking at one point in life and playful fantasy at another. The dual authorship produces a special effect here, because it suggests a halfway public form of fantasy – the role which the reader normally plays in the poem is already being played by the other poet. The excitement is much greater because it is being fuelled by the other person – which is how poetry is supposed to work, in actual fact. Because we are so free to choose, the factor of enthusiasm surges to the front – there is nothing to hold us here except our enjoyment. This is where *The Hermaphrodite Album* scores so many points and is so far ahead of the other New Age books which were being written at the time, because the fertility and enthusiasm in the work are so exciting.

The poems are like music – self-referential qualities like the sustaining of themes, crescendos, modulation, cunning variations, are pre-eminent, because the function of representation or documenting has been attenuated. Without realistic constraints, the poems can simply swim towards the most attractive idea. The key constraint is to be unexpected – the line of sight is systematically cheated, as each line is at an angle to the previous one. Each poem is like a vitrine, where fascinating objects and sensations are set in suggestive and complex groups. Titles include 'House of Keys', 'The Ice-Yacht', 'The Blind Ghost', 'Millions Gone', 'The Sword-Shaped Wife', 'Nine Sorceries'. On the first page we see:

> I have saved a skull-lamp of pale spectral honey
> It sheds light and a pawing silence it is sweet but helpless and
> > ghostly
> And there is still a mirror made of himself to hunt through
> I should never have entered this mirror but his glamour is
> > immense.
>
> I admired his shipwrecks
> It was my end's beginning

Jung wasn't some village witch-doctor; he was someone with a medical degree who could draw on the wide stream of Symbolist criticism of science in its inability to account for the process of consciousness. We should remember that the arrogance of science was much more obtrusive in the 19th century, when scientists really suffered from megalomania. I don't think Jung was a very honest or original man, but anyway the products of fantasy clearly have some origin, and we are justified in looking at the fantasy as a data source about a tiny organ. I see the writing down of the outputs of fantasy as something akin to botany – which also deals with fine points of small and delicate organisms.

I find it quite easy now to tell which poem was written by each poet. However, when I first read the book, in 1980, I couldn't – and this made the experience much more enjoyable – more uncontrolled, more overwhelming.

Reading *THA* was a moment of release for me, which led directly to writing my second book of poetry. Displaying disinhibition breaks down the reader's inhibitions and so releases their inner images, which are of indescribable variety. In that sense, this kind of poetry is selfless – it is a gateway through which readers pass to reach part of themselves. The resistance of a Christian or moralising strand to such poetry is a subject on its own. To be sure, the loss of illusions is a classic form of liberation. To cut down the subjective life in order to enforce social discipline – this is some kind of destruction of the wilderness, in psychic terms.

'That Reason be cut into, bound, reforged, charged with wild light, ionised': Iain Sinclair, *Lud Heat* (1975; 129 pp. tnbp3, AVA; cluster C)

The title refers to the legendary founder of London, after whom Ludgate is named. It is a variant on blood heat. The setting of *Lud Heat* is a season of working for the Council in the parks of Tower Hamlets, mowing and clearing rubbish, in the open air. The *heat* may refer to the sunstroke which ensued ('he was opened up to the whole horror of the sun'), via a Swedenborgian distinction between Love (=the spiritual sun) and Heat (the material sun). In the text, we find 'All the bacteria of body light have been boiled in malarial blood heat.'

Alongside the evocation of the work gang and their lore, there is a massive psychogeographical scheme whereby the churches of the great Baroque architect Nicholas Hawksmoor form an ideogram, a magical shape, trapping earth energies. 'It has been told how the Hawksmoor churches yield the symbol of Set, the tool for castration and the instrument for impressing cuneiform script onto the clay tablet(.)' This is, to be sure, deeply implausible (and the distracted shapes of sunstricken sight are hardly external), but eventually (and I first read this text in 1977) the ornate and monumental quality of Sinclair's spatial myth induces us to concede it a temporary alternate reality. This vortex of unreason is a paean to Hawksmoor's great churches (with their evocations of Egyptian and Greek sacred spaces) and a primer of the beliefs which the pilgrims of the Counter Culture, in super-suggestible states both chemical and self-willed, tried to live by. *Lud Heat* is an extraordinarily detailed and clear re-creation of the world seen during a freak-out. It seems to echo that key product of the 1950s, Barbara Jones' book on Follies: extravagant architecture is being used as a symbol of unreason, a solid external accretion of behavioural disorder. The tomb grass-strips the narrator mows include St Philip Howard, an English Martyr who was as a matter of fact the ancestor of several important folly-builders (including the brothers Thomas and Charles Howard, figuring as pioneers in Jones' work). We could mention Jeremy Reed's near-contemporary work *Saints and Psychotics*. The main sections deal with the Hawksmoor churches; parks work; a film of dissections by Stan Brakhage; an exhibition of sculpture by Brian Catling; St Dunstan, someone stumbling through turf and through a rotten coffin; sunstroke and Robert Louis Stevenson; a colleague's recollections of Ireland, problems with birds under the mower; a run (as pilgrimage) through East London. The sun imagery leads on to Egypt, via the Sun God Ra, and to a miscellany of Egyptian lore; the knowledge that the heliacal rising of Sirius marked the start of the Nile floods was the basis of priestly power. The eye of Ra leads on to 'the evidence of the eyes', autopsy, and so to the great director Stan Brakhage, who also made a film called 'Dog Star Man'. The dog star is Sirius, lord of the 'dog days', the worst heats of summer. Heat again. If you see autopsy as surgery on the dead, and connect church architecture with the imagination of the dead, you can see sunstroke as surgery on the living. Once you start on this method, it will take you a long way. I don't accept that the associations {Hawksmoor – Egypt / Ra – Brakhage / dog star} are there for anyone else, or that they were there for me when I lived in that part of London. The structure of the book is like a Sherlock Holmes story – with scenic shots of London, hints of sinister Asian rituals, lurid violence, layers of exact observation, clues by the dozen rearing up into a vast incomprehensible shape – which has been invaded by Doyle's belief in spiritualism. Sinclair's sentences are like the guitar solos of the time – they depart from foreseen lines to build layer upon layer of distortion and half-buried association, dragging the unknown into sound through unnaturally vivid detail. 'These quintessential forms operate on insect-time, fire at reptile blood-temperature: are very calm and poised to strike with scorpic venom. The eye is reptile also. It moves at speed around the frames of these parthenogenetic beings.'

The belief in the power of geometry accepts what ancient priests did with enclosing sacred space – you can argue that a shape which is not merely functional records a force which shaped it, and therefore makes that force visible. And so – that the universe is full of invisible forces. But the inspiration comes also from Sinclair's work in film – he had been something (maybe in script development? Or just producer's assistant?) for the brilliant horror director, Michael Reeve, who died in his early twenties. *Lud Heat* is in part the ruins of a huge unmade film – stable because it is a version of something already imagined in great detail, delirious in subject matter. A film has to be constructed in geometry – the map of camera shots, dictating what gets on screen, but also the disclosure of spatial information to the audience, which allows them to construct the place in which the characters move. Essentially, of course, this place does not really exist – and, in a horror film, it is filled with an invisible energy of anxiety. Like Hughes, Sinclair reaches the transcendental through horror – the last survival of the religious which was connected with popular art and not blocked by convention, by the fees due to the owners.

Lud Heat, as a work of pulp theology, asks for exegesis that could fill volumes. Unable to do this, let me mention that there is another writer on English mythology and the occult called Andrew Sinclair, and quote Brakhage, 'Architecture, then, is that which surrounds the living being and all such objectification as it has gathered – presents a womb, as it were, as well as a tomb of the mind's mathematics… externalizing numbers into space, numb thought's otherwise endless flights of fancy.'

Lost in colour, attuned to the invisible:
Hilary Llewellyn-Williams, *Hummadruz*
(2001, 162 pp.; urgency; cluster H)

This reprint edition combines the 1990 volume *The Tree Calendar* and the 1997 work *Book of Shadows*, which narrates scenes from the life of Giordano Bruno of Nola. Titles include 'Candlemas' 'Contradicting the Bishop' 'Hazel/*Coll*' 'Hunting the Wren' 'Feeding the Bat' 'In Aegypt'

'Heroic Frenzy'. There is a tradition, not older than the 1940s, which lists a tree for each month of the year and gives rise to a tree-calendar with Ash, Alder, Willow, etc. Trees are there all the year round, and it is difficult to see any connection between the trees and the months, but this fact allows arbitrary association and an exit from logic. Quite possibly the tree-names were genuinely arbitrary, just as the shapes of letters have no link to the sound they make (and surnames do not describe people); both calendar and alphabet are necessary. Experience is so miscellaneous that adding a name to any month is bound to capture some things that happened in that month. This labelling or canning is notably egocentric but is also close to the core activity of poets; time has to be captured in words and experiences have to be sharpened and made distinct from each other. The interest in trees is comparable to another poet interested in symbolism, Vittoria Vaughan.

A note on p.157 describes 'hummadruz' as "*bee-swarms in the earth*: this refers to the phenomenon ... of unknown origin, that is occasionally experienced on windless days, especially on hilltops or around ancient sites." An internet search reveals a possible etymology: "I wrote to Jenny once to ask her about my experiences and it was she that gave me the term hummadruz, which she said was thought to be a 'psychic training exercise' and had been known about since Victorian times. The term comes from 'hum' and 'drone' and 'buzz' all combined." Jenny is Jenny Randles, star UFO analyst and maestro of explaining the unknown, often against her audience's deepest wishes. The earliest reference to the word is in 1878, in a Manchester newspaper ("Here is a query for your readers. Is the term known?"). The sound is commonly related to the low frequency component of machines in mills or of vibrations in underground pipes. The poet's interest is more in a state of heightened expectancy and curiosity than in the external phenomenon of uncorrelated acoustic energy. The web also reveals a Turkish film called Hummadruz, and certainly the word sounds Near Eastern (something between hummus and nawroz, maybe).

The *bee-swarms* appear in one of the poems about Bruno and their drone or bumble is there related to the transmission of fine energies, which in the Neo-Platonist view of the cosmos was the principle whereby passive matter was given shape, emanating from ideas. The impossibility of correlating the sound to a source demonstrates the inadequacy of our senses to the processes going on around us: the cosmic process is dominated by invisible energies, for a Neo-Platonist.

In this system, sound plays a dominant role: space is not full of light but of sound, and shape is carried on messenger sounds of which our use of speech is merely an imitation.

The atmosphere is one of credulity. Silencing reason produces a quiet in which weaker impulses are unusually amplified and we can learn more about them: following the analogy with underground pipes, these delicate sounds can lead us to large scale phenomena, buried deep. Relaxation leads to intimacy, tranquillity, a chance to let the imagination flow freely and to see what it produces. The interest in symbolism, mythology and the occult is connected to a contemporary project, what might also be called New Age sensibility. The classic source on Bruno is Frances A. Yates. Of course the themes also connect with Kathleen Raine, who drew on the *Carmina Gadelica* and wrote poems about Bruno.

> Between here and the coast
> acres of sunflowers turn their polished heads:
> gold worshipping gold. Their hearts
>
> are rich oil. They thrust
> from cool nourishing darkness into light.
> ('Sun in Leo')

Where Raine is spooky, alien, and intense, Llewellyn is comforting, intimate, and tranquil. The ambience is like certain folk singers of the later sixties; the programme is one of cultural acquisition, as a function of affluence. While this is less of an imaginative stretch than actually projecting into the situation of Druid moon-watchers or 16th century heretics who got burnt in a public square, it does not make for lyrical peaks. While the writing is unusually clear, it also lacks drama. It seems to lack holes where tension could build up; it is like a brocaded quilt, warm and rich and saturated. Bright colours pick out rippling patterns.

As the Tree Calendar follows a preset pattern and corresponds to the months of a year, so (we are told) the 22 poems in *Book of Shadows* correspond to the 22 Trumps in a tarot pack. What this suggests to me is New Age jewellery of the kind you might buy in Camden Market: ornate, symbolically rich, assertive, but distinct both from symbols of a lived religion and from records of experience. Qualities like *affluent, domestic, acquisitive* are to the fore. Such objects accumulate symbolic loads because of their symmetry and highly defined pattern. Bruno was above all things seduced by analogy and symbolism, in fact he saw natural processes on the earth as a kind of symbolic re-enactment of archetypal processes elsewhere in the universe. The poem which recalls a saying of Bruno that when he was a child (in Campania) he thought there was nothing beyond Vesuvius is pointing to the limits of what we know and hinting at an immensity beyond. This is not only beautiful but points to an abiding condition of stillness and eagerness to know.

The poet connects the possessions called Book of Shadows of modern occultists to the 'shadows' of Bruno's late 16th-century cosmological works, *de umbris idearum* and so on. Gerald Gardner, inventor of modern witchcraft, had a book called the *Book of Shadows*. I think the suggested connection with Bruno is factually wrong.

The genii of a secret state: Paul Holman, *The Memory of the Drift* (2001, 19 pp.)

I reviewed this work in an essay named after Ernst Pfleumer, who found in the 1920s a way of depositing a layer of gold on the mouthpieces of cigarettes; a chance find which resonates, for me, with certain recent poetry: a thin film of something precious and oral, where painstaking technical changes open up startling futures.

>   This blur of angels
>   the trace
>   of a more brilliant
>   language. Some
>   diminish into cloud,
>   too rapid
>   [[birds' flicker
>   [   ]
>   find a common shape
>   in flower
>   star, Medusa's head:
>   their sign.

Sound is thinner than gold leaf. Holman's work is based on silence and tension, syllables surfacing fleetingly as traces of some vast psycho-acoustic energy. A note in the pamphlet, a continuous work in 26 parts, describes the process of composition: one, 'the text is drafted in a rapid improvised take'. Two, a syllabic pattern (template) is preset and rigidly adhered to, the text cut back to fit into it. "This is achieved through a long process of superimposition and erasure." One section was written over an erased poem. We are apparently gazing through a template (as a device of optical protection?) through which fragments of something much more massive are visible. The process reduces the text to nuclei which are lapidary and essential, glowing in the dark. The poet had difficulties, in a magazine, with non-isometric typefaces: i.e. where letters are different widths, so that "five letter spaces" do not genuinely equate to "the space of five letters (side by side)", and the matrix is not genuinely invariant in different typographies.

> Even to number them turned
> me stupid, docile
> enough to be a medium
> for their angelic
> discoveries.

The template is composed of cells of which some mandatorily delete the text written into them (shown by deletion marks, thus [ ]). An expanding spiral of white cycles through the second part of the book, engulfing the sonorous black, producing silence by a simple inversion.

A statement that the poet read during a reading at the National Poetry Centre said in part, "*The Memory of the Drift* is a serial work which I planned as a homage to, and critique of, the now closed history of modernism. The argument of the poem is manifested in its structure; it might stand as a lapidary text if the process of composition itself had not ravaged the transmission of content. The book falls into three broad sections: the first is concerned with the high matter of poetry, the second is a daybook, the last a meditation upon primitive democracy drawn from Montesquieu, Rousseau, and Engels."

Titles include 'the genii of a secret state' 'stargazer' 'maki nomiya' 'sexee bunnee' 'skrimsl'. I note that *skrimsl* is an Icelandic monster, chronicled in *Fortean Times*, possibly a sort of reptile living in lakes. Holman is apparently someone who studies cryptozoology while listening to techno music. (Or listens to zoo music while studying crypto-technology?) Poem xiii, 'skrimsl', also refers to Pizzicato Five

(Japanese pop band), and Josef Albers (painter and Bauhaus teacher). The reference to "Ben and Esther" is not to a doo-wop group from Stamford Hill but to two stars of the punk-adornoite scene and sworn enemies of the Romanovs. The title "genii of the secret state" includes a coded phrase, familiar to those who read *Lobster* magazine and related publications, referring to the intelligence services and their ability to make policies without parliamentary control. "Recovered memories" of various events in disobedient colonies, or deniable assassinations, may have influenced his interest in erasures.

I perceive this work as occultist because so much of the text refers to Neoplatonist and magical practices. The interest in the physical nature of writing reminds me of Neoplatonist spells, where it is important to make the ink from special ingredients. The words seem to be partly involuntary – like the inscribed spinning-tops of Neoplatonists, which produced texts outside human control.

I find it hard to define the appeal of this poetry – perfectly distinctive and pared down to the bone as it is. I came round to it because individual phrases haunted me, like phrases of music, over months. The conduct of the text throughout has a singularity and decisiveness, which both blasts it into a new and unexplored cognitive space, and locks it inside it. It is the fate of new poets to be singular before being understood. Holman poems are much more like other Holman poems than like anything else. I find these poems as compelling as certain musical phrases that drift in from no discernible source and which haunt the memory. They seem like fragments of another universe, willing to erase the contents of consciousness and lay it open to ecstatic transformations.

Naturalist Poets

Nature as a world of biological forms too diverse to comprehend is a natural metaphor for the fulfilment of our desires, a paradisiac world where variety and beauty never run out. Any desirable world is going to resemble this state as much as it can. Naturalists have a direct access to writing great poetry which less informed people do not. This endlessly serial variety offers a path away from the self – and this section lets us focus on subject matter rather than the personality of the poet.

Eleven Poems on the Frangipani:
Sacheverell Sitwell, *Tropicalia* (1972, 57 pp.)

Titles include 'Eleven Poems on the Frangipani' 'Tzintzuntzin', 'Ti-Fai-Fai (papiers découpés de Tahiti)', and 'A Charivari of Parrots'. This has a strong appeal as a collector's item because Sitwell (1897-1988) was a strange survival from another era: his last volume containing new work had come out in 1936 (as the jacket reminds us). He had once been part of native English modernism: appearing in the style-founding *Wheels* anthologies when he was still a schoolboy. We gather (from accounts in print by various of his friends) that he stopped publishing poetry because he was pained by the hostility of certain critics. We believe he went on writing poems, for distribution among his friends. This is classically eccentric behaviour – he represents an era of personal aesthetic impulses which was incompatible with the era of the art expert, of severe bourgeois knowledge, of stylistic norms enforced by didactic reprisal. (There was a whole issue of *Poetry Review* in 1968, given over to his poems – breaking the silence.) His style shows close resemblances to that of D.H. Lawrence (in poetry) – free verse, expansive in length, wandering through an inexhaustible landscape full of plants and animals. It is inexhaustible because the brain wants this flow of forms to continue, rather than because the world really is so diverse. Why do we want to catch the moments of diversity, rather than those of repetition? This is a fundamental question. His poetry is based, in design, on extravagant Victorian works of natural history, with hundreds of colour plates, not yet the work of photographers, illustrating the diversity of the world uncovered by naturalists and explorers. Any volume of modern poetry is at one level a series of arresting images – and the quality of the work depends on the constant flow of images and on their optic appeal. This flow is quite unimpacted by projection or by religious guilt-scenarios. Art opens an eye, and stops when that eye closes. The tranquillity with which Sitwell stages his exotica – flowers, birds, buildings, an entire costumed cultic society in Tahiti– produces a sensation of endless benevolent time. It offers the loss of the personality, to be reconstructed as simple wishes – amply fulfilled. Nothing here is a reflection of his personality – rather his serene gaze, which provides the integrity of everything, is a reflection of the intact and extended nature of the visible world. We have returned now to the world without didactic intent. Poetry does not need to make itself attractive by a vortex of status struggles superimposed onto its gigantic primary flows of integral organic forms. The visible world is in fact quite untouched by our personal conflicts. At the simplest level, a poet collects arresting images in order to record them in words.

The marginalisation of Sacheverell (and of his sister Edith) from the canonised version of modernism relies on a selective re-editing of what the style of 1910 to 1930, or just of the 1920s, really was. Scholars tended to pass over the ephemeral arts – Poiret's clothes, Diaghilev's ballets – because they were hard to reconstruct. Sitwell is close to the world of forms suggested by Bakst and Benois, where exoticism and endlessness, released from everyday restrictions, were an essential part of the appeal. We are assured that modernism was earnest, puritanical, and obsessed by learning – in the image of the academics who reconstructed it.

Like so many of the poets I am describing, he has a vision of beauty outside the poem, a stylized world where ordinary preoccupations vanish and a state of flow exists. Sitwell's world of flowers and rituals is less capricious and more evident than the others. Where beauty is made so plain, are we going to go to the effort of proving it wrong?

Bird Life of Waziristan: Colin Simms,
In Afghanistan: poems 1986-94 (2nd edition, 2001, with 30 pieces not in the 1995 edition; 46 pp.; tnbp3, cluster C)

The author, a naturalist, visited Afghanistan regularly to "look at thrushes and a mysterious 'brown falcon'": 'Distances ripen up, dizzy altitude. White peaks and silver edges dazzle all the while at which seems as distilled off glaciers as the rock dust on dry gorge, ridge wisp. Kiosk and minaret alike all also appearing friable as cake in the mirage or haze dazing torrents and waving willows and tilting strata and stirring stars.' (Kiosk, 'a summer pavilion or pleasure-house', Persian word.) Themes are birds, geology and land formations, local customs, and the war against the Russians. Scientists on field trips are always rushed, and the poems are the result of moments where cognitive fields came into collision: written at great speed in field notebooks, more or less on the spot, recording momentary events, and retaining the limiting conditions of precise witness. Simms builds everything on an idea – confirmed by what neuroscience I can glean from *New Scientist* – that conscious reactions are slower than instant, less mediated, non-verbal reactions, and overlay them with a narrative or fabulation. Close observation of transient events, along with a painstaking approach which exposes the overlay, teaches someone this gap. So, along with a much finer sense of time, Simms' founding framework is biogeography, which relates the behaviour of creatures to the environment around them. This draws the gaze out to very large spatial extents. Biogeography affects behaviour – of birds and men – through the mediation of cognitive models: the Simms poem describes the behaviour within a reproduced context which sets out the cognitive model. The search for precision produces an extraordinary linguistic creativity. The tracks of Russian armoured personnel-carriers (APCs) are compared to radulas, the hard 'tongues' of snails which scrape (*radere*) the rock or soil gathering nutrients. He calls the clans of Afghanistan *grains*, a technical term from the dialect of the Borders, where also it meant a kindred, an association of people by their surname and for functions of violence (where the law is weak and other grains will practice violence upon you).

'Atrak Arcs, Oxus' describes the forming of an (inland) crescent sand dune, or barchan, (bahcahn in Simms' spelling) by wind, in the Kara Qum (Black Sand) desert. In an astonishing display of virtuosity, Simms mimics the omnidirectional swirling of fine particles of sand in words, 'stinging salt crystals squeaking quarts, silica/ each grain surging, signing, ellipsing, arcing/ not finished ever, the snaking crest tumbles over ripple'. A complex geophysical process is rendered in photographic detail. The sand grains are small enough to make energy flux in the air visible: the transition from sunlight to structure is visible here. The dunes are an 'energy store'. The poem ends with a sighting of a lone fox.

In 'Mirrors beyond Mirranshah' we see swallows, and the creases of Waziristan (in north-east Afghanistan), mountains described as 'seamed scissored stiff unscanned'. They are serrated, like gears; 50 years before it (the swallow) came there, a ratel (honey badger) or bear saw a mirage (a reflection, hence the mirrors in the title). The place has autonomy because you can't get into it in winter:

> Karakorum seven hundred miles impervious through Hindu Kush
> in exclutch eggbox hachuring
> extended life sentence and oviparous pension
> Pamirs noose loosen best gearboxes
> tighten and tire suspension
> coil the births of creations the snake is viviparous

Even war is partial, but the arrival of Russians from outside invites a total response. The Hindu Kush range is impassable, and the Pamirs destroy gearboxes. They are like eggboxes because you can hear the linings crunch. In those mountains, there are (viviparous) snakes, who give birth to live young. The "oviparous pension" is what you call a "nest egg". Hachuring is a way of marking an area (of mountains?) on a map but also means imposing fine scratches – like mechanical wear and tear.

'United Service Instruments Ltd.' describes an ancient optical instrument, better in a haze than technical ones, as an Afghan agrees, who is using it to spot tiny traces, for example of a spetsnaz (Soviet special forces). Another talks about rattlesnakes, having been trained in Oregon. The device keeps them on their mettle because of its simplicity.

Simms' poetry affects consciousness because of its precision on a small scale and its comprehension of geographical space on a large scale. He has a thoroughly mimetic approach – we fall into a mimetic abyss, drawn by the vertigo of gazing into the depths of the visible world, without defensive blocks and favours. The poetry has an amazing receptivity to diverse and fleeting sense data; and is exhilarating for that reason. He looks into the flow of sand and surrenders to it, imitating the insanely rapid succession of details in high-speed action. He is travelling to the haunts of the incomprehensible to make one-take captures of the miraculous, that have the flawed quality of Marconi's first radio broadcast.

The delicate organs of plants: Elisabeth Bletsoe, *Landscape from a Dream: Selected Works 1989-98* (Internet only, at http://www.dhfurniss.eurobell.co.uk/ebcontents.htm) (and 1994 tape from Direction Poetry) (cluster H)

This Internet release is a 'room' within a virtual building, The Tower. The set consists of 7 poems: 'I was dead... (reconstructed coffin text)', 'Landscape from a Dream' 'Maiden Castle', 'Cross-in-hand', 'Rainbarrow', 'Azrael', 'Pharmacopoeia'. The aesthetic is Jungian, and Bletsoe (b.1960) can be compared with Raine, Redgrove, or Lowenstein. The poet started with a writing class in the late '80s, where the project was performance + landscape, so words for utterance which also described a larger space, to be imagined. The poems about the Dorset landscape, on show here, develop out of descriptions of Cardiff in early work (*The Regardians*), with performance as the crucible, spoken through deified figures, superhuman projections.

I think it was the Rolling Stones' 'Parachute Woman' which introduced me to the possibilities of eroticised landscape: "I break big in New Orleans, overspill Carolin'". The song conjured up images of levees being swept away, indolently, by pent-up waters; of warm torrents washing over broad plains; of the horizon vanishing as consciousness gave way. Throughout these poems, the level of sexuality is deafening and thrilling. An erotic charge is flooding the reaches of topographical documentary, with awesomely dense data points from real botany and real landscapes:

> The intricate hills a lament configuration. Lips of the downs I balance on, the calx escarpment; unlocking the puzzle below in reticulate fields, symbols to work by, a vibratory blue. Bata's valley. Greensand & clay. The clunch tower breeding expanded atolls of white coral. Farms scratched up from chalk. A negative beauty in the straightness of a Roman road that rules itself out; puritanism scored on fields of wheat. Verges bleached to blinding. The scent of coumarin from trod grass (sweet vernal, false oat and fog), fills my head with a mess of leys and leptons, plasma currents and turf giants. (...)
>
> Evershott: 'the place of wild boars'; Frome-source. Silvergleam bark of ash lightening its shadow. St Osmund's gargoyles

swallowed by their own mouths; green men vomit leaves behind their hands. The four Tetramorphs, visited by elderflower succubi, give way to creeping necrosis. Swallows shuttle mandorlas of sound, dreamnets diverting my prayers for a softening, a break in fixation. Waiting defines me. Also a deliberate turning away before the goal is reached. Reinventing myself. Flowering myself inside out. A hedge of floating calices; bride-wort & wound-wort. Broccoli in my soup and from the open mouth of The Acorn flow songs on the forbidden colours of love.

(from 'Cross-in-hand')

'Cross-in-hand' is a monologue put into the mouth of Tess Durbeyfield, in a Hardy novel set in Dorset, where Bletsoe comes from. It is one of three long poems spoken by, or for, Hardy heroines, in this set. ('Cross-in-hand' is a headless stone cross high up on bleak Batcombe Down.) Tess is walking between two places in Dorset, thinking of the fields she works in, of the broader landscape around, and of her relations with men. The great strength is less the richness of detail than the emotional continuity of line. The rational and relativising elaboration of the novels has been razed to reveal an aria, a passionate monologue of a heroine living in a world of pure emotion. Suffering is apparently the key to opera, and the scenarios are suffering heroines, victims of men. What is the concept of the suffusing detail about plants and soil conditions? Place is evoked in immersing detail, to give the experiential density of a novel. But more than that, I think a line from an old song, "Let no man steal your thyme", is a key. "Come all you fair and tender girls, that flourish in your prime". To flourish is to bloom like a flower. Thyme is "time" when sung: the song means both "don't let him take your love" and "don't let him take his love away", simultaneously, and this is also true of the monologues in this set. The poems do not just offer complexity but a figure of complexity. A metaphor for sensation. The style is open to folk symbolism, where very commonly flowering plants are used as symbols of female emotions. The profusion of small plants is used as a metaphor for rich, allover, and unpredictable sensations; they symbolise the ways in which the heroine can be hurt. The development implies a converse of this ripple of small sensitive surfaces, in sum a male figure causing pain.

The title poem has the subscription 'Dorset coast from Swanage to Kimmeridge', and is about a landscape – although perceived in erotic terms. (It is 'after' a surrealist painting by Paul Nash, with the same title.) The edges of sea and shore are written as the sensory envelope of a body, lapped in sensual waves and opening to release itself. At around the time Nash was painting, Lawrence was writing (in *Apocalypse*) about the dead cosmos of the last 2,000 years and the archaic living cosmos, seething with energies pouring down from the sun onto our bodies. The sun produces us in the same way that we produce dreams.

The languorous, supersensitive, psychic side of Gothic is evoked, a rich subjective world uttering itself through legends, spirits, children's games, spells, church ornaments, hermits, glowering beasts, and ancient country places. The central idea is possession; of heroines, and of landscapes. The body image of the heroine is projected everywhere, as the precondition of knowledge. This law of projection derives from popular art; however, it is limited in range: and the Gothic style has shifted between pop and high culture for two centuries. The gigantic, boundless, body lashes around as if in a high wind, to be held down by precise observations; we hear also 'A clot of mica, quartz, and calcite, whelk chips, arteries, alveoli of green-mauve weeds. A mussel, hair glued to a half inch core of blackwrack. (…) Brown strapped laminaria, fruiting bodies of fucous, volatile with oils, mineral traces, and mucilage. My mouth tasting salt and Helena Rubinstein's *Rose indienne*.' ('Low Season, Whitby', from the tape only) Here, exceptionally, the "I" is Elisabeth Bletsoe rather than a heroine. Precision in dealing with the outside world signals that precision in dealing with the inside world is invited; the world is full of other people's feelings, building constructions as morphologically ornate as a beach full of biotica. Attentiveness, lit by poetic language, also shows us a rich world of transient objects, displacing aged and glowering ones; her exquisite alertness to Nature is an opening to our subjective experience.

'Tetramorph' is a compound figure of the four evangelists, who are associated with the role of guarding the four corners of the bed as we sleep; in a reprise of four angel figures seen at the corners of Egyptian sarcophagi. These also had coffin texts (instructions for the afterlife) painted on them – a skin turning into flourishes of language. The coffin text of Bletsoe's vastly ambitious recreation of the soul's journey after death reminds us of Vittoria Vaughan's mummies. Vaughan refers to a 'blossoming tholus' and Bletsoe to a 'tholal web' (from the word for the beehive roof of archaic Greek shrines).

Afterword. The poet has patiently explained that *Rose indienne* is a lipstick; and that the 'tholal web' appeared in an episode of *Star Trek*. The *lament configuration* describes a puzzle in a horror novel.

The Dorset poems are now available in a book from Shearsman, *Landscape from a Dream*, and the webpages are no longer available.

Morphometrics:
Helen Macdonald, *Shaler's Fish* (2001, 56 pp., cluster C)

This piece is longer than the others, because Macdonald is clearly the most significant poet of her generation; and because it took me seven years to work out how to say anything about her poetry, and I am disinclined to shut up now.

Helen seems to regard period-mentalities as a puzzle, perhaps because of a dissociated and detached nature which finds the unconscious rules of the period she lives in difficult to follow. "[T]he beautiful insulatory/ qualities of the English Channel" likewise seems to problematise Englishness, seen as a package on offer rather than as "second nature". We could even link this to the linnet in the experiment: we are thrown at birth into a family which equips us with a behaviour set whose arbitrariness we can see but not quite reach. Perhaps this fleet-footed recession explains why the Macdonald poem, full of fascinating objects, is uninvolving, free of silent commands to feel and to identify?

Shaler's Fish has an prefatory quote from one Nathaniel Shaler about being given a fish and told to study it without any external help, presumably as a training in unaided (uncorrupted?) observation. Helen represented tomorrow for certain poets whose sense of their own idealism involved an investment, perhaps even a claim to property, over the pristine future. Such manœuvres do not give a reliable account of poetry dedicated to the transient present, to philosophical curiosity, and to a sense of surprise (and even bewilderment). The overall patterns made by the parts of the poem (which may on their own be as recognizable as a china jug, a swatch of fabric, and a bird) are distinctive and haunting. There is, sometimes, an interest in ornithology, and in the way an experience occurs simultaneously in several sensory modes. The excision of familiar teleologies, poetic or personal, has been fairly thorough. The appetite organising the poems, selecting, matching, and sharpening patterns, is of startling force.

'Hitman.doc' appears to be about a spy and assassin, the I-figure: "St Tropez/ hitman reads Merleau Ponty disassembling/ the .22 conceit." It is also named after a file type in the most popular word processing package. This is a cool assassin, with "musical thoughts on a heart/shot for the afternoon". Soft target (l.8) is one without armour, generally human, vulnerable to small arms fire. The tense and danger-defined tenor of most spy fiction allows us to register in contrast what is specific to these poems: the sense of ease, consciousness acting as a filter against banal preoccupations and their repetitive compulsions. In reality, most spy work is profoundly boring. The first lines define the tenor of the poem:

> There is no bravery involved in recognition
> existentialisms final take on globalising statements/ communism
> your perfect *petit* object/ control/ decision/ concert honest derision

It draws us into world politics, the designs of the leaders of the "Western alliance", and implicitly the acts of adjustment which get other ideas off camera, and the "mechanics" who take care of the adjustments: where "clandestine violence and economic rationality are intertwined" (Kees van Pijl), but pitches itself at the level of the individual consciousness, where choices are made and where paradoxes decline resolution. The reference to "*Lobster* 27-36 on the table" is probably about the Hull-based magazine of analysis of the Intelligence Services, rather than an academic periodical about bottom-feeders. I have *Lobster* 36 on my table. (The file format may be a mutation of title-types like 'The Arkadin Dossier' or 'The X-files'.) *Lobster* has interests in parapolitics, the secret state, transnationalised repression, psywar, disinformation, *who struck John*, "deep politics", the "tables" where business interests, bankers, officials, and the Intelligence services meet to formulate foreign policy. It has a link with the Dutch Marxist group (van Pijl, Henk Overbeek etc.) busy interpreting contemporary history by chronicling the contacts between business interests, academics, and government; an update of the old "fractions of capital" analysis, for which capitalism is not a monolithic bloc but an arena where competing interests win or lose the competition. Carroll Quigley wrote the history of Anglo-American foreign policy up to 1966, not as a vague "conspiracy theory" but as a connected story, a history of the policy-making elite. In this world,

Quigley and Peter Dale Scott are the heavyweights, the authorities on a new and exotic interpretation of history. In a poetry world abrim with unemployed ideas, who could not be interested in how ideas get turned into practical policy?

"[T]he lithe muse on extremely sharp pure speed" clarifies the word *sulphate* a few lines later. It helps the concentration at marginal moments and is a useful nutrient in paranoid projections. Whereas morphometrics turns anatomical form into information, "deep politics" studies the economy of political information. One makes manipulation possible, the other makes it visible.

If we turn back to the poem with this scheme in mind (about a Hitman, thoughts on parapolitics, details of preparation for a "job"), feelings of alarm and perplexity assail us. For, most of it is nothing to do with that. Oh. Maybe we can turn this "oh shit" feeling into an "aha!" sensation by theorising that the faithful prose data collector is just one agent in a mind which works by splitting itself, constantly, into several virtual minds, agents; that the efficiency of the rational agent is overdeveloped in people doing brain-work, and that the primary quality of poetry is to refresh the brain by rebalancing it; and that the poem is constructed in multiple planes, like a picture where there are multiple actions occurring at different distances from the observer; and that perhaps we have now seen its structure. My impression is that it is unified; that details have been broken down to a level normally unconscious to make fresh perception possible (while delaying recognition); that the order in which details happen is not essential (certainly not following a time sequence); that great care has been taken to make it beautiful and not didactic, and that indeterminacy of categorisation may correlate with a political opposition to instrumentalism; that questioning (at the conceptual level) is matched with finding (at the level of sensory detail, of which there is a great deal). This may prove useful in assessing other poems. I would also say that the poem is uncontentious; although it does not voice the slogans about unaccountability, media manipulation, etc., such ideas are part of the image complex invoked by the word "globalising". Meanwhile, the inexplicit nature of the details offered asks for curiosity and conjecture – the primal acts of the *Lobster* reader (if not of the lobster).

The second most visible plane is the question of the influence of the weather and of visual stimuli on well-being. This is "clued" by a reference to Merleau-Ponty, and we are entitled (at the risk of ignoring the post-1985 term "globalisation" and the magazine issues from the late '90s) to jump on from this philosopher to a milieu of French political violence, variously with the Resistance, the *épuration*, the OAS, or the security services taking out the OAS, or even the monarchists who killed Admiral Darlan. We think of *Le petit soldat*, perhaps Godard's best film; of OAS killers reading Sorel and philosophising interminably. The point of taking a stand was to live in the present – which brings up the contents of the present moment, the influence of objects, the air, etc. "Globalising" means generalising, in this context, as in *global statements*. (As if language were a sphere in which truth is a series of holes?) The imposition of will brings up the question of what is truly desirable, which is perhaps why we have a discussion of biophilia, EO Wilson's theory that our "good place" is the realisation of a Palaeolithic landscape which we recognise because it is "imprinted" on our unconscious; why *the fascination is less with cities*. I relax and feel satisfied, but am I justified? The degree of correlation between these themes I have named (self-awareness, assassination, parapolitics, the nature of sensation, biophilia) is not high. Either I have missed the binding theme of 'Hitman.doc' (perhaps it's really about lobsters?), or the obliqueness of the plane junctures is what gives the three-dimensional effect. In defining why the poem is so attractive, we realise that there is an overall feel that emerges from the decisions about phrase and line juncture, that it is like the camera-pen (*caméra-stylo*) which Alexandre Astruc posited as personal style in film, and that these unconscious choices also frame consciousness (and give it its quality?), but we want to avoid the phrase "inherent rightness" and its relations. Actually it seems that each separate line break is the product of a risk, a difficult balancing between unstable masses. Writing 50 brilliant lines in a poem is not "inherently" different from writing 50 lines of which one is brilliant. To shift our gaze for a moment, there are poets who practice inconsequentiality and bore us to death and poets who focus relentlessly on one object while reciting soundbites from Heidegger and bore us to death. The elements of Macdonald's style – the avoidance of "functional" awareness, the use of simultaneity, the jumps between disparate ideas, the staging of complex fields of intellectual enquiry inviting long-term attention, the reliance on personal consciousness, the preference for conjecture over stabilised facts – are available to other poets. Other poets are sensitive to nostalgia, to the odd textures of textiles or clouds. Only… we have this impression of overall perfection because she can play the music all the way through, while others give renditions full of accidents, repetitions, and drop-outs.

There may be a link between Astruc and the author of *The phenomenology of perception*, Merleau-Ponty. "What do you think of the structure of daily life?" "Maybe we can save it in post-processing."

There may be a link between the use of firearms ("assembling a 22") and observing weather conditions: *at the denser edge of the room*. The bullet is influenced by the medium it flies through. The point about long-distance shooting is that it achieves distantiation, one of the qualities of true art; philosophy becomes possible when you eliminate those messy interactions between object and subject. If you want to kill someone at a thousand yards, you have to be aware of things like moisture in the air, wind speed, tricks of the light. There is a convergence between shooting and photography, as applied optics. Accuracy of aim is also a matter of the internal consistency of the marksman: an unsteady pulse makes the barrel wobble, while inability to achieve perfect calm at the moment of firing may be a sign of emotional dividedness. The geometry of a perfect shot is a Pythagorean one, involving diet and spiritual integrity. The feedback between the self and the physical world is what phenomenology studied (or pretended to). The long throw allows us to detect very fine oscillations of the rifle, allowing a breakthrough into the fine timescale – a good place to look for the personality. Is this why the hitman is talking about the weather? Probably not.

The feedback loop between perception and muscular response action takes place in time, which is why we can detect flaws in the loop (slight oscillations of a barrel that is supposed to be steady). All psychological activity is rhythmic and takes place in the time dimension; it is behaviour in time (responses, updates to internal models, persistence of impulses) which qualifies individual minds. A poem is an externalisation of a neurological state, and presumably we are reading the various loops in the poem as indices of the brain which produced it. Attention is a voluntary thing; we are interested if the poet seems interested. This is why editing a poem to make it faster is so dodgy: if the poet signals lack of engagement with a topic, the reader will take him at his word, decide the topic was boring, and lose interest. Authenticity, quite probably, is a matter of internal relationships within the poem; if these tiny and complex numerical ratios give off the wrong sound, it's no good writing poems that move slowly (to signal "commitment"), or uttering banal benignities in a venerable voice.

The poet remarked at a reading that 'Hitman.doc' was inspired by watching films like 'Grosse Point Blank' and disliking the indulgent view of assassins which they offered. It took me years to work out how to write about these poems, and now trying to capture why I like them is too much.

blue with the reflected coldness / of strangeness :
The Meta-periphery, or Arctic Poems

After choosing the books, I found that several of them share a theme, the Arctic. Is this the kind of oddity which pleases a collector mentality? Or is there some myth drawing poets towards this quarter of the globe? If the Atlantic is the periphery of Britain, shaping the climate of the outer regions of the island, the Arctic, even further out, can be seen as the 'meta-periphery'. Perhaps outer space, as a theme of psychedelic music, is the successor to the Northern ocean – equally boundless, sustaining weightless drift, occupying the same tile of symbolic space. Arrangement by theme pulls us right away from style and back to subject matter. The North is a matter of fundamental interest – of course it is only brilliant writers who can capture the alien and make it come over in words.

Rubbing the grid off the map:
J. F. Hendry, *Marimarusa* (1978, 40 pp. CC, cluster D)

In interviews, Hendry gave two different dates for the composition of *Marimarusa*, though both are in the 1940s, and when he was living in Vienna. He published no books of poetry between 1943 and 1978. Most of the book is the title poem (subtitled 'A Polar Sonata'), in 15 sections and about 400 lines long. An epigraph comes from Lao Tse, the Daoist. Marimarusa (actually Morimarusa) is the name given by the Classical poet Philemon to the dead sea found far to the north of Britain; a preface explains that there 'despite the cold, flowers in profusion bloomed, with tropical fruits, and the secret of eternity and youth was to be found.' The landscape is allegorical:

> Over the empty schools of ocean and steppe
> Sightless blizzards stumble through the dark.
> Fountains of deception storm the senses.
>
> We are thrown back on the springs behind the seasons.
> There is no escape from the dream under the ice.

> We have tried to arrange the patterns of time
> Into a snare to capture the timeless.

Hendry invented the fruits, or added them from a myth, about the Hyperboreans. The name is interpreted as the Celtic word for dead sea (words related to the Welsh words *mor, marw*). It is not as simple as a frozen sea; it has been interpreted as a temperature barrier caused by currents, at high latitudes, which means that a ship is gripped and cannot move forward. Pytheas possibly saw this as a mixture of sea, fog, and ice: the *sunkrima* where the identity of substances breaks down. It is reasonable to take this poem as the most fully developed expression of the Apocalyptic school. In an interview from 1977 (Ryan), Hendry says he was experiencing nothingness: 'a vacuum or it can be called an experience of infinity or the abyss', and that *Marimarusa* was an attempt to describe that experience. In Vienna under the multinational control commission 'The snow was on the ground everywhere; it was a real Arctic experience living in a city which was bombed flat, and in which the people were in a state of semi-starvation.' In the poem, referential systems of knowledge break down: 'The old maps and scales were no use'. Having read Victor Turner, we can link this to myths of liminality, where oppositions are dissolved. This is presumably the explanation for the tense-system of Hendry's verse, where the elimination of precise references to transient places and moments is taken as the poetic. Indeterminacy is not simply vagueness, but the realisation of a pre-existing and shared schema. 'I suddenly realised that this nothingness... could quite easily be interpreted in theological terms as an experience of freedom.' The term 'sonata' (in the subtitle) points to music – not referring to anything outside itself, but controlled by an internal reference system. The ejection of this internal state onto the outside world and geography is a version of the Apocalyptic concern with the individual as the site of all experience. This dissolution into subjectivity, which is yet existential rather than fantasy, is akin to the abstract expressionist painting which was developing in the 1940s. Specifically, it is close to biomorphic painting; he looks in the water and sees 'liquid stars and milk', which are the birth of ice-floes becoming 'the mystery of the living cell'. This sea is not the literal, rather sterile, northern ocean, but somewhere which by virtue of its primal quality also sees the origins of life: it is what lies before everything, and consequently sees the origin of form. It is the fluid where shapes are born. Hendry also sees it as the place where time stops flowing: 'features of time snowbound in the clock-face freeze' (and on p.25 we plunge through the Tertiary era). This somewhat handicaps the development of the poem: it is an all-over condition, a state of mind. But it has a compellingly attractive and suggestive quality: it is a shimmering plane, where everything is about to happen.

Hendry succeeded in building a mythical space and did not proceed to build new things to populate it with. This poem exhausts itself by creating the picture of the incomplete, boundless, and potential – not just that the ocean is slipping and wiping itself out all the time, but that it reflects another reality, as great as an ocean but more abstract, where too every stroke is an effacement.

My personal relationship to this poem leads back through a project of recapturing the 1940s. When I was starting out, around 1973, the New Romantics were the "out group" of the dominant Movement apparatchiks, whom I detested. Naturally I thought that I might belong to this out-group. The texts had never been reprinted since the 1940s and were unobtainable at that time. My interest in Berry and Barker comes from this period. When I read James Keery's essay on the Apocalyptic roots of Prynne, in around 1999, it sent me rushing off in a new direction.

Graham also wrote a long poem based on imagery of the Northern ice. The other poems in *Marimarusa* are similar in style (and may also come from the 1940s).

Glass for talking in tongues:
Francis Berry, *Ghosts of Greenland* (1966, 84 pp.)

The main poem is a radio drama (there are only two voices) called 'Illnesses and Ghosts at the West Settlement'. Two dead characters from 10th century Greenland speak to Berry during his trip to Greenland. They are Erik, the discoverer, and his daughter-in-law Gudrid – to whom he is very strongly attracted. She went to the West Settlement with her husband, and acted as medium for a sorceress. Later, there is an outbreak of the plague in the settlement: many people die, including her husband. Helping a sick woman out into the yard one night, she sees the dead people walking towards them: one of them leers at the women, and spits something at them, but in general the dead are on their way to where they are going, and they do not pause to molest the living. In an epilogue, she returns to the East Settlement with the coffins, and argues with Erik, who marries her off to Thorfeinn Karlsefni, the discoverer of Vinland (in North America), where she spends three years. There may be a connection between this plot and G. Wilson Knight's eccentric theory in *The Golden Labyrinth*, where he says that the core of drama in general is an androgynous figure who has mediumistic gifts. In Berry's poem, these words come through the medium:

> Of the seal, of the floe, of the ice,
> About her eyes which spin glass,
> About a fish, about a tusk, about the walrus,
> About a special peg, or bone, which dances
> Both in and out, about the grass, about a flap
> A bleeding flap, or wound, and in it plunges,
>   Winces, prances,
> A thudding sire, a bull, a thing, a fire,
> About the bull, about the calf, about the eyes
>   Of spirits' wild glass.
> Seal, floe, ice, eyes, fish, tusk, bone, flap.

This is heavily non-integrated language: infantile, mimetic, repetitive, gripped by simple structures. It is an attempt to reproduce the spell-style of primitive religion – and it is interesting to compare it to Maggie O'Sullivan. It might seem simply to be the sound of weirdness, but in fact it predicts the action of the play; the peg is the 'male bone' of a walrus, which Gurdar was hammering into the wall as a peg when he fell ill – the first victim. It also relates to Gurdar's staring through the dresses of the women – and to the breaking of ice, to catch fish. The bull has to do with a better yield of calves. The witch is dressed in catskin and a necklace of glass beads. She successfully tells the future from Gudrid's spirit message.

The word 'Ward-Lock' appears three times. Having read Strömbäck's work on the subject in Swedish, I have to tell you that the 'ward' bit is a kind of female spirit, and a warlock is one who *closes in spirits* (gaining power over them).

The other long poem in the book is 'Punitive Expedition', which is a shed part of *Morant Bay*, his book-length poem on an uprising in Jamaica in 1839, which was put down with excessive brutality.

The switching of action from the polar ocean to the Caribbean is disconcerting, and gives us an insight into Berry's method: that of a weak centralising ego, throwing itself with amazing completeness into external scenes. The result is less events being filtered through a sensibility than a cataract of quite primary images, represented without filters, in mimetic fascination. Berry (1915-2006) also set large-scale poems in India and Australia. The project is not of self-realisation, but of shaping overwhelming excitations in order to gain some kind of stability. 'Outbreak' is an example of the amazing malleability of his language, its constant dissolution in order to imitate the processes it is supposed to describe. The theme seems to be an orgy in Iceland, a 'happening' – the key moment in history, someone says, is not the Incarnation, events in Olduvai Gorge, or the Russian revolution, but 'Now/ I, you; you, I'. This could be a theology of the 1960s. (Berry uses the same word, 'outbreak' for the brief revolt at Morant Bay.) G Wilson Knight is quoted on the jacket and one of the poems is for John Cowper Powys' 90th birthday – we do well to pay attention to these heretics, cranks, or mages. For, it is not so far from them to Berry, and from him to Hughes and Redgrove.

Berry, more than almost anyone else, stood for the possibilities of poetry as a high theme from which any tangible moment of history was a fall and a loss. No-one more than he has made the variation of landscape over the zones of the planet into the central theme. The exotic settings were wonderful gestures but gave him almost impossible technical difficulties. They induce a dizziness in which the mere subjects of his poems are hard to make out. They place demands on the imagination which threaten strain and exhaustion.

The encounter between this impossibilism and the discipline represented, separately, by saga prose and the confines of a radio play produced a poignant moment of perfect realisation.

Clusters moving out into space:
W. S. Graham, *Malcolm Mooney's Land*
(1970, 54 pp. CC; cluster D)

The setting of the book appears to be in a double geographical and virtual place; the name in 'land' reminds us of various placenames around the South Pole, and the poem is set in some kind of frozen continent; but it is also a philosophical place, one where the poet is isolated from outside stimuli and sees language in the pure form. The poet has gone a very long way from inhabited lands and may never be able to come back.

The mythology of the title poem has been carefully documented by Tony Lopez. He points out that the chain of Mooney's Bars had, in London in the 1940s, stocks of alcohol which other pubs didn't. Wartime shortages included beer and spirits; Mooney's were an Irish chain and could import their stock from neutral Ireland. Lopez also discusses how Graham's second book, *Seven Journeys*, in 1944, anticipates the themes of *Malcolm Mooney's Land*, and how he suppressed this work – as if he knew that he was going to need these themes.

The spectral emptiness of the ice-pack as a visual field sometimes causes the psychological problems which are induced by experiments in sensory deprivation. Such deprivation also induces hallucinations – rather accurate sealing off of the brain from external inputs, too tight for light (to quote George Clinton), is needed to assure these. This heightened activity of the brain with reduced stimuli is central to intellectual study, as we know it – a special skill which it takes children a long time to acquire. We suppose, too, that it took Europeans a long time to acquire it in history.

Within certain limits, *Land* tells you nothing. It inspires a sense of doubt, and asks you to do the rest of the work. The isolation of the Land is intimately related to the starving of the senses which is necessary to switch on the life of the free intellect. Graham's cerebral style was virtually impossible in British poetry in the 1940s – but was possible for philosophers. The closest person to his way of thinking is Wittgenstein – whom he may never have read. The merit of the poem is not what it says, but the vacuum it creates, which forces us to build shapes and hypotheses to fill it. The energy we expend doing this turns our brains on – it's like running up a mountain. This poetry is absolutely no use unless you are fresh and strong enough to make this effort – which may not be the reason why we are reading a book. Unfortunately, it is hard to make mental breakthroughs with the kind of poetry which supplies you with finished information all the time. The brain's ability to conjecture is a wonder of nature. Although the title poem is only part of the book, the whole book seems to move in the same linguistic world. Other titles are 'The Constructed Space' 'The Thermal Stair' 'Clusters Travelling Out' 'The Dark Dialogues' 'Wynter and the Grammarsow'. Bryan Wynter was a painter who lived near Graham in Cornwall.

Sociologically, the rapid extension of higher education, with its emphasis on solitary reading as a means to knowledge, has made high literacy a socially admired quality, and has produced a whole stratum of people capable of reading Graham. In poetry, the sector linked to higher education generally feels close to him. The inhabited world has drifted up to his ice-pack, so to speak. Graham is interesting because he was self-educated, and forged into the polar waters without much contact with educated people. He invented it for himself.

Graham had been silent since *The Nightfishing* (1955), a long poem about a fishing boat off the north of Scotland; already a journey into cold and isolation and the boundless, of which we can see a Polar trip as an extension. He had served an apprenticeship as a shipbuilder in Greenock, a town full at that time of construction docks; one of his poems speaks of the tightness which makes the riveted hull of a seagoing ship proof against the surrounding water; this seems to anticipate the pressure of cold and ice in *MML*. Sea fishing, in Scotland, is attended by certain taboos – things you aren't allowed to say at sea; and this too may be related to the nameless linguistic pressure of our poem.

My problem with the discourse which goes on about "what is language doing to us", language being a subject carrying out actions, etc., is that the verbal patterns in our heads apparently reflect significant relationships with other people which were partially carried out in words; the words in our heads are not just words, but symbols keyed to stored experiences – of which, other people and their actions and states of intentions were the most significant. Language doesn't come from nowhere. Making language autonomous sounds like something a highly functional autistic person would do – the kind of person Oliver Sacks tells us about. I can't persuade myself that investigating language in a completely asocial way is going to get you to the right answer. This correlates with the skin-flayingly low temperature of Graham's later poetry – the wavelengths which deal with self-presentation and interpersonal messages, with warmth, welcome, and sociability, seem to have been surgically removed. Isolation was his natural state.

I must say that the arrival of people who could think intensely in a social way, through argument and dialogue, was a huge relief. Without other people, what exactly are you going to think about? Haven't you abolished the subject of philosophy?

To be fair, we should put *Land* in the context of extremist works coming out around 1970, where the spectator was confronted with the blank future as if with an ultimatum – told to throw away the Past as if it was just packaging. Graham is the most palatable end of this genre – because he supplies a long, coherent, continuous text for the destabilised brain to latch onto.

The move into silence and reflection mirrors the move from oral literature to print. At which point – we are forced to admit that Graham liked to sing, and wrote fine ballads.

From the destroyer escort:
Alan Ross, *To whom it may concern* (1958, 83 pages)
(in Poems 1942-67)

Readers will probably find these poems in one of two other volumes: *The Open Sea* (which collects his naval poems) or *Poems 1942-67* (a collected). *To whom it may concern* is subtitled poems 1952-7. Ross (1922-2001) spent most of his life editing *The London Magazine*, which had a large circulation and was about culture in general. He was famous, which possibly distracted people from his poetry. The main work in this book is *JW51.B. A Convoy*, a poem about a convoy running military stores 'between the ice and German Norway' to Murmansk, to help the Russians survive. The first line is 'The sea, phlegm-coloured, bone-white, fuming.' Ross served on *Onslow*, a destroyer acting as escort to the ships which carried the stores. This convoy, at the end of December 1942 (a turning-point of the war in Stalingrad, North Africa, and Burma), was intercepted by a German surface fleet, which the escort saw off. The *Onslow* engages a battle-cruiser and takes direct hits; the forward magazine is flooded and a fire breaks out in the engine-room. But the icy water puts out the fire: "the elements' cancellation of each other", and the *Onslow* leaves the line of fire. The action took place in the Barents Sea, far within the Polar Circle. It is hard for an English person to see a ship without identifying with it. The ship is like the island, battered by the waves and trusting to the ocean. Life on board demands social cohesion and careful use of space – indeed, if someone is extravagant with space in a poem, it triggers all kinds of unconscious states of alarm. In the early 20th century, the naval poem was considered to be the English kind of poem *par excellence*. The reaction against this (with the wave of books around 1928 discrediting First World War patriotism) led to the obscuring of naval poems – even great ones like *JW51.B*. The major result, for me, of rummaging around in the 1950s was the realisation of how important Ross's poems were. We are likely to think about issues of masculinity here. Probably one effect of the war on culture was to push women off stage while the grand narratives of male heroism were running. We are likely to see recent poetry as deliberately privatised, in pursuit of the Christian pole of culture, rejecting the narratives of violence; and to see certain poems (by Hughes and Wevill, for example) as a recapture of warfare in symbolic and aestheticised terms. Debates about the duties of poetry distract us from a compelling and complete story, such as the one Ross tells, with its perfectly satisfying mixture of the immense (the polar ocean) and the exact and rapidly moving (the ballistics of ships moving in or out of enemy fire). A certain plainness of language is apparent; a lapidary quality which does not allow the ego of the poet, or individual feelings, to detract from the grandeur of the subject – which is little less than the boundless and freezing ocean as a figure of death and annihilation. Such a register has of course much in common with the language naval officers use for spoken and written communication. This is a great poem because it has a great subject. As with shipbuilding, the precision allows the large scale: the contrast between domestic anecdote poems and a voyage which goes all the way from Scapa Flow via Iceland to Murmansk on the Kola Peninsula, a movement on a planetary scale, makes the former seem ridiculous. Ross says in a preface 'Naval actions take shape in retrospect(.)' He is telling the story "through images ... suggesting any one person's imperfect and fragmentary experience of the whole." A certain understanding of the poetic identifies it with experiences outside Britain – a 'wider world'. In fact, Ross wrote travel books, and most of his poems are about travel – anticipating the exotic poems which are such a formula today. Titles in this volume include 'Nuraghi near Abbasanta', 'Cairo Perfumery', 'Venetian Games', 'Painted Racehorses', 'Winter Boats at Brighton'.

Ice Queen: Pauline Stainer,
The Ice-Pilot Speaks (1994, 72 pp. TNP, 60WP; cluster A)

This is marvellous poetry: step up for the on-ice spectacular of natural magic. It may offer more than a ritual staged by the visible world to amuse us: if you blow up this dazzle, you will see the Face of God. The staging is brittle, heraldic, recherché, Anglican, glassy, attentive to phantoms, constantly projecting hysterical processes into mineral form. It moves in the stylistic space between Kathleen Raine and Brian Catling. It is preoccupied with chill, bones, minerals, is properly mortified. It belongs written on vellum, clasped inside a nest of lead and black velvet. In the amazing title poem, 'The Ice-Pilot Speaks' –

> Up she rises –
> the sunken softwood ship
> with her dissolving
> cargo of sugar,
> fainter than
> the eight hooves
> of Sleipnir
> on the albumen print
> of the glacier.
>
> *Pittura metafisica*
> the mistletoe shafting
> Baldur; Borges
> feeling the pillar
> in his hotel room
> at Reykjavik,
> the Euclid of childhood
> flowing through him
> like serum.

(Albumen is a kind of size used on photographic prints in the 1850s, made from egg-whites, rather like pastry glaze; the glacier too is white, flows and sets, and takes the print of Odin's mythical horse. Baldur was shot with weapons-grade mistletoe by a blind god, Borges was blind.) As the sugar dissolves, the ship shoots to the surface – like Borges' childhood memories. 'Up she rises' is a line from a sea-shanty.

The headline images in the poem are: a shaman fitting the skin of a walrus as his drumhead; explorers (John Franklin's?) wearing 'black crêpe veils against blindness' (in an ice-field, therefore), while the astronomer is given 'four ounces of raven'; polar bears 'sweat through upturned paws' (unable to lose heat through their perfect pelts); the ship's figurehead is warm 'as though from the furnace'; Amundsen drives his dogs to death; a section about making love, a memory of cocoons at a silk farm; icebergs; a reflecting estuary; the *Titanic* on the seabed; speculations on theme music for the North (maybe an explosion on a North Sea oil-rig); mummified Inuit bodies near some hunters; a radio transmitter on the leg of an arctic tern; Eskimo ivory carvings; saint Brendan's ship with shamans in flight tangled in its rigging; Varèse's flute piece; plague; a sailor hallucinating the shape of his bride; a sunk ship being raised, with a cargo of dissolving sugar; a painting; the Edda tale of a cow licking at ice to thaw what will be Buri, ancestor of the Norse gods; poor visibility (on Brendan's voyage when he sees paradise?); the chess-game at the end of the world (also from the Edda). She likes to capture the moment when surfaces are violated and to throw away the context.

The proximate theme is a sexual act. I must admit it was only 8 years after first reading the poem that I clocked this. However – it's the only element which is close to England rather than to the North Pole; this closeness suggests that it is the centre and that everything else is just illustrations of this focal idea; it really doesn't fit as a tale of the Pole, itself. I take the phrase 'The Ice-Pilot Speaks' to be a purposive direction: all the poem is being spoken by someone who is called an ice-pilot. It is, then, someone who finds a way through pack-ice: thin leads of living water through mortal peril. I think we are authorised to see an analogy between this and the perils which beset love. Love will find a way. No better analogy offers itself within the universe of the poem. So logically we should explore this one. Imagine the human body as a boat. Even if the surrounding air is warm – it is much colder than the inside of the body. Even if society is peaceful – it is much colder than the heat of the lover for the loved one. So the oppositions hot: cold and moving: rigid (and safe: lost) are appropriate in the context of love – and as invariants translated across, and outwards, into the context of Polar exploration. At the end of the poem, we hear 'So what made our love-making/ the palimpsest/ for all successive acts' – perhaps a very clear indication that all the images fleeting by are projected onto one stable, effaced, ground. It has taken 250 lines to get this far – by any account the poem is mysterious and elliptic, and we have to trust the pilot to take us where she wants to go. The compelling quality of Stainer is simply what compels us about miracles. At one level this is just Christian poetry, capable of failing to seize us as the Church has failed. At another level, something like 'The Ice-Pilot Speaks' is so complex that successive readings yield unrecognisably dissimilar experiences. The hyper-association induced by the awe of marvellous sight has produced a text so intricate, flowing out on so many levels, so allusive, as to be incomprehensible to the mainstream readers it was marketed to. This retracing of the path to the Underground is saddening and fiercely exhilarating at the same time. The poet reminds me not only of Brian Catling, but also of saints' lives – the reliance on intense, almost psychotic, physical-spiritual experiences, hallucinatorily enhanced and isolated, everything in between burnt away, blacked out. Everything takes place on a plane of imminent death, transcendence, mutation of bodily form, sex, rapture.

The generation of space

If we look at the geography of various books of modern poetry, we see, not only that there is a location of the undemarcated wilderness in northern Scotland, but also that there is a chain of additional locations of it which heads further west and north. The south-east of Britain is a place of dense boundaries and heavily affirmed property rights. These qualities fade as we move north or west. The south-east is also where there are many, densely differentiated, statuses of individuals. By the time we have passed through Greenland (Francis Berry) and the Beaufort Sea (Aklavik, in 'Aristeas'), and the shore of Alaska (as recalled by Tom Lowenstein, who did fieldwork there), we are willing to accept that this logic of stepping-up leads ever further on.

In two of our poems (*Marimarusa* and *Malcolm Mooney's Land*), the ice appears as a primal substance, the origin of language and concepts. The answer to the riddle is that ice is mere substance without shape or colour or heat. This qualifies it as proper for the place of origins, where everything is formless, not yet separated into things.

Because the wilderness takes on wider dimensions, within the British Isles, as you move north and west, a further projection into that quadrant could seem like a trip into a more intense wilderness. There is a shift up whereby that direction means an increase of upland moors which are uncultivated and therefore undivided, and of uninhabited tracts; and, further on or deeper in, means the Atlantic, a desert waste of ocean sprinkled with windswept islands and, perhaps, with ships. I would offer this as an explanation for the fascination of the Arctic.

If there is an opposition between two terms, in a current system of classification, it is possible to extract the distance between them, redefine it as a vector, and use it to construct a third term. This can either be invented, or ascribed to a real thing which roughly fits the bill. Perhaps all oppositions can thus be used to generate fictional but comprehensible values; and literature is often derived by over-fulfilment of rules within familiar sets of language and social customs.

Poets from the *Grosseteste Review*

We have already introduced this cluster of poets when discussing *A Various Art*. *Grosseteste Review* ran to about 30 issues between 1968 and 1984, and in full flight was the flagship for intelligent poetry. These poets do not greatly resemble each other, nor are they the only ones who adorned *Grosseteste Review*. Nonetheless, it pleases me to draw attention to this link – with the aim of finding groupings within our poets, lines the reader might want to pursue when they are looking for pleasurable ways of reading.

GR suggested to the intelligent that they didn't have to be isolated and self-sufficient, and to the eccentric that fleeting and bizarre sensations could be brought back and made to slow down. It began with an orientation towards the (American) Objectivists, and evolved into a mix too rich and heady to characterise. If we did describe the ambience, we would say that it was cool, leisured, and non-confrontational; and that it felt that time spent studying perception was never wasted.

The arrival of intelligence in the Midlands:
Roy Fisher, *City* (1961; 17 pp. AVA tnbp3; cluster C)

'As far as I see it, a poem has business to exist, really, if there's a reasonable chance that somebody may have his perceptions rearranged by having read it or having used it.' Everybody now seems to agree on Fisher's brilliance, so we may as well just record his own account of the poem, from his fascinating interviews. The first point is that this is a long poem about the city of Birmingham: 'In many cases the cultural ideas, the economic ideas, had disappeared into the graves of the people who had had the ideas. But the by-products in things like street layouts, domestic architecture, where the schools were, how anything happened – all these things were left all over the place as a sort of script, an indecipherable script with no key.' But this vast stage set of facts is just the perceptions which it is time to rearrange. This is actually the first problem – what is its relationship to the actual Birmingham? The poet talks about "Rilke's Paris or Kafka's Prague or the imaginary towns that Paul Klee made up or Kokoschka's painting of towns he worked in." Birmingham is a large city given over to light industry – dominated by small firms with a small gap between owner and workers, and with a high proportion of skilled workers who could look forward to starting their own concerns. It was obscured, in cultural representations, by dominant imagery about urban ugliness and pollution, the cultural degradation of the workers, the exploitation of the workers, the depressing qualities of repetitive tasks, etc. These images largely came from outside, and Fisher's lifelong effort to write about the city from the inside has dwelt on acts of linguistic criticism – to disperse myths through which the city and its people were invisible. As he remarks in the poem, "it's never been seen" – glossing in the interview, 'the metropolitan culture, the literary culture, had no alphabet to offer for simply talking about what I saw all the time." The effect of this methodical erasure is to bring an industrial landscape into sight with almost hallucinatory vividness – a sight crowded with complicated shapes, embodying human intentionality. "They're sceptical formulations of life, systematisations; the poems are anarchic. The poems represent, if you like, an anarchic response to –not so much social issues, things which come out of society and stand out and can be put into newspapers – but to the whole rubble, the whole mass of tiny interfaced circumstances that carry you along, the present in which you exist." The work of the poems is almost ascetic – it asks for a critical act of vision, dispelling systems of projection to create a vacuum, held by a strain which creates a wealth of new imagery once the act of true perception starts. In retrospect, I can see that there was a kind of competition, at that time, to detach perception from inherited appetites, to make it reflexive so that astounding truths could be revealed about how it works – immense, quasi-industrial structures, milling and transforming.

Fisher (1930–2017) speaks further of his wish 'to make a double use of the ordinary data of sense. That is, to write about, shall we say, a city which exists in space and time and has a name and is not a city which is already mentalised or internalised in the way I was describing in my answer to your first question. I would like to be able to use names, to name names, not as brute documentation … but to have floated real things into a fictive world and use them without distancing them at all. Anyway, in that particular poem I had it in mind that very often in trying to evoke urban things I as it were dissolved things and made them strange so that I was free from the entailments of them in ordinary reality, so that I could in fact use them within the compass of my own perceptual thinking, my own way of working. The conscience I had was that this was always distorting, which I accepted. But I had an ambition to make the transaction so clean that I could just take from a thing – a street with a name to it – sufficient properties to exist verbally in my poem and at the same time to be answerable to the reality should anybody stop and look at it. I was writing about a street people could recognise, but I still was writing about a street that was in my poem and not just stupidly reported as it might be. In a very ordinary piece of documentary.' Writing about Birmingham so interestingly flashes up as a negative the image of the English writers of an earlier era – whose bias in favour of domestic scenes from middle-class families and in the South appears as a *negative hallucination*, an inability to register what is actually there. It was a small protected world – the social and mental blocks amounting to an aesthetic system.

The original edition came from Migrant, and was a turning point – a moment when a whole tier of English poets became obsolete. It is different from all later editions.

Ride the Wind:
J.H. Prynne, *The White Stones* (1969, 86 pp.; AVA CC, cluster C)

The White Stones was a revolutionary moment in English poetry, the first major publication of a whole new wave. It has an aura which no other modern work possesses. If you were going to read only one modern British book – it would have to be this one. Titles include 'The Esterházy Court Uniform', 'Thoughts on Retained Colour', 'Star Damage at Home', 'Smaller Than the Radius of the Planet'. The nature of its superiority lies in a refinement of language, a complexity which cannot be unpacked in prose without spreading over whole acres. So I am going to concentrate on a single poem, 'Aristeas, in Seven Years', about 220 lines long. The basic story is one told by Herodotus. Sometime in the 7th century BC, by the Black Sea, Aristeas goes into a trance:

> leaving the flesh vacant then, in a fuller's shop,
> Aristeas removed himself for seven years
> into the steppes, preparing his skeleton and the
> song of his departure, his flesh anyway touched
> by the in-
> vading Cimmerian
> twilight:

– leaving his body behind. He is 'snatched up by Apollo' (*phoibolamptos*); his spirit travels, by flight, to the interior of what is now Russia; and returns seven years later. We have twelve lines of Aristeas' poem about his journey, during which "his soul would issue from it [his body] and wander in the sky like a bird, surveying all beneath, land, sea, rivers, cities, nations of mankind, and occurrences and creatures of all sorts" [Maximus of Tyre]. The second story has him return, after 340 years, to Metapontus in Italy; he is following Apollo, in the shape of a crow; the Pythagoreans erect a statue to him. Apollo was associated with poetic rapture, and the flight of Aristeas may be a figure for poetic inspiration in general. His story was compared to shamanistic trances already in the 1930s: Meuli says "Like the soul of the Netsilik Atungai, his [Aristeas'] too has visited in ecstatic flight numerous real countries and peoples, has collected information about demonic beings, fantastic animals, and peoples of the dead, and has told of it in the inherited form of a poetic first-person narrative", and Prynne too links this Graeco-Scythian legend to such practices described for Circumpolar peoples of recent times. It is certainly a long way from the Scythians who lived near the Greeks, i.e. north of the Black Sea, to Siberia. (The Netsilik or Seal People are Eskimo of the Melville Peninsula in the Canadian Arctic.) What Sinor stresses about these peoples is their poverty; mobility starts in barrenness and forces them to restrict their material possessions. The bone theme recurs often in the poem. 'Aristeas' was first published in a pamphlet, which had on its cover a picture (by Muhammad Siyah Qalam, 'master of the black pencil', 14th century, from the collection of the Topkapi Museum, Istanbul) from Inner Asia of two figures, called 'The Dancing Shamans'. It includes a bibliography for the poem (which mentions the Netsilik). I associate this picture with tape recordings of ritual wrestling, collected somewhere in Mongolia or nearby, which Prynne played me in around 1980; this may be incorrect, but the figures look like wrestlers. The same picture is on the cover of a book, *Painting of the Mongols*, by M.S. Ipsiroglu, cited in the booklist. The poem is in part a description of several paintings in this work – principally by 'the master of the black pencil'.

> Gathering the heat to himself, in one thermic
> hazard, he took himself out, to catch up with
> the tree, the river, the forms of alien vantage

I think this refers to metabolism, in trance. Aristeas' fake death resembles hibernation, as a way of dealing with winter. But possibly his soul is riding up on a *thermal* – a plume of heated air. As for *the forms of alien vantage*, this sums up the poem, I think. Perhaps the word "vantage" is split out of the collocation "coign of vantage", i.e. observation point, and so stresses the contingency of all such points, the absence of a non-local, perfect, observation platform. That is, our knowledge would come from our ability to move. Conversely, our ability to produce prose may derive from our sedentary way of life – accumulating stores of knowledge. There may also be a hidden reference to Adam Smith's phrase about local advantage – there is a product suitable for every clime. Nomadism is one way of exploiting the crop cover – and analysing all points of view misses the state of permanent wandering, of a dispersed point of view.

In this first section, *a natural development* is nomadism, a geographically conditioned response to life in semi-arid zones, while *his nose filled with steam* is enigmatic, but possibly to do with the "stopping of breath". It may be that the delineation of this physiologically altered state is phenomenological: the basis of rational discourse is a certain, cool, state of the brain, but the brain can transit, or trance, into other states and it may even be easier to write poetry in one of these. 1968 was, of course, a period when people were altering their brain states in an ecologically rash way. Meuli gives us hemp, its *steam*, as a ticket into shamanistic trance. The trance-rapture thus presents an analogy to the nomadic order of being, in opposition to the farming or urban life.

singular as the larch tree brings us details of North Eurasian life, not given in Herodotus; the larch is the ridge-pole of the skin tent, poking up through a smoke-hole, which is also the shaman's mythic steps into the stars, his horse. It has steps carved on it. Compare "his staff, the larch-pole", the "singular and one axis of the errant world" – because the cosmos was seen as rotating around a pole which went through the earth and rose up to the Pole Star, or Nail Star as it was known in the North.

I believe the *double twist* refers to a fragment of Heracleitus, where he talks about the bow and the lyre, and the way their strings are tense and yet still vibrate. Aristeas flying is vibrating like a string – more, perhaps, he is like the vibration without any string. This is being associated with the crozier and the lyre, mentioned in the title of a book in the bibliography as tools proper to Apollo, as the god of lyric poetry. Meaning? that poetry was associated with shepherds. The peoples of the northern steppes were also herdsmen, of course.

god of the shepherd: Apollo was called *Hyperborean*, from behind the north wind (Boreas), and is here linked with nomadic shepherds; he was also god of poetry and the muses, as we know. This scarcely points to a Siberian origin of poetry, but that is the myth valid inside this poem. One philologist has claimed that the Germanic word *scyttan* (our *shoot*, etc.) gave rise to the ethnic name *Scyth* (zguda, Ishkuza, Ashkuz, whatever) as the definitive archers, and certainly the flight of arrows has a lot to do with the flight of Aristeas. The double twist may, accordingly, be the *compound bow*, a key innovation of the steppe area. Energy is released as elastic materials *untwist*, and propels the arrow. Or it may simply refer to the *contrapposto* of the Dancing Shamans. Ipsiroglu sums up this picture as 'The black colossi leap about with elemental force, their bodies rebounding from the ground. The movement seems to begin in the figure that turns its back to us and to be continued in the convolutions of the figure facing us. The twisting action is very skilfully conveyed by the expressive dislocation of the limbs and particularly of the soles of the feet.'

felted eagle of Pazyryk refers to a site in the Altai, in Russian Central Asia, where very ancient artefacts were found in five tombs preserved by the freezing of the soil. The eagle resembles metalwork of the Scyths, motifs known as far west as Poland – "remote animal gold". It may be a griffin, confirming Aristeas' account.

sniffing hemp as the other air: Herodotus reports Scythians burning hemp seeds on braziers in enclosed spaces, as confirmed at Pazyryk by archaeology. This is associated with the origin of steam baths in Russia. He did not realise the recreational value of this, but possibly Prynne did.

singular – this word occurs six times in the poem. The concept of 'relative position, coordinates' implies fixed spatial relations, which is what Prynne is telling us the nomads didn't have. Is their space singular because they carry their notions of order around with them? Perhaps the singularity tracks back to the moving individual, a fleeting eye-point where curtains close up what is behind in darkness exactly as they part to disclose what is ahead. There is another explanation of *the vantage is singular* (section 4). The poem Aristeas wrote was called the 'Arimaspeia'. It says the Arimaspi were all one-eyed. This means that their point of view (=vantage) was singular.

2. in name the displacement

No cheap cigarettes nothing/ with the god in this/ climate is free of duty I don't see what this does, but it's the usual prynnean lecture on paying for everything you use, repeated three times in this poem. Aristeas is looking down on the mysterious interior of Russia from the air, a point of observation that defines what can be observed, for example 'wormwood as the cold/ star, the dwarf Siberian pine/ as from the morainal deposits/ of the last deglaciation'. The reference to the 'star called wormwood' of Revelations may chime with the theme of resurrection in the rest of the poem. The *deposits* of locally thicker soil allow trees, as opposed to the typical scrubs and grasses of the steppe.

the underground sea not clear to me. This may be to do with the retreat underground attributed to Zalmoxis/Salmacis, a god of the Thracians (the people between the Scyths and the Greeks) whose fake death (followed by a rebirth) resembles that of Aristeas. Unlikely to be related to the Pink Floyd's "sounds surround the icy waters underground", of the same year as 'Aristeas'.

3. as fact

The term, as has been pointed out, is bone. "term" means end state of development. Any human stops moving, at the term of their life, and becomes bone? Turkic peoples did refer to "black bone" and "white bone" as commoner and noble clans, so bone is the human essence, the stuff of procreation. The resurrection of killed animals from their bones is a rite (practised by the Siberian shamans, quoted at the end of the section) to ensure the fertility of the wild. The refinement of trance is like a body being calcined down to the bone? Like the poet's path to exaltation?

ruinous/ as the old woman's prophecy: what old woman? at a guess, the Cimmerian Sibyl.

4. *no longer settled*

In this section we find the cloak made of birds' feathers; the Hyperborean paradise; and the reincarnation of animals assured by rituals involving bones. The feather cloak is a means of flight, what Aristeas is doing throughout the poem, also a garb of some shamans (see Martin Thom's poem quoted below). He is *settled now into length* – he is *not* settling down, the *Path* is his home, stable in that. The object of knowledge moves from state into process, good hegelianism.

The bone rite of propitiation can be described through a legend recorded of Thor. He went to visit a farmer in his sled pulled by goats. For dinner, he slaughtered the goats and stewed them. The farmer's son broke one of the leg-bones while eating. At daylight, Thor put all the bones together, struck them, and brought the goats back to life. But one of them was lame in one leg. This shows what happens if you break any of the bones. The spirits at whom the propitiation is directed in Siberia are not individual bears, they are the spirits of all bears, and responsible for the reproduction of bears, ever new, in the wild. The bear dies and returns; the flight of its spirit is something like Aristeas' – they leave their bodies behind and fly. The tale-theme of the damaged bone is found rather widely in Europe – but the *rite* is only found far to the north-east. The same story is told of the *god*, Hyperborean Apollo: in an obscure legend we hear that Apollo was killed (by Pytho), boiled in a cauldron, and resurrected – with a golden thigh to replace a bone that had been damaged.

Greek poets refer to Hyperboreans as living in a state of nature, without war or want. The poem shifts focus, now, away from a real Inner Asia and towards the place which is the land of happiness and really "out of this world". Aristeas possibly did not get this far, but he visited the Issedoni who were *near* the Hyperboreans, and Gernet draws our attention (in "La cité future et la cité des morts") to the development by Stoic writers of the old legend in connection with a feast where the foods appear magically overnight. This, the earliest idealistic political speculation, is linked with Apollo the sun-god (Aristeas' patron) and so set in a place called Heliopolis (Sun City), and Prynne has linked these feasts to the favour of the spirits, that is to making shamanistic deals with the spirits so that they will assure the unceasing fertility of the wild. Keeping the bones of (eaten) animals intact is part of a theological contract. The Hellenistic speculation about the ideal city connects with notions, elsewhere in *White Stones,* of the perfect social state: in the grip of abundance. Meuli links the ritual of laying out the bones with the origin of sacrifice. This painstaking pattern-making for the spirits may make us think of poetic language as originally a way of communicating with the gods (and written in their language?).

We read 'he watched the crows fighting the/ owls with the curling tongues/ of flame proper to the Altaic/ hillside', notice that birds occur throughout this poem, and wonder how it relates to another poem about birds with shamanistic themes, *Crow*. Aristeas' soul flew from his mouth in the shape of a crow *(ex ore in Proconneso corvi effigie)*. The combat of the birds is from a painting in Ipsiroglu's book, where the crows are fanning the fire with their wings so as to defeat the owls. It illustrates *Kalila wa Dimna,* the tale of two likeable jackals.

5. *some part of the bone must be twisted*

The history of migrations of the Cimmerians, as a typical steppe polity; their invasion of Asia Minor in the 7th century BC, the ruin it brought; their swarming linked to 'the fine chatter of small birds' near the Urals. Settled peoples regard them as "ruinous" because their whole world-view is other. The influence of geography, water regimes causing social systems. Why is the bone twisted? I suppose this to be a way of laying out the skeletons after the feast, with a direction so that they can find their way back (to reincarnate and be eaten again). It may also refer to the torsion of bones in work – a source of knowledge as it relates back physical forces acting on the body, also of course directing the growth of bones, acquiring mass in stimulus and response.

We hear of "the Land of the Blessed", as a dwelling place of the Hyperboreans, but also where poets fly to in their fits, I suppose; it is also the land of the dead where shamans show the prey animals the way back. Karl Meuli was the first to link Aristeas with these bone rituals (and shamanism), in 1935. (Or was it Erwin Rohde in 1898?) The theme of payment in the poem may start from the idea of ritually paying the ancestor spirits of the animals by the bone ceremonials. Of course, the 'white stones' (*psēphoi*) appear in a text in Revelations which has to do with bringing *people* back to life.

6. *the true condition of bone*

The first passage explains that we are in the land of the dead, 'drawing after them/ the trail and fume of burning hemp'. As Hinge points out, the hemp seeds at Pazyryk were in a *tomb. a fact so/ hard won* the poet rather majestically states that you have to work for every scrap of knowledge – which is his thesis. But he was, I suppose, challenging notions, local to the time, of never working for anything; as Vaneigem commends in *The revolution in everyday life*, I think. This is satire, not philosophy.

the figure of change, which/ is the myth and fact of extent,/ which thus does start from/ Marmora or Aklavik, right/ out of the air I don't get this but it's obviously central to what he is talking about. Aklavik is an Eskimo name, of a place in north Canada, on the MacKenzie River, and near the shore of the icy Beaufort Sea. Marmora is the sea between the Aegean and the Black Sea – and where Aristeas' home town of Proconnesus was. Presumably, both were sites of shamanic flight. *Change* is local variation? or exchange? Adam Smith on local comparative advantage as the source of tradable goods? "Air" in Greek texts corresponds to our word "climate", books on geography were called "peri aeron". Meuli quotes accounts of Eskimo shamanism to build up his case that the Scythians practised it, and Prynne's book-list cites the same accounts. The Eskimo did not have permanent settlements, and were very keen on shamanism – so both things fell out of the air.

these people have no weapons – it must be the shamans he is talking about. The word "extent" now seems to be to do with shape-shifting: we see the human body as permanent, but shape-shifters (practices reported of Inner Asia by Herodotus) do not; the "phenomenological" twist of relating rules of behaviour to the particularities of the body (perhaps the point of "vantage" he is talking about) is analogically applied to the *extent* of the skin, as the coordinates within which perception occurs. Ideas about the durability of things, stress on accumulating knowledge, may derive from the economic fact that we stay where we are and see the same field or garden out of the window in the morning. The crux-word *extent* may be decomposed to reveal the concept of boundaries: perhaps Prynne is attacking our reliance on these, as particular merely to agricultural societies. In which he resembles Deleuze and Guattari, whose whole project is based on this insight, and whose fetish word is deterritorialisation. The *extent* of an animal is related to the thermal rates of the climate, and northern animals are larger; the *extent* of land needed to support ten people also depends on climate. *any settled and complaisant fixture /on the shoreline* suggests that settling is a slump: we know that our poet wants rigour and hates complacency.

To conclude, the poem describes state formation among the Sarmatian (in Anglo-Saxon, *Sarmende*) peoples of the steppes who drove out the Scythians, and how gold supplied the symbolic objects of the royal or Golden clan; and the griffins who, in another tale from Herodotus, guarded gold, in the frozen ground in or near the Altai (=gold) mountains in Central Asia. The makeup of the soil connects us with one of the major themes of the book: details of steppe confederacies developing fearful military striking power, and overrunning nearby peasant societies: 'The Sarmatians, we are told, were armed in a different manner from the Scythians. The latter were light horsemen, primarily mounted archers, while the Sarmatians were knights in armour with the long sword, rather than the bow, as their principal weapon. Because of the mounted Sarmatian knights, it has been suggested that the Sarmatians invented the stirrup[.]" (Richard Frye) Mobility becomes striking power, and the momentary strike of military victory becomes the durable structure of feudalism. *'the gold reposed as the divine brilliance, / petrology of the sea air, so far from the shore*': dynasties in the Iranian world were marked by *khvarenah* (dialectally *farn* or *fern*), a personal and family luck, literally 'divine brilliance' and like a halo. The royal clan of the Scythians, for example, was instated by gold weapons which fell from the air; the mandate of heaven, or, Excalibur. The *sea air* is an error of Herodotus, associating displacements in Inner Asia with the incursions of the tides.

gold [...] which in the steppe was no more than the royal figment: because the Scythians didn't have an exchange economy and only used gold to make regalia from.

life and not value: the claim is that there is some qualitative difference between a pastoral empire (slaves analogous to herds) and commercial empires (such as the Roman, Athenian, British ones?) concerned with money. *we should pay them or steal*: I don't know what this means, but it's the usual Prynnean stuff about paying your dues.

The poem has, I take it, two main themes: one geographical, to do with how social customs are brought about by climatic conditions; and one to do with the state of poetic rapture, whereby Aristeas' trance is, covertly, occupied by Prynne himself in a kind of neo-Ossianism.

Aristeas learns how to fly, a basic part of a shaman's equipment; the enhanced vision which stretches over all parts of the world, the future, the hidden unborn young of the game species, etc., perhaps resembles the origin of abstract thought, thinning out to rise above the world of the senses.

Having completed the poem, we can turn back to reflect that it is a definition of the village through its opposite. 'Aristeas' is a poem *about* the classic English themes of the landscape, the weather, the village, the plant cover, pastoral song, but only as their negatives. One of the other poems in the book describes deglaciation as the origin of English society – everything follows from farming, which was possible once the soil thawed. This is why the word *thermic* appears in the first line of our poem. We would properly *think* about the village, a central imaginary object of mid-century English culture, by looking at societies who are mobile, and have no villages. The white stones may either be the hail which appears in the poem about deglaciation, or else a reference to the white stones given to the blessed in the Book of Revelations (according to James Keery's essay on Prynne). We are taken to the Altai to see the permafrost – what Britain was like 10,000 years ago. It is a hibernation like that of Aristeas in his trance. The quest of the book is to define "vantage", the influence of place on awareness – 'Aristeas' is there to show the origin of place. But the theme of the poem is also the condition of lyric poetry as pure movement – for which the flight of Aristeas' soul is a metaphor.

This was a brush with a great poem, which might have turned out better if we had a larger extent – seven years perhaps. *White Stones* has, for some of those who have read it closely, Miltonic status. The themes are continuous through the book – the style, one of majestic ornateness and fluidity.

Twelve silver instruments:
R.F. Langley, *Twelve Poems* (1994, 52 pp., cluster C)

'The original object being painted, guitar or person, was there to provoke the investigation.' (*Journals*, p.93) Langley (1938-2011) came from Wolverhampton, and did English at Cambridge in the late 1950s; a friend of Prynne, he acquired at that time the same direction of interest to Olson and Adrian Stokes (both of them close associates of Ezra Pound). This volume is his collected works to that date, the first to be published being *Hem*, in 1978. *12 Poems* includes beautiful but mysterious phrases like "I've been noticing how they needed low light and stale eyes to catch such humble cajolery" and 'Mild fingers set twelve straws on the shining wood.' I found it enigmatic at first, but with the contextual information, helpfully published in an interview (which I spent a week editing from its raw state) I can now read them, and it strikes me now as the perfect book, so beautiful, so resourceful, so finely balanced. I regard his work as sophisticated, but that begs the question of where on our palate the detector of sophistication is to be found. My proposal is to look for his quality where a puzzling anomaly meets something legitimated by long familiarity and admiration. His poems may now amount to 20, each of them differing in all essential aspects from the others. That is to say, he starts a new poem somewhere distant from all the others. This suggests that the step before writing any of the poems was to go somewhere untouched by anyone else's poems. This brings us to the anomaly. Langley is far removed from the radically alienated art of the time, which banked on incomprehension and contradiction. Rather than complete neural chaos (supposed to lead to political redemption, like winning a lottery through the utterance of randomness), he offers smooth and powerfully acquired patterns of reaction, which we are able to steer and control.

'Saxon Landings' is a discussion of the Mildenhall treasure, a hoard of silver deposited by Romano-Britons in Suffolk, perhaps under threat from disembarking Angles, as evoked by hearing a radio play about the end of the Empire in Britain. At one level, this is an experience we are profoundly familiar with. Treasure trove! Lost beauty found! silver retrieved from darkness! This has a deep conventional appeal. At the same time, it is a meditation on the impact of the Mediterranean's world of forms on the rainy Atlantic periphery, Britain for example. This aspect might connect with the ideas of Adrian Stokes, even with the title of his book *The Invitation in Art*. The Mildenhall silver, with its *repoussé* images of Bacchus, its implications of a dinner party and a convivial gathering where one might be happy (as well as rather drunk) is a natural symbol for the discovery of creativity, or simply of the ability to be happy. What was there all the time is recovered and emerges as a classical masterpiece. The leading expert on Stokes is a former pupil of Langley in Wolverhampton – another example of invitations made and accepted, perhaps.

Langley's originality is to be sought at the level of scenario rather than in the choice of vocabulary, the visual organisation on the page, or the metrical organisation. But there is no obvious stanza in the entire book. There are a whole set of lines which are predictable from the whole gestalt and Langley never bothers to write these.

Langley explains in the interview that part of 'The Ecstasy Inventories' is about a territorial pattern where 'packs fold away', wolves protecting their pack areas from the neighbouring pack so assiduously that around the boundary they don't have time to hunt the deer. The deer are safe when near the edges of two pack territories – at a fold, as he says. The poem also describes clothes 'in the press of the storm' (where a press is also a linen-fold); it is all about folds. The anomalous safe zones at the fold may be an unconscious echo of the spaces which Langley finds in linguistic terrain, perpetually drawing new and striking lines. Any classification system produces cells which are unrecognised and unassimilated. In order to articulate the unknown, the linguistic faculty has first to find it, repeatedly and nimbly moving into a sector of the cognitive landscape marked as strange and elaborate.

One of the moments in his poems is the flooding in of irrational wealth and complexity, the breakdown of control in the face of natural perceptual wealth. The inventory details in the will of Mrs Coker:

> The cuffs, collars and bedclothes
> have lace on them. The lace can be
> mentioned as strips with discs
> or wheels, as sunbursts
> of logical straps, rays, pips,
> split pods or crooked stars, as
> much as counting and nice
> as a pocketbook with every
> species, in flight, at rest,

> in colour. These inroads let
> me understand, and mark
> sharply. Over what? Over
> brilliant quietness. The path
> ends in the shadow of trees.
> In the trees I can't see the tiny
> passerines all about in the
> sparkling confusion. Or
> her cheeks. Or her chin.

are simply taken from a document, not invented. They are a found wealth of data. The runs of monosyllable nouns, a cascade like grains onto a hard surface, and in short staccato sentences, appeal to Langley.

To go back to unit structures, we can see in Langley the interest in reading *original documents* as the basis for a poem, and in the *Image*, something sensory, vivid, and carefully isolated, both of which go back to Pound. The reliance on documents features in 'Matthew Glover' and 'The Ecstasy Inventories'. The vivid sensory objects are often insects, and we have extensive details of insects observed in the Journals, which I had to review: "*Evarcha arcuata* looks violent and imposing in the tube, although I won't know who he is until I get home and look him up. I have not seen such thickened, powerful femora and tibia before. They are deep black, with the thinner part of the legs brown with black articulations. He has a bronze face and a face-mask, ear to ear, as it were, which consists of two or three lines of white hairs, the top line pulled up to beneath his huge round anterior eyes. Above this the eyes themselves have white spectacles around them. [...] It's a face that reminds me of the African ones on sale in that room off the courtyard of St Philibert." (p.59) What this may be is an escape into a smaller dimension with unexplored possibilities and an unravished autonomy. Something else he records a lot about is church decoration: 'There is a double shadow on the whitewash behind each poppy-head in the Bohun aisle. Trinities, says Jeremy. But no more flames come in, and without them, the walls around have joined up and squared the place. The three roofs, the chancel one, single beam, massive, the nave and Bohun aisle ones, with purlins and wall plates, seal into a unity, gather together overhead. [...] The west window, cut out in pure black now, has geometric tracery, quatrefoils, also two bare, straight transoms rather brutal in the side lights.' (p.39) The beetle is *arcuata*, with arches, a pun which allows us to think of the formalism and rich colour both of flying beetles and of church decoration in one visual frame. The journal is made out of the same material as the poems, and so may lead us closer to them. Are these firm and ornate visual forms acting as models for ornate and firm verbal forms?

If you aren't a megalomaniac you can't sound like Pound and Olson. This is where the investigation of the perceiving self makes such a break, through and away, possible. Langley likes to choose an ambiguous subject which remains outside exact definition while he is describing numerous clear features belonging to it. The poem remains poised between mystery and literal accuracy; but any detail we look at is clear and fluent. The calm of the finished work, with its promise of a stable and capacious external space, is what calms us. Langley's poems are full of calm objects, in this sense. Through fine balance, art enters a different kind of time, floating on rhythms of attention which are slowed, co-ordinated, and stabilised; it is directed at its objects, but is at the same time autonomous from these.

I do not feel that a cogent description of his work is yet possible. He has swallowed vast draughts of defamiliarisation and philosophical perplexity, producing an open text. The sensations he offers are remarkably rich, delicate, and abiding, even if they do not have proper names yet. As consumer advice, we can sày that someone who admires Prynne and Geoffrey Hill will probably admire Langley.

Where horizontal forces converge;
David Chaloner, *Chocolate Sauce* (1973, 39 pp., AVA, CC, cluster C)

This was published by Ferry Press – i.e. Andrew Crozier. The typeface is the same one used in *Grosseteste Review*. The cover design is beautiful, a painting by Patrick Caulfield. It consists of three flat panes in two colours, separated by three black lines which, because of their angle, we read as forming a corner – which therefore defines a room, where we read the purple panes as walls and the yellow one as a ceiling. Three-dimensional space comes and goes almost as a shimmer – tilt the oblique line a few degrees, and we have simply a 2-dimensional abstract. Without even opening the book, we are plunged into the problem of perceptions being influenced by subliminal social suggestions. A shift of perception – a new society, actually – could be as simple as a change – a tilt – in the signals and imperatives being sent to us by other people. Within the book, each poem has a date underneath it, a single day. This implies that each was written on a single day – and, perhaps, that the details were swept together by the myriad event lines of the world, so that they represent, put together, a dossier of experience not filtered by literary rules and the imperatives they embody. The title might be as simple as hedonism – chocolate sauce on vanilla ice-cream poses just such a crisp vision of pure colour as Caulfield's cover. But – a moment of prudence – there is an anecdote that Hitchcock, when asked what he used for blood in the film *Psycho*, answered 'Chocolate sauce'. So the primary optical evidence we use for constructing the world depends on the qualities of the medium through which the information reaches us. The great works of art which are the most substantial and persuasive webs of evidence that reach our brains are tissues of fictions and conventions.

In the first poem, 'Swirl', we have a swirl of wind in the tall grass; then a check, as in stanza 2 episode 2 'encroaches on the previous line', and stopped when 'a dead line arrived' – we are offered the process of writing, the poem *hesitates to open up a deeper space*. In 3, we have a discussion about how to write the next stanza, via the key problems of continuity, integrity, and time allowance. Pessimistically, the poet suggests that integrity may be 'a fictional affectation'. The next moment is just a pause (pause). In stanza 4 we return to the swirl, which in 5 is 'tying lovely knots in the wind'. All this in 18 lines.

Chocolate Sauce is an example of '60s hedonism and good taste. Affluence, leisure, and comfort weren't new, exactly, but they were new as things for the masses – they had to be extricated from upper-class models, polished over opulent centuries. The gap between the controllable square of paper on which the poet draws, and the stretches of experience, limited by the night and by the circumstances of, for example, available light, is down to a minimum. It really seems as if life could be made up of cells of designed experience – where preference and foreknowledge are tempered by the unexpected and the polymorphous, but only in comforting doses. Each poem represents a day – so that, cogently, each day represents a page. As with few other books, this one seems mobilised by a domestic device which creates poems, pulse patterns, all the time; while the poet stands off, in a dégagé way, and intervenes just enough to modulate each one, delicately, unobtrusively. It is so natural, so effortless.

The '60s hadn't really stopped in 1973 – these poems have for us the golden quality of Sixties three-minute pop singles. Political polarisation raised the stakes – poetry began to ask too much of the reader; and vice versa. The jacket has no blurb, no biography, no Ferry products list – that just wouldn't be cool. As for telling you who Chaloner is – well, you're just supposed to know. If you don't – it's more tactful not to draw attention to this. Each poem is written in an eternal present. Naturally, they are written in parataxis throughout. Each situation is unfolded obliquely through tantalising details which never quite define the edges, so that we are drawn endlessly into a space that endlessly deepens.

There was the analysis of subliminal imperatives which read them as the hegemony of a malign and alien bourgeoisie, and the analysis which saw them as means by which the good life could be reached through a wide open series of good moods and good scenes. The former came from reading the newspapers, the latter from wearing clothes with the intent of display. One seduced you into a socialist future, one scared you into it. Chaloner (1944-2010) belongs in the category of working-class dandies – so important in the Ferry/Grosseteste world. The secret of that softness and suavity is anxiety – eased by coherent and planned acts upon a medium which is malleable to them. This could be clothes and demeanour – although in fact it's poetry. If stepped up, the anxiety could be fear of political oppression – but that makes it more or less untreatable. Drawing the edges of pages around the poems like horizons – lines beyond which nothing is perceptible – Chaloner makes the manipulation and relief of anxiety entirely possible.

The poet helpfully pointed out that my interpretation of the title is wrong – he just wanted something sensuous.

A Million Forms of Water:
Nigel Wheale, *Phrasing the Light* (1994, 70 pp., cluster C)

This retrospective is a selection from 1979 to 1993. It is divided into six sections: 'The Windshield Glarestrip legends' 'Strong Lines Recessional Numbers' 'From the Versts' 'As if from the Russian' 'New York/Warsaw Transfers' 'Hearing and Calling'. Wheale has been interested in the mass media, probably because they were a kind of collective voice. His poetry frequently intercepts signals, the voice of the existing power order; it counterattacks the lying happiness of advertisements. This corporate imagery has a blatant harmony, where simplified motivation offers labour-saving solutions. Wheale sometimes plunged into the opposite effect, whereby personal consciousness, raided and doubled by new "data feeds", is shown to be riddled with contradictions. How could anyone be in intellectual and emotional harmony when they lived in a society where the tokens of everyday language had lost their worth? Wheale is engaged to two simplifying and integrating speech lines, those of political statement and lyric utterance, almost as in folksong. A post-Marxist humanist, he speaks with the personal voice, taking this as the agent which carries out the acts of questioning and choice without which there is no ethics.

This shared music rings in our ears as we read his lyric poems:

> Yeast bloom on the bullace
> bright among your murder thorns
> a blue that calls with bitterness.
> Olives of the north light, sad grapes, wineless plum
> we'll burn you with rime-frost
> before we're done.
> Then darkly gather your darker sweetness
> and extort the blue-red life of wine.
> ('Black Thorn'),

which are singularly beautiful. Continuing the duty of remembering and recording what is true, there is a poem here ('Cara Alba derelicta') about the Highland Clearances: his wife's family were cleared from Bernera, fled to Harris, and were cleared again from Harris: "roofless houses and empty livings". The truest and most precious message was one of hope:

> New times call from between the sound of words:
> for the sublimed vision of plenitude
> occurs exactly within the condition
> where it might be installed if only
> we were simply to realize there is no earthly reason
> why it should not be lived among us
> ('Cara Alba derelicta')

The title means 'dear Scotland, desolate', and comes from an inscription by David Jones. Wheale is one of very few optimistic Socialist poets in the country. The problem was of going to Cornwall and admiring the sea and the cliffs and the wild flowers and also wanting to protest against the social order. The West Coast represents the Periphery and internal colonialism, but also, more palpably, quiet, natural beauty, and a million forms of water:

> What is it that damasks the waves of this great bay
> as if with a care for each moment within the deep sad systems
> of the sea? Stone crop flares on the boulder face
> and we walk the high edge, our words leaving no mark,
> silent on the more general silence. The great sun
> is absconded beyond the waste and we navigate as if
> we were the old-time sailors, peering eyelessly to gain
> the pressure of invisible land with a facial seeing,
> the blind sight of those who move by dark of intuition
> and the common surface of their skin.
> (from 'Silent Coast')

The small space of skin-based senses and the far space of migration and the Ocean sensibly recall Wheale's concern with intimate lyric and with large-scale politics, the goal of history being reached by steps and by changes of heart which we can all make. Several poems narrate travels of a disembodied eye:

> Novalis and I were hang-gliding the walls of data
> on petroleum thermals that rose from traffic canyons far below,
> collating cloudtop with seasurface, scanning through our landsat
>   high-tensity regard
> all that viral writing across insufferably thin architecture
> matte entablatures, beige pilastering, no white.
> Novalis had the lightest keyboard touch, never known to mis-key
> and his formatting was integral song to the degree of depth.
> (...)
> ('The earth seemed unearthly')

that soars and takes everything in. This rapid flux of ideas is exciting in the same way that driving very fast in a car is; images are as fleeting as in a magazine or a filmed advertisement, and the resultant low affect also makes the critical message – of grief, of alienation – more palatable. It is as if the emotionally rejected had become the virtual, which is a mimicry of the Socialist Utopia implicit in criticism of the social order. The coloured, shimmering, gewgaw surface of a capitalist world is mimicked by the poet as a weapon against it. However smooth the transitions, the inner logic of such poems is quite different from that of a traditional poem. The composition in flakes whirling past necessitates quick recognition, easily attained by using brand names, a device borrowed from the advertising which the poem deeply hates; famous people, significant ideas, appear as 'guest stars', or samples, rapidly making their point before vanishing; architectural features flash up as quickly as if they were logos.

Wheale puts considerable faith in the abiding power represented variously by socialism, standing for an idea of happiness and goodness, and popular song, with its written form of lyric poetry. This faith is sustained by the ordinary experience of daily life, and his ability to keep faith gives the poetry its durability and sweetness.

The philosophy of everyday life:
Denise Riley, *Dry Air* (1985, 57 pp.; tnbp 3, CC, OofE; cluster C)

I lived with my children in a warm bright & harmonious room which formed the crest of a high timber scaffolding – a room on stilts. Outside it was a black night, an old railway yard, abandoned tracks, a high wind. The volume seems to me to come together in one large-scale, overarching image of a household in peril: like a ship, it is battered by the waves, it gives the poem a defined location and perspective, it is much weaker than the forces around it, and we identify with its prospects of survival. To be sure, the volume is a composite of poems that had appeared in small pamphlets (*Marxism for Infants, No Fee, Living a Life*) over several years.

Titles include 'A note on sex and the "reclaiming of language"', 'Making a Liberty Belle', 'Mastering the art of English art' and 'The ambition to not be resentful speaks'. Dry air is a personalised phrase: it inevitably refers to a person, and to their manner of speech. This self-characterisation is unusual in (poetry) book titles – although conventional for album titles. To be exact, *dry air* can only refer to the nature of a speaker's response to someone else's behaviour; it refers, always, to the rejection of someone's proposals – which could be intellectual ideas or, for example, sexual persuasions. It is not impossible that it also refers to having somewhere to go out of the rain – the 'warm room' has no roof. Wet air is not a phrase in use, but the opposite of dry, here, might be sultry, simmering, bubbly, or gasping. *Dry* means self-possessed, unimpressed, without emotional inflection, unsurprised. Puttenham's *Art of English poesie* has 'The figure of Ironia, which we call the dry mocke.'

We are within the acephalous sliding forward of the counter-culture here – a mass of human beings sharing symbolic constructions, a certain *mise en scène* of the collective experience; even if we adjust the phrase to read *feminism* or the *New Left*. We are at a specific moment in this inexorable progress, which refuted the intellectual positions of the politicians and thinkers in power in the 1960s, and was itself dialectically refuted by the arriving weight of time. The moment is one where the boundless, intermittent, collective, and subjectively unresisting space of optimistic speculation has fallen to earth, in part, as the concrete and continuous space of a single household – albeit one whose head is a New Left philosopher. The vicissitudes of the group of people in the poems – the family, to be exact – are given peculiar sharpness because we have so much at stake in the theories which they can, at any moment, disprove. Riley is writing 'history from below' in the first person. Indeed, the operation of checking and changing hypotheses is central to the way the poems are written. When I say 'we' – the belief that social customs could be re-designed and re-learnt is part of the geography around these poems.

Marxism for Infants is a joke, a reference to a joke title of Orwell's – summing up the naivety of the Left, which is less of a joke for either writer. The central figure of 'Infant' sheds a light on the whole book – intelligent but vulnerable, in real danger inside a joke. The subject of the lines ('who is...') fluctuates between Riley and her infant daughter. 'Living a Life' sounds like the Godard film, *Vivre sa vie*, with the iconic photographing of Anna Karina.

Although the house in the book has children, the absence of men is a clear feature of the book. They are not being sued – for more love, more money, more time spent at home, or more respect. They are not part of the equation. This is quite unusual for a publisher like Virago – a feminist house which, at that time (1986), meant that men were being blamed for everything, having superhuman powers ascribed to them, and being seen as the providers of all (future) bounties and concessions.

To be published by Virago at that point still meant that you were marginal, subject to unthinking abuse by right-wing columnists and comedians, and likely to outsell all the poetry published by mainstream houses. Supplying some biographical information (which is fairly clear in the poems), we can say that the book is about being a one-parent family. This means – among other things – that the mother can't go out dancing.

The difference between Riley and the typical poetry of the Counter Culture is, first, that she is experiencing events which are not arbitrarily chosen or willed – without a primary tier of aestheticisation, that is. The poems are not trophies of a liberated life. Next, that she is not 'cool', but excited and vulnerable. But further, that she is preoccupied with the consequences of actions – the affect of liberation is either absent or not being presented as the dissolution of all consequences to actions. Indeed, we could define her attitude to life as being like New Criticism's approach to a text and our responses to it – everything is being interrogated, and every point which is made consciousness is a victory. Not for nothing is the philosophy degree course at Cambridge called Moral Science. If the dithyrambic style of then-contemporary male poets corresponds to the progressive guitar solo – narcissistic, luxuriant, deliberately a secession from the 'rules' of the melody – then Riley's poems correspond to soul records: where feelings are treated as real, where the trueness of true love is the truth of the song, where not all feelings are true, where loss and bliss are very close. Dare we quote the white soul of Leslie Gore: You don't own me… I'm not one of your many toys.

It is possible that the father of the two children mentioned on the cover is off somewhere in idealistic speculations, and this is why he is not taking part in the life of the household.

Myth and Deep Narrative

One view of the modern revolution in British poetry is, not the new simplicity or new empiricism, but a breakthrough into mythic creativity, of which *Crow* is the most famous example. The truth is that the modern revolution consisted of a huge adaptive radiation into uncontrolled diversity.

This group is not really separate from what I have classified as Jungians and as occultists. The rise of this genre is intimately tied up with the decline of Christianity as a medium for poetry. There is a view based on conservation of energies in which these myths simply fill the space left by the vanishing of Christian theology and Classical mythology. But the poems in question rely on personal myths – whereas the whole concept of myth within history, and say over the last 30 centuries, was that it was collective, available in adult life because it was inculcated in children. Personal myth is something else. Robert Crawford has summed up the poetic speech of the era as *the democratic voice*. While the truth of this interpretation is borne out by very much evidence, the *sectarian creativity* of these personal myths reminds us that the era is also one of individualism and migration away from the social and public.

This cluster makes us look back to Edwin Muir, David Jones, and Kathleen Raine as figures of a mid-century pattern essentially ignored at the time.

Quick-eyed carrion hawk:
Ted Hughes, *Crow* (1970, 82 pp.)

The packaging doesn't tell us this, but the poem-sequence (59 poems, to which a further 7 were added in a second edition) takes off from a myth-cycle of north-east Siberia (Koryak and Chukchi), where Crow is a trickster god. Because crows always hang around dead things, they were seen as having foreknowledge of death: when you see the Crow, you check to make sure you're still alive. By a simple association of ideas, he has to do with souls crossing the great border from the other side – and so with birth and creation. Sometimes, he is the leader of souls, the psychopomp, who escorts the souls of the dead across the trackless wastes to their destination. The whole poem works at the level of the eschatological – with the exit from life and with the formation of things like physiology and instinct for the very first time, humans being put together from inanimate body parts. Crows are very clever birds. Everything to do with sudden death is part of this theology.

The prehistory of *Crow* is in the Apocalypse of John, where the prophet swallows the book. The book is assimilated by, and engulfed by, the body – whose parts start speaking a prophetic language where all the words are body parts and the horizon is no further away than the heated air around the skin. That is – we can consider all the parts of *Crow* as rewrites of poems from the Apocalyptic movement of the 1940s. Something like 'The Battle of Os Frontis' (i.e. the frontal bone, behind which the brain lives) presupposes (a) the course of human history is dictated by the prehistoric imperatives in the human brain (b) the subjective factor is more important than the objective one (c) the personality is the horizon beyond which nothing is visible. The trope is one very common in the 1940s. Probably, he was influenced by the Serbian poet, Vasko Popa. Poems include 'Crow's Account of St George', 'Examination at the Womb-door', 'Crow Paints Himself into a Chinese Mural', 'King of Carrion'.

A well-bred readership had hoped that Hughes' early books were a nature poetry which could be assimilated to Edmund Blunden and to a neatly hedged and chartered countryside; *Crow* set them back by showing that the descent into animals was the first step into an irrationality which no longer had any boundaries. It is the opposite of the English poetry which reports exquisite sounds made by small, hushed animals with classical educations. That is – he sets out from terminal frustration with this madrigal sound. He is the return of the repressed. He is answering the question about the origin of evil which the delicacy of pastoral bird-watchers had omitted to ask. The whole book takes place within the borders of theology – something which its Old Testament scale of violence distracted early critics from. He is asking questions about human nature – and about the nature of animals, of course. Anglicanism is unable to explain why regimes like the Third Reich and Leninism in Russia came to be – it is missing a belief in the aggressivity of humans, their will to power, the fragility of their acquired inhibitions about violence. Of course, the Crow myth can be used just as easily to justify the secondary apparatus of the common law, the structure of property, the civil order as proposed by Hooker's theology – as to propose hedonism and the careless release of instinct. Indeed, by defining violence as fundamental, it militates against the programme of liberation and discharge of instincts that was on the radical agenda around 1970.

Much of the effort of mid-century British poetry was directed into personalist religion, where the poet could get away from over-familiar Christian equations. The poets were generally feeble at original mythic thinking – and Hughes had developed this to a vast, continent-sized degree. His method of getting away from the individual personality was to use binding forms from non-literate sources. This is the basis for throwing himself into the poems – the amazing self-contained construction of verbal objects, each of which is like the start of a world. Not only the lead character, but the language itself, is primal – with a new simile in virtually every line, furiously unstable, blown around by nameless energies like leaves in the wind. Decentred, deforming into archaic patterns, constantly seizing and ejecting organs. Shaping new worlds as music shapes the air. Most poets would have difficulty doing this for the extent of four lines – Hughes sustains it for something like 2,000 lines. This heroic energy is utterly exhilarating, and gives his myths the energy they need to become self-sustaining.

1969 was (according to the historian Brian Simon) the first year in which the governmental budget for education exceeded the budget for arms. So, the older British economy was based on trade, which itself depended on seizure or defence of territory supported by force of arms. *Crow* is a graphic depiction of this process. It's quite reasonable for liberals to dislike this process, or to avert their minds from it, or to wish that things might work differently in future – but it's wrong to deny it factual status. *Crow* has mythic efficacy because it touches on knowledge available to everyone but is also provocative – it dramatises fundamental processes and forces deep strata into immediate consciousness. It is impossible to think about the civilising process unless you accept that barbarity is possible. *Herauskitzeln* – luring the violence of the system into the open – was a phrase of the Maoist Red Army Fraction in West Germany – one that could be heard in 1970. No-one would accuse Hughes of belonging to the ultra-Left – but the links between force and law, between violence, territorial power, and the State, were not fictional – and not dreamed up by Hughes.

Crow resembles the accounts of sea-fights ('Fights for the Flag') which were a staple of English poetry early in the 20th century, but a transformation has occurred – the whole has been raised to a mythic level, and the element of idealisation has been stripped away. Hughes is not interested in unit cohesion under fire, or in tender thoughts of the homeland. *Crow* is an epic with no virtue. He is in no way saying that the violence on which crows thrive is good – it is merely primal.

The force of the poem comes from releasing energy bound in structures. Because nothing is stable, we see the forces shaping cooled form – the origins of the land, the origins of anatomy, the origins of the social order. He makes the energy visible by using small self-contained deformable objects – they are total physiognomy, totally expressive, whereas most poems are mired in fact and have only a few physiognomic elements. The poem is written in the transhistorical mode – Crow lives in every millennium and every country. This is no doubt the most interesting way of writing poetry. The whole landscape is new in every poem – and is therefore totally expressive. What's strange is how the complete freedom of the *mise en scène*, its unique formal creativity, is combined with such a strong sense of destiny – of the inevitability of patterns.

Crow is composed of multiple episodes, each with its internal climax, which never lead us out of the basic situation, which are connected only by the hero and by an emotional atmosphere. Thus it resembles the TV serial – one of the typical forms of the 1960s.

I am irritated at the need to explain Hughes' poetry, which has a singular obviousness and singular greatness. One day in 1969 I was sitting a scholarship exam which involved commenting on a poem (which I now know to have been Hughes' 'Thistles'). It was a wonderful afternoon, a glimpse for a little 12-year-old of how wonderful writing could be, an abiding memory. It didn't need explaining, and Hughes has more real fans in this country than any other modern poet. Not all his poetry is at the same pitch, but *Crow* was a revolutionary breakthrough and a classic.

Breakout into myth:
David Wevill, *Where the Arrow Falls* (1973, 115 pp., cluster H)

The jacket explains that the 'Hopi maze of emergence' represents the child's path to birth; in its almost infinite possibility is 'where the arrow falls'. The Hopi are Indians of the southwest USA; the maze is illustrated on the dedication page. The first page opens with 'We have lost our natural images. All the images we make are twisted, hammered, brilliant.' This is a turning-point in Wevill's career – the transition from the careful, short, tense, ideally self-contained poems of his first three books into a huge field of continuous relations, where the semantic frame never really closes. This moment was a huge relief – collective and, no doubt, individual. The comment on the jacket that the poems are 'loosely related' cannot quite be accepted – the advance into composing on the scale of 2 or 3,000 lines was so sensational that even to claim it was inflammatory. In fact, the book falls into two tightly coherent blocks – which are also related to each other. Part 1 is a series of poems, set in the landscape of Texas, where Wevill had moved at this time. Their language is paratactic, simple, the imagery elementary and mythic. The first one is about the poet's year-old child – presumably the motive for the 'emergence maze'. In part two, the 30-page long prose story 'The Ritual', Wevill is opening the poem onto the whole range of personal experience, while simultaneously making the domestic mythical. The discontinuities in the plane of *Arrow* seem to me to be more the gaps between the discrete processing centres of the mind than moments when threads are severed, the theatre empties, and recent memories are wiped out.

One of his earlier poems was 'Birth of a Shark' – the poem contained within the physiology of an animal, temporally restricted to a moment of origin, constrained to the biologically predictable acts of the shark. Birth, physiology, and behaviour tightly specify each other – the poem is a system which clasps itself at every point, and which leaves nothing loose. *Where the Arrow Falls* is about a marriage – the theme has grown to engulf the writer, and its internal relations are unbearably rich and yet frequently loose, irrational, unseizable. It is existential, in the sense that the '50s fought for, and which, yet, no '50s poet seemed to approach. Presumably, the ability to write about personal relations without any lapse into the prosaic and economistic took a long time to develop. 'The Ritual' has moved completely into myth – we can say that while his earlier poems ejected themselves into the bodies of (violent) animals, *Arrow* ejects itself into a shared organism which is the marriage of the two central figures, which is itself vulnerable in all directions, so that the sensitive surface of the poem touches the whole environment. The relation between the use of myth and the acceptance, or grasping, of a preliterate community in which mythic thinking is still predominant, is sensitive and has called forth a range of strikingly differing solutions among British poets.

'Cawdor rose up from his day bed and shook out his hair. He stumbled to his typewriter. Day rose and fell. By nightfall he had written 300 cantos of his World. A new generation of insects had lived and died outside his windows. The sun from which he took his energy saw many people born and many injured...'

Cawdor is writing a book of the world because he is inside a marriage which is self-referential, and a world on its own; but because the book is written he can no longer invent the world but has to live in what is written.

The rise of feminism, with a burningly close look at male-female relations, made this kind of thing impossible – it became easier to write rigorously about individual experience. The risks in writing on a large scale about relationships are always high. Society came to talk more frankly, and more frequently, about emotional relations, but poetry could not make full use of these topics – the damage inflicted by people quarrelling about your right to your feelings was just too much. Fiction and distantiation were needed safeguards.

The creation myth is one of the most widespread kinds of text in world cultures. The originals have a didactic value, and must be learnt by the listener; dissolved from such context, they have the specific function of making us imagine the world when it did not yet exist. This is a worthwhile activity. I would be happy to spend a long time doing this. Ensuing themes would be wondering about the origin and growth of the individual mind, and about the origin (too) of laws and social institutions. This might lead to thoughts about recovering this freedom for long enough to remake the society we live in in a better frame. This is worth thinking about, too.

Wevill's move into myth, saturated with animal and plant imagery, bears certain resemblances to two other poets at Cambridge around the same time: Redgrove and Hughes.

Elaborated violations:
D.M. Black, *Gravitations* (1979, 80 pp., cluster D)

The OED defines gravitation as 'the attraction of one body for another', (and supplies 'the strong gravitation towards evil', as an instance). The reader is likely to find this book inside Black's *Collected Poems 1964-87*,

Myth and Deep Narrative

which includes several other narrative poems (but not his first published work, *A Theory of Diet*, already grotesque and viewing humans in firmly biological terms). The book is dominated by three long narrative poems: 'The Hands of Felicity', 'Urru and Uppu', and 'Notes for Joachim'. Each of them takes place in a mythic dimension, and deals with the social structure by fundamental violations of moral law. The author has explained that two of them are written in hendecasyllabics, an eleven-syllable line. Black (famous for almost completing training as a Freudian psychoanalyst before then beginning training as a Jungian) also wrote poems about animals and eastern religion, and his line is clearly simple forms which express a part of human complexity, and which have an excelling narratibility and self-containedness. 'Notes' is about a Franciscan monk who has a compulsion for sodomizing the 'blond, beautiful, children of his charges'. 'Urru and Uppu' is set in Uruk (some ancient Mesopotamian kingdom), and deals with two visually indistinguishable brothers. 'Felicity' is based on a Grimms' *Märchen* (fairy-tale), and starts with a stanza from the poet, who is bestridden by 'the narrative demon', and wears a demon mask. Then, it tells of a rich miller who after three years of drought, is facing revolt. A stranger offers him rain in return for 'what is behind the house' – he thinks it is the apple-tree, but in fact this is his daughter, Felicity. Ample rain comes. Three years later, the devil comes to be given his due. Felicity draws a circle around her with a spade; the circle and her purity mean she cannot be touched. The miller, in panic, cuts her hands off. The devil, frustrated, dissolves into gas. Felicity goes out into the world and finds an orchard of pear trees, behind a stream which an angel carries her over. The king who owns the orchard catches her in a net, and then marries her and gives her wonderful silver hands. Because her mother-in-law tries to kill her child, she flees again. In a moment of despair, she wants to throw the baby on the fire – and her hands grow back. After a failed war and his deposition, the king (who was obscurely complicit with his mother) spends seven years wandering to find her – when he does so, she does not want to speak to him. But at last they are reconciled, and return to the town, and their marriage, with their goods in a handcart. In the Sumerian poem, a senior court official (the chief finance officer) tells how an ancient man, Uppu, a woodcutter bankrupted by the decline of the forest, came to his door – and was the king's father. One day, the fatally poor Uppu came to his brother, a goldsmith, with a feather from a golden bird – which he claimed to have oracular value. Urru makes him promise to find and kill the bird, to please the god. His twin sons are hungry. He brings Urru, instead, two eggs – one of which, on the way, devours the other. Later, Uppu kills the bird itself, with a throwing-stick. A legend, known to Urru, is that eating the vital organs of this bird guarantees you a lifelong supply of two gold pieces a day. The hungry sons steal the cooked fowl – and eat it. Aware of their wealth (in golden beechleaves), Uppu, against his will and after long religious struggle, chases them off – to where one became king (a story recounted at the start is of their brotherly loyalty, how one identical brother saved his brother, turned to stone in the Great Forest, rather than take his place and queen).

The style is notably unambiguous. However clear-cut the events, the meaning of the events is still complicated – their impact, in three dimensions, really undefinable. We detect perhaps that the ambiguity of modern-style texts is to supply small oscillations that exhibit small forces – in fact the *fins écarts* that differentiate an exceptional personality from others.

The conscious mind deals with a small frame at any time. Filling that small frame (with involving narrative), and then visibly replacing it, we realise how small it is. The plot construction is more about thermodynamics – rate of change – than about any emission of the poet's character. We suspect – do we not? – that the obsession with building a monument to personality is what expelled narrative from the poem. Most books of poems just don't have this rapid succession of exciting events. Somehow, the turns of the poem reflect the rules of social structure in the same way that speech reflects the geometry of the mouth. In fact the wish to exhibit the personality excludes the high-energy external events which narrative demands; its quality of self-repetition excludes the uncertainty of exciting narrative. To sum up: ambiguity displaces the unexpected. More: Black's narratives are about shock and forgetting.

Black is Scottish, although born in South Africa (in 1941). His work influenced Frank Kuppner and possibly the novelist Iain Banks.

The Bloodshed, the Shaking House, by Martin Thom
46 pp. (A4, photocopied typescript, stapled; cluster C)
(published 1977 but dated 1974 in the text)

The first section is called 'The Bloodshed the Shaking House', and opens with a dream about watching a 1950s TV set showing a town in Portugal where all the men are absent fighting colonial wars. It is an influencing machine. At the beginning of the dream, the speaker sees men and women in a corridor, on all fours, playing a kind of game of chess in which they are the figures. I think this chess game is a way of visualising the social order: where our actions draw their significance from their visibility to other people, within a set of conventions which are like a game (chess for example), so that we are simultaneously conscious of our bodies and intentions from within, and of the part they play as pieces in a game visible to others. This is very helpful in thinking about social systems – which involves us in a similar double image. The significance of the passage is that it condenses something abstract and reflexive into something visual and immediate, which we can process with our visual imagination: what might be a key for Thom is the total emotional involvement in scientific enterprises (anthropological and psycho-analytical, mostly), so that the poet is talking about complex abstract ideas in a primary discourse. We can recognise this as the state of flow which Czikszentmihalyi spoke of: the poet is walking fluently through a landscape where ideas have become visible. This is what we are granted in dreams; and is perhaps how people's minds work when they are about to make breakthroughs in anthropology. I feel especially close to this, because I have spent so long trying to put social experience into conceptual form, which can be manipulated in the mill of thought; the idea of someone simultaneously living in their own mind and body, and moving in a chess game, was terribly exciting.

The influencing machine (*Beeinflussungsapparat*) comes from the 1914 account by the psychoanalyst Victor Tausk of one of his cases. It is something in much the shape of a human body, containing inner works, which influence people, in a kind of broadcast. It had human organs which acted like switches, controlling feelings in her, identical, human organs. This puts in visual form the dependence of humans on other humans: our states of mind are dependent on other people's states of mind. Even the central process of art can be thought of as a kind of influencing technology, whereby the artist's state of mind is transferred to the spectator. Again, a wonderfully vivid concrete image for an invisible process. But this is not a rational construction, it is the product of a Croat schizophrenic, Natalija A, Tausk's patient. No one has an identity wholly screened off from other people's wishes and beliefs, but Natalija, as a schizophrenic, had no protective screening at all, and this is what she was expressing in this great image. Most people have some sense of agency about their feelings, as acts which are partly involuntary and partly participatory; Natalija experienced her own feelings as alien imperatives, events happening inside her over which she had no control. That is – she was like a piece being moved in a game only, not simultaneously feeling ownership of her actions and sensations. The TV is an 'influencing machine' because it tells people what to do and feel. The rest of the poem can be seen as a sequence of images on the TV screen; it can also be read as an account of a phase in Thom's life, but one where most of the material is drawn from his study of anthropology, psychoanalysis, and myth. I know nothing about the later history of this patient, but her ability to shape telling images deserves proper credit. Thom's use of this imagery produced by mental disturbance is a crossing of deep barriers which explains, also, how he has got from academic study of anthropology (and then of psychoanalysis) to poetry. The discontinuity between *The Bloodshed* and earlier English poetry comes from his decision to use the full extent of his intellectual knowledge within the poem. The subject matter is, to be sure, ordinary human emotions and domestic relationships (the 'House' of the title), but the conceptual framework in which they are seen is wholly unfamiliar, because it embodies the efforts of a century of anthropologists to break out of Christian-capitalist mythology and think about how societies are organised, how subjective wishes knock into the complex symbolic games which all societies set up. At the same time, it is possible to take the flow of *The Bloodshed* simply as a sequence of scenes, fully realised and held together by an internal complexity and richness of relationship, which we participate in – while the idea of *what does it mean to participate? what are our desires?* is a kind of music to be heard on one part of the stage.

There are problems in paraphrasing the dream episodes in the later sections. I think this is partly because they are too uncategorised and delicate to put into recognisable terms; and partly because the paraphrase always seems to take longer than the poem. One page reads, in its entirety:

> still human in the
> arrogant
>
> net imagination
>
> closely drawn, pinned with gold structures
> an aereal cluster hanging
>
> 'no more strife'   in five tongues, more
> and more
> in the dual relation
> no one leaves
>
> the princess slept here
> her head
> on and on
> through the savage
> side of her bed
> and the iron flanks of
> the mystical horse, her father
> to birth in fields
>
> wet with the dew metaphor
> and swimming against time
> to our birth in her   You who are full of things
> and stand   dry as tinder
> living in sunlight
> cannot go ever
> fire tongue out

This is not an explanation of something else, but something that needs explaining. Perhaps this is the start of a new set of myths, setting loose further cascades of collection, explanation, and exegesis. It could be the constructivist product of montage from 5 or 6 texts, subtly joined – or a report of a dream, governed by the primary process, and using the identical principle of montage and onward flow. The whole sequence of *The Bloodshed* cannot be summarised, but possesses a fine flow, a kind of delirium in which we fly over the Eurasian uplands and lowlands, never losing impetus and never repeating effects.

Thom can be compared with Tom Lowenstein, not just because both trained as anthropologists but also because their poems have a comparable detachment from arrangements specific to 20th-century Europe, an equal willingness to talk about the deep patterns of human behaviour, and an equal openness to myth.

Reference to the quoted passage shows clearly a liminal condition. The features which the reader finds most difficult – the absence of a concrete situation, the deletion of everyday purposive activity, the suspension of realistic limits, the timeless setting full of eternal and founding objects – are the most clearly linked to this condition. Indeed, the setting of the poem at the level of the most generalised ideas – about how the mind works, about how humans relate to each other – and simultaneously at the level of mythical actions and processes, shows how ideas and myths are related; natives of a liminal landscape.

The Middle Passage:
David Dabydeen, *Turner* (1994 TNP tnbp1, cluster B)

Dabydeen (b.1957) comes from Guyana, and belongs to the Indian ethnic group, who came there as indentured labourers in the 19th century. Guyanese politics are much about the conflict between Indian and Afro-Caribbean ethnic groups. Guyanese politics have turned out exceptionally unfavourably – Guyanese intellectuals and artists have found it a good place to leave, which has been to the advantage of the British scene in many ways. This volume is a compound of a new poem, 'Turner', and a selection from Dabydeen's previous volumes. These are largely set in Guyana, and in Guyanese patois – remote from Standard English forms. They describe the village life of Asians (known locally as East Indians) in the countryside. They are picturesque realism, showing strong descriptive powers.

The main poem is about 950 lines long, and its point of departure is a sea painting by Turner – 'Slavers throw overboard the dead and the dying.' At lower right is the head of a man, thrown overboard, drowning. A Note explains that 'My poem focuses on the submerged head of the African in the foreground of Turner's painting. It has been drowned in Turner's (and other artists') sea for centuries. When it awakens it can only partially recall the sources of its life, so it invents a body, a biography, and peoples an imagined landscape.' The whole poem thus comes from the mouth of someone dead – the head in the painting. The date is roughly 1810, and the world around the poem is the real world of that time – with sugar plantations around the Caribbean yielding high profits, and the slave trade in West and East Africa leading to the devastation of entire regions, as most slaves were captives of war, and the firearms supplied by Americans and Europeans made the wars easy to win.

Not only the painter, but also the owner of the cargo, and the ship's doctor, are called Turner. This is extremely confusing. Turner's painting was of course anti-slavery in emotion – the sight of someone drowning arouses our sympathy, and automatically makes us think of escape; which draws our attention to denial of freedom, and to the will of someone else, which decreed that this dying man should be confined on a ship by force. Because so many different characters are called Turner, and because he never speaks in his own voice, it is hard for us to know what he is feeling, and so to read the emotional situation which obtains at any moment.

The theme of the Atlantic crossing is bound to remind us of Edward Kamau Brathwaite, an exile from Barbados, whose masterpiece *The Arrivants Trilogy* (published 1967–9) was one of the great achievements of the 1960s. The setting moves into liminal space: it is the founding of Guyanese society, a moment when memories were wiped away and when small things had a permanent influence on the way of life that was coming into being. The theme rises to the level of the entire nation simply because it is at the origin and because it is non-localised: the sea crossing is where everybody comes from, so a poem about the sea crossing belongs to everyone, and by virtue of that becomes a national poem and an epic. The narrator cannot belong to any parish of the new land – because he never completes the crossing, he has drowned (and his role as non-living, speaking, head is a liminal one, where oppositions are deleted and the eternal forms become visible). Much of the poem describes village life in Africa, before the enslavement of the speaker and his family. Dabydeen is little concerned to recount the politics and economics of the slave trade – with which every reader is familiar; the tenor of his poem is much more pictorial and mythic. It is also surprisingly optimistic – the evocation of pastoral life in an unidentified part of Africa is like a landscape painting, secure, agreeable, and full of incident. Much of it describes unfamiliar plants and animals – the exoticism which is a general feature of post-imperial writing about the empire, as also of cinema. This aspect may remind us of Francis Berry or Sacheverell Sitwell.

Because the whole *mise en scène* is mythic, the character Turner may follow the rules of myth. In this case, the white man appears by necessity, as the (evil) stepfather of Guyanese society – which was summoned into being to service white-owned plantations. In mythic discourse, individuality does not matter – and hence the merging of identities serves to mix the functions which add up to one role, of paternalistic authority. In this role, the painter emerges not only as someone speaking to the political opinion which was about to abolish the slave trade (in British ships), but as someone speaking *for* the African victims – whose voices we do not hear – and instead of them. This is a possible explanation.

The Dominance of the Optical

So much of the change over the last 400 years in the way the West lives has to do with ever-improving optical processing. In small errors getting smaller lie gigantic possibilities. The deceptive qualities of light reveal that we are just microbes with archaic sensory organs sampling a universe too complex for them. While also permitting artists to arrange grandiose illusions. Poetry is not a visual art but relies on visual processing: poets are clinging to the edge of a whole universe of visual data as the power of cameras and computers explodes.

In White Ink: Mimi Khalvati, *Entries on Light* (1997, 90 pp. 60WP, cluster A)

The idea of the book is that each poem is about light – 90 of them. They are like entries in a diary.

Khalvati was born in Teheran (in 1944), and her first language is Farsi. We would expect infelicities of language from an English-learner – this is a false expectation, since her smoothness and grace in using language are quite remarkable, and in fact she seems to have these qualities more than anyone else.

Light appears as a liminal substance – it is continuous, like a fluid, and it joins things together. Continuity seems to be one of the great values here. Actually, and not being ironic, Khalvati could be declared as excessively English – she is more interested in smoothness and the fluency of social intercourse than in conflict, drama, or extreme emotional positions. The steady change of light is not seen as a drama, but rather like the months in some Burgundian Book of Days, eagerly and accurately carrying out its changing tasks of bouncing off things and recording, momentarily, their shapes and colours.

> Light's sharpening
>   knives of water
> I long for the coolness
>   of a room downstairs.
> White grapes. A morning
>   cigarette. To take

    umbrage behind hessian
      blow on a glass
    of tea, sugarlump held
      between my teeth, taste
    how bitterness
      too quickly sweetens.

There are certain conventions about poets having arrived from warm countries – a kind of mandatory exoticism, intimately related to the way seaside holidays are portrayed in posters. Unusual food, too, is often implicated. We have been devastated by those poems like idyllic resorts being devastated by uncontrolled tourism. Khalvati is unusual because she steers away from these globalising formulae to produce, instead, poetry which expresses intelligence and character at every point.

Normally, we can detect points in a poem where it would be possible to improve it – the poet has got involved in a scene with a thousand factors, and has unsurprisingly failed to scan and integrate all of them. This is apparently quite impossible with Khalvati – she has such grace in using the language, such an ability to view a phrase from all sides before releasing it, that every passage is stylistically perfect.

Light is something that makes you forget what came before it. Because light has to do with changes across time, drawing attention to it refers to someone's state of alertness in general, the neatness with which their brain moves out of one attentional state and switches, completely and integrally, into another one. We do not find that light appears here as a metaphor for the infinite love of God, as in Christian theology (led by Dionysus the Areopagite, perhaps); for the unattainable, for what dizzies and overthrows reason. Instead, it appears as rather a calm substance, in general. It is not a source of purged knowledge, which reveals paradoxical truths because it is puritanically cut off from the filtering and projecting industries of social perception – the whole stormtrooper/puritan drama of avant-garde painting has been led away and left there. This light is not harsh and does not, brutally or criminologically, reveal more of the visible world than our customary gaze as it flickers over the familiar. Her earlier books were called *In White Ink* and *Mirrorwork* – both seeming preoccupied with light, which we can consider as the white ink, which is brilliant but soon becomes invisible.

In the poem on page 58, the leaf which the tulip seems about to lose is compared to a part of the pigeon's plumage, as it perches on a red-tiled roof, grooming a second pigeon; the red is picked up as the red coat of a little girl playing football. We move to empty lots which reach out to waterways running between mill towns (i.e. canals), as if the urban tracts could be a river, and office workers do their jobs on its banks. In the poem on p.86, the poet says how much she dislikes the eye of longing, and the eye of fantasy: a clue to the stability of the poems, which is being offered as something suited to the human species. She expresses puzzlement at the fantasy images of a Northern world of fairy-tales – implicitly connecting such counter-sensual fantasy to a dimness of light which makes the results of the senses incomplete. Longing and fantasy necessarily fragment us. In another image of plumage, we see the Simurgh (a Persian fairy-tale bird, *murgh* being bird), flying over the Alborz Mountains (in Persia), and fostering a human being (presumably) for three years. This is compared to the language itself, as a kind of foster bird for Khalvati (and stranger to her than English!). The Simurgh gives the foster-son a feather from her back to light as a rescue beacon: this is the light which ties the poem into the scheme of the book.

The use of light seems related to an affection for textiles, defined by their colours. The poet has written about the painter Pierre Bonnard, and the domestic intimacy which we associate with Bonnard seems related to her stylistic ideals. The individual snatches are windows on a remarkably abiding and stable and profound scene which is in no way vulnerable to discontinuities of illumination. Light is transient but the poems, themselves transient, are glimpses of an abiding reality. It is as if the breaks between the poems (each one a moment of inner awareness and external illumination) were rehearsals for change and separation – true detachment can ride over the events of separation from loved ones and from pleasure. For this reason, none of the poems offers a turning point or a threat which excites us by peril – each one is benign and secure, like a Bonnard painting.

This is dissimilar from any other poetry of the period.

The secret life of objects:
Peter Didsbury, *The Classical Farm* (1987, 71 pp. TNP)

Didsbury (b.1946) lives in Hull and this was his second book. Titles include 'Truants', 'A Winter's Fancy', 'Death of Pan', 'Scenes from a Long Sleep', 'Vesperal', and there are two epigraphs, from two antiquarians, Aubrey and Walpole, positing Yorkshire as a picturesque and mysterious wilderness: 'Oh! What quarries for working in Gothic!'. Typical imagery includes the Humber estuary. The basic method is of fixing reality before interpretative frames have classified and categorized it, isolating primary features, and recording these features in a serial way, such that multiple interpretations are possible during the course of the poem, and the interpretative framework, invisible and eliminated, paradoxically stands out starkly as if read by infra-red light. These are poems about cognition, unable to supply sentiment or morality. That is, the same basic method as with Christopher Middleton and Roy Fisher. The release of information across time is the essential part of the poem's design. Any discussion of *ostranenie* will shed light on Didsbury.

Sometimes the scene is bizarre and inexplicable: in 'The Drainage', a Yorkshire parish is bound by frost, a man goes round cutting the skins off cows and stitching them together. 'The Rain', recounts the Eddic myth of the creation of mankind by a cow licking the ice (to release the grandfather of the Æsir gods), in a surreal Northern dialect which is and isn't like the way people speak in the North. He is interested in the secret life of objects:

> Edifying Lectures at Dusk
> float in and out of the windows like paper planes,
> the kind whose bombload is held to resemble
> the light reflected from jams in the pantry,
> pear halves stacked like syrup in jars,
> the breath of apples in the air raid shelter
> and the sound of the clock in the hall that is ticking like fruit.

and we can link this to his second profession as an archaeologist (a modern antiquarian), where inanimate and dumb objects are arranged in patterns which provoke a conceptual breakthrough into speaking and becoming evidence. The title poem shows a plain of allotments lit by a burning school – set alight by the pupils, it becomes a 'massive antique stove of brick'. 'All will come by wisdom on this spacious classical farm.' One of the seekers of wisdom has had an allotment there for sixty years. In the last seven lines, an I narrator comes in, describing himself building a fire on his allotment, in a cone: it creates fertile detritus, and is a model for 'its great Platonic master', the burning school. Ambiguously, this might mean that the school cultivates its pupils – just as cultivation makes gardeners pupils of the earth.

Often, the poem is a verbal account of an image, perhaps a photograph, which has several interpretations – its relation to a possible three-dimensional reality is ambiguous. In 'Glimpsed Among Trees', we start with a house suddenly becoming visible to someone kneeling on his allotment, pulling a plantain. We hear about some of the layout of the house, about a boy's room full of toys. His father leaves 'lemonade and cooking Marsala' to go sticky in a glass, which 'the blue-painted god of the morning' picks up and carries to the top of the house, to enjoy the prospect. What we hear is actually 'It is this broad prospect... which the kneeling man has knelt to cultivate', and a similar chain of turns in which the optical becomes an object uncoils for another 60 lines. We hear much about a glass button which has been lost in the soil for 80 years, 'Quartz from the lips of the tide shines like diamonds, then dies/ but this has been up and down in the earth, and has learned a thing./ Its stored reflections will always include the poles of the ferry at Hell'. The house seems to be one of a row which has drifted off to the wrong position, which is about to be returned: 'We shall take this festering street and sail it home at last'. This perhaps records the optical effect of houses on flat low-lying ground near the sea, which sometimes appear to be standing on water. The writer appears at several moments to be musing on his own reality through identifying with phantoms who may not regard him as real (but merely optical). There is a reference to someone cataloguing phenomena (in tens) in order to convince himself of his own existence, and the insidious fluency of the poem may be connected with the idea that consciousness is naturally intermittent, and the narrative faculty exists to stop up the gaps.

The picture around Didsbury is confused because although he is painstakingly original and is using techniques of estrangement, he is not recognised by the Underground as one of theirs. His poetry is clearly hard to write and each poem demands a new idea. The count of his poems is small and easily overviewed. At his best, as in this volume, each poem starts from a weird point of approach to develop a weird but entire world.

A City of Glistening Organs:
Michael Ayres, *Poems 1987-92* (1994, 70pp.)

Perception is not yet meaning; what is no longer perception, is no longer trustworthy. Six out of twenty-four poems here set out from works of visual art. In 'The incredible shrinking man', the victim-hero is seen almost as an effect produced by playing with lenses:

> The body first.
> All the intricate imbroglio of muscles
> shrinking down to the innards of a watch,
> then scaled down further.
>
> This is the micro of all his considerations.

Once everything has been reduced to a picture, one can then view both the scene and the I as designed objects, enhanced in post-processing. This narcissism is the most common, cheap, discourse of our society, copiously available in advertisements, which Ayres exhibits to gun down: 'In a drowned, aquanigrescent light/ he holds her skin: /Obsession for the body/ c.1986'. Obsession is also a brand name; the careful dating signals the transience of wishes, their negation by the forces of imitation which aroused them. It would be perverse to say that the models in photographs, in advertisements or for shows, are not beautiful; Ayres's purpose is to write beautiful poems. He loves the fluids around the body – light as perfume: *two corpus resting/ complete with drifting/ starfish hands/ on a seafloor of desire waves in upper light/ ripplingly striate, with soft bars*. The drowned girl, painted by Caravaggio, in 'The Dyer's Hand', oddly anticipates 'Pool' (1994) in its link of water and sexuality. The embracing medium is the lover's body, and the moment when inner and outer fluids merge is the rippling transverse and longitudinal muscle contractions called ejaculation.

The quality distinguishing ads from art would be their brevity. Ayres has nothing to do with short forms: the autonomy of the work of art is located in its length; the resultant legato, long smooth curves of language, reminds me of the 'labyrinthine clarity' of New Order. They are opulent, even: the momentum of large-scale symmetrical forms, swept like the side of a liner, carries the reader away. He wants that 'classical skin veneer & inside a city of glistening organs'.

The scenes critical of the Government are numerous; in 'Raw Materials' there is a mention of 'Mussels/ changing sex on a polluted coastline', and an evocation of greedy and violent landowners as the human reality of a 'pastoral' English landscape; in 'Docklands' the liquidation of the old community in London's docklands makes way for an imaginary new financial quarter ('whatever has power survives/ when the powerless goes to the ground'); in 'The famine in Africa' he evokes the burning of cattle infected with BSE, a brain disease causing dementia, as a result of gross failures of control in the livestock industry. Perhaps he is treating politics from an optic point of view, as media distortions: the fate of the image within a data-processing medium. He is comparing the visibly decaying urban fabric with an imagined ideal which would resemble the symmetry and opulence of the verse cadence.

In the Eighties, the poets experienced the urge to be sleek, coherent, highly finished, persuasive, to avoid being written off with the incoherent, unwelcoming, wholly negative, etc. work with which Sixties radicalism climaxed and died. Disruption had any effectiveness for the audience only in the short term. The audience stopped having the conversion experience. It seems likely that Ayres too is caught between the wishes to engender alarm, by means of contradiction, and for political purposes, and to engender tranquillity and artistic bliss, by means of long smooth forms. His political poems have a curious aestheticism, whereby the lighting, cutting, and patterning of the material is more fascinating than the political reactions it might arouse. This is the flip side of political art wasting its effectiveness by being ugly and grubby.

Ayres likes the method of composition around repeating key lines. This is a feature of oral, non-composed music as repetition with variation; it recurs in contemporary music based on programmable synthesizers. The cyclicity points away from the idea of efficient information content, denies a straight line of progress, and redirects attention to the texture of the poem. Recurrence binds the poems as they avoid a logical structure; it allows a loose flow of sense without drift. The willingness to exploit data from television, advertisements, the newspapers, paintings, etc., caused breaches of tonal 'envelope', which were solved, later on, by minute attention to editing; as Mies van der Rohe is said to have spent endless time designing the corners of his skyscrapers, the point of transition between two planes. The covering of links, false transitions, which in propaganda, or television news, would be seen as inauthenticity, thus becomes in poetry the sign of aesthetic autonomy and elegance: the glaze.

I think what this poetry brings is like an advance in electronics, where everything becomes more highly defined and less jerky. Michael Ayres is confident about what he wants to see, the surface of the language is continuous and full, he is not showing us what makes him anxious or angry but what he loves. Truly, this is like listening to the endless curve of techno music after years of jagged punk rock. He is not showing us alienation, but something attractive and desirable.

Ludic Poets of the 1980s

As I claimed in my book *The Long 1950s*, there was a change of regime in the 1980s so that empirical domestic anecdotes stopped being the only poetry tolerated by the official organs, and a wave of new poets arrived to write a poetry which was not evidence about sociological process but was playful, genial, secular, imaginative, original, and amusing. These poems were not meant to say important things, not to be the utterance of someone with knowledge of Fate, but avoided moments of destiny so as to have time to explore the picturesque and the odd. They were not critical but invitations to a game.

They were often discussed under the fashionable rubric of post-modernism, and their local ancestry was the work of George MacBeth and Edwin Morgan. Morgan had, indeed, been writing poetry of this kind in the 1950s. I was unable to establish a firm date for the change, but the appearance of poems by Kuppner and Ash in a 1983 anthology edited by Michael Schmidt points to a date when such poetry was technically possible but not yet identified as a new trend. Other poets who emerged in the 1980s writing poetry which can generically be compared to these are Jeremy Reed, Jo Shapcott, and Robert Crawford. One line of approach is to talk of the textual machines which were described by French structuralist critics, linguistic programs which generate texts at a level outside the ego of the writer, either above (as a shared resource) or below (as a unit in a psyche seen as made up of hundreds of autonomous units). Another line is to look at the pop world of about 1979, dominated by the monotonous, compressed, and aggressive sound signal of punk rock, breaking up into the far greater variety, if also of less intensity, of the 'new wave' and bands like The Cure and Simple Minds. Another line is to look at the left-wing Counter Culture which had made the running in the 1970s, with its intrusive demands on the content of art, and even on the content of individual consciousness, and to see a rollback from this revolutionary intensity into self-indulgence. The Counter-Culture had after all offered a model of individual liberation, and the new ludic poetry was coming up with the fruits of that liberation. Other lines of explanation are no doubt possible. The artistic validity of these poems is the best explanation for why they were written, and why they were written in such quantity.

To say 'of the 1980s' is flawed because it implies that an idea is only valid for a few years. On the contrary, the real map of poetry in a given year includes poets who set out in each of the previous five decades, and styles continue to be fertile.

Bean-soup and Coarse Red Wine:
John Hartley Williams, *Canada* (1997; 114 pp.; TNP)

The book is divided into sections called 'Bean Soup' 'Pistol Sonnets' (in 3 books), 'Canada' and 'Deuce'. There is an epigraph from Benjamin Péret: *Canada canada mon petit Canada*, which already reveals a grand loss of scale under the force of caresses. At one point, the poet (b.1942) glosses Canada as "Kwakiutl word meaning 'exit'." The poems in this section belong to the genre of virtual landscape, constructed from media imagery and full of *adunata*, impossible things. They have flamboyantly long lines, and are Tall Tales from the chamber of imagination; an expansion of the third word of the title of 'Big Rock Candy Mountain':

> A typical Canadian girl has a nose like a pigeon, a mouth like an eel, a jaw like a silk ear, hair like cognac, eyes like a hockey game, breasts like mother, a waist like General Wolfe, thighs like tennis spectators & a voice like parliament.

This is close to oral poetry. We do not resist quoting his great line 'O normality, dearest and least understood apparition from the vegetable kingdom', which simultaneously gives away the whole nature of this book and reminds us of Brian Marley and Rosemary Tonks. The volume slides on one long glissade of paradox, hyperbole, yarn-spinning, lust, parody of 19th-century eloquence, lessons on non-existent worlds, romantic dreams, extravagant rambles, dream connections, exotic cities. These burlesque erotic phantasies would not be credible without the tilt brought by the sheer volume of talk. Clouds weigh as much as 50,000 tons (according to a poem by Michael Ayres), and Williams' talk weighs as much as a whole restaurant.

Williams lived in Berlin from 1976 until his death in 2014 and had a generous view of eastern Europe from there – of the poets who mix surrealism and folk tradition. He fields torrents of data without being didactic – a poetic response to the academic era. Titles include 'Amours de Garage' 'Could Have Been Me... Actually... It Was' 'The Brain of the Tragedian' 'Kissacop' 'Twelfth Century Rag'. This is the non-desexualised male, blown up to twice life-size with verbal energy and demonstrating skill and prowess like a fish about to invent legs. The return to the prowl, to display, to maps of the city constructed entirely in terms of erotic potential: zones of chill and being out of place; fertile zones where potential partners look for an opportunity to drop precautions; tropical belts where elemental forces disport themselves like domestic floods, cyclones, and stampedes: 'ejaculatory mists of steam & plaster'.

At the highest crest of affairs, lulled by the peaceful beating of blood, we see things that can't really happen. The Péret quote evokes for us the splendours of 1920s Surrealist poetry; the litany of male chat-up lines, the grand flow of afternoon seduction in words.

The pistol sonnet is uncredited here, but I know the rules are 14 lines and writing in one take, spontaneously, because of a note the poet sent me circa 1995, which I have unfortunately destroyed. The Pistol Sonnets come in 3 sets of 32 (more or less), and the last poem in each book is a double sonnet. Phew. Hope that clears things up. 'I was queuing outside the Museum of Forms.' Time limits give this the aspect of performance: 'pistol' implies both 'under the starting-gun' and 'very rapid in action' (as in Polly Pistol, a character played by Kim Novak in a forgotten film called *Kiss Me, Stupid*). This free space suits someone for whom poetry is completely natural and the need is to get rid of fogs of tired impulses and to get back to zero, the stream at the mountain top, structureless structuring energy. These sonnets fire from the zero plane, the moment after pure blankness – the field prepared by a kind of street cleaning machine. The chat-up chat, ancient as the worship of the moon. Of which, 'I have a right to expect it', as that Moloko song has it. It requires an enormous forward impetus – enough to sweep two people off their feet – yet has to be light enough to be redirected at a moment's notice on realising that she really won't go with that, (and didn't last time she heard it). These requirements strangely match the structure of surrealist verse – it never loses balance because it can so plausibly claim that it was about to change direction anyway. Although supposedly directionless, surrealist poetry is often an erotic litany flowing on a scale which can drown entire towns. The unconscious operates entirely through metaphors and seems to think about nothing but sex. In 'Red Bean Soup and Garlic', we hear of a club in Novi Sad where someone plays saxophone like Sonny Rollins, freezing cold, a hut where the poet carouses and eats red bean soup with garlic. The zest with which he undertakes life in Belgrade (an autobiography in the volume *Ignoble Sentiments* tells us that he took a job there in 1968) points to a belief in himself and other people which is very pleasurable to watch. Faced with all the possibilities for misunderstanding and alienation, he simply dives into the jazz club and has a rare old time. The gap between Williams' ideals and the life he actually leads doesn't seem very obtrusive. Throughout, there is an intimacy with the You figure, a buoyancy and generosity. The modalities of the sensuous – garlic, paprika, red, Rollinsesque saxophone, heat and snow – seem to hit the richest parts of the spectrum in each case. This is because Williams has such an appetite for the riches on offer – he has a mimetic capacity and when garlic is available he turns into a garlic-shaped lump of appetite. When snow is available, he turns into something with a multiple crystalline mouth. The poetry is close enough to his pulse-beat to match these transformations.

Turkish Restaurant Anecdotes:
John Ash, *The Anatolikon/To the City* (2002; 140 pp. Carcanet)

This is two books in one (because *The Anatolikon* had been published separately). Anatolikon is a pseudo-Greek word for 'an epic account of Anatolia'. 'To the city', *eis ten polin*, was the Greek phrase which became Istanbul or Stamboul – where Ash lives. A city of twelve million people, as he points out. The poems are primarily about Ash (b.1948), but then also about life in Turkey. Title include 'Elegy, Replica, Echo' 'Aunt Petka's Earrings' 'Under Mount Anamas' 'Forgotten Orchestras' 'The Displeasure of Ruins'. He explains in the poems that, as a rather eccentric and impulsive child in Manchester, he read about Byzantium and conceived a desire to live there – as he did some thirty-five years later. In a sense, then, he is living inside a fantasy. He is writing travel poems – although, like many travel writers perhaps, he felt like a stranger where he grew up. The aspect of moving into a fantasy life based on exotic and splendid architecture is traditional, and to a certain extent it is the emotional fantasy of English Christians of living in the Near East of the first two or three centuries of our era which accounts for the rich variety of Near Eastern architectural types to be found in our cities – as churches, but also, even more strangely, as banks, town halls, etc. This by its nature vacant splendour of fantasy architecture was utterly likely to be occupied, imaginatively, by those who live much in fantasy, because of an excess of intelligence and a lack of engagement with the real society around them. Exotic details of doctrine and architectural detail, and exotic words describing them, were the stuff of life for many members of the Church of England or the Roman Catholic Church. In fact, it is music in which his real emotional release is found.

'My Poetry' is about being described as an experimental poet and how indignant he is about this, how he thought it 'was just my heart talking', and ends with an apostrophe to 'Ah, sadness and freedom!'. A twin poem, explaining to avant-garde readers how his work isn't really personalised, convergent, and comfortingly familiar, is not present. But surely he knows that the apostrophe sounds like 19th century drama – that its apparent directness and grand sincerity are so stylised as to be a comic spoof – invoking the conspiracy between actor and audience while satirising the role as written. Ash is not interested in poetic theory, and his poems are free because they sound like no-one else's voice, and yet not free because they curl back to sound like his own voice all the time. It is the contrast between his feelings and the environment which makes the poems interesting, and this contrast is the source of his vivid stream of language, where frustration, surprise, indignation, nostalgia, and fantasy are the motifs of each poem. To a certain extent, he lives in a foreign city, in a narrow circle, because of the threat of competition from other people who are equally frustrated and voluble, and would make his possession of this niche of spoilt charm insecure.

It seems implausible that we are willing to listen to a poem about the difficulties of a taxi ride to a tempting antiquity, or to a poem about the unreliability of plumbing in Istanbul. Surely no-one expects a city which grew by a factor of twelve within one human lifetime, where there was never enough room, to have American-style plumbing. Furthermore, the poet could live in America if he wanted to. You would really have to pull out something exceptional to make the audience sit still for this. And, in fact, Ash does – 'To the Plumbers of Asia' is a virtuoso fake catalogue-ode on the stylistics of plumbing, running through neo-traditionalists, Symbolists, Expressionists, and neo-formalists, to climax with

> O plumbers of Asia,
> it is your lyrical and improvisatory
> compositions that most delight me,
> filled with the sadness of flooded basements.

By redefining failed engineering as art, he redefines artistic style as an extravagant and personalised failure – and makes his own art a success.

The churches embody theology, which itself embodies a social order of norms taught to children. The churches invite assimilation and imitation. The elaborate instructions and moving patterns of the social order are ludicrous for him partly because of their incorporation of heterosexuality as part of their meaning – leaving him, right from childhood, in a position of not matching. A whole series of omissions follows – the dance rotates, slowly and comprehensively, to leave him alone, on a dark heath, for weeks, waiting for a partner to come and lead him back into the dance. The ornate and finished intricacies of music and Byzantine architecture are, in effect, compensations for the absence of a social order which would give him something worthwhile to do and say. The individualism which this leads to is suitable for a lyric poet – it dissolves the social order, to leave us alone with the poet, in an island of warmth, where the poem is as large as the meaningful world. It is perfectly clear what we have to say and do in the poem – we have to comfort the poet and try to coax him into remaining cheerful and afloat.

500 Willow Pattern Sight Gags:
Frank Kuppner *A Bad Day for the Sung Dynasty* (1984)
(TNP; 2004 + 40 lines; cluster D)

Poem 1 runs:

> The elderly statesman trudges wearily over the bridge;
> He was expected in the palace more than twenty-five minutes ago;
> Surely that is not his penis he holds in his hand?
> From the bedroom of a house in Germany I once saw trees
>   exactly like that.

A book (by Osvald Sirén), of reproductions of Chinese paintings, struck Kuppner in a second-hand bookshop. The poems – 501 of them – are all quatrains, all set in an imaginary China, all mis- or at least para-readings of the paintings in Sirén's book. The poet looked at them 'feeling certain that the whole story was not being told'. There is also 'A Technical Note' with ten more quatrains describing the technique of the quatrain. Even the form is taken from one commonly used by translators from Chinese – mis-reproducing some original metre, possibly tied to music, which we can only see as a kind of fog. Within this fog, mis-recognitions are common. Many of the characters are misreading the situation they are posed in. Often, we get two or three – absurdly incompatible – interpretations of the same scene. Perhaps the basis of humour is misunderstanding – to be exact, the click moment where you lose an understanding and before you replace it with another. This double-take may explain how he can pull off so many gags in four lines.

Sections are named 'A bad day for the Sung dynasty', 'Soft laughter and distant music' 'Yellow River dreaming' 'The Moment Passes' 'The same laughter, further away'. This may be of interest to some people – Kuppner (b.1951) has stated that the first part of his name is Polish, the second Czech, and the third German. His family must have come from Silesia, or close by. Anyway, he was born in Glasgow and has, he says, 'ever since, nurtured the hopeless dream of one day living in Edinburgh'.

As is the tradition of Western orientalism, the scenes offered have a consistency and aesthetic perfection which real-life scenes can never have. The idea of basing poems on paintings (even imaginary ones) is similar to Sitwell (q.v.). The plainness of diction, the exoticism, and the endless elaboration can be compared to D.M. Black. Kuppner combines the notion of a labyrinthine artificial world with finely imagined, sharp detail – a winning combination. The key to writing fantasy, which neither writer nor reader wishes to end, is to give a sense of rapid local movement and change – an urgency sufficient to distract the reader from the generous endlessness of the whole. In the context of the 1980s, and a decaying manufacturing and seaport city, the endless development belongs with endless leisure – and unemployment. The enforced inactivity of some very intelligent people was conducive to elaborate, endlessly varying, social games. In such conditions, the unemployed graduates of Glasgow could become world leaders in the exploration of leisure. The indifference to politics belongs to a milieu where everyone has had their say about how bad things are, far too often and far too loudly. Luxury and distraction are things profoundly to be wished, from culture – people don't need to be reminded of the fact that they have no money. There is absolutely no didactic or moral intent.

I am looking at an account of Bamforth Films – a forgotten Yorkshire company which began producing lantern slides in 1860 and gradually moved into the cinema, before pulling out again to specialise in coloured comic postcards. 'Alike in laughter-creating qualities and photographic qualities they are unequalled' – a good description of Kuppner. The spectacle of simple pictorial gags coming to life and opening up a window onto a bizarre and uncontrollably moving world would please this poet.

> In stances familiar from photographs of modern golfers,
> Two men on an old stamped tile go about their harvesting;
> Above their heads swim fish as large as themselves;
> The left-hand side of the stone has been badly chipped.

Each scene has to be set up, made the background to some startling and piquant event, and rolled up again, with dazzling speed. Attention has to be drawn to the wholly visible action at the front of the stage without drawing attention to the edge of the scenery, where the whole scene disappears into nothingness. A labyrinth is being painted, fitted up, and dismantled, as we move through it, so that although we cannot see the edge of this landscape of drunken poets, intriguing courts, moonlit gardens, officials on journeys lasting months, ravishing courtesans, and visual misinterpretations, it is barely longer than our own bodies.

Because each poem is the same length, we become sensitised to the approaching end of the poem. This creates a very strong rhythm – the same organisational moment keeps on recurring, with varying verbal shapes leading up to it. The rhythmic effect sharpens our sense of the fine variations – and draws attention to Kuppner's virtuosic ability to make each of 501 poems run differently from the others. The stronger our expectations, the more vivid the surprise at a new twist.

The Neo-underground

This section, along with the one on non-discursive poetry, gives us a chance to evaluate the poets, mentioned several times, who appeared after the peak of the underground in the late 70s.

Bourbon Street Coolerita in a white halation paying back its chains: *Alar*, by Kevin Nolan (1997; 21 pp., cluster C)

Defying chronological probability, this is both a direct response to *The White Stones*, and what may be the most brilliant debut of the decade. Perhaps in the seventies and eighties he was wandering through the cultural beach party wearing sunglasses so cool he couldn't see what was going on. Several passages see Nolan in blackface; already Karl Marx had compared the Catholic Irish to the Negroes (within the terms of nineteenth-century colonialism, of course). The protagonist accepts pop culture with a certain fastidious wood-kern cimarron swagger, is possibly the owner of a bar in the wharfside area:

> He goes down to the dock. Honky business,
> the hours of daylight strike him; the pleasures of the harbour
> fall coin after coin, little crotales of white joy
> tiled in crab-joint. He takes up the shoreline,
> Esquerita humming in the juke slot: the
> ferry comes in daylight, midwise invisible,
> in a white halation playing back its chains
> as yokelore, living memory,
> chuckle-headed phantom of a ship becoming ashes.

Esquerita? The major influence on Little Richard. Crotale is a rattle-snake. Nolan meanwhile occasionally sounds like a lyric by Sly and the Family Stone that got away into the backstreets. Perhaps there is a connection between the pop obsession of Cambridge poetry, as it was developed in the 1960s, and the concern with philosophy; the imperatives of immediacy and rapid change demanding as speaker a mind whose contents are essentially unstable, therefore moving in the zone of errors and paradoxes surrounding Western thought, which is also where new ideas and awareness come from.

The longest poem is 'Seven Last Words of Roy Cohn', an elegy to the much hated figure of Joseph McCarthy's young special assistant in prosecuting Unamerican Activities; later a friend of Hoover. McCarthy's roughneck flair revealed the psychotic at the basis of politics, just as rock and roll swept away the base of the stately and professional American entertainment industry. Cohn died of AIDS in 1986; Nolan's tribute is allusive but allows no hiding place:

> Dealing green bills into black robes, (she sue the judge, Roy sue the furrier, then the ermine all dine with Roy) some other big *chiffre* a late hit as the ex-future Mrs Roy in a blanquette of arum, *as the stars align the principles of man – if you're indicted, you're invited* to sip Old Fashioneds in Dubrovnik '62 with Cal who looks neat in cerise frock, sequinned shadow and liner. Cabochard is it drifting up from his knuckles? Givenchy? ("Cal you old biohazard!") organdy memory and void the papers around him – is he safe?

Roy Cohn and Esquerita (and J.J. Hunsecker) add up to a special theory of the 1950s: a Greil Marcus-style secret history which doesn't exactly cut to a Wranglers ad; maybe one day we will interpret the nineties in terms of Kevin Nolan and Karlien van den Beukel. We got out of a world where the people were misled by evil silver-tongued corporate lawyers like Cohn to enter a bright new world owned by evil silver-tongued corporate lawyers. The Fifties was a time of repression and bad consciences, and so is ours. Equally part of the 1950s was Cleanth Brooks' theory (in *The Well-Wrought Urn*) that paradox was the natural condition of poetry; a design precept which, when taken to the max by Cambridge academics in the sixties, produced the engulfing psychedelic shimmer of *The White Stones*. Every straight line is given a spin, every object is swept away by a ceaseless flux; defying the deadness of what is fixed in writing. There is a kind of aura surrounding any significant work of art, a neurological jitter as we perceive the outline of the complexity of form which is *ipso facto* too much for us to make out in the onset; the precondition for total attention is a rapid bulk impression of incomprehension, the eluding of attention. Engineering appliances are described in terms of their capacities, that is their limits, or, more precisely, the boundary lines where their behaviour becomes unpredictable and complex. Introspection necessarily plunges to the system limits of the mind: where it is inconsistent, paradoxical, arbitrary. What happens to the rotatory energy of a drill-bit when the shank of the drill snaps?

The impact of *Alar*, and of certain other masterpieces of the Cambridge Sound, is like the emergence of complexity theory by gazing at areas of the physical world which had previously been written off as too perplexing or fine to measure: the arrival of a new instrument capable of fixing much finer time-intervals opens up an entire new world of phenomena, for which no words exist in our inherited language.

Arriving just a couple of weeks after Prynne's sensational return to form in *For the Monogram*, *Alar* offers us the vivid image of Counter-Cultural transcendence.

Plastic in Waste Heat:
Peter Manson, *Birth Windows* (1999; 18 pp., cluster D)

The Scottish poetic avant-garde in 1999 consisted of Rob MacKenzie and Peter Manson (b.1973). *Birth Windows* is a milestone in Scottish literature. When I published a poem of Manson's, around 1996, I couldn't actually understand it, but I found it beautiful and haunting. Two translations in *Birth Windows* point us to Mallarmé, and for rapid recognition this is a useful name: evoking a fastidious approach to language over tiny extents, polishing the setting of words until the fabric of familiarity collapses and we fall through into a microdimension of strangeness without apparent limits. Local passages have a clear meaning but when they follow each other the larger meaning is either hard to guess at or highly strange. The outcome is dense and has a unique flavour. If we look at the short poem "In vitro" we can see something of how he works.

> Exploded from the vent
> of ephemeral glassware
> rather than garlanding its bitter vigil
> the neck breaks off, uncut.
>
> I know well two mouths never drank –
> not my mother's, no lover of hers –
> never with this Chimera,
> me, sylph of the Petri dish!

A decanter that's tasted no wine
but long widowhood
grudges with dying breath

– o funereal kiss! –
that the dark
should spawn roses.

The title means in glass, referring to processes being observed in test tubes; in the poem, it seems to mean, more narrowly, *in vitro* fertilisation. The speaker is the offspring of this procedure, IVF. The poem is a series of negations and paradoxes, partaking in fact of a rather 17th century rhetoric; the figure which has an "I" pronouncing a series of impossibilities (*adunata*) is actually not unknown to Latin literature as a riddle form, and the whole is close to an Anglo-Latin riddle, "Roscida me genuit gelido ex viscere tellus", where the thing speaking about its "birth" is a gold ring. Such riddles were usually inscribed on objects, where their shape followed the three-dimensional anatomy of the object. Manson's poems seem to follow, tightly, the surface of a wrenched and perforated 3D space. The theme seems to be the bitter fate of the "mother", the test-tube. Rather than receiving a hymeneal garland (as part of the wedding-rite), it is broken. The birth was not the result of two people making love (stanza 2); the speaker was produced in a Petri dish (containing nutrients for a culture, usually of bacteria). A "Chimera" is three kinds of monster in one body; in biology, an organism produced by two sperm fertilising the same egg; here, the offspring of glass and flesh – of dual nature. Sylph is glossed as "an air spirit", so perhaps the reference is to the "open air", external to a maternal *matrix*, where the fertilisation took place. The dying breath of the decanter (=test tube with fertilised ovum) is some air trapped in it. The "roses" (stanza 4) are the pinks of flesh, now blossoming in the "dark" of the womb where the ovum will become a baby. 'In vitro' is quite a close translation of Mallarmé's poem 'Sonnet' (published in *Poésies* in 1899). The speaker is apparently a glass nymph – cut off at the neck and attached to a ceiling (in mid-air, hence 'sylph') – a glass gas-mantle? 'Veillée' is less 'vigil' than 'party' (which does involve staying awake). Obviously, 'Petri dish' has been supplied by Manson. The "grudging" may simply be that the mantle supplies light and chases away the dark.

As with music, it is individual passages that haunt me which persuaded me to come back to the poems:

The walls' burden, Erato, appended
as who will speak, linear gold

Collapse thought down to the sixty
words you own, dumb in impaction

An epitaph's outflow in beeswax,
the twice-reddened wick

—

speechcraft

– I enjoy these words as decorative arrangements of geometrical elements before discovering what they signify. The whole poem, 'Widows and Orphans' (speechcraft was section I) seems to be about the structural merging of buildings and people, with implications of poverty and constraint, often involving physical destruction and transformation through fire. I think two themes of the pamphlet would be extreme physical situations (structuring an anatomy), and sudden illumination (the word *wax* appears three times). The phrase *Kirlian snapshot* might be thematic; Kirlian was a Russian technician who took photographs by ultrahigh voltage flares, in which auras became clearly visible. This was an extreme physical situation. The pattern of unbearable bursts of light breaking through darkness may be indicative for the opacity of the style, and its perforations. *Dumb in impaction* might be language reaching for density to reproduce what is most rigid, captive, but finally breaking its dumbness. "Hoverers' cunning frees revels/ frozen a thousand seasons" (section II) may refer to bombers – as the house burns, the flames dance. Section IV may be about bodies entombed in volcanic ash at Pompeii.

The title poem is about the death from malaria of Borso d'Este, of the ruling dynasty of Ferrara. I think the 'birth windows' are the decans, 36 divisions of 10 days (the year's round) of astrological significance. These were detected, by Aby Warburg, as the programme for a cycle of mural paintings, partially preserved now, made in the Palazzo Schifanoia for Borso d'Este. The poem doesn't have much to do with astrology, but if we link glass, transparency, and birth (as themes of 'In vitro'), perhaps the point that birth makes you transparent to shaping astral forces (a quasi-light) may shed light on 'Birth Windows'. Another poem is called 'Vitrification Anxiety'.

Manson's poetry is obscure and soaked in light imagery. The allure of this cryptic togetherness is the deeply romantic one of sharing a private world. Language refined to this point offers the prospect of exit into a new world. The fantasy behind it is the beguiling one of creating a language which is completely unlike anything else and which offers a unique experience for sharing. I believe Manson's style arises out of emotional and poetic impulses and is adapted to the poet's personal communicative needs and restrictions.

The guiding fantasy features a conventional style which thousands of young poets use and which will therefore cause anyone using it to vanish. The affect of this extremely exotic and transmuted style, developed as a reaction against vanishing by conformity, has therefore to do with a strong awareness of the marketplace and a strong fear of it. This style is like a fish which is exhibited, when caught, because it looks too strange to be eaten. It is an expression of living in Glasgow knowing the poetry reader wants tales from pretty little villages and not any Glasgow stories. It builds in the expectation of rejection but raises the stakes: seeking an intimacy which goes beyond desolation to totality. The Kirlian flash of light stands for the communication act of such a poetry where the discursive surface has been impacted until it mutates at molecular level.

People round mob-like / open into a column:
Jeff Hilson, *Stretchers 1-12*, *Stretchers 13-33*
(2001-2; 33 pp. together)

Stretchers is a sequence of 33 poems 33 lines long, a number referring to Hilson's age at the moment of composition, but also, teasingly, to the age of Christ. An epigraph reads "I live on the island where people shout 'It is they!' at the voyagers as though they knew of their coming and feared them." A stretcher is a tall story, one that stretches the truth. 'Arminian stretchers of the royal prerogative were caressed and preferred', OED. The name also refers to the tall format of the poems, and perhaps to the arms of the Cross. The line length fluctuates slightly around 8 syllables. The regularity of pattern allows us to get in synch with the poem – catching the pace is quite different from finding coherence. Indeed, *Stretchers* is a completely free associational pattern, a luxurious drift from one thing to another. The point is companionship – free association is just about the most intimate thing you can share. The poem is one long string of irrational, domestic, but also captivating slips or jumps from one idea to another. In Stretcher 8, we find roughly 20 snatches, mostly resembling a proverb or homely saying. Most, that is, take an object or process but seem to give it a behavioural meaning. It starts 'an english bond the long/ and short will make a summer/ havoc'. 'English bond' is a way of laying bricks – seen from one side, you do see an alternation of long and short (known as headers and stretchers). But when in l.6. we hear 'a flemish bond is a castle that's out in time', it's apparent we haven't got a theme or a discursive meaning. The opposition of two classic ways of laying bricks does not carry any semantic load. Such binary forms – pairs, illustrations, sound echoes, puns – are frequently used here to pull the poem along. Everything rolls off the tongue – a kind of melisma. The poem ends with 'people round mob-like/ open into a column', which could be an echo of the building theme – or just the result of entropic drift. We could envisage the whole thing as a failed phonetic reconstruction of some forgotten piece of folklore: 'the green knight nape bone's/ honour's gone and connected to/ the scrape bone belongs to jesus' – where folklore by definition is a clutching at what has been forgotten several times, propped up by metre and commonplaces. If the mark of the aesthetic is to be non-functional, then the faculties of passive registration, association (and stringing-on) are central to poetry as art – and don't need a purpose. Indeed, these processes are going on underneath a poem even if it has an overt intent. I associate *Stretchers* with Harry Smith's 'Anthology of American Folk Music' (on Folkways, originally 1952) – the model of stringing nonsense together within a numerical form that repeats, and keeps asking you to string new ideas on, seems relevant (and Hilson does quote one song from Volume 2, Bascom Lamar Lunsford's unexcelled 'I wish I was a mole in the ground', recorded in North Carolina in 1928). Traditional songs do like a style that uses proverbs or generalisations to illustrate the theme. I see this as basically oral poetry and can hear parts of it being sung in a playground. Who could resist 'these use handy little biscuits/ to add more windows all over/ wandsworth'? It also couldn't be further from Zukofsky (whoever heard of an *affable*

Objectivist?) – on whom Hilson is writing a doctoral thesis. What is being stretched is perhaps the small frame of attention these moments demand, extendible indefinitely – a point becoming a line. I hadn't realised up till now how much we needed someone who would be a cross between a Shakespearean clown and *The Basement Tapes*.

Short Strings Strung Together :
Nondiscursive Poetry

Archaic Virtue seen through glass panes: Ian Hamilton Finlay

Just this once, we're going to throw away the technique of careful first-hand examination of an object right under my eyes, and rely on memories gathered over many years. This is because I don't have access to any Finlay objects. I could go to Stonypath, but it's several hundred miles away, and the weather up there is cold and damp just now. So this is going to be a conceptual review. A key moment in my image of Finlay is one reported by Derek Stanford, in his memoir, *Inside the Forties*. Stanford was an officer in the Pioneers battalion in which Finlay (1925-2006) served late in the war, and recalls that he had already been the leader of a strike at the art school he attended – as a teenager. His career has been attended by uproar, contestation, and rows. The Pioneers were a non-combatant unit filled, at the time, with conscientious objectors. The word, in military language, comes from the mediaeval units who used to cut down trees and make traversable paths for the army; it means *flatteners* in Italian. By 1943 they seem to have been, in line with tradition, involved in forestry – looking after stands of trees which were going to produce the timber for the many Army applications which required wood as a raw material. This scene of ethical virtue, in primitive material conditions, engaged in outdoor work protecting growing things, seems to point forward to his activity as a gardener – a conceptual gardener. In 1945, he was more interested in painting than writing poetry. Fascinatingly, Stanford reports Finlay's enthusiasm at that time for *Un rappel à l'ordre*, by Jean Cocteau, a 1926 book promoting the neo-classicism which was such a feature of the French scene in the 1920s, and after; it was variously associated with homosexuality, stage design, Picasso, the resistance to Picasso, Surrealist painting, etc. Finlay later produced a postcard pack called *Rapel*. Finlay's vision, as developed in the 1960s, is specific, if ramified: a Classical garden whose ornaments recall the stern Republican virtue of the early years of the French Revolution, of Robespierre and Saint-Just; themselves massively influenced, in their oratory and legislation, by the idealized virtues of Republican Rome, codified by the Senatorial opposition to the 2nd century BC rise of dictatorship, a form of monarchy and arbitrary rule; a political theory taken fully fledged from an even older tradition, that of Greek civic virtues, brought to a rhetorical peak in the cult of Tyrannicides, men of exemplary virtue who assassinated, even at the cost of their own lives, the destroyer of republican freedoms. The revolutionaries harked back to republican Rome and Finlay picked this up as a continuation of linking Cocteau and that neo-classical, anti-subjective moment of 1923 or so. In 1978 Finlay renamed his garden at Stonypath, Lanarkshire, Little Sparta. The most martial, traditionalist, ascetic, and indeed communistic of the Greek republics was Sparta. It was thought of as rustic and archaic, as well as being Doric, which is why we associate the tribal name Doric with those qualities: rusticity is also central to Finlay's project. We can see that his discourse is one of interesting complexity, even though it uses proverbs and conventional graphic symbols, such as the Doric column. The Scots language is often called Doric, because those virtues are common in Scotland.

Perhaps dishonestly — at least thriftily — I am using Finlay as an opportunity to discuss a whole cosmos of art which is somehow poetry — even though it is quasi-verbal and quasi-nonverbal. Is it poetry? we would speak of Little Sparta as a garden which has some mottoes in it, or perhaps as a folly. But we do speak of concrete poetry and sound poetry. This field is stretched between the most avant-garde and the most industrial of pictorial output. Concrete goes back to a coinage by Theo van Doesburg circa 1929 — he was objecting to the word *abstract*. This was picked up by Max Bill, instructor at the Bauhaus and anti-Hitler exile, who worked further on it and gave a lecture on it in Brazil. His concept of involving words in design was quite practical — this is the strand of graphic design which gave us, for example, the image-lettering integration on album sleeves, cereal packets, and the Coke can. I think many of these designs are beautiful — in any case, this has been a most fertile area of commercial design. In Brazil, the word was picked up by two brothers, Augusto and Haroldo de Campos, who evolved a 'concrete poetry'. This was a hot item in the Rio de Janeiro of the 1950s, and influenced the other hot item, bossa nova; I am informed that when Antonio Carlos Jobim composed 'One Note Samba' he was thinking of concrete poetry — where the form and the concept are one. This strand became high concept avant-garde — an international fashion slightly later, in the early 1960s. It reached Germany through a Swiss writer, Eugen Gomringer — his work *konstellationen* was published in 1953. He was also editor of the trade magazine of the packaging industry in

Switzerland. Presumably this showed the work of the graduates of the industrial design school of which Bill was director. You can't write off concrete poetry without writing off industrial design and advertising. I am looking at Stephen Bann's catalogue essay for a Finlay exhibition at the Institute of Contemporary Arts in 1992 – there are some watering-cans, which Bann points out are a description of Thermidor – a name which means 'hot month', also used for a right-wing coup in July 1794, which deposed Robespierre. The water is supposed to cool this heat. This way of meaning is truly Doric – cheap, plain, robust. 'The watering-cans clustered in the wheelbarrow are not simply a promise of refreshment for the parched ground, but also an allegory of the Jacobin leaders being carried in a cart to their execution', as Bann tells us. The blood of heroes waters the shoots of the revolution. The show was called 'Instruments of Revolution', of which the watering-can is just one. Many of the pieces in this show were poems (blasted) on glass.

The limits to Finlay's artistic scope are obvious. His work is didactic and moral. It has a studied simplicity of means and rigidity of method. These bring it the serenity of Roman inscriptions while denying it the mimetic power of living language. It is austere but lacks persuasive power. But it does sometimes reach a genuinely conceptual power – the cover designs for *Littack* being an example. He is not a profound thinker, preferring proverbs and puns. The problem with concrete poetry is to confine one's gaze to the horizon where it has something to show – and not overshoot. There is a whole learning curve here. Concrete and sound poetry represent either a protruding loop – like the tag with which you rip off a can lid – of a whole new universe of symbolic activity, or else a blank where articulate language has been erased – like a squashed insect. It is mean to misread a work of art simply because we have patterns of expectation which are not appropriate to it. We have to understand it before judging it, I think. There are many things we have a right not to expect.

A distraction in the field around visual poetry was a sociological structure which induced a certain minority group to invent a rule inside which they were superior to everyone else – and everyone else was a mug, a sucker, etc. This structure had to alight on an element of artistic technique in order to realise itself. Among hundreds of other things, visual poetry was victimised in this way – so that people would strut around pronouncing that *the sentence is dead discursive poetry is old-fashioned using words to write poetry with is comic we are more sophisticated than everyone else*, and so on. This kind of self-confidence only survives among cliques tiny enough to generate and sustain their own ignorance. Of course, while each clique was small, there were also many such cliques. The metaphor of *I'm above* or *ahead of* other poets was a favourite. We reach for our copy of 'I'm five years ahead of my time' (by the Third Bardo, 1967), and perhaps wonder where the Third Bardo were in 1972. But, what a great record!

Deviant or original style is, often enough, generated by negative commands – dominated by its resolution not to re-acquire elements of music or language, and so become 'conventional'. Personally, I find the attack on linguistic poetry annoying and I have never encountered any sound poetry from England that turned me on. The idea of a world of infinite variation patterned by ways other than meaning is really there and it's not even controversial. I mean, how can you not like Little Richard. *Awopbopaloobopalopbamboom.* The story in the 1950s was 'the adult world is messed up and uncoded para-verbal activity is the start of a new world which says goodbye to the traumas of the Past', and if you apply that to Little Richard and doo-wop you can see it's a valid point. What is sad about Sound poetry is its character as a margin, negated by its negation of music and language. Any sound which isn't musical will do, apparently. The creative process is obscured by the effects of clique competition.

Finlay's designs are suitable for gardens, and are often found in the grounds of public buildings. They have a low information density. This is in fact implied by the transfer to a three-dimensional space, which would simply be overwhelming if covered with signs. In fact, signs are planar – as a rule. Why do we discuss this field of endeavour as poetry and not as garden design? Gardens imply rest, a psychological activity which is large-scale but diffuse; and a move into archaic conditions. We come across his statements unexpectedly, while wandering curved paths – the ideal moment is one of discovery when we are expecting nothing but a bush. Simple proverbs appeal to us when we are in a state of rest.

The word *discursive* means talking at length – something a writer presumably has to do. The root (Latin for run) suggests ease and fluency – but we have ambiguous feelings about people who can talk well. In Welsh, *sgwrsio* means 'to talk nonsense at length'. By non-discursive we mean poetry which has been led by negative commands to produce language which is less developed (or, freer) than fully organized speech. The Doric tribes left no literature, but presumably had proverbs – these were laconic, which means 'from Lakonia', the province where Sparta is. Finlay likes proverbs (or even single words).

As we rush forward to label this as incomplete or underdetermined information, what springs to mind is Roman Ingarden's dictum that Indeterminacy is the hallmark of modern poetry, and that modern poetry is growing ever more indeterminate. Recognising that Roman Ingarden and In Doric Garden are different things, we are going to talk about some poets, probably influenced by Sound and Concrete Poetry. The earliest description of Sound poetry seems to be in Nicomachus of Gerasa's *Excerpta de musica*: *sigmois te...* "hissing and lipsmacking and inarticulate and discordant sounds they call 'in code'". These were *theurgoi*, workers of magic, in around the 2nd century AD (though the sentence I am quoting is held to be a 5th century forgery). Again, we seem to be in the realm of cults of the Late Empire – this is the association, if it is not waste energy leaking into a loose connection in my brain. These gabblings are closely related to the alphabet magic described in Franz Dornseiff's book. The magic which flourished in the Hellenistic world liked to adapt the plane written on into a visual design – so like the visual organisation, compulsive and anti-rational, of so many small press productions of the 1970s. These are images and sounds which I unfortunately cannot reproduce. Back files of the magazines AND and Spanner shed a great deal of light on them. The poets discussed are post-non-discursive, they have advanced out of non-verbal extremism into linguistic form – singular and startling. The concepts of indeterminacy and earliness (getting back 'before' classification, 'before' social roles, etc.) are important to most of them. They partake of the myth of the uncoded.

Extreme Noise Cold Waveband Django Il Bastardo Blink: *Obscure Disasters*, by Adrian Clarke (1993; 70 pp., cluster C)

OD is preceded, in this volume, by *Spectral Investments*: these are the latter parts of a trilogy, *The Ghost Trio*, begun with *Ghost Measures*. The trilogy consists throughout of lines of four words, with certain exceptions which are of eight words each. The preset line-model is a row of blanks, hence ghost measures, but the spectre in question is more like the Geist in Hegel's system. The effect of these insistent and asyntactic incisions in continuous verbal material is like a beatbox:

> politics occulted pronomial freeze
> frames narrative ellipsis exit
> to clarify the door
> slammed contextual by default
> in Armorica the analogue
> absolute magnitude bibliographic in
> another perspective a closed
> system speeds up to
> proliferate the factual summary
> at the event horizon
> (from OD, 3)

The lines are of course anisometric in syllable or stress count; the real rhythmic principle is not on show.

This poetry uses indeterminacy as its resource. Such absolute clusters give us noncontrastive overall contexts rather than differentiated, pinpointed, moments. There is a traditional separation of realms between prose – hypotactic, precise as to time and person, abstract, orthogonal – and poetry: paratactic, sensuous, emotionally direct, based on an identification, whether of choral delivery or not, which blurs the gap between persons. One could, then, claim that the lack of articulation of this kind of text makes for ancient chases and coverts of poetry. However, Clarke includes a kind of self-reflexive commentary which takes the place of metalanguage:

> syntax articulates a land
> fit for generative trees
> (OD, 15)

(these are a kind of diagram for describing syntax).

> an encoded
> effect emotional literacy traces
> back script to hieroglyphic
> a drive to obliterate
> schizophrenic as a last
> resort through a dark
> cloud of dependent clauses
> (OD 1)

At moments Clarke appears to be replacing the reviewer. However, the level at which signature emerges has been pushed back, from sociological self-labelling, to something more like the physiological self-sameness of someone's walk or the way their eyes scan. The metaphor 'back', with its set of '(more and less) primary', 'irreducible, full of potential, incorrupt', 'pristine' etc., is what underwrites the aesthetic worth of such a speech conduct. The before is the straight thing which Mark E. Smith, in his album named *Perverted by Language*, left unnamed.

Spectral Investment may refer to colour spectra, if we consider Gerhard Richter's painting. Investment (*investissement*) is a word dear to Deleuze and Guattari and replaces older psychoanalytical words like projection, attachment, and object-choice. How can these two words fit together? If we invest in a spectrum, that implies a line of continuous variation from which we freely select a band, or wavelength, to identify with; locating our body image in these external hollows. The difference between what we identify with and what we don't is in fact spectral. This *découpure* is the act of making meaning. In the form of identification, it is also the central act of orthodox British poetry. We may well think of the competitive and agonistic elements of jazz, its ruthless demolition of sticky pop love affairs and accepted forms, its elevation of process which at the same time invests it into adornment and display.

Disconcerting or neoclassical, *The Ghost Trio* may be an extrapolation, to an extremity, of an early sixties style, based on paratactic units and frequent montage or splices. Lingering ideas of singing or self-presentation have been replaced by a diction which in four features – the insistence of arbitrary rhythmic blocks as a binding element, sampling of captured textures, reliance on high-contrast juxtaposition to supply forward motion, jeering at other performers – resembles the dance music, of the period when the text was being composed. The encounters with other people in his poems seem to be Leone-style duels.

One can find the extent of this diction in a merely topographical way, but I don't think its aesthetic possibilities are finite; the sweeping away of a set of ultimately Hellenistic techniques merely reveals that juncture is an abstract unbound function which can be realized in an unlimited number of ways. Clarke is little interested in affective states, but instead satirical and social in orientation.

as birdflight intersects to guess the colour of the heart:
Sean Bonney, *Notes on Heresy* (2002; about 38 pp.; cluster C)

The letter A (for us this is not a crime
    or C (is musk, ambergris, bruised lingum
    or F (witchcraft business

Notes on Heresy is an account of spiritual truth being put down by conspiracies of power. "Heresy" is everyone who deviates ideologically – mediaeval witches, Ranters, prophets unlicensed by the diocese, anti-globalisation protesters, lyric poets. The epigraph on the last page is 'the bourgeois international insists upon the monopoly of violence', the one on the first page is 'talking about poetry to a dead hare' (related to an action 'How to explain pictures to a dead hare', by the German charlatan, Joseph Beuys). Themes include the Elizabethan poem 'Tom O'Bedlam'; beggary; witchcraft trials such as those of Ann Bait; imps; the history of markets; conviviality and truly public space.

The ranter Abiezer Coppe, the Dadaist Hugo Ball, the Situationist Raoul Vaneigem, appear as tutelars. One of his characters, Ann Bait, arraigned in Morpeth in 1673, used to transform herself into a cat, a bee, a hare, or a greyhound – or, refused to deny this in court. The transformations resemble those of Eurasian shamanism – and whose legends are they? There is a hare in heresy – it is also hearsay, something as unreliable as individual consciousness, equally fleeting and pursued. 'It is the hare in the saying.'

Heresy is a breach of group feeling, the integral home of art – but it's all too true that the experts in the sacred have also been the persecutors of deviants. If Bonney resembles anyone, it's probably Ulli Freer. Both poets think a political poem shouldn't sound as if it was written by a policy professional (whose processes are infected by economism and by power politics), and want to go back, to a time before the alliance of possessive individualism and rational calculation (to sustain early imperialism). The phrase *are as archaic as birdflight intersects to guess the colour of the heart* is probably a keynote. The discursive surface is missing altogether – as if every right-angle had been replaced by a curve. The composition is in flakes, often effaced or overlaid, scantly orthogonal, carefully unclassifying and non-syntactic – calling on us to use intuition as the path, as meaning leaks out at us through a dozen channels. *but tell but me/ from where do you come// from trade-routes, from nowhere/ a spark or a light/ like strange sparrows.* If you can't follow the link from free movement across the earth, social flow, water as silver, quicksilver, silverfish – just relax. The *mise en page* is playful and diverse, with a coherent project of interrupting the forward motion of logic – this is his form of protest. Attacking habits of projecting emotional states onto other people is part of an attack on habits – the aesthetic project itself. The expectation of failure by unconventional people is also the expectation that the poem will not succeed – will not put us back in touch with our own idealism and optimism – which is the very thing we want. My notes of hearing Sean read definitely say that I heard a strong repetitive rhythm, not necessarily related to the syntax – but emotionally compelling. The poem takes a broad sweep of different periods and mixes them up – producing a blurred target but taking us to where everyday oppositions are dissolved. Thus, the structure embodies the intellectual point. We presumably see the weird graphics (over-writing of print, shifts of size, arbitrary windows through texts which we do not see complete, etc.) as a threat to the orthodox and symmetrical typeset page analogous to the threat to the body-image offered by witches transforming themselves into hares. Bonney identifies this moment of intolerance for deviation from patterns very precisely; it has to do with the repression of creativity – and, for me, with the demands of work, inducing a dominance of the left hemisphere and the triumph of anxiety over expressivity. What do you do with a text which reproduces *itself* virally, with errors of transmission at every stage? Which has ejected its own anatomy? I don't think the factual basis of Bonney's poem is too strong – but if you get hung up on facts, you end up deciding that you can't judge the war on Iraq until after it's happened. Maybe lyric poetry at this time is limited to what is viral and heretical – what doesn't turn the self into an object of knowledge. While lyric poetry is more diverse than theories like, I am offended by pseudo-lyric poetry which is really didactic and self-seeking. What I find so attractive about this poetry is that it values intuition, but is never authoritarian; is resentful, but never angry; ecstatic, but mild – Sean always seems to be listening to a music, and offering it for us to hear.

Bonney is now associated with Writers Forum in London, a group focussing the non-discursive tradition in Britain. However, he comes from Manchester, a poetry scene I know nothing about. His earlier work (what I saw of it) was Blakean beat poetry.

Expanded Documentary

One of the variables in poetry is the size of the nozzle which brings in new information. The limit of range was one of the ways in which the aesthetic, i.e. the poetic, was delimited from the non-aesthetic. To open the poem up to the uncontrolled flow of information was to alter its basic rules. English poetry had gone through a romance with documentary in the mid-century which had become a failed project; its materials were available as scrap which could be taken up as the matter for a radical critique. Poets such as Selerie are inspiring because of their fascination with trackless material.

Half a Century of Shared Gestures:
Gavin Selerie, *Days of '49* (1999, 134 pp.; tnbp4, cluster C)

On Scott Walker's wonderful *Climate of Hunter*, there is a track 'Rawhide' where he sings of "Cro-Magnon herders" and a fearful tale of slaughter, and we momentarily see history as going wrong right at the origin of the species, that succeeds by eliminating its kin. *Shutting down here.* The neurotic richness of denying history, and cherishing an unreal personal alternative sequence (a fabulous wealth of internalised and private event patterns), is attractive: for awareness to coincide with reality would produce a certain flatness. But that soft non-passive nucleus, (containing critique, personality projections, advocacy of just causes, aching grievances, private world-models) which makes a poet's "uniqueness component", dissolves going backwards: by the time we reach 1949 there is no point being "personal". You can say, "if only they'd gone for workers' control and not for state corporations!", but the real course of events is accepted, psychologically. Of course, it is possible that the common sense of that time is no longer here, dispersed by the choices available in a consumer society, where people have "lifestyles", broken up into volatile subjectivities. Poetry reached this state early. *Days of '49* is a beautiful and warming volume. (There are some pieces by Alan Halsey, but I am only reviewing the parts by Selerie.) Both poets were born in 1949, and on reaching 1999 wrote this birthday volume of poems and prose collage drawn from newspapers, films, writers' letters, BBC policy documents, and novels of 1949. That is, it is a nostalgic mélange: there is only so far you can go with this collective and familiar material, but the stitching is never stupid, and its charm and affable inclusiveness are quite overwhelming. Thrills whose names are Ingrid Bergman, W.S. Graham, William Sansom. The final poem, however, is an account of Gavin Selerie's experiences since 1949. "To vitreously chime and ring. Electric jism. Not spasmed with a mojo hand. Not cheap factualism. Fezzed unlikely the grey doctor tells how to arrive. Ask anybody infected with talk on the steps of the Chalmette obelisk. A hundred years of shared gestures. You could go into every kind of stone. Taller than stars. But this is a chamber in a block of quartz, intelligence over glitter, vaulted. One sentence pulls a whole page along." The complementarity of the two paired rhapsodes is "a hundred years of shared gestures" and quite beautiful. In passages like this they are special agents in the universe of pulp, an amazing web of scenes and characters. (Shards from *The Naked Lunch* and, oh, that little country boy who "played a guitar just like ringing a bell", the glass of "vitreous" magnetically erected as a quartz pyramid where its bell becomes a chamber of state?) William Burroughs, in Algiers Louisiana, in 1949, confronts a pyramid, a symbol of African magic which foretells the Interzone and spins him into the African mojo of a blues song. Does the obelisk foreshadow "towers open fire"? Or maybe it's a radio mast? Of course, the form is delicately borrowed from '40s patterns like Mass Observation and surreal documentaries like *Listen to Britain*: available light plus montage technique. You spin the radio dial and all the scraps from all the serials link up to make a story. "She emitted a gleam of animal magnetism like a searchlight held inexpertly by a child." One of the strengths of *Days* is that it is so open in structure that it doesn't need to stamp the poet's style on every frame: the magazine market favours poets who are rapidly recognizable, and so self-repeating, so as to compete (for memory space). *Days of '49* applies a personalised *caméra-stylo* of editing to found language and to ordinary and collective experiences: it is not dominated by personality and so has a value which continues even when the poets leave the room. It deals as much with collective fantasy (politics, cinema, also music, as Parker and Soho's Archer Street where the jazz musicians hung out waiting for a gig) as with flat grey facts.

Things like photography have made an excess of data available, and this has been a major stimulus to reflexivity, which may thus be intimately linked to documentary, which is superficially its opposite. The excess also invites collage technique.

Days is so brilliant that it points to a whole possible new road for poems which incorporate what is in the newspapers. Next time – they should be today's newspapers and not those of 1949. The original attraction of alienation was fear that someone well-adjusted would repeat the news and in the upshot be no different from the newspapers. That is, unsaleable pulp by tomorrow.

Feminist Poets

Feminism in literature records three key experiences, of disentanglement from emotional commitments, deflation and spreading wings.

disentanglement
In order to move into a new society you have to disentangle yourself from the set of roles you are playing in the existing one, and from the attitudes that match those roles. In a literary context, this resembles critical thinking, the perforation of texts. The desire for approval was more typical of women's social equipment in the old society, but came to be seen as ultimately conservative and inhibiting, a judgement which included pre-1970 women's poetry.

deflation
A common expression of this was taking a myth and rewriting it so as to damage the central roles and empty it of meaning.
 The purpose is to disable male egos and so male narratives. It would be inappropriate for a male to read feminist literature and feel cheerful, accepted, or satisfied. If you so triumphantly perforate the world of someone else's wishes and attachments, you may find someone else perforating your little world. In fact, by legitimating this moment of demolition you may find it becomes the central act of the poetic culture.

spreading wings
the experience of authenticity as the pay-off for struggling to escape from inherited psychological patterns. More ideal, less conditional, in poetry. Often takes the form of enacting prestigious stories with yourself in the starring role. Often takes the site of idealised states and heretically rewrites them.

 The trouble with political idealism at one stage was the lack of reality, of sensory and three-dimensional depth, in what it represented. The society of 2009 bears many resemblances to the proposals of feminists in about 1975 at sites where it is totally different from the society of 1975. In an earlier book I avoided the use of the word *feminist* because of its implications of unfairness in reporting facts and of hostility towards half the species. I still find this area difficult; taking a partisan view is tantamount to rigging the evidence, so I would rather describe poets as perceptive, critical, steady, intelligent, etc. than *feminist*. All the same the feminist presence in poetry since 1970 is huge, and a large share of the most credible poetry of reportage is feminist. An implication of a political bias would be that very weak poets are hailed as good because of their political stance, and that a large number of poets saying the same thing can be counted as political strength rather than literary tedium.

A Huge Fund of Loving Sarcasm:
Judith Kazantzis, *Selected Poems 1977-92*
(1995, 246 pp.; Angels, Purple; cluster A)

I take it we all set out from the point of view that there could be a better state of society and that generally in art we prefer to be granted hope and to find in our own feelings and thoughts the elements of this better life. Further, that this hope is so besetting that art which deals with anything else may fail because we are distracted from its message by the more important one of hope. Despite this it is possible – as laboratory tests have shown – to write unsuccessful left-wing poems. One path to this goal is to decide that the experience of millions of people is essentially similar and then to write poems which are completely predictable in the literary sense and also treat their human subjects as if the inevitability of Big Statistics made their lives predictable too, and to top it their lives are tragic because, of course, they are led under capitalism. Kazantzis (1940-) was one of the first feminist poets to write excellent poems in the genre, and sets out with a childish view of the world – this is the distinctive feature. When in a poem from *Mine Field* she encounters Mister Punch, the puppet figure, in a booth on the beach, she sees in his thoroughly childish phallicism and violence a reflection of oppressive and unrestrained behaviour by adult males. Realising this, she does not proceed to scold in adult terms but operates at the childish level – developing her own script. The poem shows a formula which recurs often in her work, of concrete details and a sharply defined social situation, which is overlaid by another dimension, of wishes which are simultaneously weak and yet visibly able to shape the landscape we are seeing. She likes to write versions of myths, fairy tales, and popular legends, which is indeed a feature of hundreds of feminist writers:

> Leda, the inside out lady of the swan
> wants to knuckle the cold
> rotter who fluttered her to bed.
>
> Caught in the infinite wiggle
> in a mesmerisation of paint
> here she is, propped in her voluptuous stay
> maddened
> for all who like a good sex object
> shielding her feathered friend.
> ('Leda and Leonardo the swan')

and this throws us into the childhood of a new society – where we are, as long as the imaginative world of the poem lasts, childish versions of a kind of adults who do not exist yet. These experiences of potential, of shifting out of cognitive norms, and distortion compete with ideas, are incompatible with them, but perhaps draw on the same invisible resources. The painting referred to is 'Leda and the Swan', (painted about 1505-10) by Leonardo da Vinci, now destroyed but known from copies. The 'wiggle' might be the curve of the swan's neck, a very flexible and acquisitive organ. The painting shows happy little babies wriggling out of the shells from which they have just hatched. The biology involved is ridiculous – in one of those internal contradictions which suggests that the whole of the existing culture can be replaced. The lurch is typical of Kazantzis' poems.

A number of these poems depict people realistically and yet satirically, in terms of the objects which locate them in social space (i.e. through their acquisition patterns) and the habits which guide them. Take 'A Sussex Lady' –

> Remember the mermaid-tail roofs
> and the black-eyed chapel
> of Lewes, like a duck
> on a bank between the cars.
> Remember the slur of the Ouse
> towards and away from a deep
>   and obedient pond,
> netted by road, wire pole.
> You can see the pure sports cars

seed in the valley
like lilies; from Beddingham Beacon.

It is worth comparing these scenes with Betjeman, who had something of the same sharp eye. Betjeman perpetually used pastiche rhythms, never really escaping parody, and while this lathered his poems in familiarity and nostalgia and was comforting, it drowns them in unreality – which is one reason why Kazantzis' poems are so much better and more vivid. We do not find in them a sense of social reality as dreary and horrifying, but also the evocation of contemporary English reality is so recognizable and sharp as to be undeniable. In 'One a.m., November' we hear about the vibration of a dishwasher at night,

putting my feet sleepily
in the caftan of a chic and rumpled night
down to a Moorish pink-breasted
kitchen, the light wrapped in
kingfisher colour horn

the explosions and whistles
right in my ear upped and drove me

in a poem which demolishes my theory that domestic anecdote is always boring because it is compelling. In the line *experienced, vibrant dishwasher* we find what seems most likely to be a sort of advertising copy for a wife as produced by a focus group: *experienced, vibrant, dishwasher*. The line comes out of a huge fund of loving sarcasm. In the dark of night the dishwasher starts resonating so that its kinetic energy shakes the machine and gives rise to a loud rattling noise. *The cat bunches on the very edge of the pingpong table/ lulled/ by the swish and wallow of saucepans* – fascinated, it leans towards the sound – perhaps recurring to a maternal purring sound. So the cat is apparently inventing techno music. At the end of the poem, the sound has gone, and the cat discovers that *there is no god.*

It is hardly worth pointing out that Kazantzis is a left-wing intellectual, as it becomes obvious through reading the poems that an exceptionally clear intellect is guiding the knowledge released by the poems (and such features, common in childish speech, as repetition, egocentricity, lack of logic do not feature). This sly choice of simplicity allows the poems to form a surface that retains integrity; abstract ideas are only allowed in through a filter that lets them fit into the integrating world-view. We can see this simultaneously as a move out of alienation and a sly side-step into Aesopian language. The left-wing points are made in such simple language that the vessels of unjust power have no defence they can make. The political points are obvious (or at least they are ones I deeply identify with) but the style allows for originality. There is no point being eccentric about politics, at least not if you are interested in politics. Every poem is close to dreams or fairy-tales and data like abstractions, citations from legislation, and social statistics never appear. That kind of discourse is not only designed to remove ambiguity but is also behaviour typical of people with high status and high levels of education: the poems ask us for assent on different grounds than because we have been driven into a corner. The large-scale work is the 'Poem for Guatemala', about 350 lines long, relating to a war by the government against its own people, a theme also featured on the cover of *Eucalyptus*.

Kazan means bucket. Kazantzis is not related to Elia Kazan (*né* Kazanoglu) or Nikos Kazantzakis. I have not read all the individual volumes (on grounds of cost), but the poem which first convinced me that Kazantzis deserved close attention, a wonderfully nimble and comprehensive reflection on nuclear war called 'Progenitor', is not here (though it is in a book called *Touch Papers*). It is a reasonable bet that there are a lot of important poems which have not been collected here.

Nine Fine Flyaway Goose Truths:
Bernache nonnette, by Grace Lake (1995, 15pp CC, OofE, cluster C)

Bernache is a barnacle goose, so called because its young were supposed to grow out of barnacles which then became eels (in a variant, the barnacles grew on trees). *Nonnette* is also a kind of goose – actually, the same kind of goose – called "little nun" because its nests were nowhere to be found in northwest Europe, being safe in Greenland, and consequently its sex life was a mystery to Europeans. Tales about gooseberry bushes probably have the same folk-myth source. The theme is sexuality, coming into season, bearing, breeding, dreaming about the child's growth and birth, but only by periphrasis, substitution, fantasy, and camouflage. I think the phrase 'jars of tadpoles for aversion therapy' is a reference to the male essence. Grace Lake (a.k.a. Anna Mendelson, 1948–2009) wrote to me that "'Bernache Nonnette' is a concept that has found a name – Barnacle Goose, St. Bernach was an Irish monk who tried to settle a fight in the South of Wales. Nonnette is also gingerbread, & 9 of anything." Berdacus came to Wales and then I think Cornwall, floating around the legendary Atlantic shores in his coracle. It was the unfindableness of barnacle goose nests which led to the saw about a wild goose chase, and indirection, elusiveness, looping around, wild flights, resolutions withdrawn by subterfuge at the last minute, are structural rules in this book. The mystery nesting sites full of fluffy barnacle goslings are a figure both of some Mother Goose fairy-tale land and of a terrain of poetic fantasy, perhaps the society where we want to live. Fairy tales about female sexuality and reproduction, a kind of Mother Goose Gorgon; on waters where the wild tales spawn. Human sex life is a mystery too.

'Collegiate cooling her heels flapped by a stream of torrid bananas, motorized/ Adjacent gazette, gassy, classy & yet, determined to leave with a spick if you please/ Where is my piano the gangway awaits the conflict's secure it's pouring with rain/ Champagne's on the brain her name is charmaine she wears pink pyjamas/ She's going insane and when she arrives she'll catch fish alive and checkout again,/ & again those maniacal, driven or not, unite to declare that red must rot.' This is a dazzling rendition of the high life in six lines, a kind of hot jazz, but I think what the poet is thinking, much more darkly, about this dashing fashionable socialite-suffragette undergraduate type, as a threat, because of her superficiality, effortless (sexually mediated) social power, her selfishness; a danger to a middle-aged woman for all sorts of reasons, but among other things as a figure projected onto, a never-lived youth relived, a fable of lightness and gleam; while Lake renders this dazzling lamé folderol out of 'Flying Down to Rio' to maximum effect, different emotional currents are under the surface, and in fact give it its shimmering quality. But almost immediately we move on to the next thing. The scene with the dressing-gown ('he found her in a dressing-gown, red, velvet, sitting in a kitchen knitting him/ Not breakfasting no not her, but complaint walked in with a tumblerful of peruvian gin') is played for laughs, but again I suspect there is a much darker emotional layer beneath, perhaps a relationship ending, perhaps a moment of extreme frustration with this man, the realisation that a whole life has to be given up and left. Aboutness is not one of *Bernache*

Nonnette's main qualities. It's hard for me to talk about it, knocking nails in with my head, without crumpling its lighter than air swing.

Grace wrote, "'She Walked' is me, frogmarched off the Essex campus in 1970 by a fellow poet who didn't want me to be either single, younger than him or a Writer (…) I had been handed over – in the middle of a vast lyrical metropolitan exequy's composition (incepted by me & in the process of being incised upon paper) by a group who were writing for Tariq Ali's *Black Dwarf* who wanted Politics not Poetry – to a strange flat in Stamford Hill where I was seized by a group armed with stolen chequebooks & weapons." At one level, *Bernache Nonnette*, and I think the whole of Lake's poetic work, is a critique of the determinism of left-wing discourse around 1970 and ever after, including official feminism, how it creates a new imaginary State which imagines the population in the bureaucratic terms of the old one, how it skimps the impossibility of imagining 58 million people as human agents by imagining them as quantities, like money, which can be housed and planned for. This is not an opposition of true/untrue or good/bad, but one of levels of porosity and granularity. Lake is a social poet, writing against something always being said. A lot of people, in the sixties, found the style of Marx and Freud about as credible as a speech by Harold Wilson; most of the poets who began in that decade, you could say, were attacking official knowledge. The problem was then to create a poetry which was simultaneous and constantly shifting and irrational but never falsifiable, seductively fluent, never slipping back into informativeness to explain what was going on, and, if Lake has found the perfect answer, it shouldn't be too hard for us to remember the question.

We discovered at an event in 2017 that the "exequy" exists and was among the documents seized by the police in the preparation for the Angry Brigade conspiracy trial in 1972. Lake's family are now trying to recover it from the police lock-up.

Menna Elfyn, Eucalyptus: Detholiad o Gerddi 1978-94 (1995; 107 pp. with facing translation into English)

Elfyn (d.o.b. elusive, first publications around 1976) wrote a manifesto-essay for feminism in Welsh literary criticism 'Trwy lygaid ffeministaidd' (published in *Sglefrio ar Eiriau*, 1992), which says among other things that "Except it's not a work of art that reveals its truth to everyone who looks at it. But what is the truth? Here is a proposal that we accept a plurality of judgements and standpoints as an infallible compass. As in anything, it is natural to human nature to try to accumulate strength and orthodoxy in his or her judgement and it is natural for people to look at things differently, given that we are such different human beings." The curious thing about this essay is that it makes absolutely no criticisms of Welsh literature or society, normally thought to be male-dominated and to reinforce rigid role constancy. A pendant to this is that the feminist authorities cited are all American or French: the English oppressor does not feature and we are not likely to have the subversive thought that feminism came to Wales from England and is an offshoot of English radicalism and its progress in Wales is going to encourage a more Anglo-Saxon social style. Elfyn's feminism is delicately positioned so as to be compatible with nationalism. The claim to occupy the high attainments of post-structuralism (so that assets held by a Welsh person become Welsh national assets) is made locally acceptable by stripping out of those assets any elements of radical critique which they possessed at source: Welsh literature is being re-described in Continental terms but no critique of either the original aristocratic or later Puritan texts or the nationalist canon of literary history is actually being made.

In *Eucalyptus*, titles include 'Song of the Voiceless to British Telecom', 'National Year of the Bat', 'Arsenic and Gold at Dolaucothi'. The title poem is about a report of the scent of eucalyptus trees giving people relief in Baghdad after bombing in the Gulf War of 1991, and the wood of the trees being used as fuel as the electricity supply was cut by the bombers.

The cover has some blurbs and a collage of images which may make a thematic statement about the book. The collage includes Nelson Mandela. A march is shown of people holding a very long banner saying 'Cymdeithas yr iaith' [society of the language], whose goal was to persuade Welsh people not to speak English (I think the further goal of getting English people to speak Welsh was not advanced), along with a logo which I understand shows the tongue of the dragon. There is a leaf with a drawing and a handwritten text – perhaps a tourist curio. The text says 'the eagle man Agulach stands for the day labourers and is associated with Quetzalcoatl and Maya culture'. Quetzalcoatl (the plumed serpent) is Aztec but if the source is southern Mexico it could also be in the Mayan cultural zone. There is a piece of knot-work imitated from a mediaeval Hiberno-Saxon manuscript – the drawing has little heads, which appear to be of birds, so it is actually a zoomorphic interlace. It is surely there as a symbol of celticity – only historians view the style, with its links to the jewellery the Saxons brought from the Continent, as Hiberno-Saxon. There is a picture of a dove with a sprig in its beak – a symbol of peace. There is a snippet from a Welsh text, with words each in a different colour, which is evidently some kind of declaration of the rights of women. A photo of a woman holding a newspaper called *Y Faner* (the banner). There are manuscript pages from Elfyn's poems. Mayan, dove, interlace – that is three birds. Elfyn's previous selected poems was called *Aderyn bach mewn llaw*, a little bird in the hand. There is a detail from an oil painting, perhaps around the 16th century, showing a scene of violence with a king looking down on it from a throne raised on a stage (?), so probably the massacre of the Innocents; the perpetrators are men. I cannot identify two of the graphics precisely but I think one of them (the edge of something showing tips of the feathers of a very stylised bird) is from a Mayan codex and so both of them are Central American. Taken to the 1980s, these images certainly refer to genocidal acts of fascist dictatorships and to the actions of American finance, arms and expertise supporting them in their endeavours. Secondarily, to the role of the British government as a key ally of the Americans. The painting probably appears to show the massacre of entire villages in the ethnic Mayan regions of Guatemala during the 1980s (and possibly is a Flemish representation of Spanish atrocities in the Low Countries). Reaching a bit further, we can possibly put fingertips on a casting of Wales, subjugated by the Act of Union in 1536, as oppressed by the English in a way analogous to the oppression of Central America by the Spanish and then by feudal elites with a key political link to American capitalism. The reference, that is, to fearful violence in Guatemala, Nicaragua, Salvador, and Colombia has an occult suggestion that the Welsh relationship with England was imposed by violence, so not voluntary when entered into, and so that terminating it would not breach any good principles of public law. Am I going too far? Well, Central America is rife with countries with very small populations – as weak as Wales on the international scene. The Mayan bird (from a head-dress possibly?) corresponds to the other image, of Celtic knotwork – so that both may fall into the category of 'indigenous art of small peoples discerpserated by imperialism'.

We can sum it up as the pin-up board of 1980s leftism. Any connections to the world of advertising with its gloss and invitations to realise your wishes through high technology are totally missing. The invitation is to enter into the feelings and wishes of other humans and to change your life by having them enter into yours. This *is* thematic for the poems. Feminism is not on show in the collage but that is because there is a lack of unambiguous feminist visual symbols. The four faces shown at a recognisable size (there are some marchers too) are all female. One is a woman whose face is whited up to show up a CND logo traced in black – evidently for a protest against nuclear arms.

These are plain symbols. However, these poems were written in Welsh. Nothing in the collage suggests any critique of life in Wales. Except, that is, for the prevalence of English, as symbolised by the Cymdeithas yr Iaith banner in one of the photos. These are very good poems. What makes them is the freedom of association or defamiliarisation in the texture of the lines, which redeems the more obvious aspects of the compassion and emotional projection which are also a great strength but could slip into sentimentality.

In the poems, the political critique is always of things being done by foreign governments. It can therefore be stitched back into the inherited nationalist position that anything done by the government in London is inherently bad (and that large countries are inherently domineering and unrestrained). Elfyn is writing in a style which sets aside the most treasured metrical inheritance from the Dark Ages but is avoiding anything which could cause another split in the small band of Welsh readers by setting up an alternative version of politics and history – and so avoids making us rethink any standard models. Her poetry is persuasive without having anything much to persuade us of.

The other avoidance is of a critique of the traditional Christian ethical beliefs in Wales. This implies that Elfyn's line of sympathising with the weak will become stitched back into a traditional Christian line of charity, compassion, refusal of self-aggrandizement, and good works. This is not necessarily to criticise the Christian line, with all its artistic successes, but again it precluded any real intellectual challenge. The conclusion which offers itself is that solidarity and communalism are overwhelming in Wales and that the activities of satirising the powerful, questioning values, plunging into autonomy and self-definition, working out the root of the social order, are fruits of Anglo-Saxon individualism and are not on the market west of Offa's Dyke. The blurb refers to the poems as *digyfaddawd*, uncompromising; but they seem to be compromised in a very specific way, that the critique is all of English or Americans who were acceptable enemies in Welsh Wales. No critique of Welsh society, no self-critique.

The use of such familiar images allows the poems to go through exhilarating originality and elusiveness of language and after being reunited in a creative act by the reader to connect with major structures of the public life and with the possibility of structural change, hoped-for and at least partially visible to the imagination. The difficulty of language so to speak enacts the task of imagining a different and common future.

In 'In an Old People's Home', the poem is founded on the ambiguity of the word *llen* in Welsh: *tynnu eich llen* can quite well mean 'draw the curtain', and this would mean either opening onto a stage or else opening a home (which becomes a picture) or else drawing the curtain on a life. (Tynnu, Latin *tendere*, means pull, stretch.) But llen also means cloth or sheet, and *tynnu* also means draw (like draw a picture). Most of the poem is about the old people drawing pictures, an activity to fill the day. But this is presented in terms of *llen*, of sheets on a clothes-line (same word as the *line* the pencil is drawing). The tone of the poem is exemplary piety and sympathy, just what you would expect; but this is hidden behind the playful nature of the language and the almost riddling style. The people are presumably drawing a clothes-line. The poet shows herself sorting the drawings but the word she uses could also mean *untangling* clothes-lines or clothes. The empty clothes are as if the roles which the people can no longer play. The poem might not have started if not for the resemblance between the word *llen* and the word *llun* (picture): the clothes line *tynnu*'s the clothes and the pencil *tynnu*'s the *llun*.

Elfyn originally refused to have her poems translated into English but adapted after a certain time and is now very successful in English-language versions. The rhythm is free verse, without the traditional verse structure of Welsh. The style is perfectly adapted to a protest poetry drawing on the intimacy and warmth of a small group at a reading, notably close to English and American models and notably hard to relate to any Welsh poetry before 1970. Elfyn has also edited two volumes of Welsh poetry by women; the one I saw, interestingly, is entirely in free verse.

Conventionally Breaching Conventions

I was looking, on a magazine stand in Waitrose, at a magazine cover featuring Nicole Kidman. She is wearing very little except some high boots and a body which is tight, black, and skimpy – and staring boldly at the camera. The text beside the photo says "Kidman – still breaking all the rules". Exactly what rules does it break for a female film star to appear on a magazine cover in revealing and restricted clothes? But the proposal is that you don't sell a million magazines by blazoning "Nicole Kidman behaves in a traditional way which would please her bank manager".

Evidently there is a branch of mainstream poetry today which essentially breaks the rules. It chooses rules selectively and leaves a much larger set of them rigorously intact. Equally, there are a large number of women who need to be told twenty times a day that they are breaking all the rules to avoid depression and panic. The discourse around women's poetry suggests that they need to be told "you're breaking all the rules" as often as they need to be told "you are thin". The feminist plan of converting women to hedonism and seeking to maximise personal pleasure (rather than seeking approval from others all the time) succeeded only at the cost of being rolled up with a straightforward capitalist project of getting people to consume as much as possible by breaking down various inhibitions, which had to do with avoidance of seeming selfish (among other things). It is sensible in this case to be behind the marketing project – mid-century poetry is full of examples of people inhibited from self-realisation, and we can't treat those inhibitions as an imperishable national heritage. It is a common sight now to see young women in gangs competing with each other to drink as much as possible, show as much flesh as possible, and make as much noise as possible. This is wholly in line with the direction of poetry since the 1960s, of smashing through the old bourgeois inhibitions. The problem I often find with this impulse is that it has lost all its radical potential and simply become something vulgar, ostentatious, and bullying.

There seems to be something unfair about saying that for Prynne, Raworth, Allen Fisher to break all the rules of poetry is radical but when someone whose style is orthodox breaks the conversational conventions by talking about sex all the time, talking about themselves all the time, making as much noise as possible, etc., it is not radical. Liberation means doing what you want to do, and what people want to do, in Nottingham at least, is not esoteric and not remote or unattainable. No one wants to hear that they are conventional. But clearly if you break rules in the way that a mass of other people are doing, in the same hours of Friday night, and in the same pubs and clubs, you are also being conformist. It occurs to me that the distinction between linguistic innovation and breaking rules of propriety and good order may be quite hard to grasp. It is one of the essential distinctions for insiders.

I should clearly unwrite a large section of my previous work by observing that this new mainstream, which was not a distinct phenomenon until the 1980s (I think) is quite free of the conditions which guaranteed the tedium of an earlier mainstream, the one which was growing rank in the 1950s and was still being written and published into the 1980s. It compares more with the industrial product of TV or cinema, something highly effective (and turned out in quantities just because it is effective). This is where we have to resort to literary history – the 'central current' is good in good periods and bad in bad periods.

Kiss Kiss Bang Bang:
Vicki Feaver, *The Handless Maiden* (1994, 55 pp.; 60 WP, cluster A)

There is an interview with Feaver (b. 1943) on the Net, originally in *Magma* magazine in 1988, which credits her with "her poems now celebrate extremes of femininity from sensuality to violence". These are not feminine traits by definition. The phrase could be rewritten to say *runs the gamut of states normally subject to deep inhibition*, and this would yield a latent result, that the states of mind are impersonal, because what differentiates drives and produces the personality is the layer of social learning which encodes inhibitions; and that the latent message is *indulge yourself. do not fear disapproval. carry out fantasies to excess*. This takes us rapidly to the core of the matter – that Feaver's poems genuinely are melodramatic, disinhibiting, and exciting, but also that this area, if left alone by English poets over quite a long stretch, is one which is quite densely colonised by other forms of art, such as cinema and crime novels, and indeed the tabloid press. If we accept that these drives, sexuality and aggression, are innate and fundamental, that explains why Feaver's range of themes is narrow and the number of her poems is few, but also why their appeal is strong and rather easy to grasp.

There are two famous Bible stories of women killing men: Jael and Sisera, and Judith and Holofernes. Feaver offers us poems on both of them. These are stunning poems, and their intensity is reached by great concentration, which is related to another quality, that they do not add anything to the inherited tableau of these righteous and murderous women, as recorded in numerous poems and paintings. If we compare it to the Anglo-Saxon poem on Judith, it is apparent that Feaver's version has much less information. (We could add other such Bible stories, for example Esther getting Hanuman hanged and Salome and Herodias collaborating to get John the Baptist beheaded.)

Judith was not killing Holofernes for personal reasons but for political ones. He was Assyrian, she was Hebrew. Feaver leaves this detail out. She would *rather* we thought Judith was chopping a man's head off because she felt like it than that she was doing it for political reasons. The overriding imperative is to say *I am not other-directed*, because that is what the target audience want to hear, every hour on the hour. The story has been redesigned to be a single situation at flash-point, with one individual wallowing in an emotion, with the sounds of other impulses, other people's voices, shut out with miraculous thoroughness. These are powerfully compressed and high-impact poems, ruthlessly focused on elemental if unoriginal passions. It is hard to see the poems as celebrations of murder. Shock is not pleasure.

There is a poem on her mother making crab-apple jelly, out of frustration at the fruit going to waste, which I read the week after my mother confessed to having made fourteen jars of crab-apple jelly, for a similar reason. The poem says that the jelly is of little use, but that is too pessimistic. Is there a link between the wildness of the crabs, so unlike the cultivated varieties (which don't come from England anyway), and the underrated drives which Feaver's other poems are about? Probably not. Anyway this is a charming poem.

The title poem retells an old story (Grimms' no. 31) also retold in Kazantzis' 'The Handless Queen' and in a poem in D.M. Black's book. The pattern seems to be reduction of a narrative composed of a more or less long sequence of events into a single scene with a strong emphasis on a central character. Modern poetry has problems with narrative. Black starts from the raw folkloric material but makes long complex narratives.

When the poems are so compressed there is no point writing about them at length.

Moniza Alvi, *Carrying My Wife* (2000; 158 pp., 60WP, cluster B)

Carrying My Wife is published in an edition, in 2000, which scoops up two previous books, of 1993 and 1996, so that the poems were written throughout the 1990s. Titles include 'Man Impregnated' 'My Wife and the Computer' 'The Old Woman Who Lived in a Shoe' 'A Bowl of Warm Air' 'Hindi Urdu Bol Chaal'.

Alvi (b.1954) is of Pakistani origin and the central thing with her poetry is the reversal of expectations as a character is faced either with Pakistani reality contradicting English expectations or with the opposite. The appeal of the work is initially that the poet is not interested in British crimes against the people who were going to become Pakistanis in 1948, or otherwise in British crimes against people from Pakistan who had travelled to Britain. These acts are not in doubt but they are not on stage here to push the poetry into a realm of grievance, accusation and remedy. Something as simple as switching off nationalism makes us relieved, relaxed, and somehow innocent. The second stage of the appeal is the vividness of the imagery she shows: the naivety of the character with respect to what they are seeing recreates naivety for us and makes every detail clear and new.

>   I pictured my birthplace
>   from fifties' photographs.
>   When I was older
>   there was conflict, a fractured land
>   throbbing through newsprint.
>   Sometimes I saw Lahore –
>   my aunts in shaded rooms,
>   screened from male visitors,
>   sorting presents,
>   wrapping them in tissue.
>   ('Presents from my Aunts in Pakistan')

There is a history of estrangement which shows it as a radical poetic step in around 1960, ridiculed and reviled by the cultural managers in power. Later it became a prestige object for poets who wanted to slip into that realm where they could be detested, in as pompous terms as possible, by the managers they detested. It became a chic asset, a symbol of being "with it". Rapidly it migrated into the mainstream and became something which spectators could give a knowing verdict on "Ah, that's estrangement you know." It relates primarily to the bafflement of people in trying to understand someone essentially foreign and finding that projection of your own state of mind onto them could be misleading. The poems calm this anxiety and derive pleasure from it by seeing it in a particular way. They are *very* far removed from a simple didactic project of explaining as much about Pakistani and Anglo-Pakistani culture as possible. That would be prosaic. They are not there to supply literal information. Instead they stage the bafflement. This is applied both to a Pakistani in England, or to an English person in a Muslim country, but also to an Anglo-Pakistani trying to understand Pakistan. Imagining someone we are not is a source of literary pleasure, indeed is close to *the* source of literary pleasure.

The information supplied is like a naive painting, simple and sensory but free of cynicism or critical reactions. In the poem just quoted we hear of 'candy-striped glass bangles', a peacock-blue shalwar kameez and an orange one, denim and corduroy, and a camel-skin lamp. In the poem just before it we hear a list of spices and of a kind of silver leaf to drop on *khir*, a kind of rice-pudding. The objects are part of relations between people, reminders to help with the code governing social acts, rather than merely sensory gluttony. The syntax is of extreme simplicity and the vocabulary also suggests the way a child might use language. Several of the characters have problems with everyday speech:

> I had the feeling she was grappling
> with a completely new language.
> Eventually it was clear to me
> she couldn't move from room to room
> without a dictionary in her hand.
> Every word I uttered, she looked it up,
> then mouthed it to herself.
>
> ('Lizard Tongues')

The charm of the poems is to return the reader to a childlike state of surprise and surmise, where every detail is precious because we understand very little of the society we are living in, but we have the means to acquire understanding of it. And we are showered with gifts to keep us content.

Deryn Rees-Jones, *The Memory Tray (1994);*
Signs Around a Dead Body (1998)

The cover of both books shows a painting by a surrealist woman painter, highly coloured, biomorphic in appearance but altering the known rules of anatomy, showing with a smooth and illusionist surface of paint a weird and mythological scene. They look almost interchangeable, but in fact one is by Leonora Carrington and one is by Remedios Varos. The point that you can be radical without being personal is teasing. Titles include 'Song for the absence of her lover's Voice', 'Midnight Beach at Sizewell B', 'The Oral Tradition', 'From his Coy Mistress', 'A Brief Inventory of Facts About Snow'. Her style may be connected to the work of two younger Welsh poets, Samantha Wynne-Rhydderch and Zoë Brigley.

My method as a critic depends on isolating distinctive features of any poet, reflecting upon them until they can be described as clearly as possible, and looking for pervading imagery which shows an unconscious stratum of the imagination. The work then moves on to setting out this knowledge in words. This method does not work when someone has no personal traits. This is the case for Rees-Jones (b.1968). It is simultaneously true that her work is highly sensual, and sexual, and emotionally highly coloured throughout.

The key to Rees-Jones' work seems to be in another work, her anthology of modern women's poetry. This is a classic of its kind. If we see her as a prudent classifier of poems, someone covering the whole range and carefully sifting to find the best, the work falls into place as something diligent and discreet and based on the findings of a survey. It is like a set of government recommendations on how to write poems in these times.

The other view is that this method is so efficient, so developed after decades of battering and detailed modification, that it reliably turns out effective poems, in the way that a studio band in some soundproofed room of the 1960s or 1970s could turn out an efficient backing without either being original or stamping a personality on the song – and indeed that a great mass of art, in records, film, TV, etc., is produced by just such professionals, using anonymous but boundlessly effective methods. So that in fact the apparatus of originality and experiment in art is tangential to writing about emotions, and so in many ways to artistic impact as well. Rating Rees-Jones' poems low would be equivalent to low-rating the whole world of contemporary poetry. As I mentioned, she has picked the freshest and most effective techniques.

An exception is the title poem, 'Signs Around a Dead Body', which has no obvious intention, and where the poet seems to lose control in the face of a complex of images that generate mystery and momentum. This is less efficient than the other poems but more interesting.

The idea of *memory tray* is intriguing: it promises to task memory and to saturate us with the evocation of unusual and intricate objects. The source, not mentioned, is in Kipling: the hero of *Kim* is trained by being shown a tray of objects and being asked to describe them from memory once the tray is taken away. Kim is a young child. All poetry gives us words and asks us to remember objects we can no longer see. The question is how ideas do in this exercise. In 'Song to Noise' we have a catalogue:

> I call on you in the whisper of the dying,
> In the rush and creak of water in the wainscot pipes.
> I call on your lawnmowers, vacuum cleaners,
> Your ill-tuned radios, your television sets.
> I call on the wetness of fingers circling a glass.

This is good, but how many other poems with this design could you find in two hours or so in a library? The pressure of sensory detail and the immediate situation leaves no space for abstraction, and leaves the poem too stuffed to move, without intellectual potential. The difference between Rees-Jones, and dozens of other educated poets who focus their poetry on the ego and the impression of a personality, and the intellectual poets of mid-century, is a vast topic and exists on many planes at once. However, one thing gets to the heart of it: in order to make abstraction possible you have to wipe out the surface of bourgeois domestic reality with all its continuity and viscosity. There has to be a gap, an emptiness. Precisely this emptiness causes the poetry reader a feeling that their comfort is at risk and that they have to get away as quickly as possible. This new poetry is not even on the same plane as W.S. Graham, Roy Fisher, or David Jones. But it offers comfort and welcome.

'Sheep Piece' shows two lovers in a field. A sheep kicks a Polaroid camera lying nearby and it takes a picture. The poems gives us a page on the lovers, then a page of monologue by the sheep, then a page of monologue by the camera about its feelings as the picture spreads and the image blushes with colour. This is indisputably original: there are no other poems about a sheep taking a photograph. The idea of having a sheep speak a poem is unpredictable, unfathomably eccentric. But this originality has no political potential, it is not connected to a critique of how everyday life is constructed or to the dominant assumptions of the social order. It steps away from a norm without wanting to replace it. Rees-Jones shows no interest in ideas. She is not interested in sheep, or in cameras: the point of the poem is simply to be original and in control and nothing more.

The question of the new poetry which emerged in the 1980s having moved to the cell which was occupied, in 1955 or so, by W.S. Graham and David Jones is fraught. My feelings about it are probably clear, but the arguments could go on forever. Evidently the reading public had problems with Graham and Jones, as earlier with Eliot and Pound, and then with Prynne and Allen Fisher. The excess of knowledge and ideas did not reach them simply as pleasure.

Rees-Jones lives in Liverpool but has family connections with North Wales. As the author points out, *deryn* means 'bird' in Welsh, as in Elfyn's *Aderyn bach mewn llaw* (aderyn is the dictionary form). In the poem 'The Oral Tradition', 'So ends this branch' is a quote from the 12th century prose text *Mabinogion*, divided into four branches: *Ac yuelly y teruyna y geing honn yma o'r Mabinogy*.

Afterword

I grew up hearing critics who said that the tedium of mainstream poets was due to their inability to challenge the political system (which also provided the fabric of everyday life). But there is a completely different line which argues that the problem with the mainstream (in 1940 to 1980, even 1920 to 1980) was writing about subjects which were of no interest to the poet. Rees-Jones' poems are emotionally frank, often about themes of love and sexuality, in a way which mid-century poets found impossible. This is a big question, but the problems of mid-century were there on many planes at once. Any analysis relying on a single cause needs detailed testing. Maybe you don't need to make a dramatic exit either into radical politics, experimental form, or into intellectual ideas? Maybe in a society which has personal liberty and frankness in discussing feelings you can write significant poetry without any exit into negation and abstraction? These questions may have seemed closed but now they seem open.

We started out with the image of a clash where the reader denies the text a subjective opening (and is presumably denied a pleasurable artistic experience). Rather than explore this derelict ground, I went on to discuss roughly 70 books all of which I liked.

Having read all this exposition of detail you might hope to find a shared pattern. This hope is unworthy of us and must be thrown away. The diversity of the texts is too great. I field this as a way of justifying my inability to make generalisations about the period – it's too split up for generalisations to be valid. *I own this pattern and it is not there.* This seems to be the basic situation of cultural historians, always hoping to find something they can stretch between texts like a curtain between hooks. "I'm a part of it's a part of me", Traffic used to sing in the psychedelic heyday. But perhaps poets are part of a dozen different things which are outside the realm of poetry.

I am sure that the rapid transition from one book to another is the thing poets least want – after you describe their book they would ideally like a silence of several hours for reverence and due absorption of the Important Messages. The rapid shifts of focus may be exhausting but have the advantage of foregrounding the diversity so that people have to admit to its existence and have to discard their comforting and controlling fantasies of order. If I find the subject to be inconsistent and irregular it is appropriate to record that rather than impose some grid of grandiose (and egoistic?) symmetry.

The clashes between poets and readers surely amount to failed readings, and the poetic realm exists because of successful readings, when language pulls us out of a lonely subjectivity. When poetry is so diverse it is a great problem for the reader to grasp the genre of the book they are reading, so that they can apply the right artistic grammar. It pays the poet to be certain what he or she is about. Indeed, it may be constitutive of a successful reading that poet and reader lock themselves into a precinct of certainty which is quite different from the shifting cognitive patterns all around them and untouched by the "collapse of shared norms" which is supposed to have happened in the 20th century.

Bibliography

General works

Contemporary Poets ed. Thomas Riggs, (Detroit: St James Press, 2001) has entries on most of the poets concerned. Essential background also in Ryan, M.P., *Career patterns in poetry* (thesis, University of London, 1978), and Görtschacher, Wolfgang, *Little Magazine Profiles: the little magazines in Great Britain 1939-93* (Salzburg: Salzburg University Press, 1993). Orr: Peter Orr, ed., *The Poet Speaks* (interviews) (London: Routledge and Kegan Paul, 1966)

Let me invite you to my website, www.pinko.org. This has a lot of supplementary material. It includes a literature survey of many books about modern poetry (as 'Reception Hall'). More material is available at angelexhaust.blogspot.com. Other books are part of the project, abbreviated as follows:

DSMT: *Don't Start Me Talking*, ed. Tim Allen and Andrew Duncan (Salt, 2006);
and by Andrew Duncan:
CP, *Centre and Periphery in Modern British Poetry* (Liverpool University Press, 2005; 2nd ed, Shearsman Books 2016);
FCon, *The Failure of Conservatism in Modern British poetry* (Salt, 2003; 2nd ed. Shearsman Books 2016);
Scene, *The Poetry Scene in the '90s* (published on the Internet at www.pinko.org);
Origins, *Origins of the Underground* (Salt Publications, 2008);
Heresy, *The Council of Heresy* (Shearsman Books, 2009);
The Long 1950s (Shearsman Books, 2012).

Together they form a comprehensive account of British poetry 1960 to 1997.

Groups and Boundaries: The Poetic Field Around 1995
Agenda An Anthology, The First Four Decades 1959-93, edited William Cookson (Manchester: Carcanet, 1994)
Angels of Fire: an anthology of radical poetry in the '80s, edited Sylvia Paskin, Jeremy Silver, Jay Ramsay (London: Chatto and Windus, 1986) see longer review at http://angelexhaust.blogspot.com/2010/04/history-of-temporary-oral-poetry.html
Purple and Green: poems by 33 Women Poets (no editor, Sheffield: Rivelin Grapheme Press, 1985)
The New Poetry ed. Michael Hulse, David Kennedy, David Morley (Newcastle upon Tyne: Bloodaxe Books 1993) see longer review in *Angel Exhaust* 11 (1994).

Completing the Picture: Exiles, Outsiders, and Independents, ed. William Oxley (Exeter: Stride, 1995)

Out of Everywhere, linguistically innovative poetry by women in North America and the UK, ed. Maggie O'Sullivan (London: Reality Studios, 1996) see longer review in *Scene*.

60 Women Poets, ed. Linda France (Newcastle upon Tyne: Bloodaxe Books, 1993)

The Stumbling Dance, ed. Rupert Loydell (Exeter: Stride, 1994)

Dream State, edited Daniel O'Rourke, (Edinburgh: Polygon, 1994)

Contraflow on the Super-highway edited by W.N. Herbert and Richard Price, (London: Southfields Press and Gairfish, 1994)

The Urgency of Identity, contemporary English-language poetry from Wales, edited by John T. Lloyd (Evanston, IL: TriQuarterly Press, 1994)

The New Makars, edited Tom Hubbard (Edinburgh: Mercat Press, 1991)

A Various Art, edited by Andrew Crozier and Tim Longville (Manchester: Carcanet, 1987) Many of the poets included are discussed in *Origins of the Underground.*

the new british poetry, edited Allnutt, D'Aguiar, Mottram, Edwards (London: Paladin, 1988)

Conductors of Chaos, ed. Iain Sinclair (London: Picador, 1996) see long review in Angel Exhaust 10 and 11.

London/Cambridge: There is an anthology of the London school, *Floating Capital* (1991, ed. Adrian Clarke and Robert Sheppard), and some information on "group theory" is supplied in Angel Exhaust (periodical, London) #8, *The Blood-soaked Royston Perimeter*, Royston being a station between the two towns.

Lexicon

Firth, JR, in: Jones, WE and Laver, J., eds. *Phonetics in Linguistics. A Book of Readings* (Harlow: Longman, 1973)

Jones, Robert Owen *Hir oes i'r iaith* (Llandysul: Gwasg Gomer, 1997)

Lakoff, George *Women, fire, and dangerous things* (Chicago: University of Chicago Press, 1987)

Ardener, Edwin ed. (and contributor), *Social Anthropology and Language* (London: Tavistock Publications, 1973)

There is more discussion of exceptionalism at http://angelexhaust.blogspot.com/2010/03/coherence-and-exceptionalism-if-there.html

Metre

Hartman, Charles O. *Free Verse* (Princeton: Princeton University Press, 1980)

Couper-Kühlen, Elizabeth. *An introduction to English prosody* (Tübingen: Niemeyer, 1986)
Halliday, M.A.K. *Language as Social Semiotic* (London: Edward Arnold, 1978)
Cruttenden, Alan *Intonation* (Cambridge: Cambridge University Press, 1986)
Gimson in Jones, WE and Laver, J., eds. *Phonetics in Linguistics. A Book of Readings*. (Harlow: Longman, 1973)
Attridge, Derek *The Rhythms of English poetry* (London: Longman, 1982)
Giegerich, Heinz *English Phonology* (Cambridge: Cambridge University Press, 1992)
Gasparov, M.L., *A history of European versification* (Oxford: Clarendon Press, 1996)

The Concatenator
Gernet: Gernet, Louis, *Anthropologie de la Grèce antique* (Paris: François Maspero, 1968).
sociologists: I am thinking primarily of Henri Lefebvre, but there is also the school of ethnomethodology.
Lowenstein: *Eskimo Poems*, translated by Lowenstein (London: Allison and Busby, 1973)
Binford, Lewis: *In Pursuit of the Past* (London: Thames and Hudson, 1983)

Formations of Taste and Attitudinal Learning
Jonathan Barker, *Poetry in Britain and Ireland since 1970: a select bibliography* (London: The British Council, 1995.)
introduction by Michael Cookson to *Agenda* anthology [details above]. Memoirs in tribute issue of *Agenda* to Cookson in 2003 (Vol. 39, No. 4). Copies of *Nine* (periodical, London) on file in Cambridge University Library. Objectivists: see anthology *The Objectivists* by Andrew McAllister (Newcastle: Bloodaxe Books, 1996). historicism: see Patrick Heron, *Painter as Critic* (London: Tate Gallery, 1998), John A Walker, *Cultural Offensive* (London: Pluto Press, 1998).
innovations visible around 1970: see my book *FCon*, pp. 44-52.
Schmidt: *Poetry Nation* 1 (periodical, Manchester: 1973). For Formalism, see my discussion in *The Long 1950s*. empirical: Conquest, Robert, 'Art of the Enemy' (*Essays in Criticism*, journal, London, volume 7, 1957). Easthope quoted from *Englishness and National Culture* (London: Routledge, 1999), pp. 185 and 187.

A Section on Black and South Asian Poetry
the new british poetry ut supra
James Berry, *Hot Earth Cold Earth* (Newcastle: Bloodaxe, 1985)

Wells, J.C. *Accents of English* (Cambridge: Cambridge University Press, 1982)
Bailey, T Grahame, *Teach Yourself Urdu* (London: EUP, 1956).
Rai, Amjit, *A House Divided, the Origin and Development of Hindi-Urdu* (Delhi: Oxford University Press, 1984)

Noble Relics

David Jones: the poem was reprinted in *The Sleeping Lord* (Faber, 1974). see Foreword by Thomas Dilworth to *Two Wedding Poems* (London: Enitharmon, 2002); see the introduction to *The Anathémata* (London: Faber and Faber, 1952) for Jones' statement on his art. Dilworth's book *The Structure of Meaning in the Poetry of David Jones* (Toronto: University of Toronto Press, 1988) has a detailed account of *Visitation*.

George Barker: see his biography by Robert Fraser (*The Chameleon Poet*, London: Jonathan Cape, 2001), and my essay in *Origins*.

F.T. Prince: see interview with Stephen Devereux, published as a book by the National English Literary Museum, South Africa, 1988. Perfectly satisfying interview at book length, telling the story of this poet who has reached the heights so many times.

Philip Toynbee: author's note in *Two Brothers. The fifth day of the valediction of Pantaloon* (London: Chatto and Windus, 1964); see my essay in *Scene*.

Christian Poets

General books I found useful were Wilkinson, Alan, *Dissent or Conform: War, Peace and the English Churches 1900-1945* (London: SCM Press, 1986), Loudon, Mary *Revelations* (London: H Hamilton, 1994), Norman, E.R. *Church and Society in England 1770-1970* (Oxford: Clarendon Press, 1976), Leech, Kenneth and Williams, Rowan, eds. *Essays Catholic and Radical* (London: The Bowerdean Press, 1983).

Euros Bowen: see *Barddoniaeth Euros Bowen*, cyfrol 1 (Abertawe: C. Davis, 1977) by Alan Llwyd. *Trin cerddi* by Euros Bowen (Y Bala: Llyfrau'r Faner, 1978). *Myth and Ritual*, ed. S. H. Hooke (Oxford: Oxford University Press,1933). Interview in *Ysgrifau beirniadol* VI, ed. J. E. Caerwyn Williams (Dinbych: Gwasg Gee, 1971). Paul Tillich quoted from 'Protestantische Gestaltung' in *Auf der Grenze* (Stuttgart: Evangelisches Verlagswerk, 1962).

George Mackay Brown: see book by Alan Bold, *George Mackay Brown* (Edinburgh: Oliver and Boyd,1978), and interview in Christopher

Carrell, ed., *Seven Poets,* (Glasgow: Third Eye Centre, 1981)

Christian problems are described in more detail in *The Long 1950s.*

The Atlantic Periphery
see *Centre and Periphery* for discussion of the influence of geography on poetry.

Roland Mathias: the richest source is the many issues of *Anglo-Welsh Review* (periodical: Pembroke Dock) edited by Mathias in the 1960s and 1970s and reflecting his curiosity about history.

Alexander Hutchison, interview in DSMT.
Peter Manson, interview in DSMT.

Jungian Poets
For a non-hagiographic account of Jung, see Noll, Richard, *The Jung Cult: Origins of a charismatic movement* (New York: Random House, 1997) and *Aryan Christ: the secret life of Carl Jung* (Princeton: Princeton University Press, 1994)
Redgrove: see my essay in *FCon.*

Poetry of the Evanescent Present
Rosemary Tonks, my piece in *FCon*; interview in *The Poet Speaks.*
John James, see my reviews in *FCon* and *CP.*

Occultist, Mantic, and Eccentric
Kathleen Raine: on Neoplatonism, Lewy, Hans, *Chaldaean Oracles and Theurgy* (Paris: Etudes Augustiniennes, 1978). Yates, Frances, *Giordano Bruno and the Hermetic Tradition* (London: Routledge and Kegan Paul, 1977). See my long essays on Neoplatonism and Raine in *Heresy.*
Whiteley, Sheila *The Space Between the Notes* (London: Routledge, 1992)
Iain Sinclair: see my essay in *Origins*
Llewellyn-Williams: references as for Raine. look up string <hummadruz> on the Internet for some interesting stuff.
Data on Gardner in Hutton, Ronald, *The Triumph of the Moon* (Oxford: Oxford University Press, 2000).

Naturalist Poets
Sacheverell Sitwell: Pearson, John, *Façades: Edith, Osbert and Sacheverell Sitwell* (London: Macmillan, 1978)

Colin Simms, see my essay in *Centre and Periphery*. See *The Oxford Companion to the Earth*, eds. Hancock, Paul L. and Skinner, Brian J. (Oxford: Oxford University Press, 2000) p. 5 on the barkhan.

Elisabeth Bletsoe: see interview in DSMT.

The Meta-periphery: Arctic Poetry

J. F. Hendry: interviews in Ryan *ut supra* and in *Chapman* (periodical: Edinburgh), no.52, 1987. See *Origins of the Underground* (and references there)

Francis Berry: see my essay in *Origins*;

Strömbäck, Dag Alvar, *Sejd. Textstudier i nordisk religionshistoria* (Stockholm, 1935)

W. S. Graham: see Tony Lopez's book *The Poetry of W.S. Graham* (Edinburgh: Edinburgh University Press, 1989) and *The Night Fisherman: Selected Letters of W.S. Graham* (Manchester: Carcanet, 1999)

Alan Ross, see his autobiography, *Blindfold Game* (London: Collins Harvill, 1986)

Stainer: see my essay in *Long 1950s*.

Poets from *Grosseteste Review*

See my essay on the Ferry/Grosseteste School in *Origins*.

Roy Fisher, see his book, *Interviews through Time*, edited by Tony Frazer (2nd ed., Bristol: Shearsman Books, 2013)

J.H. Prynne: see *Nearly Too Much*, by Reeve, N.H., and Kerridge, Richard (Liverpool: Liverpool University Press, 1995);

Keery, James, 'Schönheit Apocalyptica', in *Jacket* symposium edited by Kevin Nolan, www.jacketmagazine.com.

Sinor: Sinor, Denis, ed., *The Cambridge History of Early Inner Asia* (Cambridge: Cambridge University Press, 1990). Gernet, Louis, 'La cité future et le pays des morts' [originally 1933] in *Anthropologie de la Grèce antique* (Paris: François Maspero, 1968). Bolton, JDP, *Aristeas of Proconnesus* (Oxford: Clarendon Press, 1962). Meuli, Karl, 'Scythica' (in *Gesammelte Schriften*, Basel: Schwabe, 1975). Frye, Richard N., *The Heritage of Persia* (London: Weidenfeld and Nicolson, 1976), p.177.

R.F. Langley, see interview in DSMT; a previous essay in *Scene*; his *Journals* (Exeter: Shearsman, 2006)

David Chaloner, see interview in DSMT

Denise Riley: see my essay in *Centre/Periphery*

Nigel Wheale, see his statement in Denise Riley, ed., *Poets on Writing* (Basingstoke: Macmillan, 1992)

Myth and Deep Narrative
Ted Hughes, see Sagar, Keith M. *The Art of Ted Hughes* (Cambridge: Cambridge University Press, 1975)
David Wevill: see interview in *The Poet Speaks*

The Dominance of the Optical
Michael Ayres, see presentation on shearsman website URL www.shearsman.com [*No longer online*]

Ludic Poetry of the 1980s
John Hartley Williams, see his autobiography in *Ignoble Sentiments* (Todmorden: Arc, 1995).
John Ash, see my essay in *FCon*.
Frank Kuppner, interview in *Talking Verse*, ed. Crawford, Robert *et al.*, (St. Andrews: Verse, 1995).
see chapters in *The Long 1950s* for a discussion of style changes occurring in the 1980s.

The Non-discursive Poem
see 'A primer of the avant-garde' in *Council of Heresy*.
Dornseiff, Franz *Das Alphabet in Mystik und Magie* (Leipzig: Teubner, 1922)
Finlay: Abrioux, Yves, *Ian Hamilton Finlay: A Visual Primer* (London: Reaktion Books, 1985);
Stanford, Derek, *Inside the Forties* (London: Sidgwick and Jackson, 1977)
Ingarden quoted in *Rezeptionsaesthetik: Theorie und Praxis*, ed. Rainer Warning, (Munich: W. Fink, 1975)
Sean Bonney, see interview in DSMT

Expanded Documentary
Gavin Selerie, see my essay on *Azimuth* at www.pinko.org . Interview previously at Shearsman website, www.shearsman.com
Fisher, see interviews in *Marvels of Lambeth* (Bristol: Shearsman Books, 2013)

Feminist Poets
Elfyn: *Sglefrio ar Eiriau* (ed. John Rowlands, Llandysul: Gomer, 1992)
O'r Iawn Ryw (Dinas Powys: Cerddi Honno, 1991) is one of the anthologies she edited.

Conventionally Breaking Conventions
Feaver: *Magma* 13, Winter 1998, includes a full interview with her by Vicci Bentley, on line here http://www.poetrymagazines.org.uk/magazine/record.asp?id=3900

Index

Abetz, Otto 95
Adams, Anna 27
Adorno, Theodor 100
Agard, John 110, 111
Agenda (magazine) 35, 36, 94, 97, 98
Akbar, Emperor 151
Albers, Josef 189
Alciati, Andrea 151
Allnutt, Gillian 17, 20
Allott, Kenneth 81, 83, 86
  Penguin Book of Contemporary Verse 81, 82
Alvi, Moniza
  Carrying My Wife 303–304
  'Lizard Tongues' 304
  'Presents from my Aunts in Pakistan' 303
Angel Exhaust 47
Angels of Fire (group) 37
Anthologies
  60 Women Poets 30, 31–32
  Agenda, an Anthology 1959-93 35–36, 96, 97
  Angels of Fire 37–38
  Completing the Picture: Exiles, Outsiders, and Independents 27
  Conductors of Chaos 23, 25, 45, 50, 97
  Contraflow on the Super-highway 34
  Dream State 33
  Eleven British Poets 36
  Exact Change Yearbook, The 47
  Floating Capital 47
  Ladder to the Next Floor 47
  Mingling of the Streams, The 47
  new british poetry, the 17–22, 108
  New Lines 87
  New Lines 2 91
  New Makars, The 33, 42–43
  New Poetry, The 24, 25–26, 38, 45
  News for Babylon 120
  Other 47
  Out of Everywhere 28–30, 31
  Poetry with an Edge 47
  Purple and Green 30, 31, 38–41
  Some Contemporary Poets 103
  State of Independence, A 47
  Stumbling Dance, The 32–33
  Urgency of Identity, The 41–42
  Various Art, A 23, 24, 43–44, 216
Antonioni, Michelangelo 43
Apocalypse (movement) 141, 152, 240
Apollinaire, Guillaume 168
Ardener, Edwin 51
Arif, Iftikhar 117, 118
  The Twelfth Man 117
Arts Council of Great Britain 120
Ashbery, John 93
Ash, John 26, 261
  The Anatolikon/To the City 264–266
Astruc, Alexandre 200, 201
Athanasius 140
Auden, W.H. 124, 141
Ayres, Michael 262
  Poems 1987-92 257–260

B

Bakst, Leon 173, 191
Ballets Russes 173
Ball, Hugo 284
Bamforth Films 267
Banks, Iain 246
Bann, Stephen 279
Barker, George
  True Confession of George Barker, The 131–133
Barker, Jonathan 82, 83
Barrett, Syd 177–181
Bartlett, Elizabeth 40
Bauhaus 189, 278
Bendon, Chris 42
Benois, Alexandre 191

Benveniste, Asa 168
Beowulf 81
Berger, John 89
Bergman, Ingrid 287
Bergvall, Caroline 28
Berry, Francis 75, 124, 252
   Ghosts of Greenland 205–207
   Morant Bay 206
Berry, James 115, 117
   'Chain of Days' 116
   'Happy Goodbye Sun' 115
   Hot Earth Cold Earth 115
   'In Our Year 1941 My Letter to You Mother Africa' 116
Berry, James (ed.)
   News for Babylon 116
Beuys, Joseph 284
Bible Dictionary 140
Bibliography of Poetry in Britain and Ireland since 1970 82
Bill, Max 278
Binford, Lewis 80
Black, D.M. 267
   A Theory of Diet 245
   Collected Poems 1964-87 244
   Gravitations 244–246
Blake, William 174, 175
Bletsoe, Elisabeth
   Landscape from a Dream 194–196
   'Cross-in-hand' 195
Bloodaxe Books 35
Blow-up (film) 43
Blunden, Edmund 240
Bodkin, Maud
   Archetypal Patterns in Poetry 160
Böll, Heinrich 145
Bonnard, Pierre 255
Bonney, Sean
   Notes on Heresy 284–285
Bourdieu 29, 30
Bowen, Euros
   Cerddi rhydd 137–141
   'Sodiac' 138

The Seven Trumpets 138–140
Brakhage, Stan 183
   Dog Star Man 183
Brathwaite, Kamau 109
   Arrivants, The 251
Breton, André 168
Brigley, Zoë 305
British Poetry Revival, The 20, 22, 25, 148
Brooks, Cleanth 270
   The Well-Wrought Urn 270
Browning, Robert 57
   'The Guardian-Angel: a Picture at Fano' 57
Bruno, Giordano 184, 185, 187
Buile Suibhne Geilt 163
Burroughs, William 287
   The Naked Lunch 287
Butler, Alban
   Lives of the Saints 163

C

Cabral, Amilcar 109
Calvert, Phyllis 176
Campbell, J.F.
   Lebor na Feinne 175
Campos, Augusto de 278
Campos, Haroldo de 159, 278
Caravaggio 258
Carcanet (magazine) 102
Carcanet Press 101, 102, 103
Caribbean poetry 19
Carmina Gadelica 175, 186
Catacomb (magazine) 94
Catling, B. 23, 183, 212, 214
Caudwell, Christopher
   Illusion and Reality 160
Caulfield, Patrick 231, 232
Celan, Paul 180
Césaire, Aimé 109
Chaloner, David
   Chocolate Sauce 231–233
Chaucer, Geoffrey 59

cheek, cris 28
Clarke, Adrian
    Obscure Disasters 281–283
Clausewitz, Georg von 136
Close Reading 81, 102
Cocteau, Jean 277
Cohn, Roy 270
Columba, Saint 159
Conan Doyle, Sir Arthur 183
Conquest, Robert 87, 88, 89, 96
    'Art of the Enemy' 91
    'The Rokeby Venus' 91
Conran, Tony 154
Cookson, William 35, 94, 96, 97
Coppe, Abiezer 284
Corcoran, Neil 21
Couper-Kuehlen, Elizabeth 63, 64, 67
Cox, C.B. 102, 106
Cox, C.B. (ed.)
    Black Papers 103, 104
Crawford, Robert 26, 35, 239, 261
    Spirit Machines 158
    The Second Life 158
Critical Quarterly 102, 106
Cromwell, Oliver 109
Crozier, Andrew 22, 23, 43, 44, 231
    High Zero 22
Cruttenden, Alan 58, 59
Cure, The 261
cynghanedd 137

D

Dabydeen, David 77, 111, 112, 113
    'Coolie Odyssey' 112
    Turner 250–252
D'Aguiar, Fred 17, 18, 108
Daumier, Honoré 144
Davidson, John 34
Davie, Donald 21, 101, 106
Deleuze, Gilles 226
Diaghilev, Serge 191
Didsbury, Peter

The Classical Farm 255–257
Dilworth, Thomas 124
Doesburg, Theo van 278
Donne, John 146
Dornseiff, Franz 281
Draycott, Jane & Saunders, Lesley
    Christina the Astonishing 162–163
Duhig, Ian 35
Duncan, Andrew
    Centre and Periphery 110
    The Long 1950s 261
Duncan, Robert 93
Dunn, Douglas 26

E

Eagleton, Terry 101
Early English Lyrics 59
Easthope, Anthony 98, 99, 100
Edwards, Ken 17, 22
Elfyn, Menna
    Eucalyptus: Detholiad o Gerddi 1978-94 295–299
    'Trwy lygaid ffeministaidd' 295
Eliade, Mircea 124
Eliot, T.S. 81, 111, 124, 129, 141, 307
Engels, Friedrich Wilhelm 188
Ennius 125, 144
Essays in Criticism (1957) 87

F

Fanon, Frantz 109
Farocki, Haroun 99
Feaver, Vicki
    The Handless Maiden 301–302
feminist poetry 20, 289–299
Fergar, Feyyaz 27
Ferry Press 231
Finch, Peter 42
Finlay, Ian Hamilton 277–281
Fisher, Allen 300, 307
Fisher, Roy 136, 256, 306

City 216–219
Fortean Times 188
Foscolo, Ugo 129
France, Linda 31
Fraser, Robert
  biography of George Barker 132
Freer, Ulli 284
Friedman, Milton 95
Fry, Christopher 153
Frye, Richard 226

G

Garvey, Marcus 109
Gascoyne, David 25
Gasparov, M.L. 59
Gernet, Louis 78
Gibson, Wilfred 121
  'In Fifth Avenue' 108
Gidal, Peter 75
Giegerich, Heinz
  English Phonology 64
Gilonis, Harry 163
Gimson, A.C. 59
Godard, Jean-Luc 200
  Vivre sa vie 237
Gomringer, Eugen
  konstellationen 278
Goodby, John 35
Graham, W.S. 25, 205, 287, 306, 307
  Malcolm Mooney's Land 179, 207–210, 214
  Seven Journeys 208
  The Nightfishing 209
Grass, Günter 144, 146
Gray, Edmund 97
Gray, John 71
Grosse Point Blank (film) 202
Grosseteste Review 43, 98, 216, 231
Guardian, The 101
Guattari, Felix 226
Guest, Harry 27
  Lost and Found 147–151

'Brittany, c. 2300 BC' 148
'Enchanted Acres' 149
'Memories of the Sinagua' 149
'The Sixth Elegy' 148

H

Hakim, Khaled 75
Halsey, Alan 286
Haslam, Michael 137
Hausmann, Raoul 159
Hawksmoor, Nicholas 182–184
Hegel, F.W. 93
Heidegger, Martin 200
Hendry, J.F. 25
  Marimarusa 179, 203–206, 214
Heracleitus 220
Herbert, W.N. 34, 35
Herodotus 220, 221, 225, 226
Heron, Patrick 93
Hill, Geoffrey 35, 94, 136
  Speech! Speech! 144–146
Hilson, Jeff
  Stretchers 274–276
Hitchcock, Alfred 133
  Psycho 232
Holman, Paul 33
  Memory of the Drift, The 187–189
Holmes, Sherlock 183
Homberger, Eric 106
Hooke, Samuel (ed.)
  Myth and Ritual 140
Hubbard, Tom 42
Huchel, Peter 103
Hughes, Ted 207, 211, 244
  Crow 239–243
  Gaudete 75
Hulse, Michael 25
Hutchison, Alexander
  Deep Tap Tree 150–152
    'Construct by Simple Succession' 151
    'Impresa' 150
    'Mr Scales walks his dog' 151

Huxley, Aldous 108, 121
Hymes, Dell 53

I

Informationists 34, 159
Invasion of the Body Snatchers (film) 84
Ipsiroglu, M.S.
  Painting of the Mongols 219, 224

J

Jackson, Tony 168
Jamal, Mahmood 113, 114
  Silence in the Mouth of a Gun 114
  Sugar-Coated Pill 114
  'Work-in-progress' 114
  (as editor of) *Penguin Book of Urdu Verse* 114
James, John
  Berlin Return 166–168
  The Welsh Poems 167
James Thin (bookshop) 43
Jandl, Ernst 159
Jobim, Antonio Carlos 278
Jones, Barbara 175, 183
Jones, David 25, 35, 36, 97, 235, 239, 306, 307
  Anathémata, The 126
  'The Fatigue' 124
  The Sleeping Lord 124
  The Tribune's Visitation 124–127
  'The Tutelar of Place' 124
  'The Wall' 124
Jones, Glyn 153
Jones, Peter 102
Jope, Norman 33
Jouvenel, Bertrand de 95
Julian of Norwich 176
Jung, Carl Gustav 160, 180, 181, 194, 239

K

Kazantzis, Judith
  Selected Poems 1977-92 290–293
Keery, James 227
Kennedy, David 25
Khalvati, Mimi 149
  Entries on Light 253–255
  In White Ink 254
  Mirrorwork 254
Khan, Nusrat Fateh Ali 118
Kinloch, David 35
Kipling, Rudyard 306
Kiss Me, Stupid (film) 263
Knight, G. Wilson
  The Golden Labyrinth 206
Kramer, Hilton 97
Kuppner, Frank 246, 261
  A Bad Day for the Sung Dynasty 266–268

L

Labour Party 103
Lake, Grace (aka Anna Mendelson)
  Bernache nonnette 293–295
Lakoff, George 50, 53
Lambert, Margaret 175
Langley, R.F. 52
  Jack 52
  Journals 228
  Twelve Poems 228–231
La Tène 154
Lawrence, D.H. 156, 162, 190
Layard, John
  The Lady of the Hare 160
Le Corbusier 90
Lefebvre, Henri
  Philosophy of Everyday Life, The 44
Left Review 102
Lenin, Vladimir Ilyich 89
Levi, Peter 136
Lewis, C.S. 90
Littack (magazine) 279
Llewellyn-Williams, Hilary
  Book of Shadows 184

Hummadruzz 184–188
   'Sun in Leo' 186
   The Tree Calendar 184
Lloyd, John T. 41
Lockwood, Margaret 176
Logue, Christopher 14, 75, 94
London Review of Books 94
Longville, Tim 43
Lopez, Tony 208
Lowenstein, Tom 71–74, 194, 214, 250
   Filibustering in Samsāra 71–72
Loydell, Rupert 32
Loy, Mina 171
Lucie-Smith, Edward (ed.)
   British Poetry since 1945 82
Lyle, Rob 94

M

MacBeth, George 75, 261
   'A Light in Winter' 75
   'Driving West' 75
MacDiarmid, Hugh 34, 124, 157
Macdonald, Helen
   Shaler's Fish 197–201
Mackay Brown, George 77, 136, 175
   Fishermen with Ploughs 141–142
MacKenzie, Rob 271
MacLean, Sorley 157
MacVean, Jean 36
Malatesta, Sigismondo 95
Mallarmé, Stéphane 271, 272
Manson, Peter
   Birth Windows 271–274
Marcuse, Herbert 100, 156
Marcus, Greil 270
Marechera, Dambudzo 18, 111
Marley, Brian 262
   Springtime in the Rockies 168–170
     'Bargain Basement Sonnets' 169
     The Luminous Band of Stars 170

Marley, Brian & Benveniste, Asa
   Dense Lens 168
Marx, Enid 175
Marx, Karl 269
Masefield, John 79–81
Massey, Alan 36
   'Leechcraft' 97
Mass Observation 287
Mathias, Roland
   Snipe's Castle 152–155
     'Lowbury Hill' 153
     'The Anchorite' 152
Matthias, John 148
Maurras, Charles 106
Mead, G.R.S. 96, 160
Merleau-Ponty 199, 201
Mickel, Karl 107
Middleton, Christopher 256
Milton, John 227
Montesquieu 188
Mont Pelerin Society 95
Moore, Nicholas 25
Morgan, Edwin 33, 34, 53–54, 261
   'A Little Catechism for the Demon' 54
Morley, David 25
Mottram, Eric 17, 20–21, 23, 25, 37, 93, 97, 106, 148
Movement, The 21
Muckle, John 17
Muir, Edwin 87, 142, 143, 175, 239
   'The Horses' 142
   Variations on a Time Theme 143
Mulford, Wendy 28
Mussolini, Benito 94, 95

N

Nagy, Imre 145
New Left 17, 36, 237
New Order 258
New Right 95
New Scientist 71, 192

Nietzsche, F.W. 106
Nimbus (magazine) 95
Nine (magazine) 94, 95
Niven, Alistair 120
Nolan, Kevin
  Alar 269–271
Nott, Kathleen 149
  Landscapes and Departures 126
  Poems from the North 126–130
    'Absolute Zero' 127
    'Internecine Love' 128
    'Manichee's Black Mass' 129
Novak, Kim 263
Nuttall, Jeff 37

O

Objectivists 43, 97, 98
O'Brien, Sean 45, 46
O'Hara, Frank 93
Okri, Ben 111
Oliphant, Margaret 159
Olson, Charles 93, 98, 228, 231
Origen 155
O'Rourke, Daniel 33
O'Sullivan, Maggie 28
Our Time (journal) 102
Overbeek, Henk 198
Over, Jeremy 170
Oxley, William 27, 28

P

Page, Jimmy 180
Partisan Review 101, 105
Paskin, Sylvia 37
Pasolini, Pier Paolo 103
Pater, Walter 76
Penguin Books 30
Péret, Benjamin 263
Perrie, Walter 180
  By Moon and Sun 155–157
Pfleumer, Ernst 187
Picasso, Pablo 97

Pink Floyd 177–179, 222
  'Astronomy Domine' 177
  Piper at the Gates of Dawn 177
Piontek, Heinz (ed.)
  Neue Erzählgedichte 79
Pizzicato Five 188
Plato 175
Plotinus 175
PN Review 36, 47, 101, 102, 103
Poetry London 176
Poetry Nation 102, 104, 105
Poetry Review 21, 26, 82, 83, 190
Poetry Society of Great Britain 21, 22
Popa, Vasko 240
Portishead 173
Pound, Ezra 36, 94, 95, 97, 98, 156, 171, 230, 231, 307
  Cantos, The 96
Powys, John Cowper 162, 207
Prévert, Jacques 168
Price, Richard 34
Prince, F.T.
  Dry-points of the Hasidim 130, 163
Prynne, J.H. 45, 46, 228, 300, 307
  For the Monogram 271
  The White Stones 218–227, 269, 270
    'Aristeas, in Seven Years' 218
Puttenham, George
  Art of English Poesie 237

R

Raine, Kathleen 87, 124, 143, 160, 179, 186, 194, 212, 239
  The Hollow Hill 174–179
  The Year One 175
Raleigh, Sir Walter 173
Ramsay, Jay 37
Randles, Jenny 185
Raworth, Tom 68, 300
Redgrove, Peter 194, 207, 244
  Apple-Broadcast, The 161–163
Redgrove, Peter & Shuttle, Penelope

The Hermaphrodite Album 180–182
Reed, Jeremy 261
   Saints and Psychotics 183
Rees-Jones, Deryn
   Signs Around a Dead Body 305–307
   The Memory Tray 305–307
Reeve, Michael 184
Reeves, Gareth 102
Resuscitator (magazine) 167
Rickword, Edgell 101, 102
   Essays and Opinions 1921-31 102
Riley, Denise
   Dry Air 236–238
   'Marxism for Infants' 237
Roberts, Lynette 153
Robinson, Alan 21
Rodney, Walter 109
Rohde, Erwin 224
Rokeby Venus (Velázquez) 90
Rolling Stones, The 194
Rollins, Sonny 263, 264
Rorty, Richard 53
Rosch, Eleanor 50
Ross, Alan
   Poems 1942-67 210–212
   To whom it may concern 210–211
Rousseau, Jean-Jacques 188
Russell, Peter 94

S

Sacks, Oliver 209
Sade, Marquis de 144
Sansom, William 287
Schmidt, Michael 36, 101, 102, 105, 106, 107, 261
Scott, Sir Walter
   'Marmion' 58
Selerie, Gavin 286
   Days of '49 286–288
Senghor, Leopold 109
Sglefrio ar Eiriau 295

Shakespeare, William
   Hamlet 119
   Twelfth Night 51
Shapcott, Jo 26, 261
Shaw, Robert B. 101, 106
Silver, Jeremy 37
Simms, Colin 52
   Poems from Afghanistan 52, 191–193
Simple Minds 261
Sinclair, Andrew 184
Sinclair, Iain 17, 23
   Lud Heat 182–184
Sirèn, Osvald 266
Sisson, C.H. 106
Sitwell, Edith 191
Sitwell, Sacheverell 124, 252, 267
   Tropicalia 190–191
Skelton, John 60
Sly and the Family Stone 269
Smith, Adam 220
Smith, Harry
   Anthology of American Folk Music 275
Sneaker Pimps 173
Socialist Workers' Party 103
Spengler, Oswald 125
Spicer, Jack 93
Stainer, Pauline
   The Ice-Pilot Speaks 211–213
Stephens, Meic 41
Stevenson, Robert Louis 183
Stokes, Adrian 105, 228
Surrey, Earl of 59
Sutherland, Helen 97
Symbolism 76, 140, 141, 160, 181

T

Tennyson, Alfred, Lord 57
Thomas, Dylan 152, 153
Thom, Martin 73, 179, 223
   The Bloodshed, the Shaking House 247–250

Thompson, E.P. 89
Thrilling, Isobel 40
Thwaite, Anthony 21, 136
Tomlinson, Charles 87
Tonks, Rosemary 168, 262
  Emir 165
  Iliad of Broken Sentences 165
  Notes on Cafés and Bedrooms 167
Toynbee, Philip
  Pantaloon, or, the Valediction 133–135
Turner, J.M.W. 250

U

Ungaretti, Giuseppe 35

V

van den Beukel, Karlien 270
  Pitch Lake 171–173
  'The Spectacle is a Map of This New World' 172
van der Rohe, Mies 259
Vaneigem, Raoul 284
van Pijl, Kees 198
Vaughan, Vittoria 185, 196
Villiers de Lisle-Adam
  Axel 96
Virago (publisher) 237, 238
Virgil 88

W

Wainwright, Jeffrey 103
Walcott, Derek 109
Walker, Brenda 117
Walker, John A.
  Cultural Offensive 93
Walker, Scott
  Climate of Hunter 286
Warburg, Aby 273
Webb, James
  The Occult Revival 174

Wells, Robert 103
Wevill, David 211
Where the Arrow Falls 242–244
Wheale, Nigel
  Phrasing the Light 233–236
  'Black Thorn' 234
  'Cara Alba derelicta' 234
  'Silent Coast' 235
  'The earth seemed unearthly' 235
Whyte, Christopher 143
Wieners, John 93
Williams, Charles 36, 87, 88, 90
  Taliessin through Logres 88
Williams, John Hartley 13, 26, 45
  Canada 262–264
Wittgenstein, Paul 208
Woolf, Virginia 134
Writers Forum 285
Wyatt, Sir Thomas 59
Wynne-Rhydderch, Samantha 305
Wynter, Bryan 209

X

X, Malcolm 109

Y

Yates, Frances A. 186
Yeats, W.B. 174

Z

Zukofsky, Louis 93, 275

www.ingramcontent.com/pod-product-compliance
Lightning Source LLC
Chambersburg PA
CBHW021833220426
43663CB00005B/226